Action, Intention, and Reason

ACTION, INTENTION, AND REASON

R O B E R T   A U D I

Cornell University Press

Ithaca and London

First published 1993 by Cornell University Press.

Library of Congress Cataloging-in-Publication Data

Audi, Robert, b. 1941
    Action, intention, and reason / Robert Audi.
        p.   cm.
    Includes bibliographical references and index.
    ISBN 0-8014-2866-1 (alk. paper). — ISBN 0-8014-8105-8 (paper)
    1. Act (Philosophy)   2. Intentionality (Philosophy)   3. Will.
4. Free will and determinism.   5. Responsibility.   6. Reason.
I. Title.
B105.A35A839   1993
128'.4—dc20   93-22578

Printed in the United States of America

To My Sister and Brother

Contents

Preface

This book brings together eleven of my essays in action theory published since 1971 and three written specially for this volume, including the initial overview, which is meant to introduce and interconnect the later sections and to outline my general position in the field. I have produced the collection in the hope that, brought together as they are here, the individual chapters develop and defend a general position in action theory that cannot be clearly seen in any single chapter or part of the book. This position is intentionalist about the nature of action, which is viewed—at least in the clear cases—as behavior that is intentional under some description; the position is causal and nomic regarding explanations of action by appeal to such intentional elements as beliefs and desires; it is compatibilist about free action and moral responsibility; it is internalist about the grounds of rational action, which is seen as rooted in psychological elements accessible to reflection; and it is holistic about the nature of rationality.

Within each part of the book, the essays are ordered chronologically. This is their natural order: many develop accounts, ideas, or distinctions introduced in my earlier work. This cumulative development of my position is not accomplished without some overlap, but where overlap occurs, there is some gain in both the continuity of the book and the comprehensiveness with which some of the important questions are treated.

For permission to reprint the previously published material I thank the editors of the journals listed here. Chapter 1 originally appeared in *Philosophical Studies* 24 (1973): 1–21 (copyright © 1973 by D. Reidel Publishing Company, Dordrecht, Holland; reprinted by permission of Kluwer Academic Publishers); Chapter 2, *Journal of Philosophy* 70 (1973): 387–403; Chapter 4, *Metaphilosophy* 2 (1971): 241–50; Chapter 5, *Journal for the Theory of Social Behaviour* 9 (1980): 227–49; Chapter 6, *Philosophical Review* 95 (1986): 511–46 (copyright 1986 Cornell University; reprinted by permission of the publisher and the author); Chapter 7, *American Philosophical Quarterly* 11 (1974): 1–14; Chapter 8, *Canadian Journal of Philosophy* 19 (1989): 246–66; Chapter 9, *Ethics* 101 (1991): 304–21; Chapter 12, *Australasian Journal of Philosophy* 68 (1990): 270–81; and Chapter 13, *Philosophical Perspectives* 4 (1990): 227–44. Chapter 11 first appeared in Gottfried Seebass and Raimo Tuomela, eds., *Social Action* (Dordrecht: D. Reidel, 1985), pp. 243–77 (©1985 by D. Reidel Publishing Company; reprinted by permission of Kluwer Academic Publishers).

Only minor changes have been made in the previously published work, and these are chiefly to give the chapters a common format and to put the notes into a uniform style. I have resisted the temptation to make revisions; but it is appropriate to mention a few of the extensions and defenses of my views published elsewhere: to Part I, especially the account of intending, "Intending, Intentional Action, and Desire," in Joel E. Marks, ed., *The Ways of Desire* (Chicago: Precedent, 1986) is particularly relevant; to Part II, "Inductive-Nomological Explanations and Psychological Laws," *Theory and Decision* 13 (1981), and "Mental Causation: Sustaining and Dynamic," in John Heil and Alfred R. Mele, eds., *Mental Causation* (Oxford: Oxford University Press, 1992) add support; regarding Part III, especially Chapter 8, "Self-Deception and Practical Reasoning," my book *Practical Reasoning* (London: Routledge, 1989) develops many of the main ideas; and some major points in Part IV are supported by "Weakness of Will and Practical Judgment," *Noûs* 13, no. 2 (1979), and "The Architecture of Reason," *Proceedings and Addresses of the American Philosophical Association* 62, supp. vol. no. 1 (1988), reprinted in my *Structure of Justification* (Cambridge: Cambridge University Press, 1993).

In working out the positions defended in this book, I have learned much from other philosophers and from my students. I cannot name them all; they include audiences to whom I have given papers and authors of papers presented at conferences, in my own department, in the National Endowment for the Humanities Summer Seminars I have held, and, particularly, in the NEH Institute on Human Action that I directed in 1984. This book has also benefited from my reading, and sometimes talking with, a number of the authors referred to in the notes (and many not referred to or discussed because of limited space). I particularly acknowledge William Alston and Alvin Goldman, each of whom, through their writings and discussions with me, provided an early and enduring stimulus to my work in action theory, beginning in the middle 1960s. I have also been fruitfully discussing action theory for many years with Michael Bratman, Robert Kane, Paul Moser, Raimo Tuomela, Michael J. Zimmerman, and, especially, Hugh McCann and Alfred Mele. On many occasions, I have profited from discussions of one or another major topic in the field with Frederick Adams, Lynne Rudder Baker, Myles Brand, the late Hector-Neri Castañeda, Wayne Davis, Jorge Garcia, Carl Ginet, Robert Gordon, Brian McLaughlin, Jeffrey Poland, Aaron Snyder, Eleonore Stump, Barbara Von Eckardt, Arthur Walker, and Margaret Urban Walker. For detailed comments on the new essays I thank Frederick Adams for comments on the Overview; Hugh McCann, Raimo Tuomela, Michael Zimmerman, and, especially, a reader for Cornell University Press, for reactions to Chapter 3; and Harry Ide, Tomis Kapitan, Robert Kane, Lawrence Brian Lombard, and Hugh McCann for criticism of Chapter 10.

ROBERT AUDI

Lincoln, Nebraska

Action, Intention, and Reason

Overview: Reason in Action

The theory of action is both philosophically interesting in itself and pivotal for several other fields of philosophy. It is crucial for the philosophy of mind because any adequate account of our mental powers must extend to a theory of their connection with action. It is important for the philosophy of science, especially the social sciences, because an adequate theory of human behavior must either employ some concept of action and explain its connection with motivation and cognition, or show, as no one has even come close to doing, that our behavior can be understood apart from these crucial notions in action theory. And action theory is pivotal for ethics in several respects: ethical theory needs a conception of free action and its relation to moral responsibility; it needs a moral psychology, notably for understanding such phenomena as practical reasoning, weakness of will, and self-deception; and, if it is to address the classical problem of the relation between morality and rationality, it requires an account of rational action.

The territory of action theory may be conceived in relation to four major problem areas, each encompassing a number of subsidiary topics. The first is the nature of action. One question here is conceptual, concerning what an action *is* and what sort of analysis of action is best; another central question is metaphysical, concerning the ontological category to which action belongs. A second major problem is to account for the explanation of action, particularly for explanations by appeal to motivational and cognitive elements in the agent, such as desires, intentions, and beliefs. A third problem is the issue of free will, which concerns the nature of free action and, especially, whether, if determinism is true, we can be either free in performing actions or morally responsible for those we have performed. Insofar as moral responsibility is a normative notion, for instance by implying that a certain kind of assessment of action is *warranted*, the problem of free will belongs to the normative theory of action, which is also a concern of this book. The central question in that domain indicates the fourth major area of action theory: the nature and grounds of rational action.

With respect to each of these four major areas, there are basic theoretical divisions in the philosophy of action. Regarding the nature of action, one important view is that an action is an instantiation of an act-property by an agent at a given time; another (more widely held, and perhaps dominant, at present) is that actions are particulars— events, to be sure, but susceptible of many different descriptions in essentially the same way as "shoes and ships and sealing wax." On the former, fine-grained conception, my writing this now and my moving my (writing) fingers are two different actions, since the property of writing is different from that of moving one's fingers.[1] On the latter, the coarse-grained view, there is one thing I am doing now, which may be described in either of those ways (among many others), just as we may describe a tree as the maple closest to my house or as the tree I pruned last October.[2] In the case of the explanation of action, the largest single divide is between those who hold causal theories and those who hold one or another kind of contextualist view. The causalists, in turn, divide into those who maintain that there are genuine laws connecting actions with the motivational and cognitive factors that explain them and those who interpret this explanatory relation as causal, but not nomic in that sense. The contextualists, who are heavily influenced by the later Wittgenstein,

[1] This view of events has been strongly associated in metaphysics with Roderick Chisholm and Jaegwon Kim, and has received its most important defense and development in action theory from Alvin I. Goldman in *A Theory of Human Action* (Englewood Cliffs, N.J.: Prentice-Hall, 1970).

[2] This view, given an influential formulation by Elizabeth Anscombe and later defended and developed by Donald Davidson, is often called the Anscombe-Davidson view. See esp. G. E. M. Anscombe, *Intention* (1957; Ithaca: Cornell University Press, 1963) and Donald Davidson, "The Logical Form of Action Sentences," *Journal of Philosophy* 60 (1963). I should also mention the component view of action, represented by a number of philosophers, including Irving Thalberg, *Perception, Emotion, and Action: A Component Approach* (Oxford: Basil Blackwell, 1977). See also Judith Jarvis Thomson, *Acts and Other Events* (Ithaca: Cornell University Press, 1977), and Lawrence Lombard, *Events: A Metaphysical Study* (London: Routledge and Kegan Paul, 1986).

emphasize a different aspect of everyday explanations by reasons: denying that reasons are causes, they stress the ways in which actions are made intelligible in the light of the reasons of the agent.[3]

The central division with respect to the problem of free will is more widely known: it is between *compatibilists*—those holding that determinism is consistent with the existence of free action—and *incompatibilists*—those denying this. Regarding normative action theory, the two most prominent categories of theory are *instrumentalism*, which takes the rationality of an action to be entirely a matter of how well it serves (how good an instrument it is for realizing) the agent's basic desires no matter what they are, and *objectivism*, which places constraints on those desires or indeed on any grounds of rationality. Such theories maintain that actions which are rooted in elements lacking rationality cannot themselves be rational; however subjectively appealing the object of a basic desire may be, that object may not be objectively worthy of desire.

In this book I develop detailed positions on all four problem areas except the ontology of action. The main reason for this asymmetry is that the principal contributions of the book can accommodate either the fine-grained or the coarse-grained ontology (or various intermediate views, such as the component approach). As it happens, however, the essays written before 1980 tend to be worded to fit most readily with a fine-grained approach, and the later ones tend to be written in a way that is more easily combined with a coarse-grained view. In Chapter 6, I explicitly compare the two by showing how the account of acting for reasons is neutral between the two ontologies. Regarding the conceptual analysis of action, while no chapter is devoted wholly to this task, Chapter 6 provides an account of intentional action, especially of the kind that, being performed for a further end, is not intrinsically motivated, that is, not performed "for its own sake," as are things we do purely for pleasure. I refer, of course, to individual action; *social action* is a different thing and cannot be assumed to be reducible to individual action. My conviction, however, is that social action, such as a government's signing a treaty, is at least largely comprehensible in terms of individual actions, and if that is so, then

---

[3] Donald Davidson, from "Actions, Reasons and Causes" onward, has tended to be a non-nomic causalist, whereas, in Chapter 1 and elsewhere, I defend a nomic account. For references to him and others (on both sides) see Chapter 1. Contextualism is discussed, and its proponents examined in Chapters 1, 5, and 11.

the omission is less serious from the point of view of presenting a reasonably comprehensive account of human action.[4]

On the explanation of action, my view is nomic and qualifiedly causal: actions are both explainable by appeal to laws (of a special kind) and causally grounded in what explains them. On the problem of free will I defend my own compatibilist account, though I do not espouse determinism. And on the problem of rational action I develop a pluralistic objectivism that countenances a variety of rational grounds of action.

This overview indicates how all these positions are developed and interconnected in the chapters to come. It makes some points not made in them (at least not explicitly); and it is intended to be both intelligible to readers who have not studied those chapters and useful to some who have.

I. The Intentionalistic Grounds of Action

Intentionality has been thought to be the central mark of the mental; but even if it is not that, it is central to the sorts of elements which, in everyday contexts, explain our actions. The very term brings *intending* to mind: intending is an intentional attitude in the usual sense that it is directed upon a content (and in that sense on an object); and it can explain at least those actions we perform with the intention of achieving an end, say writing to a friend with the intention of inviting her to a party. Wants, beliefs, and a multitude of other psychological attitudes play similar roles in explaining actions. There is no end to the number of actions explainable by (true) statements indicating that one wanted something, where the context makes it clear that one had a belief to the effect that the action would (or might) contribute to getting it. Since I argue that wanting (which I take to include desiring as a special case) and believing are fundamental to intending, I begin with the notions of wanting and believing.

The Basic Elements of Motivation

Citing what we want is one of the most straightforward ways of explaining why we did something. But when we seek a philosophical

[4] For an account of social action that supports the individualistic hypothesis I have suggested, see Raimo Tuomela, *The Importance of Us*, forthcoming from Stanford Uni-

understanding of wanting, we find considerable difficulty. Chapter 1, "The Concept of Wanting," is written in the conviction that a philosophical analysis of the concept of wanting cannot be both illuminating and entirely non-circular. For reasons made clear in the chapter, it seems impossible to provide an account of wanting without appeal to believing, and believing, in turn, is not adequately analyzable apart from an appeal to wanting.[5] What this chapter does, then, is to develop a quite different kind of account, one in which the notion of wanting is explicated in terms of the general relationships that are conceptually fundamental to wanting. These concern, above all, its connection with believing. First, believing is the main element that *directs* desire in leading both to actions aimed at realizing desire and to the formation of further desires, particularly for things we believe to be means to realizing strong desires we already have. Second, desire is linked, via believing, with disappointment and pleasure, as where these arise from suddenly realizing (hence believing) that we cannot have (or will have) something we wanted. Even independently of believing, desires are connected with a tendency to avow them and with the content of fantasy, thought, and free conversation: in ways the chapter describes, desire tends to produce those avowals and to influence that content. We tend—even if we often do not act on the tendency—to say what it is that we want and to think about getting it.

Each of the relationships just sketched is expressible in a schematic generalization about wanting. The most important is to the effect that (under certain conditions) we tend to do things we believe will contribute to getting what we want.[6] What is the status of such generalizations? They may seem analytic, since they may appear "true by definition." Reflection reveals how unfruitful it can be to classify propositions like these in terms of the analytic-synthetic distinction. It will not do to call this schematic proposition analytic; for one thing,

---

versity Press; and for a contrasting point of view see Margaret Gilbert, *On Social Facts* (London: Routledge, 1987).

[5] This is argued in my essay "The Concept of Believing," *Personalist* 53 (1972).

[6] It is difficult in a brief formulation to do justice to the variety of generalizations that can instantiate the schema. One might believe the action necessary for the end, for example, or sufficient, or both, or neither. There must simply be a suitable "promotional" relation. Chapter 6 discusses the possibilities under the subheading "Connecting Beliefs." It *is not* necessary for the agent to conceptualize the object wanted *as* wanted; one can want something prior to developing a conception of wanting, hence before being able to want something under a description involving wanting.

the proposition is, in the context of the entire set of such propositions, testable, and for another there is no plausible explicit definition of wanting with this proposition as a part in the way *being female* is part of what it is, by definition, to be a vixen and, as part of that definition, warrants saying that 'all vixens are female' expresses an analytic proposition. On the other hand, because the schema expresses "part of what we mean" by 'wanting,' it cannot be considered merely synthetic. It turns out, I argue, that such generalizations are lawlike (nomic); and, taken together, they express a commonsense psychological theory—this use of 'theory' does not have the genetic implication that anyone postulated these generalizations to explain phenomena; the term is used in the functional sense that the generalizations provide a network of testable propositions in terms of which we can classify, explain, and, to some extent, predict action and other behavior. These propositions are constitutive of the concept of wanting, rather in the way that the basic lawlike propositions in which a theoretical scientific concept figures are constitutive of it.

This approach has an important implication for understanding want-explanations, indeed any explanation equivalent to one, such as 'She did it *in order to make her car safer*'. These explanations may plausibly be taken as elliptical versions of inductive-nomological covering-law explanations, though it must be granted that giving them does not imply having the relevant constitutive generalization *in mind or ready to formulate:* even in the simpler case of explaining why a hand is swollen by noting it was stung by a bee, one need not have in mind, or ready to formulate, the generalization under which the swelling is subsumed, say that bee stings tend to produce (persistent) swellings shortly after they occur. The point is that to give such a purposive explanation comprehendingly one must be able to back it up, at least on reflection, by an appeal to the sort of relationship expressed by the generalization, which I shall call the *purposive principle,* an apt name if the principle is as pervasive as it seems and 'purposive' is understood broadly enough to include anything wanted. To deny that a want tends to produce actions believed necessary to realize its object would normally be to show a failure to understand what wanting is; and to see the relevance of citing a want to explaining an action is in part to be prepared to invoke this principle in elaborating one's explanation, or at least to appeal to the relationship it expresses.[7]

[7] If I am right about how such action-explaining generalizations can figure in our explanatory practices without being explicitly formulated by people explaining actions

It turns out, I think, that the notion of believing is to be accounted for by the same sort of theoretical construct approach to explanatory concepts. Notice that the purposive principle just discussed is equivalent to one in which believing is more prominent: if one has a belief to the effect that performing an action—*A*-ing, for short—will tend to produce some state of affairs, *x*, then if one wants *x*, one tends to *A*. Similarly, we can explain action (for a further end) as well by appeal to the crucial (instrumental) belief as by appeal to the motivating want: if she did it because she wanted to make her car safer, she did it because she believed it would make her car safer, and vice versa. This equivalence confirms that believing and wanting are *both* crucial in explaining actions, and our ability to shift between them as just illustrated supports my thesis that people who explain actions in the normal ways at least tacitly understand the purposive principle partly constitutive of both.

There are, of course, other such constitutive propositions for believing. Some of these propositions connect believing with avowal of the proposition in question: we tend to avow what we believe. Some connect it with inference: we tend to believe, in an inferential way, obvious consequences of what we believe. Some connect it with perception: under certain conditions, if one can see that (a proposition) *p* is true, one tends to believe it is. And there are other cases. But again, we find that we cannot fruitfully give an illuminating non-circular analysis (for example, because wanting, which is intelligible only in relation to believing, must be invoked to understand when believing will actually lead to action); and again, the constitutive propositions are, taken together, testable in a way appropriate to their status as theoretical generalizations.[8]

The Cognitive and Motivational Elements of Intending

We have seen some reason to think that wanting and believing are important in understanding action. But intending is often thought to be *the* basic action concept, perhaps because it seems central in

---

in the light of them, then some of the insights of the simulation approach to understanding action (on which one understands another's behavior by a kind of simulation of relevant aspects of it) may be accommodated. Certainly a grasp of the relationships expressed in these generalizations can be a partial basis for success in simulation. For a valuable discussion of the simulation approach see Robert M. Gordon, "The Simulation Theory: Objections and Misconceptions," *Mind and Language* 7 (1992).

[8] In "The Concept of Believing," I present and defend a theoretical-construct account of believing quite parallel to the account in Chapter 1.

intentional action. It is certainly of immense importance. I argue in Chapter 2, however, that it can be adequately understood in terms of believing and wanting. They are absolutely indispensable to action theory, and if we can understand intending by appeal to them, our overall view of action is both better unified and more economical. Let me briefly indicate the shape of this conception of intending.

What we intend to do we typically expect to do and often plan to do; it is not enough to hope to do it. Chapter 2, "Intending," argues that although confidence that one will *A* is not required for intending to *A*, one must at least believe that it is probable that one will *A*. This does not imply that one must have a probability belief: I refer to a *disjunction of beliefs*—for example, that I will, or that I certainly will, or that I am bound to by tomorrow—not to a *disjunctive belief*, such as the belief that (either) I will or I probably will.[9] The point is that we need some minimal cognitive condition to capture the difference between intending and merely hoping, and to express the way in which intending implies a sense that the action is, as it were, part of one's future. Indeed, without this condition it is hard to explain the role of intentions in planning: we normally plan on the presupposition that we will do what we intend to do.[10]

If intending is cognitive in embodying what we might call a fulfill-ment-belief, it is certainly motivational in implying a tendency to perform the intended action. A natural thing to say is that what one intends to do, one wants to do. Some have resisted this, especially on the ground that one can intend to *A* out of a sense of duty to *A*, yet not want to do it. It is true that there are unpleasant duties which, in some contexts, we would deny wanting to do; but there is surely a broad sense of 'want'—one encompassing desires for things purely

[9] The wording in Chapter 2 may not always make this plain, but the overall thrust is that some appropriate belief to the effect that one will *A*, even if it is only that one probably will, must enter in; any number of specific beliefs will do, including a belief that it is certain that one will.

[10] For discussion of this matter, see Michael E. Bratman, *Intention, Plans, and Practical Reason* (Cambridge: Harvard University Press, 1987), which adopts a similar condition; and for discussion of plans and planning theory, as well as defense of some of the central points in Chapter 2, see my "Intention, Cognitive Commitment, and Planning," *Synthese* 86 (1991). Other aspects of this chapter are defended in Chapter 5 and in "Deliberative Intentions and Willingness to Act: A Reply to Professor Mele," *Philosophia* 18 (1988). Mele's *Springs of Action* (New York and Oxford: Oxford University Press, 1992), also discusses plans in relation to intention and contains a treatment of intending which contrasts with mine. Different cognitive conditions on intending and intentional action from the ones I propose are defended by Frederick Adams, "Intentional Action: The Simple View," *Mind and Language* 1 (1986).

as a means to others—in which we would generally avow just such a want. Chapter 2 argues this at length, noting, for example, the breadth of 'What do you want to do today?', which can evoke a list of actions including unpleasant duties. In any case, the relevant notion of wanting is the one explicated in Chapter 1; surely intending satisfies the set of lawlike propositions it argues are constitutive of wanting.

The conception of intending that emerges, then, is of an attitude that, whether it arises from practical reasoning or from decision or even from an "automatic" reaction, as in responding to a sudden crisis on the highway, is a special marriage of the conative and the cognitive. The cognitive element is a belief, very roughly an expectation of fulfilling the constituent want, that is, of A-ing; the conative element is (normally) a want *on balance,* that is, one stronger than any want the agent, S, has for something S believes incompatible with realizing the first want.[11] This view not only explains the role of intentions in planning but also explains why we normally cannot intend to do things we believe incompatible: it is normally wants on balance that are constituents in intending, and we cannot want, on balance, each of two things we believe incompatible. Similarly, because a want on balance normally either has no motivational competition in the agent or has prevailed over the competition it had, we can explain why people tend to do (or try to do) things they intend: what we intend is typically something that we predominantly want to do.[12]

The Volitional Conception of the Will

Quite apart from whether one regards wanting or intending as the fundamental (or most fundamental) practical attitude, it is clear that

---

[11] The agent only normally wants on balance to do the intended thing because one may temporarily forget a stronger incompatible want and thereby form an intention to do something one would not intend to do apart from this lapse.

[12] There is a great deal more to say about the account of intending, and I have extended it, as well as replied to criticisms by Hugh McCann and Alfred Mele, in "Intending, Intentional Action, and Desire," in Joel Marks, ed., *The Ways of Desire* (Chicago: Precedent, 1986). It has been noted, for example, that on my view not every intentional action is intended, since one might intentionally A merely in the hope of achieving something, without intending that. One point made in that essay is that the *typical* cases of intentional action are intended, and that a name can well emerge from typical cases; another is that my view does not imply that intentional action ever fails to be rooted in *intentionality,* which seems the more important point. In any event, we must surely avoid conflating intending with such weaker attitudes as hoping.

an account of the explanation of action must still explain how *either* of these, or indeed any dispositional mental element, can yield action. Intentions do not execute themselves; wants do not by themselves yield the actions they motivate. I may want ever so much to stop by the roadside for fresh fruit; if I do not see any, or at least have the thought that there may be some nearby, I drive on. Wants on balance, particularly when they form the motivational core of intentions, may indicate the direction of the will; but something active, such as a decision that now is the time to stop, must activate them. This is one among other places where volitions seem essential posits in action theory.

Volition, unlike wanting or intending, is a technical notion; and despite considerable agreement over the roles volition is to play, there are many conceptions of it. Chapter 3, "Volition and Agency," presents several of these conceptions. One way to achieve an overall understanding of volition is to think of it as tailor-made to answer Wittgenstein's famous question, "What is left over if we subtract the fact that my arm goes up from the fact that I raise it?" One plausible answer is: volition, whether conceived, generically, as willing or, more specifically, as trying or as a kind of mental doing. Whatever volition is, it lies in the category of events, hence is a candidate for what triggers such dispositional states as intending. Chapter 3 sketches various conceptions of volition; but rather than argue for any one of them as the best, I prefer to lay out the philosophical problems that motivate volitional theories and then explore how well an alternative view can deal with them. These problems include, in addition to the two mentioned, the difficulty of explaining what happens to make one falsely believe one has raised one's arm when it is anesthetized, yet, though one does not raise it, one takes oneself to obey a doctor's order to raise it.

This anesthetization case is analogous to an important one in epistemology. Just as a natural explanation of why one is surprised by the arm's not rising is that one does (or experiences) something normally involved in raising one's arm—namely, a volition—it is natural in the case of Macbeth's hallucinating a dagger to say that he saw all he normally does in seeing a dagger, but without there being any such physical object before him to be (literally) seen. In the latter case we posit something like sense-data as fundamental in perception: they are the basic items perceived, or at least are basic in perception. In the former, we posit volition as fundamental in action: it is the basic thing done, or at least is basic in action. This is an important analogy. Chapter 3 shows that there are alternative explanations in both cases. For instance, whatever normally accompanies one's intention to raise one's arm in cases in which one takes oneself to be doing it could give one the *sense* of doing it, just as whatever normally happens in one's visual field when one sees a dagger can give one the visual sense of seeing a dagger. It does not follow in the perceptual case that one actually sees something non-physical, and it does not follow in the behavioral case that one does (or experiences) something volitional.

Even if the evidence for volitional accounts is inconclusive, they would be a reasonable choice in action theory if there were not more plausible competing accounts of the crucial problems that motivate them. The final section of Chapter 3 sets out a guidance and control model of action. This model allows that volition may play some role in action but does not give it a central role. This model shows, for example, that the execution of intentions can be explained in terms of events we must already countenance: sudden thoughts, decisions that now is the time to act, perceptual cues such as glimpsing a beautiful fruit stand, and other events. Ordinary human actions need not ride upon the prior action, or respond to the underlying command, of an executive will; they may be triggered by any of a number of events, and they are monitored and guided by cognitive, motivational, and perceptual factors. This conception is developed further in Chapter 6, which shows how, even apart from volition, actions may be under the control of the reasons that produce and sustain them.

II. Explanation by Reasons

Chapters 1 to 3 show the enormous importance of wants and beliefs in understanding both action and intention. Indeed, insofar as volition is important in action theory, wants also play a role in understanding it. Volition will surely imply wanting to bring about its object, and, like intending, it will doubtless imply some positive cognitive attitude, such as taking the action in question to be possible: willing, as opposed to mere wishing, does not extend to what one takes to be out of the question. There is far more to be said, however, to explain and develop the suggested nomic conception of commonsense explanations of action. That is the business of Chapters 4 to 6.

Intentionalistic Understanding and Nomic Connections

Many philosophers might agree with my view that the purposive generalization, which links wants to actions performed in order to satisfy them, is both central to the commonsense concepts of wanting and believing and a crucial underpinning in everyday explanations, but deny that the generalization is testable. Chapter 4, "Intentionalistic Explanations of Action," critically responds to a prominent line of argument from the premise that wants and beliefs are "logically" connected to the actions they explain, to the conclusion that they cannot be causally (or nomically) connected to them. After all, this *logical connection argument* runs, since an agent's tending to A is part of what we mean by the agent's wanting something and believing that A-ing is necessary to getting that thing, it cannot be a contingent fact, and must indeed be true a priori, that when one wants something and believes A-ing is necessary to getting it, one tends to A.

What Chapter 4 does, above all, is argue that the relevant kind of connection of meaning is a kind exhibited by some nomic principles and hence does not entail either metaphysical necessity or a priori status. Consider, for example, the generalization that (normally) a magnet exerts a force on iron filings brought near it. This tendency is surely "part of what we mean" by 'being magnetic', but the generalization is testable. We have other ways of identifying something as magnetic, and we can thereby non-trivially predict that something so identified will exert the expected force. Similarly, there is a theory of magnetism, and, on the basis of it, there are various ways in which the concept of magnetism is connected with others.

The general lesson here is that, for an important kind of concept— I suspect any concept that is explanatory in the way wanting and believing are—what expresses its content is not a single condition providing a synonym or analytic equivalent, but a pattern of connections each expressible in generalizations that are lawlike and testable. In part because dispositional factors such as wants and beliefs are not events, in the strict sense in which a (non-agent) cause is an event, generalizations like the purposive one linking wants to actions need not be considered causal.[13] But this generalization supports subjunctives, for instance 'If I wanted x, I would have A-ed, which I believe would have gotten me x'', and it has at least some predictive as well as some explanatory power. One may complain that a mere tendency generalization is not truly a law;[14] but even if that is so, such a generalization can still be law*like*, in a way that both precludes a priori status and likens it to generalizations used in at least some of the sciences.

Two Concepts of Explanation by Reasons

The positive picture of action associated with the logical connection argument is sometimes called hermeneutic. The picture derives in part from the later Wittgenstein and emphasizes the way in which an explanatory appeal to reasons makes the action it explains intelligible in the context of the explanation. When we explain what someone has done by appeal to a want or by saying, for example, that she gave a long assignment in order to give her students more practice, we exhibit the *meaning* of the action for the agent. Chapter 5, "Wants and Intentions in the Explanation of Action," both meets objections by some writers in the hermeneutic tradition and shows how the nomic intentionalistic account I propose can accommodate their plausible positive claims. In responding to the objections, I make a number of points. Let me amplify just two.

First, it is essential to distinguish between a concept's being explicable only in relation to others and, on the other hand, its instances being known only through the explicative elements. Absolutely nothing I have said implies that we normally *know* what we want, or believe, only through the sorts of relationships needed to explicate wanting and believing, for example action aimed at realizing our wants. Others may have to know what we want in this way—and that we use the relevant relationships in making inferences about others confirms my account—but I can know, non-inferentially, what I want. I grant that it can be part of the concept of a mental state in

---

[13] Chapter 5 indicates how, when a substance, for instance a scythe, is intelligibly said to cause something, for example a cut, an event involving it may be posited as the intended cause in the strict sense. Similar points can be applied to agents as causes, but there the case is more complicated. Chapter 10 gives references to defenses of agency theory.

[14] I deal with this objection in "Inductive-Nomological Explanations and Psychological Laws," *Theory and Decision* 13 (1981).

general, as opposed to wanting or believing in particular, that the subject tends to have non-inferential knowledge of that state; but a contingent basis of such knowledge is also consistent with my account. Whether a concept is theoretical, then, in the wide sense relevant here, is one thing; how its instances are known is another.

A second issue concerns the possibility that on my account one can intend to do something that one believes one will be compelled to do. It is true that the account allows this; it even allows that I intend to do something that I believe I will in the end do unintentionally. Here it is essential not to infer from the oddity of self-ascribing such intentions to the impossibility of having them. Usually, *saying* one intends to A suggests that one presupposes one will A intentionally and—if one does not take oneself to be under some kind of duress—freely. But note that in the odd cases we are considering S wants, on balance, to do the deed and would, other things equal, do it freely and intentionally if not interfered with. I have called such intentions *passive* to indicate their special character (though the passivity may lie more in the agent than in the intending). But it seems clear that passive intentions do express the relevant "commitment" of the will; they simply differ in the surrounding cognitive context. In Chapter 6, I argue that it is a mistake to import beliefs about how one *will* A into the content of the intention *to* A. An intention to A, despite anticipated abnormal circumstances, is still (typically) an intention simply to A. Suppose I believe that by making a sudden (but important) left turn, I will lose the friend who is following me; I can still intend to make that turn, without intending to lose the friend, whom in fact I may hope will see the turn in time.

My proposed reconciliation between the nomic and hermeneutic views can now be put simply. A nomic relation between intentional states and the actions they explain is compatible with semantic and other culturally determined relations between the *contents* of those attitudes and the *types* of actions in question. My wanting to get fresh fruit and my believing that this stand has it may nomically explain (or even cause) my stopping, quite consistently with the fact that the existence of a fruit stand here is sufficient, given the goal of getting fruit, to make intelligible an action of the type, stopping at this stand, for anyone who has that goal. The action-type, stopping at a fruit stand, is intelligible as a means to the goal, getting fruit; my action-token, my stopping at a specific time, is both intelligible and explainable as guided by my believing this instrumental proposition, toward satisfying my want, which in turn expresses this goal. It is because I have the want and belief that the action-type in question *has* meaning for me; and the meaning relation is, as the hermeneuticists maintain, crucial to the intelligibility of the type of action performed in the context.

We might even go further beyond what is in the chapter: because wants and beliefs, as intentional attitudes, are individuated by their content, they would not be the attitudes they are apart from that content. Wanting to x is different from wanting to y, even if these actions are (in fact) identical, as where meeting one's advisor, which one wants to do, is identical with meeting the person who will make one anxious for the next fortnight. Content therefore plays at least an indirect role in giving desires whatever generative or causal power they have. It is in virtue of its content that a want points to something as a goal to be sought by the agent; it is in virtue of its content that an instrumental belief indicates to the agent what action will realize that goal. The specific causal powers of these attitudes, then, are partly determined by their content, and that is the very factor which, on the hermeneutic view, enables them to make action intelligible.[15]

The Causal and Explanatory Power of Reasons

Acting for reasons is a central element in human psychology and may be *the* distinctive characteristic of agents. What sorts of things constitute reasons for acting? I have so far spoken in a way that might leave doubt about whether such reasons are intentional states, for instance wanting, or, instead, the contents of such states, say the

[15] In speaking of content I mean intentional content, the kind expressed by infinitive clauses as illustrated or by subjunctives like 'I want that my advisor approve the material'. There are also *de re* wants, so called because they are *of* the thing wanted in a relatively direct way compared to the former (*de dicto*) cases. If I want, regarding a fellow citizen I see at a meeting, that he support my motion, and, if he is the man who undermines what he supports by his manner of promoting it, I may be said to want the promoter-spoiler to support my motion, or, less misleadingly, to want, regarding him, that he support it. But while wanting, of x, that it be F is equivalent to wanting, of y, that it be F where $x = y$, the 'that'-clause remains intentional; if, e.g., his supporting my motion happens to imply his spoiling it, we may not conclude that I want him to spoil it. The logic of want-attributions raises interesting technical problems, but needs no further treatment here. For further discussion of mental content and of the causal power of the mental generally, see John Heil and Alfred R. Mele, eds., *Mental Causation* (Oxford: Oxford University Press, 1992). My "Mental Causation: Sustaining and Dynamic," is one of the essays in that collection especially relevant to the explanatory role of intentional concepts and their contents.

goal constituting the content of a want and expressed by the infinitive phrase typically used to specify what the want is for, for example 'to promote philosophical thinking'. Since these are two quite different kinds of things, the former being a psychological entity and the latter some kind of abstract one, I call the former a reason state and the latter a reason proper. The latter is the kind of thing that any number of us can presumably share, since we can want precisely the same thing, whereas we cannot be in the (numerically) same state, but only in the same kind of state. Since acting *for* a reason is in some sense a causal notion, and abstract entities are not terms in causal relations, reasons proper are not causes. Thus, actions for reasons, which are in some causal way responses to reasons—the 'for' surely means roughly 'on account of'—must be responses to reason states, which, unlike abstract contents, can be causal factors. But an adequate account of action for a reason should also bring out the role played in such action by reasons proper. That role is in part to provide the kind of intelligibility just described in reconciling nomic and hermeneutic approaches. Chapter 6, "Acting for Reasons," characterizes this role further. Its main business, however, is to sketch the kinds of reasons there are in the domain of action and to give an account of what it is to act for one.

There are at least five kinds of reasons important in action theory. First, there are reasons to A, illustrated by the (normative) reasons there are to preserve world peace. Second, there are reasons for S to A, for example for *me* to worry about doing the conference; these are the person-relative normative reasons applicable specifically to the agent (even if they would be equally reasons for another person in exactly the same position and are reasons for certain other people, such as others who have learned of my problem). A third category comprises reasons S *has* for A-ing, which are personal, but need not be normative, as where they are ignoble motives or arise from false beliefs: from ill-grounded fear one can have a reason to avoid someone, though, normatively, there is none, and one can, after discovering the facts, say that one no longer has any reason for the avoidance. Fourth, there are reasons *why* S A's—explanatory reasons—and these can be merely causal, as where anger (nonpurposively) explains why someone is yelling. And there are reasons *for which* S A's—the richest kind, which must also be at least explanatory and personal: we cannot act for a reason we do not have or for one that plays no explanatory role in our action. These are the reasons that are of greatest importance in action theory.

Acting for a reason is a complex and elusive notion. Plainly, an explanatory condition is required: a want expressing the reason and a belief connecting it to the action must jointly provide an explanation of why the agent did the thing in question. But far more is required. Agents have a sense of their reason(s) for acting, and to capture part of this sense I propose an attribution condition: S has a non-inferential disposition to attribute an action for a reason to the motivating want and the connecting belief. We find on reflection, however, that if this want and belief produce an action in the wrong *way*, we have behavior that is merely an effect of them, not action that is a response to them. Chapter 6 devotes considerable effort to ruling out accidental and wayward causal connections.

In very broad terms, action for a reason is, above all, action under the control of reason: it is a discriminative response to one or more reasons of the agent, guided by the agent's beliefs, and made intelligible by the content of the motivation and cognition underlying it. This is a causal conception; and while it is consistent with the nomic account of action-explanation presented in earlier chapters, it does not entail that account. One could try to develop a causal account of actions which is not nomic, or one could argue for a nomic account different from mine. I believe that something like my highly qualified nomic construal of such explanations provides a good interpretation of how actions are explained by reasons; but the account of acting for reasons given here does not require that interpretation.

III. Freedom, Determinism, and the Scope of Responsibility

Even when we understand what action is and how it is explainable by reasons, we may be quite at a loss to understand what it means for an action to be free. An action for a reason, even if it must be autonomous in the sense sketched in Chapter 6, need not be free. The problem is compounded if we try to frame a conception of freedom that permits actions to be *both* caused and free, especially if we allow that they may be nomically caused in the way they would be if determinism should be true. There are also degrees of freedom in action and corresponding degrees of responsibility for it. And there are specific problems about the extent to which special liabilities, for example self-deception and weakness of will, may affect responsibility, as well as about its scope. The four chapters in Part III address mainly these problems.

Freedom in Action

Free action is worth wanting, and the notion would be of interest even if it were not crucially connected with moral responsibility. In action theory, however, the impetus to understand free action comes substantially from ethics, specifically from the widely held conviction that, for what one does unfreely, one is not morally responsible— roughly, not appropriately considered in the dimension of assessment ranging from blameworthy to praiseworthy. As 'unfreely' suggests, we often understand freedom in action by ruling out its underminers. I believe that, in any case, free action is best understood in contrast with compelled action: our intuitions about compulsion are clearer, in part because compulsions are quite definite by comparison with freedom as the normal status exhibited by countless kinds of actions. The strategy of Chapter 7, "Moral Responsibility, Freedom, and Compulsion," is, in the context of its relevance to moral responsibility, to explicate free action as uncompelled action.

It has been widely held that moral responsibility for an action presupposes its being freely performed. I argue against this, noting how, if one's duty is to guard a missile launcher even at the cost of one's life, one could be subject to a kind of pressure that renders one's giving the launch combination unfree, yet leaves one responsible for doing so. Granted, in the terminology of Chapter 6, the action is autonomous, being under the control of reason, even if the motivating reasons are products of coercion. This sort of case raises the question of *degrees* of compulsion, and I go on to argue that it *is* true that the guard could have done otherwise, in the sense relevant to moral responsibility; for one thing, a morally sound person could reasonably have been expected to *do* otherwise—to make a different autonomous choice, we might say.

In part because of the normative role played by compulsions as at least prima facie excusers, I argue that where certain kinds of motives play a major role in producing an action, it is not compelled; I call these motives of personal gain. If I would not have done something had it not seemed to bring me gain (as opposed to, say, protection from harm), I can hardly have done it under compulsion. Other conditions required to understand compulsion are non-motivational; we must, for example, acknowledge the compelling effect of certain interferences with the brain.

The account of freedom and compulsion which emerges provides for both a general conception of compulsion as undermining freedom and for a stronger kind of compulsion: strict unavoidability, the kind implied by 'could not have done otherwise' as used to attribute an excusatory degree of compulsion. In explicating 'could have done otherwise', I give a non-conditional account: one can do otherwise provided one's action is not explainable in a way that implies the strong compulsion that goes with strict unavoidability. This contrasts with a conditional construal, on which one can do otherwise provided that *if* things had been different in a certain way, one would have done otherwise. The contrast is important for understanding both responsibility and the free will problem in general, in ways brought out in Chapter 10. If, however, anything close to my account of freedom and responsibility is correct, freedom does not rule out—although it also does not entail—determinism, or even the limited thesis that actions are deterministically caused, that is, subsumable under exceptionless laws of nature. My account is thus compatibilist.

Self-Deception, Rationality, and Responsibility

Self-deception has been widely thought to manifest irrationality and to constrain our freedom. One way to assess its significance for action is to examine its effects on practical reasoning, which is crucial for much of our rational action. Chapter 8, "Self-Deception and Practical Reasoning," does this, proceeding from accounts of both self-deception and practical reasoning.

To be self-deceived, with respect to a proposition, p, is roughly to know, unconsciously, that *not-p*, yet to avow sincerely, or be disposed to avow sincerely, that p, and to have at least one want motivating this condition, specifically one that explains (in part) both why the belief is unconscious and why one is disposed to avow that p. Given the understanding of wanting and believing developed in Chapter 1, both may be unconscious, that is, such that S does not believe (at least consciously) that S has them, and in general cannot, without special techniques, find this out; but otherwise unconscious wants and beliefs behave as one would expect. This point is crucial: it enables us to understand much self-deceptive behavior in the same purposive framework applied in earlier chapters, and it explains how self-deception, by influencing wants and beliefs, can affect practical reasoning.

I take practical reasoning to be, in the most general terms, reasoning undertaken to determine what to do. More specifically, it is an inferential process containing at least one motivational premise—such as that I want to plant low-maintenance perennials—and at least one cognitive (connecting) premise—say that going to Campbell's is necessary to find them—to a practical judgment as conclusion—for example that I should go to Campbell's. Now clearly self-deception can supply, by virtue of its constituent want, a motivational premise. It can also influence the reasoning process. It may even lead to an agent's doing practical reasoning that serves as a rationalization.[16]

From the point of view of freedom and responsibility, the most important thesis of the chapter is that actions emerging from self-deceptive practical reasoning are not necessarily either irrational or unfree. Indeed, the chapter makes clear how self-deception, rationalization, and other prima facie excusatory or at least extenuating influences on action can play a considerable role in producing an action while doing little if anything to reduce the agent's moral responsibility for it. This is in part because action influenced by self-deception—especially if it emerges from practical reasoning—can be under the control of reason in a way that makes the application of moral standards of responsibility appropriate. More generally, it is because compulsion, as described in Chapter 7, is simply not implied by the sorts of influences that self-deception most typically has on action. Diminished responsibility is a subtler matter; and the chapter provides a number of categories of influence on action. These are meant to help in determining the extent to which self-deception, rationalization, and similar potential extenuators actually reduce responsibility.

The Sources and Scope of Moral Responsibility

So far, in discussing freedom and responsibility, I have considered mainly the nature of free action and its relation to moral responsibility.

[16] The notion of rationalization is sketched in passing in several chapters; I have given a full-scale account of it in "Rationalization and Rationality," *Synthese* 65 (1985). For

Might we also be responsible for our character? This is a central question for Chapter 9, "Responsible Action and Virtuous Character."

Three kinds of responsibility for traits of character must be distinguished here. There is *generative responsibility*, which is responsibility for having produced the trait in question, say self-control; this is a trait one can develop. There is *retentional responsibility*, which is for retaining the trait, for example sloppiness; even people who (being badly brought up) could not help becoming sloppy can change their ways. And there is *prospective responsibility*, which is for developing the trait, for instance supportiveness in place of dominance. We are generatively responsible for relatively few of our traits; but we are surely retentionally responsible for some of them and, given normal powers of self-development, may be responsible, prospectively, for acquiring other traits. These may include some virtues, such as honesty and industry; the higher the ideals to which one is committed, the wider the range of traits one may have a responsibility to cultivate or produce in oneself. Two theoretical points in the chapter bear mentioning here.

First, responsibility (of any kind) for traits is by and large traceable to responsibility for action. For instance, if one is retentionally responsible for sloppiness, this is owing to responsibility for omitting to exercise more care, and so forth; and to be prospectively responsible for becoming supportive is a matter of responsibility, say, to try sufficiently hard to help others. Second, the roots of responsibility, in all three kinds of case, seem internal, in the sense that they are constituted by something the agent does, or can do, at the level of internal mental or decisional action. Even if one does nothing to cause oneself to be sloppy, one can resolve to improve and can monitor one's performance with that end in mind. Generative responsibility for deviousness can derive from rehearsing ways to get around people; retentional responsibility for sloppiness can trace to omitting to exercise care, for example by deciding it is not worth the trouble; and prospective responsibility for becoming supportive can focus on one's ability to resolve to help other people.

If there is a reason for this internal rootedness of responsibility, it

---

valuable discussion of both self-deception and rationalization, see Brian McLaughlin and Amelie Rorty, eds., *Perspectives on Self-Deception* (Berkeley: University of California Press, 1988); and Alfred R. Mele, *Irrationality* (Oxford: Oxford University Press, 1987), esp. chaps. 9 and 10, and "Recent Work on Self-Deception," *American Philosophical Quarterly* 24 (1987).

may be the sense that, when one does what one should internally, the crucial step is taken: if the world is too recalcitrant for one's effort to yield the desired result, this is not one's fault (or responsibility). If I decide to do my duty and set myself on the initial path, a sudden paralysis, or an external barrier imposed by others, will prevent my succeeding; but I have done all I can. An internal conception is readily combined with a volitional approach to action but does not require it: volition is not the only internal element that can serve as a basis of responsibility. On the other hand, an internal theory of responsibility can make various uses of volition, even if it does not take all action to be volitionally grounded.

Knowledge and Freedom, Necessity and Necessitation

Chapters 7 to 9 portray moral responsibility in a way compatible with determinism. But as I grant in Chapter 9, it is odd, insofar as one thinks of an action as determined by factors extending backward before one's birth, to speak of the action as free. It is also odd to speak of an action as both free and causally necessitated. To be sure, since the lawlike propositions that I take to underlie actions are tendency generalizations, they do not imply that, given the generative motivation underlying an action, an action of that kind *invariably* occurs. But I have not ruled this out, and compatibilism entails that freedom is consistent with the existence of universal laws underlying action. The main purpose of Chapter 10, "Modalities of Knowledge and Freedom," is, by drawing on crucial epistemological analogies, to clarify the sense in which, if determinism is true, actions are necessitated.

The central distinction is between (1) the (nomic) necessity of general laws and of the conditional propositions that are instances of them, and (2) the necessity of individual events (assuming there might be such necessity). The point is easiest to see by analogy. Consider the claim that if you know, you can't be wrong. This can be rendered as, for example, 'It is necessary that if you know that p, then p' or, more idiomatically, as 'If you know that p, then p must be true'. Similarly, a conditional proposition instantiating purposive generalizations of the kind I have defended might be rendered—if we imagine enough qualifications built in to make it universal—either as 'It is (nomically) necessary that if I want on balance to plant perennials and believe this requires going to Campbell's Nursery, then I will go there', or, more idiomatically, as 'If I want on balance to plant perennials and believe this requires going to Campbell's, then I must go there'. Now, despite the obvious truth of 'If you know, you can't be wrong' on *some* interpretation, it does not imply that knowing entails that the proposition known must be true, that is, is necessarily true—which is not so: some known propositions are not necessary. Why, then, must we suppose that causing implies that the effect necessarily occurs? Knowing *necessitates the truth of what is known;* but the necessity here is in the *relation* of entailment between knowing and being correct, *not* in the correctness of what is known. Similarly, causal necessity governs the relation of cause to effect, not the occurrence of the effect. My action may be necessitated without being necessary: it may be necessarily brought about by, and so necessarily linked to, its cause, without being in itself necessary. Granted, if its cause were unconditionally necessary, it too would be necessary. But, I argue, there is no good reason to say that the causes of our actions are themselves any more than necessitated by antecedent causal factors which, in turn, "could have been otherwise."

The overall conclusion is that incompatibilism undeservedly gains from the power of our idiomatic ways of expressing certain modalities, and that a causal account of action, even if determinism is assumed (which it need not be), does not imply that it is unconditionally necessary that we do any of the things we in fact do. We may act for reasons in the normal ways and with all the implications of responsibility that, when we are uncompelled, this carries.

IV. Reason, Value, and the Rationality of Agents

The first three parts of this book bring out the nature of reasons and their importance both for understanding action and for appraising the agent's responsibility for action. But the ten chapters in question touch only briefly on what constitutes a rational action. In the light of what they show, it is clear that rational action is (at least in general) a kind of action for one or more reasons. But in what sense, if any, must the reason(s) be good, and how must rational action be related to a reason in order to be rational in virtue of that reason? These are among the central questions of the concluding three chapters.

The Sources of Value and Rationality

The most widely known approach to rational action, deriving above all from Hume, is instrumentalism. Instrumentalism is roughly the view that the rationality of an action is determined by how well it serves the agent's basic desires, whatever they are: since there is nothing a rational agent must want, even if there is much we naturally do want, there are no substantive constraints on the content of basic desires. In Chapter 11, "Rationality and Valuation," this view is examined and shown to be most plausible for action-types. That an action of a given type, say reciting a poem, would best serve my basic desires, for instance by providing pleasure to someone I care about, may count toward its rationality *for me*, that is, give me a reason to perform it; but unless I do this *for* a reason appropriate to its optimality in satisfying my basic desires, my particular act, the action-token, is not thereby made rational: I could instead have done the deed for a different and inadequate reason, say to show off, when I had much less desire to show off than to provide pleasure to the person I care about.

It turns out that a plausible instrumentalism needs a causal condition, as well as a way to account for both the quantity of satisfaction of desire that an action will yield and its probability of yielding that quantity given different possible outcomes. A natural direction to take in providing such an account is toward a quantified instrumentalism: rational action does not merely serve intrinsic desire, but *maximally* does so, roughly in the sense that when both the possible desired consequences of relevant actions are taken into account by assigning to them both a value and a probability, a rational action emerges as one that yields at least as high a score as any available alternative.[17]

When we consider how probabilities have been invoked in the maximization of expected utility frameworks for assessing rational action, we find still another problem: we normally do not *have* all the needed probability beliefs, as opposed to dispositions to form them. Typically,

---

[17] A numerical example is provided in Chapter 11 in connection with a decision about surgery. See pp. 283–84.

if I think that mailing a letter will get it to its destination in three days, I act on this belief when I want to get it there in three days. I do so quite apart from believing, as I may or may not, that, say, the probability of success is .95. And even if I compare mailing with faxing, I may not think in terms of probabilities, but simply in terms of, say, greater speed versus higher cost and a less sharp copy. Indeed, I would not be able, given what I know, to arrive at reasonable probabilities here, for example of a sharp appearance of a faxed copy.[18]

Even a causal version of instrumentalism which takes account of these problems about belief faces many further difficulties. One is the possibility that a basic desire to which an action is subordinate is irrational; another is that the belief connecting the action with the crucial desire(s) may be irrational. We do not regard drawing a conclusion as rational if the premises in which it is grounded are irrationally held, or if they do not adequately support it. Why should it be different in the case of action, where the grounding desire is analogous to the premises in reasoning and the rationality of the connecting belief is analogous to the degree to which the premises support the conclusion drawn from them? Many thinkers would accept such an analogy, and I go on to explore a plausible view—the information-responsiveness conception of rational action—that incorporates criteria for rational desire. This view constrains basic desires: they are rational provided that full exposure to relevant facts and information would not change them. The view is an improvement, but it leaves open the possibility that a desire "wired in" artificially is rational simply because inextirpable.

My own position is more objectivist than the information-responsiveness view. As in other cases, I propose to learn from an epistemological analogy. I argue that just as sensory experience justifies some non-inferential beliefs, certain other kinds of experiences, such as enjoyable ones, render intrinsic desires for such experiences rational. Intrinsic desires for things are wants for them "for their own sake," though the term is misleading in that it allows wanting them in virtue of their being enjoyable. Very roughly, if an action is well grounded in a rational desire—where such grounding also implies that one has a rational belief to the effect that the action will satisfy the desire—then that action is rational.

---

[18] The distinction here—between dispositional beliefs and mere dispositions to believe—is developed and defended in my "Dispositional Beliefs and Dispositions to Believe," forthcoming in *Noûs*.

Since valuations are like desires on this point—in that they are motivational states, are belief-guided in a similar way, and can take the same range of objects as wants—I apply the same conception to them. Here, too, rationality is well-groundedness. This view is objective insofar as it allows certain properties, such as being enjoyable, to count toward rationality for any person. But it is also pluralistic, since it places no restrictions on the range of experiences and activities that can be enjoyable and indeed allows other properties to count toward rationality. Just as there can be an objective epistemology that gives perception a special place in accounting for justified belief yet allows for alternative rational views of the world, there can be an objective theory of value and rationality that allows for different rational preferences and for contrasting rational actions on the part of different agents.

Reason and Will: Incontinence as a Challenge to the Theory of Rationality

Can we use the well-groundedness account of rational action just stated to understand how weakness of will affects the rationality of actions exhibiting it—*incontinent actions*, for short? I think so, and argue for this, though in different terms, in Chapter 12, "Weakness of Will and Rational Action."

The notion of weak-willed action from which I proceed is roughly that of uncompelled action against one's better judgment. Such action will normally be intentional, but one could act incontinently by doing something knowingly, yet not intentionally, that is against one's better judgment. One might disappoint a friend as a regretted consequence of helping another friend at the time the former hoped for assistance (for similar reasons, I think, rational actions need not be intentional). Typically, if one does something against one's better judgment, such as agreeing to meet someone earlier than one can reasonably expect to arrive, one exhibits some kind of failure in rationality. But must incontinent action be irrational?

Consider Alfred, a conscientious referee who judges that a paper, despite imaginative content, must be rejected because of flawed scholarship, which he finds downright irritating. When the time comes to check the rejection box, he cannot bring himself to do it and, without reversing his original judgment (or bringing it to mind), checks the box for allowing revision. It could be that, because of intellectual values deep in his nature, his relenting, rather than recommending straight rejection, could actually be the rational thing for him to do. Owing to redeeming features of the paper which somehow failed to inform his original judgment but have shaped his overall attitude, the judgment might not be as well grounded as the sudden decision to recommend allowing revision. Alfred might of course see this on reflection and cease to feel, for example, cowardly. But the point is that he makes a perfectly normal judgment on the basis of certain high standards; and if, at the time, we determined rationality wholly in terms of that, we would have to regard the ultimately better-grounded decision as irrational.

Reflection on this case and others leads me to formulate three models of rational action, each of which is compared to counterparts in the theory of justified belief. One is a *fidelity-to-premises model,* which says that the rationality of an action is a matter of how well it serves the desire(s) actually motivating it—its motivational premises—in the light of the belief(s) actually guiding it. A second model is inspired by a conception of the will (perhaps considered the representative of practical reason) as properly directing action; on this *executive model* an action is rational provided it is properly grounded in the relevant practical judgment, say that one ought to punish the child. The third model, the *holistic model,* construes the rationality of an action as determined by its relation to all of the agent's relevant motivational and cognitive states. Thus an action rational on either the fidelity-to-premises model or the executive model might be irrational because it does not take account of desires *other* than those determining the practical judgment, desires more important to the agent, or more rational, or both.

The holistic conception can be developed along the lines of the well-groundedness view of rationality articulated in Chapter 11. Although that view gives to the actual grounds of action a special place in determining its rationality—something almost any plausible view of rationality will do—it takes account of a much wider set of motivational and cognitive elements by recognizing that either kind of grounding element can be affected by *defeasibility.* Most obviously, a rational belief that *A*-ing will achieve my end will not render the action rational if I am overlooking a temporarily forgotten belief that *B*-ing will do so far better, and I know I can also perform *B.* My oversight regarding available means defeats the would-be rationality of the action. Similarly, even if *A*-ing satisfies a perfectly rational basic desire with optimal efficiency, if I rationally believe that some other action would satisfy a stronger and equally rational basic desire, it would not be rational (certainly not fully rational) for me to A. Here the defeater is an oversight concerning an achievable end. The details of such an account are numerous, and difficulties remain, but a holistic well-groundedness view enables us to see that even if incontinence always counts to some degree against the rationality of an action, the final determination of rationality in action must take account of far more.

The Internal Grounds of Rational Action

If a well-groundedness view of rational action is sound, then we may be able to learn something further from the analogy between rational action and justified belief. On one powerful view of justified belief, its justification is internal in the sense that what justifies it is something to which the believer has access by reflection or introspection, as contrasted with perceptual evidence or testimony, which require external sources of information. Now if the elements in virtue of which actions are rational are above all the agent's wants and beliefs (but in any case elements accessible to introspection and reflection), then rational action should be an internal concept much in the way justified belief apparently is. Thus, what makes an action rational is something like its justifying grounds in the agent's mind, including desires it is aimed at satisfying, as opposed to its being, in a certain way, externally successful, say in actually satisfying the desire(s) motivating it. This is the view developed in Chapter 13, "An Internalist Conception of Rational Action." Let me explain.

As argued in Chapter 6, we can normally know non-inferentially what we want and believe, and we tend non-inferentially to attribute our actions to the explaining wants and beliefs. We do not normally need inductive evidence, and certainly not external perceptual evidence, to become aware of our wants and beliefs. If so, then we have the appropriate internal access to the grounds of our actions. To be sure, we need access to other motivational and cognitive elements to get an adequately holistic picture of the rationality of our actions, but there is no reason to think we cannot achieve that. Notice, however, that the internalist conception of rationality implies only that we need internal access to the actual grounds of the rationality of our actions, not to grounds for *knowing* that these actions are rational. For that, we would need the internal capacity not only to be aware of our grounds but also to know that they *are* the actual (explaining) grounds of our action, which implies knowledge of causal connections. I argue that it is reasonable to suppose we have this capacity, but having it is not a requirement of the basic internalist view proposed.

This approach brings us back to something fundamental in action theory: the rootedness of action in the agent, not just in the body but in the mind. If action orginates internally (even if in response to external events), if its grounds are internal, and if, in addition, it is aimed at satisfying wants, which are also internal, it should not be surprising if its rationality is determined by factors that are internal, in a sense implying their accessibility to reflection, including self-directed monitoring of one's consciousness. This is not to suggest that a rational agent can be indifferent to the external world; but what is to be learned from that world must be reflected internally in order to yield rational beliefs and rational desires. When the reflection is undistorted, externally successful actions are possible; but it is their internal well-groundedness that makes them rational.

V. Conclusion

Human needs are innate and quickly give rise to desires. The first desires in a child's life produce responses, or disturbances, that seem unguided by belief. But very soon beliefs arise, and, guided by them, children learn to direct their behavior in ways that satisfy desire: agency has come upon the scene and with it, in roles about which there may always be dispute, volition. When desire and belief come together in the way that creates a motivated expectation of behavior, we have the beginnings of intention. Action for reasons occurs, and we can explain such action by appeal to reasons.

In the fully developed human agent, there is not only action for reasons but the activity of explaining actions by appeal to reasons for them. This rests on a grasp of the relations—nomic, I think—between the wants and beliefs of the agent and the actions they in some sense produce. These elements express reasons for which we act and, in themselves, constitute reason states. Action for reasons is a discriminative response to such elements; it is grounded in them in a sense that implies a special kind of causal relation through which the action is under the control of the agent's rational faculties.

Actions for reasons divide into the free and the unfree, though there are degrees of freedom which make some actions difficult to classify. The division between the free and the compelled must be made, I argue, in terms of the kinds of factors that explain action. We cannot say simply that an action nomically caused by antecedents is not free or that one not so determined is free. But if causation itself does not undermine freedom, many kinds of causes do. These include coercions by others, fears from within, and natural forces. Still, not every pressure from others or every dark force from within eliminates freedom; and responsibility extends both to actions produced by unconscious desires, as with self-deception, and, beyond action, to certain traits of character. Even if an action is causally necessitated by antecedents, they need not be the kind that compel; they may be quite ordinary motives. Beyond that, and equally important, they need not be unconditionally necessary. Mere conditional necessity will seem a threat to freedom, I believe, only on mistaken interpretations of natural law.

When we act for a reason, it need not be for a good one. It may seem that so long as we are efficiently getting what we most deeply want, we have a good reason and are acting rationally. But this instrumentalist view takes no account of the possibility that some basic desires may be irrational, others rational. Surely there are experiences that are—or at least may be rationally believed to be—worth wanting for their own sake. If so, then rational action should be understood in part in terms of satisfying desires of this sort: efficiency alone does not yield success if the end it achieves is of no value, and it does not yield rational action if the agent has no ground for taking the end to have some value.

We are built so that normally our practical judgments are good guides to rational action, even in a sense that seems to go beyond yielding efficient means to satisfying our basic desires considered simply as brute motivators. But we may be seriously mistaken in judgments about what we should do, and, if we are fortunate, act against them when we are. Sometimes we are fortunate in this way: nature has not entirely trusted us to our own judgment, and our natural leanings against an ill-considered or unwise judgment will sometimes prevail. Our success as rational agents is to be judged holistically, in relation to all of the wants and beliefs relevant to an action. These may go beyond those that explanatorily and causally ground an action, just as the factors relevant to a justified belief may go well beyond the premises on which that belief is based. But they seem to be potentially within our purview and internally accessible to us. This gives us much to work with both in understanding and in criticizing our actions. Not only can we act for reasons, we can also improve the reasons for which we act and thereby achieve higher and higher standards of rationality. It is along causal lines that information by which we guide our actions flows to us from the world and is reflected in our beliefs; and it is along causal lines that the power of our desires, guided by our beliefs, enables us to change the world. Our freedom and our rationality come not from escaping these causal lines, but from traveling them in the right ways, from the right kinds of motivational sources, to reasonable ends.

PART   I

DESIRE, INTENTION, AND VOLITION

Chapter 1

The Concept of Wanting

The concept of wanting is one of the most important in the domain of the philosophy of mind. Wants figure prominently in the explanation and prediction of action and in the description and assessment of persons. The notion of wanting also seems to be an important element in a number of other philosophically interesting concepts: pleasure, happiness, satisfaction, preference, valuation, interest, and others. Wants, like beliefs, are paradigms of the kinds of things cited as reasons for action; and though there is much disagreement about how wants and other reasons for action are related to the actions they rationalize, it seems obvious that we cannot understand what it is to act for a reason without understanding such concepts as wanting and believing. There has been much debate over whether wants and beliefs may be construed as causes of the actions they explain. I shall assume that such writers as Donald Davidson,[1] William P. Alston,[2] and Alvin I. Goldman[3] have achieved at least their negative purpose of showing that the major arguments against a causal theory of reasons are unsound. But I believe that there is more to be said in (1) explaining why those arguments are unsound and

---

[1] Donald Davidson, "Actions, Reasons, and Causes," *Journal of Philosophy* 60 (1963).

[2] William P. Alston, "Wants, Actions, and Causal Explanation," in Hector-Neri Castañeda, ed., *Intentionality, Minds, and Perception* (Detroit: Wayne State University Press, 1966).

[3] Alvin I. Goldman, *A Theory of Human Action* (Englewood Cliffs, N.J.: Prentice-Hall, 1970).

(2) clarifying the relation that wants and beliefs do bear to the actions they explain. Moreover, so far as I know, we do not yet have a satisfactory account of the concept of wanting. My aim is to develop such an account and through it to make a contribution to (1) and (2).

I. Wanting as a Theoretical Concept

People are often said to have done something simply because they wanted to, or even more commonly, because they believed it would lead to something (else) they wanted. Let us call wanting in this 'action-explaining sense' wanting in the primary sense. The other senses—for example, 'lack' (Her account was found wanting) and 'need' (The garden wants watering)—are far less important, especially in descriptions, explanations, and predictions. Wanting in the primary sense will be my concern. I shall not attempt, however, to give an explicit definition of the concept. For reasons that will emerge later, I believe we must explicate 'wanting' in some other way than by constructing a standard necessary-and-sufficient-condition analysis. But what alternatives are there?

One possibility is what we might call a theoretical construct analysis; and my proposal can be so called, since it construes the concept of wanting as analogous, in some very important respects, to such theoretical concepts as the concepts of an electron, a magnetic field, and an energy level. I shall make no attempt to define 'theoretical concept', but I shall assume that whatever else we say about theoretical concepts they derive their 'meaning' from the main lawlike propositions in which they figure. I shall not defend this view or try to define the notion of a lawlike proposition, but it should be of some help to say that I shall consider a proposition lawlike only if it supports counterfactuals and has at least some explanatory power. I hope to specify the main lawlike propositions in which the concept of wanting figures and to clarify the sense in which they are explicative of this concept. Thus, if it *is* fundamental to theoretical concepts that they derive their meaning from the main lawlike propositions in which they figure, then my account of wanting, rather than simply presupposing the notion of a theoretical concept, should make some contribution to clarifying it.

Alternatively, my task might be regarded as the formulation and exploration of the rules constitutive of the game in which 'want' functions. What I call explicative propositions would then be regarded as object language formulations of these rules, which, in Sellars's terminology,[4] we may call material rules of inference. To understand the concept of wanting would be to understand these rules; and to employ the concept, for example, in explaining actions, would be, in large part, to reason in accordance with them. This is compatible with maintaining, as I do, the parallel thesis for the main lawlike propositions in which the concept of wanting figures, namely, that the content of the concept is a function of its role in a nomological framework connecting it both with behavior and with other psychological concepts. I prefer to emphasize the nomological interpretation of the account that follows primarily because doing so brings out important analogies, which are often overlooked or denied by philosophers, between the concept of wanting and theoretical concepts.

Let us begin with the difficulty of deciding *what* lawlike propositions are crucial for explicating expressions of the form 's wants *p*', where S ranges over persons[5]—but for concreteness will often be replaced by 'Sam'—and *p* ranges over states of affairs (that-*p*) and over human actions and human activities (to *p*).[6] I shall not discuss this difficulty at any length. One procedure is of course to seek conceptually true completions of the schema, S wants *p* if and only if . . .'. And there are various other procedures. But whatever procedure we use, it seems reasonable, in constructing what I shall call the explicative set for wanting, to ask what propositions are such that whoever employs (as opposed to only understanding or merely mentioning) the concept of wanting must believe them. The force of the 'must' is this: if Sam failed to believe one of the explicative propositions, then, provided he understood all the concepts essential in them besides wanting, we could reasonably say either (1) that he does not fully understand what we (normally) mean by expressions of the form 'S wants *p*', or (2) (a somewhat remote possibility I shall hereafter

---

[4] See, e.g., Wilfrid Sellars, "Inference and Meaning," *Mind* 62 (1953).

[5] I do not deny that animals and prelingual children have wants in *some* sense, or that non-human rational beings might possibly have them; but my concern is with 'wanting' as applied to human beings who are fluent speakers of a natural language.

[6] I assume that wants for "things," e.g. for money or prestige, can be adequately expressed in this terminology, but I do not argue this. Nor do I discuss the related questions of the individuation of wants and of actions, or the complicated question of the precise logical form of 'want' sentences.

ignore) that, though he does understand this, if he uses these expressions at all he does not take them to have the force we normally take them to have, especially in explanation, prediction, description, and avowal.

Before introducing the explicative set, let me indicate some of the everyday patterns of inference that suggest the propositions I include. We often say such things as that because Sam wants p he will do A when he discovers that it will get him p. And if we know S wants p and is soon to find out he cannot have it, we usually conclude that he will be disappointed upon learning this. Similarly, if we know S wants p but is not expecting it, we usually suppose that he will be pleased to discover that it will occur. Wants figure even more frequently in contexts of explanation. By pointing out that Sam wants very much to get p, we can explain his harping on the subject of p. And we sometimes explain S's finding it unpleasant to talk (or think) about *not-p* by noting that he wants it. Furthermore, if S confides that he enjoys daydreaming about getting p, one good explanation of his enjoying such daydreams is that S wants p. We should also note a connection between wants and their avowals: barring deception, when S says he wants p, we believe him; and when we think he wants something, we usually expect him to say so when asked if he does. These points suggest a variety of connections between wanting and on the other hand feeling, thought, and action. I shall try to formulate these connections as precisely as I can without in effect proposing a rational reconstruction of our concept of wanting. Whether the explicative propositions I set out are the only ones constitutive of the concept is too large an issue to take up here. But I believe the comprehensiveness of the set makes my assumption of its completeness not implausible.

II. The "Laws" of Desire

Let me proceed, then, to the explanation and defense of what I propose as the explicative set for wanting:

W1 If *S* does or would find daydreaming about *p* pleasant, and *S* believes that there is at least some considerable probability of *p*'s occurring,[7] then, under favorable conditions, *S wants p*.[8]

W2 If (1) it would be (or is) unpleasant to *S* to entertain the thought that *p* is not (or probably is not) the case, or the thought that *p* will not be (or probably will not be) the case, and (2) *S* believes that there is at least some considerable probability of *p*'s occurring, then, under favorable conditions, *S wants p*.

W3 If *S wants p*, then (1) *S* tends to think (reflect, muse, or the like) or daydream about *p* at least occasionally, and especially in idle moments; and (2) in free conversation *S* tends to talk at least occasionally about *p* and subjects he believes to be connected with *p*.

W4 *S wants p* if and only if: for any action or activity *A* which *S* has the ability and the opportunity to perform, if *S* believes either (1) that his *A*-ing is necessary to *p*, or (2) that his *A*-ing would have at least some considerable probability of leading to *p*, or (3) that his *A*-ing would have at least some considerable probability of constituting attainment of *p*, then *S* has a tendency to *A*.

W5 *S wants p* if and only if: given that *S* has not been expecting *p*, if *S* now suddenly judged (or suddenly discovered, realized, or the like) that *p* is (is becoming, will become) the case, then *S* would immediately[9] tend to be pleased, joyful, or relieved about this.[10]

W6 *S wants p* if and only if: given that *S* has been expecting *p*, if *S* now suddenly judged (or suddenly discovered, realized, or the like) that *p* would not be the case, then *S* would immediately tend to be disappointed about this.

W7 *S wants p* if and only if: under favorable conditions, *S* has a tendency to avow that he wants *p*.

---

[7] This belief is required, I would argue, both here and in W_2, if we are to distinguish between wanting and merely wishing. One's estimate of the probability of *p*'s occurring may of course be based at least in part on the assumption that one does something to bring it about. The relevant notion of considerable probability is of course flexible, but this will not affect my arguments. The limiting case here, which can be approached but never reached, would seem to be believing *p* to be "factually impossible."

[8] This proposition, like W_5 and W_6, represents a development of one proposed by Richard B. Brandt and Jaegwon Kim in their important essay "Wants as Explanations of Actions," *Journal of Philosophy* 60 (1963): 427.

[9] The notion of immediacy here is not that of strict simultaneity; it is intended primarily to rule out cases in which *S*'s being pleased (or disappointed) is brought about ("mediated") by some belief (or want) that arises with or after the relevant judgment (discovery, etc.), such as the belief that the non-realization of *p* will lead to something *S* wants even more: this might make thinking of *p* unpleasant.

[10] As the discussion will show, the right-to-left constituent of W_5 must be qualified by 'under favorable conditions'.

First of all, a comment on 'under favorable conditions' and 'tendency'. I grant that these *can* be so construed as to trivialize the propositions in whose formulation they appear; for whenever an apparent counterexample is found, it may be claimed that, say, conditions were unfavorable. Hence, anyone using 'under favorable conditions' or 'tendency' should say as much as possible about what counts as unfavorable conditions or inhibiting factors. Yet given our present knowledge one cannot be exhaustive here: else we would need neither 'under favorable conditions' nor 'tendency'. But if tendency generalizations and those qualified by 'under favorable conditions' are not strong in implying that when the states of affairs specified in their antecedents occur then it is very probable that the states of affairs specified in their consequents will also occur, the generalizations are strong in implying that when the former occur and the latter do not, some explanation can normally be given and is often called for if the generalization is to be reasonably maintained. In specifying some of the relevant unfavorable conditions and inhibiting factors, I shall argue that W_1–W_7 meet this requirement. I cannot here consider the whole explicative set; but in concentrating on a representative subset of these seven explicative propositions, I shall make clear how we might specify the relevant conditions and factors for the whole set.

Let us start with W_1. Usually, when one finds it pleasant to daydream about something, say a walk in the country, one wants it, though often not on balance. But suppose one has enjoyed something to the point of satiation. One might still find it pleasant to daydream about repeating it. If for example, I very much enjoyed a trip to Capri, I might find it pleasant to daydream about going there. Yet it need not be the case here that I want to go to Capri, though perhaps I have something like an idle wish that I could conveniently go there. A second kind of unfavorable condition would be finding daydreaming about something pleasant because one finds it simply amusing; thus, S might find it pleasant to daydream about his favorite comedian enlivening a dull play which S recently had to sit through. Often such a daydream would imply wanting, but not always. But these may well be the principal unfavorable conditions for W_1; they seem infrequent compared to the favorable conditions, and when we can reasonably assume that the former two are absent, we can make quite probable inferences in accordance with W_1.

Now consider W_5, beginning with the left-to-right constituent (W_{5L}). Surely most of the time when one wants something, say a free weekend, one is pleased if one suddenly discovers it will come about. But though there is almost certain to be some reaction on the part of someone who wants p, to the sudden realization that it will occur, the reaction need not be that of being pleased, joyful, or relieved. When one indignantly thinks that p (e.g. an end to a war) is long overdue, one might be angry or at most mollified. Second, when S wants something she believes incompatible with p as much as or more than she wants p, S might well fail to be immediately pleased upon discovering that p has come about. The incompatible want here, that is, the want for something S believes incompatible with p, may be simply to avoid certain aspects of p, say the unpleasant aspects of keeping a promise. Thus, the tendency specified in W_{5L} may be inhibited by certain emotions and by a want incompatible with S's want for p. But when we can reasonably assume the absence of such inhibitors, which seem to be the most important kinds of inhibiting factors for W_{5L}, we can make quite probable inferences in accordance with it.

We also frequently make inferences in accordance with the right-to-left constituent of W_5 (W_{5R}). If, for example, people are pleased to discover that p will occur, we usually infer that they want p. But here too qualifications must be added. Suppose that Alica, a teacher, is pleased to discover that a former student Terence, will get a certain fellowship, though she has been unaware that he has even been a candidate for it. We might reasonably conclude that Alica has wanted things in general to go well for Terence, but not that she has wanted him to win the fellowship. Moreover, one might be pleased to discover that it is sunny simply because one likes a sunny day. Possibly these examples illustrate the only kinds of unfavorable conditions for W_{5R}. Such conditions are admittedly common; but often their absence can be reasonably assumed, and it appears that we can then make fairly probable inferences in accordance with W_{5R}. Note also that, in both unfavorable cases, though being pleased does not imply wanting p, it does seem explainable in terms of *some* want. To like sunny days, for example, is in part to tend to want them to occur.

W_4 is probably the most important in the set, since failure to believe it would indicate a more serious lack of understanding of 'S wants p' than failure to believe any other member of the set. Should we recognize unfavorable conditions for W_4? It could be argued that W_{4L} would not hold when one mistakenly believes that one lacks the ability or that one lacks the opportunity to do A. Suppose I want to go to my office but mistakenly believe that the roads are too icy to permit my driving there. Do I have a tendency to drive to work? For the ordinary sense of 'tendency' the question seems deviant. But as I am using 'tendency' the question is whether I am in a state such that I would drive to work unless something interfered; and here it seems reasonable to construe my mistaken belief as an inhibiting factor. Does W_{4R} hold? There might be one exception. Certainly in the normal case in which believing that A is necessary to p leads one to tend to do A, one wants p. But what ought we to say of a *habit* of doing things believed necessary to some end, such as a bricklayer's habit of doing (on the job) whatever he believes his boss wants him to do on the job? Perhaps one could not acquire this habit without in some sense wanting to do what one's boss wants done on the job, yet one could certainly retain the habit for some time after no longer wanting to do this. But it would then be at least misleading, and probably false, to say without qualification either that the bricklayer tends to do what the boss wants done on the job, or that he does whatever it is *because* he believes it necessary to doing what his boss wants. For these statements normally (and the latter perhaps always) imply, what is not here the case, that he acts in order to fulfill the wishes of his boss. Hence I shall not regard this sort of habit as an unfavorable condition. If, however, one added an under-favorable-conditions clause for this case and the above case of mistaken belief, this would be essentially consistent with my position.

Another prima-facie objection to W_{4R} is that if one believes doing something is necessary to fulfilling an obligation, one will normally tend to do it, even though one does not want to fulfill this obligation. But this objection does not apply here because I am concerned with wanting in the primary sense: an action like this can certainly be explained as having been performed in order to fulfill an obligation; and though we sometimes contrast wanting to do something with feeling obligated to do it, often we treat feeling obligated as involving wanting. We often say, regarding some task which we do not enjoy but feel obligated to perform, things like 'I'm working late; I want to study these applications'. Indeed, for any case in which I A in order that p but would usually say I did not want p when asked whether I do, we can imagine some context in which I could quite naturally avow a want for p. In the question 'What do you want to do today?', 'want' often has this broad range.

These remarks make clear what sorts of unfavorable conditions and inhibiting factors seem most important for W_1 and W_5; W_4 will be discussed in detail later. Though the lists are not exhaustive, it is clear that the relevant conditions and factors are certainly not too numerous to be taken into account in ordinary reasonings about people. These conditions and factors represent chiefly the effects of emotions, beliefs, and incompatible wants. Moreover, reflection will show that the interfering factors for W_6 are very much like those for W_5; similarly for W_1 and W_2, and for W_3 and W_7. Thus, understanding the qualifications built into the pattern of inferences exhibited by W_1–W_7 is easily within the reach of normal speakers of a natural language.

In putting W_1–W_7 forward as the core of a theoretical construct analysis of the concept of wanting, I am not suggesting they are all equally important. I have suggested for example, that W_4 is more important than any of the others. The sort of importance I refer to is primarily a function of how serious a lack of understanding of the concept of wanting one would show if one did not believe the proposition in question. There are various ways in which a person can manifest a failure to believe one of the explicative propositions. I might reject as groundless the inferences that they warrant; these are not unguarded inferences, but only inferences made on the assumption that at least the principal unfavorable conditions are absent. Second, I might regard one (or more) of the propositions as having too many exceptions to be generally reliable in reasoning about people, and I may thus only rarely reason in accordance with it. In the first case, I would show a more serious lack of understanding of 'S wants p' than in the latter. But it should be remembered that even if I were to fail to believe, say, W_2, this would not by itself provide grounds for saying without qualification that I do not understand 'S wants p': not fully understanding does not imply not understanding at all. And as this suggests, if the reason for my not believing one of the propositions is that I believe a proposition differing from it only in what may plausibly be considered minor respects, again we need not take this to show any substantial lack of understanding of 'S wants p'.

In the light of the foregoing discussion of W_1–W_7, I want to offer some argument for the thesis that a person's not believing one or more of them would give us good reason to say that the person does not fully understand the concept of wanting. I shall consider only W_5 and W_7; W_4 will be examined later, and the remaining propositions can be treated in the same way as W_5 and W_7.

Suppose I casually mention to Ann that Jim will be pleased to discover the increase in the library budget. Even if Ann did not know anything about his interest in the library, she would normally infer that he had wanted the increase (or at least some such benefit to the library). But suppose Ann for some reason thinks Jim will not be pleased and asks why I expect him to be. The answer might be (in accordance with W_{5L}) that he had wanted the increase. If she now said, 'That is irrelevant', I would be rightly puzzled, and in just the way one is when someone seems not to understand what clearly needs no explanation. If Ann had said, 'But he wanted even more for the money to go to the museum', she would be citing one of the relevant inhibiting factors, and her reply would not imply any failure to believe W_5. We should also leave open the possibility that she cites some inhibiting factor, such as extreme depression, not mentioned above. But for Ann to reject as groundless—not merely as inconclusive—the inference here warranted by W_5 would surely give us good reason to say that she does not fully understand 'S wants p'.

Similar examples can be found for W_7. Indeed, our belief of W_7 is so strong that when, in people's hearing, we have seriously avowed a want for p, if they denied that we wanted it we would usually take them to be questioning not our self-knowledge but our veracity. Moreover, if we believe S wants p, then, provided we think him honest and open, we expect him to say so when asked. Now suppose someone said that though S is fully honest, his having said he wants p is no reason to think he does want it; or that though S wants p and is disposed to reply honestly to 'Do you want p?', we have no grounds for expecting S to avow the want when asked. Clearly this would give us good reason to say that the person does not fully understand 'S wants p'. Granted there are wants most of us would tend *not* to avow, such as wants to harm others. But this is compatible with our having a tendency to avow such wants. One point of using 'tendency' is to indicate that the thing in question may occur only when it represents, so to speak, the resultant of competing forces.

III. The Nomic Status of the Constitutive Patterns

We come now to the question whether it is really plausible to regard W_1–W_7 as lawlike. One may grant that not all scientific laws are universal; but can a proposition with an under-favorable-conditions clause or tendency qualification be genuinely lawlike and have predictive and explanatory power? The answer, I have been suggesting, depends largely on what we are able to say about the nature and range of the unfavorable conditions and inhibiting factors. If we can specify the principal kinds of unfavorable conditions and inhibiting factors, then the inferences we make in accordance with W_1–W_7 can be highly probable, so long as we have a good idea how to ascertain whether any of the relevant conditions or factors are present. Recall that even a large number of scientific laws of universal form are known not to hold under certain conditions. Galileo's law of free fall, for example, in addition to being only approximately true, does not hold even for bodies in a vacuum except where there is no interference, such as the influence of a magnetic field. It is true that in cases like these we have a much better idea what may interfere than we do for W_1–W_7. Yet can we, for all or even most scientific laws, list, without a blanket phrase like 'under normal conditions', all the cases in which it will not or may not hold? At least typically we cannot, especially when a law has not been extensively and diversely tested, nor accounted for by a comprehensive theory.

Connected with the question whether W_1–W_7 are lawlike are other questions about what sort of analysis they provide. The very word 'analysis' will suggest to some philosophers the question whether W_1–W_7 are analytic or synthetic. In dealing with this question I propose to distinguish two senses in which 'analytic' seems to be used. (1) Propositions analytic in what we might call the strict sense are those reducible to logical truths by putting synonyms for synonyms; for example, if we can assume that 'vixen' is synonymous with 'female fox', then 'All vixens are female' is reducible to 'All female foxes are female', in which only the logical terms 'all' and 'are' figure essentially. Though the notion of a logical term is not altogether clear, for my purposes it should be enough to say that, roughly, a logical truth is a proposition true solely by virtue of the meanings of the logical terms in which it is expressed. (2) I propose to say that a proposition is analytic in the weak sense if (and only if) it is neither strictly analytic nor a logical truth, but is an explicative proposition in the way in which W_1–W_7 are and hence may reasonably be said to express "part of what we mean by" at least one of the concepts figuring essentially in it. Weakly analytic propositions seem to be a subclass of those Sellars calls "logically synthetic, yet true *ex vi terminorum*,"[11] but I prefer not to call W_1–W_7 true *ex vi terminorum* because this, like 'true by virtue of meaning', suggests to many philosophers strict analyticity.

Now it is by no means obvious that a proposition analytic in the weak sense cannot be lawlike and in principle testable when taken together with other, systematically related propositions. Nomicity does not require isolated testability. Thus, to point out that each of W_1–W_7 expresses part of what we mean by 'S wants p' is not a good argument against their constituting the core of theoretical construct analysis of the concept of wanting. I shall attempt to support this claim by arguing that W_1–W_7, taken together, are testable; and I shall begin by arguing that none of the set is analytic in the strict sense.

If we concentrate on W_4, which is the best candidate among W_1–W_7 for a proposition analytic in the strict sense, we soon find that there is no synonym for 'S wants p' whose substitution for this would make W_4 a logical truth. It might seem that we could reasonably treat W_4 as *the* definition of 'S wants p'. But this would imply that one could understand 'S wants p' even if one did not believe the other propositions of the set—unless we could show, as we surely cannot, at least that there is a strictly analytic connection (1) between S's wanting p, and each of the necessary conditions for wanting given in W_3 and W_5–W_7, and (2) between each of these conditions and the tendency specified in W_4. On the other hand, precisely because a person who does not believe one of the propositions can be reasonably said not to have a full understanding of 'S wants p', they cannot be regarded as simply synthetic, where this precludes weak analyticity. For they do not express merely contingent facts about wanting, but are, so to speak, constitutive of our concept of wanting. Suppose we did regard W_4 as an explicit definition. Could someone want p without satisfying the righthand side of W_3 and W_5–W_7, and could anyone satisfy the righthand side of these propositions without wanting p? Moreover, though I cannot argue this by canvassing all the possible analyses of 'S wants p', I suggest that if we regard W_1–W_7 as incapable of being analytic in something like the weak sense, we shall be left without a remotely adequate way of saying what it is to want something.

Let me now argue in another way that W_4 is not strictly analytic. We

---

[11] Here I refer to Wilfrid Sellars, *Science, Perception, and Reality* (London: Routledge and Kegan Paul, 1963), p. 319; but cf. his "Inference and Meaning," esp. p. 21.

can certainly envisage a situation in which (1) Sam has been day-dreaming about having a camera of a certain kind and has been finding this pleasant; (2) when he learns that this kind of camera is no longer available, he is disappointed; and (3) upon discovering later that such cameras will be reissued, he is pleased. Here we would have good reason to say that Sam wants a camera of this kind. But suppose that even when he wants nothing he believes incompatible with getting such a camera as much as or more than he wants to have the camera, he fails to buy it. We would immediately wonder whether he lacked the ability or the opportunity. Yet even if he had the ability to buy the camera, for example, ample money, and the opportunity, for example, in passing his favorite camera store when he is free to stop there, he might not stop there and buy the camera. That this is possible seems especially clear if we do not assume that he wants the camera very much; for then we can easily conceive his simply forgetting temporarily about the camera or his being occupied by thoughts of something else even while noticing the camera store as he passes. If, in the kind of circumstances specified, this sort of neglect occurred in a number of people, we could perhaps reasonably raise the question whether to make some revision in the explicative set.

What sort of revision? If W_4 is partly constitutive of the concept of wanting, then it cannot be disconfirmed in the sense that its antecedent is straightforwardly satisfied and its consequent not satisfied. Insofar as we are inclined to countenance the possibility that it does not hold, we are countenancing the possibility of a change, though not necessarily a substantial one, in our concept of wanting. The change might be the minimal one of expanding the range of inhibiting factors for W_4; or we might revise W_4 more substantially, for example by decreasing our (now quite high) estimate of the probability it confers on the inferences it warrants; or we might adopt either of these alternatives for whatever propositions in the set have figured in our questioning W_4 (here W_1, W_5 and W_6). But because the propositions of the set are logically connected in the way they are, revising any one of them implies revisions in the others; for example, all the implications of wanting exhibited by W_5–W_7 are nomologically equivalent to the implication on the righthand side of W_4. These considerations show how W_1–W_7, like a group of logically related high-level theoretical principles in a scientific theory, are none of them testable in isolation from all the others (at least not in isolation from *some* other propositions that give us reliable ways of identifying the state of affairs specified on one side of a given member of the set, independently of identifying the state of affairs specified on the other side). Nor can we make a sharp distinction between envisaging disconfirmation of these propositions and envisaging a change in our concept of wanting, even if the change is such that we can still reasonably speak of our concept as *of* the same thing, in this case wanting. Of course, since W_1–W_7 do not represent a scientific theory, much less one that is being systematically tested, even if disconfirming evidence were to arise, it is likely that it would be only gradually and quite unselfconsciously assimilated by the linguistic community.

Of course, we *can* say that Sam does not really want the camera, or even that he has some subtle psychological inability to buy it; but these would not be the only possible alternatives, particularly if we add that he has said that he wants the camera and is known to be honest. For while we are not in a position to say that the only things that can prevent him from stopping at the store are lack of ability or opportunity or, on the other hand, a competing want or a belief that some other action would be a better way to get the camera, these are the main interfering factors for W_4 and seem to be the only ones relevant here. If, as is surely conceivable, we could rule out these and perhaps a few other possible factors but could not simply deny that Sam wants the camera, then we might reasonably deny that he has a tendency to buy it except possibly at certain times, for example when he has just had an enthusiastic conversation with someone about its merits. Or, perhaps more likely, we would simply not know what to say,[12] since in any case we are prepared to deal with, the implications of wanting specified by, say, W_{5L}, W_{6L}, and W_{7L}, occur together with the manifestations of wanting specified by, say, W_{4L}. But if W_4 were analytic in the strict sense, we ought to be able to say without hesitation that either Sam does not want the camera or he has a tendency to buy it.

Here is a further argument for denying that the explicative set for wanting contains only or even primarily strictly analytic propositions. Consider some of the logical consequences of the set which would have to be strictly analytic if W_1–W_7, or most of them, are:

---

[12] For a detailed discussion that explains some of the reasons for saying this, see Alston, "Wants, Actions, and Causal Explanation." That paper also shows why 'wanting' cannot be non-circularly defined in the ways that appear to offer the greatest promise of such a definition.

1. If, given that S has not been expecting p, he would immediately tend to be pleased to discover that p would occur, then, under favorable conditions, S has a tendency to think or daydream about p at least occasionally and to talk about p at least occasionally in free conversation. (From W_5 and W_3)
2. If S would immediately tend to be disappointed to discover that p would not be the case, then, if S has the ability and opportunity to A, and believes that A-ing has at least some considerable probability of leading to p, S has a tendency to A. (From W_6 and W_4)
3. If daydreaming about p is pleasant to S and S believes that there is at least some considerable probability of p's occurring, then, under favorable conditions, if S believes that A-ing is necessary to p, S has a tendency to A. (From W_1 and W_4)
4. If it is *not* the case that S has a tendency to think or daydream at least occasionally about p and to talk at least occasionally about p in free conversation, then, under favorable conditions, it is not the case that if S discovered that p would be the case, he would immediately tend to be pleased to discover this. (From W_3 and W_5)

Statements 1–4, which are unified by W_1–W_7, are very far from strictly analytic. They do not seem obviously true at all except insofar as we think of them as logical consequences of W_1–W_7. Indeed, they appear so clearly testable that the reasonable conclusion seems to be that whatever strictly analytic appearance W_1–W_7 may have should be attributed, not to their being such, but to our daily reliance on them in making inferences about people, and to their status as explicative propositions in the sense I have specified.

IV. Circularity and Testability

One other problem which should be discussed in defending my account is suggested by Brandt and Kim when they comment on the terms used in their discussion of wanting:

For example, 'pleasant' probably has to be explained as meaning something like 'an experience that the person would like (wants) to prolong or repeat'. Thus, there is a kind of circularity in some of the statements (a) to (f), considered as explanations of the meaning of 'wanting'. But there is nothing objectionable in this. On the contrary, it only confirms our view that the statements (a) to (f) represent a small common-sense theoretical network which interrelates wanting and experience of pleasure and displeasure among other things. The circularity only serves to enrich the scope of the scheme. One would find oneself in difficulty over this only if one wished to assert that the statements (a) to (f) were definitionally analytic.[13]

Brandt and Kim do not elaborate further on this circularity, and they leave us with several pressing questions. First, it is not at all clear how the circularity they speak of "only serves to enrich the scope of the scheme" and why it would be a problem *only* if one wished to take the explicative propositions as "definitionally analytic." If, for example, the only thing we could say in explicating 'pleasant' were that pleasant experiences are those we want to prolong or repeat, then our circle might be too small to enable us to make any progress toward an explication of wanting. But as it is—and Brandt and Kim probably have this in mind—we can say far more than this in explicating 'pleasant'. We can in various ways bring in the notions of satisfaction, of certain sensations and feelings, of a tendency to repeat the kind of activity in question, and of a tendency to talk frequently about this kind of experience and to evaluate it positively. In explicating these notions we may have to reintroduce the notion of pleasantness, for example, in explaining 'satisfaction'. But if we need to say that satisfaction is normally pleasant, we can also say (among other things) that it is normally accompanied by cessation of a certain kind of striving; and the circle thus gets larger until no term is the only term, or even the most important term, used in its own explanation.

With respect to this sort of progressively expanding circle we can in part justify including, say, a tendency to avow the want for p in the explicative set as a necessary condition for wanting. The problem arises thus: one is not avowing a want if one is simply mouthing the words 'I want p'; one could use other words, and, at least normally, one must *believe* something to the effect that one's words have a certain meaning, that of 'I want p'. Moreover, though I shall not try to argue this here, I do not think we can explicate 'believing' without appeal to the notion of a want. Hence we again seem to be in a circle. But when we recall how many concepts enter into the explication of 'S wants p', the circle no longer appears so small as to make W_7 useless in explicating "S wants p'. One can to a substantial degree

[13] Brandt and Kim, "Wants as Explanations of Actions," p. 429.

explain 'S wants p' on the left side of W_7 using notions like those of daydreaming and a tendency to perform certain actions; and one can to a substantial degree explain 'S wants p' on the right side using the notions of being pleased, being disappointed, and exhibiting certain patterns of thought and discourse.

A further point, and one more important in defending my analysis of wanting, is implicit in this attempt to show that W_7 is not vitiated by circularity: even if one or more notions occurring on one side of W_1–W_7 do have to be reintroduced in explaining the meaning of those occurring on the other side, we can reliably identify the states of affairs specified on either side of the propositions independently of identifying the states of affairs specified on the other. Hence the propositions, taken together, are testable; and indeed, using them we can make numerous non-trivial predictions. It is well known, for example, that using W_4 (together with one or more of the other propositions) we can often predict successfully that people will do things they believe necessary to something they want. Let me add, as another argument for the testability of W_1–W_7, that there are ways of reliably identifying wants not suggested by W_1–W_7. As Brandt and Kim suggest, a heightened tendency to notice certain things may indicate wanting; and it may well be that, as they hold, people who want p have a heightened tendency to notice things they believe are means to it.[14] And we can surely discover many further possibilities for identifying wants.

In concluding this section, I want to discuss an objection some philosophers would be inclined to press. They might grant that none of W_1–W_7 is strictly analytic yet deny that, even taken together, they are disconfirmable. For, the argument would run, because the propositions are as it were constitutive of the concept of wanting, if experience convinced us to cease drawing inference in accordance with them this would only show that we no longer meant by 'S wants p' what we now do. Hence W_1–W_7 would be in no sense disconfirmed; they would simply be found, to some degree at least, inapplicable to the world,[15] and speaking of their disconfirmation would only obscure the fact that the sentences expressing them would now express

[14] Ibid., p. 427.
[15] The phraseology of this sentence is suggested by Norman Malcolm's defense of the apriority of a near-equivalent of W_{4L}. His grounds are very similar to those offered for the objecstion I consider. See his "The Conceivability of Mechanism," *Philosophical Review* 77 (1968).

different propositions. This argument raises many questions; but there are two points which, though they deserve more discussion than I can give them here, should avert it. (1) If one considers the sorts of revisions of the set that have been mentioned, it should be clear that not all of them—for example, not all acknowledgments of new kinds of inhibiting factors—would require us to say that we no longer mean the same thing by 'S wants p'. Certainly some revisions of the set, such as the total exclusion of one or more members, would give us reason to speak of such a change in meaning; but it is not at all clear under what conditions such talk is warranted, and a good deal of minor revision may be accommodated by a set as flexible as W_1-W_7 with no resulting change in meaning. (2) More important, even if we grant the objection, it does not imply a relevant *difference* between the explicative propositions and all scientific laws in which theoretical concepts figure. On my view, it would be reasonable to argue that the concept of an electron has undergone some changes in the course of this century as a result of the discovery of new laws concerning electrons. Following the objection, one *can* say instead that we have simply had a series of different concepts. But this implies a way of individuating concepts that is more stringent than any we generally employ and very uneconomical. Second, there seems to be no sharp distinction between considering revision of the explicative set for a concept and envisaging the adoption of a different concept. In any case, even if one insists that accepting any disconfirmation of the explicative set for a concept entails adopting a different concept, one cannot show that (all) scientific laws *differ* from explicative propositions in this respect: that the former are, and the latter are not, susceptible of disconfirmation.

V. The Explanation of Action by Appeal to Desires and Beliefs

In closing, I should like to make explicit how my account enables us to answer the important question of what sort of explanation is given when an (intentional) human action (or activity) is explained by citing a want of the agent. My thesis is that when we explain an action (A) by appeal to a want, where we assume or presuppose—as we normally do in explaining actions thus—that A was performed in order to satisfy the want, we are tacitly appealing to W_{4L}. Specifically, we make it clear that *S* wanted something and believed either (1) that his *A*-ing was necessary to getting it, or (2) that his *A*-ing had at least some considerable probability of leading to it, or (3) that his *A*-ing had at least some considerable probability of constituting attainment of it. In addition, we of course presuppose that the agent had the ability and the opportunity to *A*. Thus, in giving such explanations we convey information implying that the agent satisfied the antecedent of W_{4L}; and this information, taken together with W_{4L}, implies that in the absence of inhibiting factors the action was to be expected. Our (normally tacit) acceptance of W_{4L}, then, provides the explanatory connection between the action we explain and the wants and beliefs we invoke in explaining it; and such explanations are non-trivial because W_{4L}, far from being strictly analytic, is part of a fairly comprehensive set of systematically related lawlike propositions. Moreover, I suggest that not only 'want explanations', but in-order-to explanations of action and also explanations of action appealing to beliefs, intentions, purposes, and other intentional factors, may very often be considered similar to want explanations in resting on an appeal to W_{4L}, or something very close to it. When we say, for example, that Ann went out in order to get wine, we imply that she did so because she wanted wine and believed that her going out was necessary to, or that it would (might) lead to, getting it; and here we have the kind of explanation I have been discussing.

I am not maintaining that want explanations and other intentionalistic explanations of action are causal, though I hope my view provides one plausible interpretation of the often vague claim that such explanations are causal. My view is that when we explain actions by appeal to one or more wants of the agent, the explanation we are giving may reasonably be regarded as an elliptical version of an inductive-nomological explanation,[16] a kind of explanation quite similar to

[16] Paul M. Churchland has argued, using a strategy similar in some ways to mine, that the sorts of explanations of action I am speaking of are deductive-nomological. He does this by representing a near-equivalent of W_{4L} as a universal conditional (call it L) whose antecedent specifies that the agent has the ability and the opportunity to do *A* and has no overriding wants nor a belief that some other action would be a preferable way to achieve *p*. This seems to me not unreasonable, and I am far more concerned to argue that the explanations I have specified are nomological than to argue that they are inductive. But (1) for reasons apparent in Sections II and III of this chapter, I doubt that we should take W_{4L} as universal, nor do the inferences we ordinarily make about people imply that we believe L, (2) even if, by taking the already vague notions of ability and opportunity even more broadly, we can make it plausible to include L in the set, we would then stretch the analogy with scientific laws that is implicit in

what Carl G. Hempel[17] has called inductive-statistical explanation. Roughly, an inductive-nomological explanation of an event is one that subsumes it under a non-universal lawlike generality, in the case of W_{4L}, a tendency statement. A slightly weaker thesis would be that when we give want explanations of actions, (1) we normally convey, or assume, in the context of explanation, enough information so that by appeal to W_{4L} an inductive-nomological explanation could be constructed; and (2) we normally take responsibility for conditions obtaining under which such an explanation would be possible, even if weak. To take responsibility for something in this sense does not require that one have evidence that it is the case. To take responsibility for a condition is to be disposed to recognize the relevance of certain complaints to the effect that it is not the case and to reply to them in certain ways. If, for example, one explains S's going to Chicago for a weekend by saying that S wanted to visit a friend, one must, if one is to avoid incurring the charge that one does not understand want explanations, be disposed to recognize the relevance of such objections as, 'But S wanted to avoid Chicago even more than he wanted to see that friend'. The stronger thesis seems to me more plausible than the weaker thesis; but even if further investigation revealed that the latter is the most one could show, that would require few substantial changes in my position.

Often want explanations are weak because no information conveyed in giving them implies that nothing would prevent the want (and belief) in question from leading to the action they are meant to explain. But the arguments of Sections II and III of this chapter suggest that such explanations can also be quite strong and that we know what sort of information to seek in order to strengthen them. In any case, the degree of probability with which the explaining propositions imply the occurrence of the event explained is not crucial, nor do we have any way of precisely assigning a probability here. If we believed that a certain type of explanation could never provide a probability of more than, say, 0.50, we would hesitate to call it inductive-nomological; but given the contextual information that often accompanies want explanations, they frequently seem far more probable than this.

Much more could be said about the implications of my account and

---

calling it a universal lawlike proposition. See Paul M. Churchland, "The Logical Character of Action Explanations," *Philosophical Review* 79 (1970).

[17] See Carl G. Hempel, *Aspects of Scientific Explanations* (New York: Free Press, 1965), esp. the title essay.

indeed about wanting in general. For instance, the account has far-reaching implications for the issue of how, if at all, there can be unconscious wants, for the nature of our knowledge of our own and others' wants, and for the notion of want strength. The account also helps to distinguish wanting from wishing (which does not require that S believe that the realization of his wish is possible), intending (which normally requires that S want *on balance* to A), hoping (which requires that S not strongly believe p will occur), and other psychological cousins. As examples like these suggest, the concept of wanting figures in many other psycholgical notions; and partly for this reason, an account of wanting is an important step toward a systematic treatment of psychological concepts. Furthermore, if my account is basically sound, it reaffirms the impossibility of distinguishing philosophical from scientific propositions on the basis of the analyticity of the former and the contingency of the latter; it exhibits an often overlooked or underestimated continuity between commonsense and scientific conceptual frameworks; and it shows that philosophical analysis cannot always successfully proceed by the construction of explicit definitions.

Perhaps enough has been said to foreshadow along what lines these various implications of my account of wanting can be brought out in detail. Moreover, I hope that I have adequately defended at least the plausibility of the *sort* of analysis developed here. I should also like to think that the explicative propositions I propose are adequate to the concept I have set out to clarify. But I am certainly not determined to cling to every detail; and if it is right at all to conceive of my account as a theoretical construct analysis, then it should not be surprising if, with the growth and spread of our psychological knowledge, certain changes of detail are called for in what to philosophers might seem a rather short time.[18]

[18] For helpful comments on earlier versions of much of the material in this chapter, I am indebted to Alvin I. Goldman and especially to William P. Alston. I have also profited from discussion with Laurence BonJour, Douglas Browning, Hardy Jones, and Alex Mourelatos.

Chapter 2

Intending

The subject of intention has been very much discussed by philosophers.[1] But I believe that we do not yet have a satisfactory general account of the concept, and a good deal remains to be said about its relation to other psychological concepts. How are intentions related to beliefs and wants? How does intending differ from hoping and from expecting? Must intentions arise from practical reasoning? Must they be directed toward actions one believes to be the best way to achieve one or more of one's ends? These are the main questions I shall discuss. They are central to the subject of intention in the sense that adequate answers to them provide the basis for a general account of intending. Drawing on the points that emerge in pursuing these questions, I shall propose such an account. I shall consider both end-directed intentions—that is, intentions to bring about Φ (some state of affairs) *by* A-ing (some action)—and simple intentions, that is, in-

[1] See, e.g., G. E. M. Anscombe, *Intention* (1957; Ithaca: Cornell University Press, 1963); Hector-Neri Castañeda, "Intentions and the Structure of Intending," *Journal of Philosophy* 68, no. 15 (1971); Roderick M. Chisholm, "The Structure of Intention," *Journal of Philosophy* 67, no. 19 (1970); Paul M. Churchland, "The Logical Character of Action-Explanation," *Philosophical Review* 79, no. 2 (1970); Brice Noel Fleming, "On Intention," *Philosophical Review* 73, no. 3 (1964); Stuart Hampshire, *Thought and Action* (New York: Viking, 1960); Anthony Kenny, "Intention and Purpose," *Journal of Philosophy* 63, no. 20 (1966); Norman Malcolm, "The Conceivability of Mechanism," *Philosophical Review* 67 (1967); and Jack W. Meiland, *The Nature of Intention* (London: Methuen; New York: Barnes & Noble, 1970).

tentions to *A*. But in both cases I shall omit discussion of conditional intentions, for example, intentions to *A* if asked to do it.

I. Intending, Believing, and Wanting

Let us start with the question of how intentions are related to beliefs. It seems clear that if *S*—Sally, let us say—intends to bring about Φ by *A*-ing, she must have some belief about the likelihood that her doing *A* will achieve Φ. It might be thought that she must believe that doing *A* "is a way for [her] to bring about Φ."[2] This is too strong, however. If a man's car is stalled, I may intend to help him by driving to the nearest service station, even if I do not believe that by doing so I definitely will help him. Should we say that *S* need only believe that her *A*-ing is a possible way to achieve Φ? This would be too weak. For if I believed the chances of my helping the motorist by driving to the station were very slim, I could be properly said only to hope to help him by doing so. To distinguish intending to bring about Φ by *A*-ing from merely hoping to bring about φ by *A*-ing, we need to require that *S* at least believe her *A*-ing will be a probable way to achieve Φ. There are some people who will not say they intend to do something, or bring about a state of affairs by doing something, unless they are quite sure that they will do, or bring about, whatever it is. Others use 'intend' less stringently. But we do not normally say things of the forms, 'I intend to *A*' and 'I intend to bring about Φ by *A*-ing', unless we at least believe it probable (in the sense of 'likely') that we will *A*, or bring about Φ by *A*-ing, where *S* believes her *A*-ing, or her bringing about Φ by *A*-ing, to be *probable,* only if she believes they are more likely than not. Note how odd it is to say such things as "I intend to go to your paper, though it is not likely that I will make it," "He intends to visit us for the weekend, though he does not believe it probable that he will come," and "She intends to surprise him by coming early, but believes that as likely as not her coming early won't surprise him." In these cases, surely, the person hopes but does not intend. It is true that, before games, people sometimes say they intend to win, where one would think they would believe it is more likely that they will lose. But that this is normally

[2] Churchland, "The Logical Character of Action-Explanation," p. 231.

taken as an expression of confidence supports my contrast between intending and merely hoping.

This is not to deny that one can both intend and hope to *A*. That may occur when one intends to *A* but is somewhat uncertain whether one will succeed. One may also intend and expect to *A*; indeed, typically, we expect to do what we intend to do. But perhaps I might intend to speak to Judy in Boston, yet not expect to speak to her there, because I might think the chances of her being there are barely better than even. It is clear, on the other hand, that I may expect to *A* without intending to. On the basis of experience, I may expect to hurt a student's feelings, but not intend to do so.

Some philosophers have held that intending to *A* implies believing that one will try to do it.[3] Presumably, they would also want to hold that intending to bring about Φ by *A*-ing implies believing that one will try to bring about Φ by *A*-ing. Both claims appear mistaken. Suppose I intend to raise my hand. If he knows he has the normal control of his limbs, he would surely not believe that he will try to raise his hand. Similarly, I may intend to do something, for example, greet Judy, *by* raising my hand, even if I do not believe I will try to greet her by raising my hand. Nor will it do to say that intending to *A* (or bring about Φ by *A*-ing) implies either believing that one will, or believing that one will try to, *A* (bring about Φ by *A*-ing). For I may believe simply that I will probably (effortlessly) do *A*, for example, wave to someone likely to pass. Then I would believe neither that I will definitely wave nor that I will try to. Often, we believe we will try (successfully) to do what we intend to do. But it appears that trying need not enter into an account of intending.

The question of how intending is related to wanting is more difficult than the question of how it is related to believing. Clearly *S* can intend to do things which, in at least most contexts, she would honestly say she does not want to do. We might thus conclude that intending does not entail wanting. The natural reply, for many philosophers,[4] is to hold that, though intending does not entail intrinsic wanting, it does entail wanting that is intrinsic, extrinsic, or

[3] Hampshire, *Thought and Action*, p. 134. D. M. Armstrong seems to hold the related thesis that *A*-ing intentionally entails having tried to *A*. See his *A Materialist Theory of the Mind* (London: Routledge & Kegan Paul, 1968), p. 151. Examples of the kind I have given in criticizing Hampshire's thesis show that Armstrong's thesis is also false.

[4] Fleming, "On Intention," seems to be employing this distinction. See esp. pp. 307–8. For a discussion of it, see Alvin I. Goldman, *A Theory of Human Action* (Englewood Cliffs, N.J.: Prentice-Hall, 1970), esp. pp. 49–63.

partly both. I shall suppose that S wants Φ (purely) extrinsically if and only if her sole reason for wanting it is that she believes realizing it is necessary to (will, may) realize something else that she wants; whereas S wants Φ (purely) intrinsically if and only if she wants it solely "for its own sake," which is roughly equivalent to her wanting Φ in such a way that even if she believes that Φ is necessary to (will, may) realize something else, this belief is neither part of her reason—if she has a reason—for wanting Φ, nor necessary for her retaining the want for Φ. We should ask, then, whether extrinsic wants are merely a philosophers' construction or whether there is a use of 'want' in which it ranges over what philosophers have called extrinsic wants, as well as over intrinsic wants and wants that are partly both.

Let me try to illustrate such a use. Suppose that I am visiting Elaine in New York for a weekend and that on Saturday morning she asks me what I want to do that day. In reply, I might say that I want to see the paintings at an art opening, go shopping, eat at a Chinese restaurant, and spend the later evening at her home. By contrast, if she asks me, as I am about to get out of her car at the gallery, whether I really want to see such garish stuff, I might honestly say, "No, but it's a duty." Must we suppose that my wants have changed? I think not. For her question, in the context, might well be aimed at finding out whether I *intrinsically* want to see the paintings. But in the morning Elaine, as a good hostess, was concerned to help me accomplish as much as possible of whatever I wanted to do, regardless of whether the wants were intrinsic; and in the context of such a concern, 'What do you want to do?' can range over things that one intends to do, takes to be duties, and would in most contexts say one does not want to do if asked whether one does. Of course, we also ask, "What do you intend to do today?" But when we are assuming that S has not made up her mind what she will do, 'What do you want to do?' is more natural. For we are leaving open whether she will form intentions to do all she wants to do. That we can and usually do leave this open in asking, "What do you want to do today?" shows that the question is not merely an equivalent of 'What do you intend to do today?'

Note also the breadth of 'What do you want?' when asked of someone who intrudes. The answer may be 'To deliver a message', even if the messenger is embarrassed to interrupt and "didn't want" to deliver it. But to reply "I don't want anything, I simply have an obligation to deliver a message" would be at best irrelevant pedantry. There are indefinitely many other cases in which the answer to 'What do you want?' confirms that people want to do things they intend to do but would seem, prima facie, clearly not to want to do. For instance, imagine that Paul, intending to pass the salt to Ann, taps Tom, who is conversing avidly. Annoyed at being interrupted, Tom might say, "What do you want?" It would be quite correct for Paul to reply, "I just want to pass the salt, if you don't mind," even if he too was annoyed at being interrupted to pass it.

We may learn more about the relation between intending and wanting by reflecting on Anscombe's view that "the primitive sign of wanting is *trying to get.*"[5] I take this to imply both (1) that trying to get (or do) something entails wanting to get (or do) it and (2) that at least one way we learn 'want' is in contexts in which someone is observed trying to get (or do) something, for instance, trying, by stretching, to reach a high place. (1) and (2) are quite plausible. It seems equally plausible to hold that (3) intending to A (bring about Φ by A-ing) entails being disposed to try to A (bring about Φ by A-ing) if certain obstacles should arise; and (3) would support the view that intending entails wanting. Suppose S enters a bookstore for rare editions on her lunch hour and is asked by the attendant to sign the guest book. Seeing no pen, S might take out her own, intending to sign with it. If we assume she is in a hurry and is also reluctant to get on the mailing list, it might seem that she in no sense wants to sign. Suppose, however, that her ballpoint pen will not write, and picture her trying to sign by holding it at various angles and scratching back and forth to make the first letters of her name. It now becomes natural to say that she wants to sign, and we can imagine her husband, who has just arrived, saying "Why on earth do you want to sign? You'll just get more mail." One could object that the wanting to sign did not arise until S found she could not readily do so. But it is surely more plausible to say that S's trouble in signing simply provides an occasion for *saying* she wants to sign. One might also object that in this context 'want' simply means 'intend'. But this need not be so. For one thing, 'Why do you want to sign?' would have the same force and appropriateness even if both S and her husband, each knowing that pen and thinking there were no other writing implements available, believed S was quite unlikely to succeed in signing. Then S

[5] Anscombe, *Intention,* p. 68.

might hope, but would not intend, to sign. That this sort of case is possible may in part explain why, when we do not see what reason someone trying to *A* might have for doing it, we can always ask, "Why do you want to *A*?" but not always, "Why do you intend to *A*?"

I am not maintaining that these considerations about intending and trying prove that intending entails wanting. But, taken together with the other considerations set out on the relation between intending and wanting, they at least make it quite plausible to hold that intending entails wanting. Even if one accepts the entailment, however, one may object that 'want' is being taken so broadly that the entailment is trivial. I would deny this, though I grant that in the light of the examples brought forward the entailment is not surprising. Moreover, it is surely not trivial that there *is* a sense of 'want' with respect to which the entailment holds. And in any case, even if the entailment were trivial, an account of intending that in part rests on it need not be trivial. For the notion of intending is a good deal more complex than even the broad concept of wanting I have illustrated; the latter is at least fairly well understood;[6] and this concept of wanting is important in understanding many psychological notions in which the concept of intending is not a constituent.

If it is true that intending involves beliefs and wants in the way I have suggested, one might well think that *S*'s intending to bring about Φ by *A*-ing also implies that (1) *S* does not believe some alternative action to be a preferable way to achieve Φ, and (2) *S* does not want anything she believes incompatible with her bringing about Φ as much as or more than Φ,[7] that is, does not have an equally strong or stronger incompatible want, as I shall call it. But neither (1) nor (2) follows from *S*'s intending to bring about Φ by *A*-ing. Take (1) first: I might believe flying would be a better way of going to St. Louis than taking a train; yet I might intend to go there by taking a train because I have promised not to fly in bad weather. There are also cases of temporary forgetting which show that (1) does not follow from *S*'s intending to bring about Φ by *A*-ing. Even if I believe that adding a pinch of curry to the meat is a better way to give it piquancy than

---

[6] I have discussed wanting in this broad sense in Chapter 1. Other treatments of wanting are cited there. See also Churchland, "The Logical Character of Action-Explanation."

[7] Churchland, "The Logical Character of Action-Explanation," seems to think (1) follows from *S*'s intending to bring about Φ by *A*-ing; and he holds a thesis rather close to the claim that (2) also follows.

adding pepper, I may temporarily forget this preference and form the intention to give the meat piquancy by adding pepper, which, let us suppose, is visible and nearer at hand. One may object that at the *time* I did not believe curry preferable. But if I had been *asked* which I preferred, I might have unhesitatingly said "curry"; and if I had seen curry, I might have used it even over some protest in favor of pepper. One might claim that this at most shows that I was *disposed* to believe readily that curry was preferable. But I myself would probably say that I had forgotten curry was preferable; and I would describe myself as reminded of this rather than as, say, rediscovering it. It seems more reasonable, then, to allow that one can temporarily forget to take into account something one believes. Indeed, it appears that we need to say something like this to preserve the distinction between (i) ceasing to believe a proposition (as when one becomes convinced it is false) and then coming to believe it again (as when cogent arguments for it are later given), and (ii) simply failing to take account of a proposition one believes and then being reminded of it, as in the case of temporarily forgetting that a payment is due.

Similar cases show that (2) does not follow from S's intending to bring about Φ by A-ing. For S could temporarily forget, or at least temporarily forget to take into account, a want of hers stronger than and incompatible with her want for Φ, yet still form the intention to bring about Φ by A-ing. Suppose Sally wants to read the newspaper after breakfast and also to water the flowers after breakfast. The latter want might be stronger than and incompatible with the former; but especially if it is her habit to read the paper after breakfast, she might temporarily forget that she wants to water the flowers, and might spend all her free time reading the paper. It might be clear during her breakfast that she intends to read the paper; yet she could also want more to water the flowers. For instance, she might truly say, as someone informs her that she has forgotten to do it, that she would certainly have done it instead of reading the paper if she had only remembered it; and if this person said to Sally, as she read her paper, "Don't you want to water the flowers?", she could correctly answer, "Yes, I had forgotten I wanted to do that," and immediately get up to do it. These responses on her part would strongly confirm the view that she wanted to do it more than to read the paper.

Perhaps the relation between intending and, on the other hand, wanting and believing, can be seen better by considering how intending is connected with practical reasoning. One plausible suggestion is that for *S* to intend to bring about Φ by *A*-ing is for her practical reasonings to be concluded in favor of bringing about Φ by *A*-ing.[8] But suppose I deliberate about how to give my daughter a pleasant evening and conclude that the best way is to take her to a good play. This is compatible with my believing that the chances of finding a good play at the time are quite slim; but then I would have only a hope and not an intention here. However, if we add to the notion of *S*'s practical reasonings' being concluded in favor of bringing about Φ by *A*-ing, the requirement that she believe at least that she probably will bring about Φ by *A*-ing, then, barring exceptions from temporary forgetting, the condition would be at least normally sufficient. The same holds for simple intentions. One might object that we should not count as practical any reasonings on *S*'s part from which she concludes in favor of *A*-ing (or bringing about Φ by *A*-ing), unless she believes that she probably (or very likely) will *A*. But surely it may be rational and quite practical to conclude in favor of a course of action with only a hope of carrying it out, particularly if the antici- pated effort of attempting it is justified by the envisioned reward of success.

Is it necessary for intending to *A* (or bring about Φ by *A*-ing) that one's practical reasonings be concluded in favor of *A*-ing (bringing about Φ by *A*-ing)? It appears not. Does my intending to brush my teeth after eating on a particular evening require that I have reasoned about, or even thought about, doing so? It would be easy to answer this if '*S*'s practical reasonings' being concluded in favor of *A*-ing were not ambiguous. But it could mean '*S*'s having reasoned about whether to *A* and concluded—without forgetting this, or changing her mind, up to the time in question—that, on balance, she ought to *A*'; or, it could mean something like: (1) *S*'s having, at *some* time, reasoned about doing things of the same action-type as *A* (for example, brush- ing one's teeth after eating), or about things *S* takes to involve *A* or actions of that type; and (2) *S*'s having concluded—without forgetting this, or changing her mind, up to the time in question—that on bal- ance she ought to do things of the type *A* (or things involving either *A* or actions of that type). If we take '*S*'s practical reasonings' being concluded in favor of *A*-ing' in the first sense, then, as the above example shows, the notion does not express a necessary condition

---

[8] This view is proposed by Churchland, "The Logical Character of Action-Explana- tion," p. 231.

for S's intending to do A. If we take the phrase in the second sense, one might plausibly claim that it does express a necessary condition. But some things we intend to do are not this closely connected with our practical reasonings. Imagine a city dweller, Leo, on his first walk in the forest. He might impulsively reach out for a sprig of red berries, intending to pick them, though he has never thought of picking berries before. He might also have the intention to please his wife by taking them to her, even if he has never thought about taking her flowers or plants. One may insist that he must have thought something like "Wouldn't it be nice to take those to Mary?" But, even if he must have had some such thought, this implies at most practical reasoning in a quite attenuated sense.

It appears, then, that practical reasoning is not the only route to intentions. Another common source of intentions is decision. Deciding to A requires some minimal consideration of whether to do it, but not practical reasoning. If Tom says, "Shall I take her flowers?", pauses, and then asks for a bouquet of roses, he has decided to take her roses, even if in the moment he paused he engaged in no reasoning and simply looked at the various flowers. Agreeing to do something is another way we commonly form intentions. However unreflectingly I (sincerely) agree to Elaine's invitation to coffee at ten, I have formed the intention to join her at ten. On the other hand, the city dweller who impulsively reaches for the berries may have just suddenly wanted them. Intentions can arise out of wants that simply crop up; and the intentions may be as fleeting as such sudden wants and as momentary as a quickly abandoned delusion that one can do some splendid deed.

II. A Cognitive-Motivational Account of Intending

If we take into account the various points that have now emerged, perhaps we can understand intending in terms of wanting and believing. The following would avoid at least the problems so far raised:

I. For any person, S, any action, A, and any state of affairs, Φ, S intends to bring about Φ by A-ing if and only if

(1) S believes[9] that she will (or that she probably will) bring about Φ by A-ing; and

(2) S wants, and has not temporarily forgotten that she wants, to bring about Φ by A-ing; and

(3) either S has no equally strong or stronger incompatible want (or set of incompatible wants whose combined strength is at least as great), or, if S does have such a want or set of wants, she has temporarily forgotten that she wants the object(s) in question, or does not believe she wants the object(s), or has temporarily forgotten her belief that she cannot both realize the object(s) and bring about Φ by A-ing.

The parallel for simple intentions would be this:

II. For any person, S, and any action, A, S intends to A if and only if

(1′) S believes that she will (or that she probably will) A; and

(2′) S wants, and has not temporarily forgotten that she wants, to A; and

(3′) either S has no equally strong or stronger incompatible want (or set of incompatible wants whose combined strength is at least as great), or, if S does have such a want or set of wants, she has temporarily forgotten that she wants the object(s) in question, or does not believe she wants the object(s), or has temporarily forgotten her belief that she cannot both realize the object(s) and A.[10]

[9] I am assuming that S's temporarily forgetting this kind of belief is not possible. But perhaps it is. If so, we must add 'S has not temporarily forgotten' here and in (1′). Furthermore, in the interest of simplicity I omit here and in II any reference to S's believing that she is (probably is) bringing about Φ by A-ing, or simply A-ing. One might think intentions are always future-directed. It could be held that though we say such things as 'I'm doing what I intend to do', we really mean something like 'I'm doing what I intended to do and I intend to continue'. But suppose that, at t, when I see Leo, I intend to warn him. Can't I wave at him at t′, still intending to warn him, and believe at t′ that (since he is now responding) I am warning him? No doubt intentions are typically future-directed, but it *seems* that not all of them are.

[10] One may object that I and II are too broad because they may be satisfied by a person who has not decided to A. But some of the above examples show that intentions need not arise from decisions. There is, however, a related objection we should note. Suppose I want (on balance) to go to a certain meeting and believe that I probably will, but know there is a chance I will not be offered travel funds, in which case I would not go. Do I intend to go? Certainly I could not in good conscience say so to someone I believe will count on my going if I say I intend to. But if Alfred is merely curious about my plans and asks me if I intend to go, it would surely not be wrong to say "Yes" or "Yes, though I'm not yet certain I can." It might also be correct to say, "I intend to go if I get funds," and those who use 'intend' quite stringently might insist that I have *only* a conditional intention here. I am inclined to dispute this. For one thing, if it were so, we ought to add 'if'-clauses to an implausibly large number of our avowals of intention, since we often believe some particular interference may

Although there is no reasonable way to specify just how long a want or belief may count as only temporarily forgotten, I and II are meant to disallow permanently forgotten wants and beliefs. For these are surely not wants or beliefs S *has*. A want or belief may be *temporarily* forgotten at t only if (i) S has it at t and (ii) there is a later time t' at which she has not in any sense forgotten it. Regarding the possibility that S has, but does not believe she has, an equally strong or stronger incompatible want, I take it that this is possible at least when the incompatible want is unconscious, even if only in the rather everyday sense in which certain wants S would hate to acknowledge may be unconscious, for example, S's wanting to seem superior to her peers. Concerning the quantification into opaque contexts in I and II, unfortunately the sort of account I am attempting seems to require this; but I shall try to justify some restrictions on substitution in intention contexts beyond the usual restrictions on substitutivity of codesignative terms in opaque contexts.

Even though I and II seem to avoid the problems so far raised, they may appear too broad. Suppose that at a restaurant I intend to order lobster tails and believe that in ordering them I will be ordering the most expensive item on the menu, though I am not concerned with their price. Must I also intend to order the most expensive item on the menu? I am inclined to say no. One could say that I have a "non-purposive intention."[11] But it is doubtful whether these are intentions properly so called, though one may call them intentions if one keeps in mind that they are *that* sort of intention. Do such "intentions" satisfy I or II? I believe not. Do I *want* to order the most expensive item? No, for it just happens that lobster tails are the most expensive item: my believing that they are is no part of my motivation to

---

prevent our doing whatever it is. But if the logic of intending could be shown to justify the objection, we could add a condition that averts it. A first approximation would be: S does not believe that there is a particular condition such that (i) there is a substantial chance that it will not be fulfilled, and (ii) if it should not be, S cannot (or on balance ought not to) A.

[11] See Meiland, *The Nature of Intention*, pp. 7–11. What he calls non-purposive intentions seem equivalent to what Bentham called oblique intentions. Let me add that in suggesting that non-purposive intentions are not intentions properly so called, I am not denying the validity of the inference from (1) S intends to A, (2) S believes that $A \doteq A_1$, and (3) S is rational, to (4) S intends to A_1. I am denying the validity of the inference from (1), (3) and 'S believes that by (or in) A-ing he will A_1', to (4). With perhaps a few exceptions—probably some involving S's temporarily forgetting that $A = A_1$, inferences of the first sort are valid. Inferences from (1), (2), and '$A = A_1$' are of course invalid.

order them. If a teasing companion said, "He wants to order the most expensive item on the menu," I could justly protest, "That's not what I want at all; I just really like lobster tails." But consider a somewhat different case, discussed by Chisholm. Suppose that a man "acted with the intention of killing a stag and had no other goal than that, but he knew that by killing the stag he would kill the king."[12] Chisholm thinks it is not clear whether the agent acted with the intention of killing the king. My question is a bit different: does the agent, at the time he intends to shoot, intend to kill the king? To make the case more definite, suppose that he believes the bullet will go through the stag's neck into the king's heart but that he does not to any degree want to kill the king. Now it is very hard to imagine someone who in this case would not want at all to kill the king and would regard killing him as a mere by-product of killing the stag. But this is possible if the agent is perverse. Can we say, then, that he would here not intend to kill the king? Certainly we cannot say that if he kills him in this way it would be *unintentionally;* for this suggests that, say, the agent made a mistake or acted in ignorance. And we would certainly disallow 'I didn't intend to' if uttered as an *excuse;* for his not having intended such an act would clearly not be an excuse. But for someone as aberrant as the person imagined, it would seem that we can truly say that it is not the case that he intends to kill the king.

A different set of problems is raised by conditions (2) and (2'). Some writers have held it to be necessarily true that "I cannot intend what I cannot do."[13] But this seems too strong. Couldn't Hobbes have intended to square the circle? Yet even if the claim is too strong, possibly some weakened restriction of the same sort should be added to I and II. It will help to consider an illustration: "If I cannot play the harpsichord I cannot intend to play it."[14] This is initially plausible. But perhaps its plausibility derives from our assumption that if one is in one's right mind, one would not believe one could play the harpsichord without knowing how. Suppose, however, that under hypnosis S is made to believe (falsely) that she can play it. Now imagine S, no longer under hypnosis, sitting down to play. As she reaches out to play, is it false to say she intends to play? She would certainly say she intends to. To be sure, for *us*, knowing her delusion,

[12] Chisholm, "The Structure of Intention," p. 639.
[13] Annette C. Baier, "Act and Intent," *Journal of Philosophy* 67, no. 19 (1970), p. 650. Cf. Castañeda, "Intentions and the Structure of Intending," p. 462.
[14] Baier, "Act and Intent," p. 649.

it is peculiar to say this. But this may be partly because the more informative thing to say is that, poor creature, she thinks she is going to play. We would *not* say, however, that she thinks she intends to play. Moreover, we assume that normal persons are typically not deluded about what they can do, and hence saying someone intends to *A* normally carries a strong suggestion that she can, or probably can. This is another reason why it is peculiar to say *S* intends to play.

One way to deal with such cases is to add clauses requiring something like this: that *S*'s belief that she will *A* is not the result of delusion or of an irrational assessment of the evidence concerning her ability to *A*. But if any such restriction were warranted, it would sometimes be appropriate to tell people that they do not intend to do what they sincerely say they intend to do; and if one cannot intend what one cannot do, it would often be appropriate to tell someone this. But if telling people this is ever appropriate, it is not when they mistakenly, or even both mistakenly and irrationally, believe they can do what they cannot. Suppose that an old woman cannot accept the impending death of her sister, an obviously failing terminal cancer patient. If she says she intends to save her sister by taking her to a better climate, would anyone who did not doubt her sincerity (or self-knowledge) deny she intends to save her sister by doing this? Surely the right thing to say to her is that she cannot save her sister that way.

It may be objected that we can tell people they are not going to do what they say they are going to do, and that 'I'm going to *A*' is equivalent to 'I intend to *A*'. They are not equivalent, however. 'I am going to *A*', like 'I shall *A*', and unlike 'I intend to *A*', implies that I believe I definitely will. There is a use of 'I am going to *A*' in which it entails 'I intend to *A*', but this does not save the objection. For if the reason we do not accept 'I am going to *A*', in this use, is that we believe the speaker cannot do it, we say something like 'You're not going to succeed.' Thus, normally when *S* says to her child, 'Oh no you're not going out tonight!', she does not mean to deny that the child intends to go out, even if she believes the child cannot. It is in part the child's intention that disturbs her. She is denying the child permission to go out and thereby denying that the child will go out. Indeed, she may later say to her husband, 'He was going (intended) to go out, and for the third night in a row'. Clearly, the denial of 'I'm going to go out' was not a denial that the child intended to do so.

Another question we must consider is whether the suggested account is too broad because it appears prima facie possible that S might satisfy I or II with respect to an action, yet not believe she will perform it intentionally; and one might then wonder whether she intends to do it at all. Suppose Sally satisfies II with respect to insulting Leo, whom she abhors, but believes that she will be unable to avoid grimacing when she meets him and that she will thus insult him, but will be doing so neither voluntarily nor intentionally. It is tempting to say that, even if she satisfies II with respect to insulting Leo, she merely consents to it and does not intend it. But recall that, if Sally satisfies II here, she must (with rare exceptions not relevant here) want to insult Leo when she meets him, more than she wants to do anything she believes incompatible with this, *including* such things as abstaining from grimacing to wait for a better occasion for insult. In this light, it is plausible to say that she does intend to insult him (by grimacing). For we now see that she not only is motivated to insult him when she meets him, but also wants to do this more than to do anything she believes incompatible with it.

One may protest that Sally cannot intend to insult Leo in this case, because one cannot intend what one believes one cannot help doing.[15] But, even if this view is correct, she does not believe categorically that she cannot help insulting him, only that *if* she enters the situation she intends to enter with him, then she will not be able to help insulting him.

But the view seems false. Imagine that, after a quarrel with my sister, I believe that I will not be able to help asking her forgiveness. If I also want to ask her forgiveness more than I want anything I believe incompatible with doing so, it would seem that I indeed intend to ask her forgiveness, and one can imagine planning a way to do so. Consider also one hunger striker saying to another, regarding food which embarrassed officials are offering, 'Do you intend to accept food tomorrow?' It might be perfectly proper to answer, 'Yes, I can't possibly hold out longer than that.' Thus, one can intend to do what one believes one lacks the power not to do. And it appears that if S really does satisfy I or II with respect to an action she believes

---

[15] Baier seems to think this. See, e.g., "Act and Intent," p. 657.

she will not perform intentionally or will be unable to help doing, she nonetheless intends it.

III. Intending, Intentional Action, and Responsibility

Even if there should be no counterexamples to the account, there remains the question whether it is fruitful to explicate 'intending' along the lines of I or II. Chisholm, for one, prefers to explicate 'action' in terms of 'intending', rather than conversely.[16] Moreover, the notions of wanting and believing are quite complex. Is it any help to make them central to an account of intending? Let me make two points in reply to this.

First, the notions of wanting and believing seem to be of such general philosophical importance that philosophers would wish to explicate them even if they could be avoided in explicating 'intending'. Second, in part because actions are not necessarily intentional,[17] there need be no circularity involved in using the notion of action in explicating that of intending. Indeed, it is noteworthy that Chisholm, who does not presuppose the notion of action in his account of intending, does take as primitive 'He brings it about that—in intending to bring it about that . . .' (pp. 634–35). This is a locution one might well wish to be able to analyze; and perhaps it can be understood largely in terms of the materials employed in I and II.

There are, I believe, other ways in which the account of intending summarized in I and II is helpful. Consider the question of how the notion of intending is related to the notion of intentional action. It is natural to assume that intentional actions are those brought about by intentions. For simple intentions, this view is false. First, we normally cannot explain why S A-ed (where her A-ing is intentional) by citing her intention *to do it*, though we normally can explain an intentional

---

[16] Chisholm, "The Structure of Intention," pp. 634–35.

[17] For instance, a man's wife might properly reproach him for shameful actions at a tea, referring to his (unintentionally) spilling a drink, putting his cigar in a candy dish, and sitting on someone's hat. Moreover, even if actions were necessarily intentional, what would follow is at most that an account of intending that uses 'action' could avoid circularity only if 'intentional action' could be explicated without appeal to the notion of intending. Goldman, *A Theory of Human Action*, gives a plausible explication of just this kind.

action by citing an intention *with which* S performed it.[18] Second, some intentional actions are neither preceded by nor accompanied by intentions to perform them. Imagine that, as Sally is target shooting, a silver fox appears fifty yards beyond her target. Her companion, Ann, seeing her aim that way, might say, "I hope you don't intend to shoot that beautiful thing." Now if Sally knows she is so bad a marksman that her chances of hitting the fox are very slim, she might hope to hit it, but not intend to; and she would probably answer with something like 'I'm going to try.' Nevertheless, if she does hit it, the game warden could rightly say she did so intentionally. It may appear that all intentional actions are brought about by end-directed intentions. But a person humming just because she feels like it may be doing so intentionally, even if she has no further intention, such as to inform someone of her presence. The shooting case also shows that not all intentional actions are brought about by end-directed intentions: Sally shoots at the fox with the hope of hitting it; she does not have the intention of hitting it. Notice, however, that she does shoot at it because she wants to hit it, and her shooting at it is intentional. Hence the case also shows that, contrary to what has been argued,[19] 'S A-ed with the intention of bringing about Φ' is not equivalent in explanatory force to 'S A-ed because she wanted Φ'.

Thus, the account we have been exploring shows that the relation between the notion of intending and that of intentional action is not so close as one might well think, though the paradigms of intentional action are those performed with some further intention. Yet the account also makes clear why end-directed intentions should have the explanatory power they do. For one thing, we very often explain actions by appeal to the wants and beliefs of the agent. Indeed, it has been plausibly argued that all intentional actions are explainable by appeal to S's wanting something and believing either that her performing the action will constitute (or amount to) realizing it, or that her performing the action is necessary to (will, may) realize it.[20] Even if this needs important qualifications, certainly we very often do explain actions by appeal to such wants and beliefs; thus, it is

[18] This point and the distinction it employs are brought out by Malcolm, "The Conceivability of Mechanism." See esp. pp. 59–62.

[19] For example, by Churchland, "The Logical Character of Action Explanation," p. 231.

[20] Goldman, *A Theory of Human Action*, argues for this view. See esp. pp. 49–76. For explication and defense of a revised version of this thesis see Chapter 6.

easy to see why end-directed intentions, as conceived according to I, have the action-explaining power they have: intending to bring about Φ by A-ing entails both wanting Φ and believing (at least) that by A-ing one will probably achieve Φ.

The account of intending summarized in I and II also accommodates the point that intending to do something is non-contingently linked with doing it, in the sense that it "is part of what we mean by 'intending X' that, in the absence of interfering factors, it is followed by doing X."[21] This is an important view. I shall not attempt to defend it. My point here is simply that it is just as plausible to make the same claim regarding the connection between (1) the wants and beliefs with which I and II equate intentions and (2) the actions they are intentions to perform. For instance, surely *part* of what we mean by '*S* wants to *A* (more than she wants anything she believes incompatible with A-ing) and believes she will A' is that, in the absence of interfering factors (such as insurmountable obstacles), S will A.[22] Thus, I and II partly explain another important aspect of the logic of intending.

A further desirable consequence of the account of intending I have suggested is that it disallows certain initially plausible inferences that might be—and sometimes are—used in giving excuses. Consider some examples. People who are accused of intentionally doing what they claim was an accident may plead that they never thought about doing it, implying that they thus could not have intended it. But clearly the wants and beliefs constituting intentions can arise (and vanish) momentarily; they need not emerge from practical reasoning or from thinking about the intended action. People might also plead that they do not have some reprehensible intention because they have some strong incompatible want. Leo might say that he does not intend to deprive a member of his staff of credit for an achievement because he very much wants people to know just how good a staff he has. I and II make it clear, however, that this inference is invalid. He might still have a stronger incompatible want to take credit for the achievement himself.

There are many other questions that a comprehensive account of intending should treat. But the account I have proposed seems ade-

[21] Charles Taylor, *The Explanation of Behavior* (New York: Humanities, 1964), p. 33.
[22] I have argued for this at some length in Chapter 1. But, for reasons indicated there, the "meaning relation" between wants (or beliefs) and actions is by no means such as to rule out the possibility that explanations of action by appeal to the agent's wants and beliefs are either causal or nomological or both.

quate to simple and end-directed intentions, and it helps us answer a number of interesting questions connected with intention. It helps us, for instance, to see how intending is related to wanting, believing, trying, and practical reasoning; to distinguish intending from hoping and from expecting; and to assess various forms of inference in which the notion of intending figures. If the account accords with our intuitions about intending as well as it appears to and has the further advantages I have suggested, it may be a significant contribution toward a general theory of intention.[23]

[23] For helpful comments on earlier versions of this chapter I am grateful to Paul M. Churchland, Hardy E. Jones, Norman Malcolm, Jack W. Meiland, and John O'Connor.

Chapter 3

Volition and Agency

In one form or another, volitionalism has been perhaps the dominant theory of action since Aquinas and quite possibly since Aristotle. Gilbert Ryle did much to chase it underground, and in the two decades after his publication of *The Concept of Mind* (1949) the position was not widely defended. But a powerful theory with deep historical roots is not easily demolished; and volitionalism—by which I mean a theory of the nature of action which gives a central place to one or another kind of willing—has been considerably refined in response to Ryle and other critics. By the 1970s, many philosophers writing on human action had shown that Ryle and other detractors refuted at best only unsophisticated or implausibly strong versions of volitionalism. In the 1980s, the volitional theory was developed further, and in current philosophy of action it is perhaps the most widely held view, at least regarding the immediate antecedents of action. Despite the prominence of volitionalism, however, there remains much unclarity both about the basic notion of volition and about its surrogates and close cousins. The theory should be assessed in the light of the wide range of problems that motivate it, and an appraisal of this kind is apparently still needed. Proponents of volitionalism usually develop the theory in relation to only a few of these problems, but volitionalism cannot be adequately evaluated apart from its overall contribution to answering the full range of important questions on which it bears. My aim here is to trace some major conceptions of volition, to articulate the main problems that motivate volitional theories, to assess volitionalism as a response to those problems, and to propose alternative solutions to them.

I. Some Varieties of Volitionalism

Even if we suppose that, in line with a long-standing philosophical tradition, volitions may be conceived as *acts of will*, this leaves us with much to clarify. For one thing, no plausible volitional theory posits a substantive will capable of its own acts; and if volitions are acts of any sort, they are acts of an agent. It turns out, however, that about all we can presuppose regarding the basic ontological classification of volitions is that they are in the category of mental events. We then find great diversity. Some volitionalists, such as Hugh McCann,[1] conceive volition as action; H. A. Prichard goes so far as to argue that *only* volition is action.[2] By contrast, Hector-Neri Castañeda denies that volitions are actions, at least in the (usual) sense in which actions are doings.[3] Volitions have also been characterized as components in every non-primitive action, and hence as useful in explicating such action.[4] They have even been functionally characterized, in terms of mediation between their causes and effects, so that their intrinsic nature is left unspecified.[5]

[1] Hugh J. McCann, "Volition and Basic Action," *Philosophical Review* 83 (1974): 451.

[2] See H. A. Prichard, *Moral Obligation* (Oxford: Clarendon Press, 1949); on p. 190, for example, he says that "to act is really to will something." Cf. Jennifer Hornsby, *Actions* (London: Routledge and Kegan Paul, 1980). She says that "all actions occur inside the body" (p. 13), and that "[e]very action is an event of *trying* or attempting to act, and every attempt that is an action precedes and causes a contraction$_i$ [where 'I' means 'intransitive'] of muscles and a movement$_i$ of the body" (p. 33).

[3] See Hector-Neri Castañeda, *Thinking and Doing* (Dordrecht: Reidel, 1975), esp. chap. 12, where he says, "If the reader wants to speak of mental acts, then volitions are acts, but they are still not doings" (p. 310).

[4] Douglas Odegard, for example, says, "A volition consists in willing an event to occur. It is therefore an action and cannot be used to explain what action in general is. But it can be used to explain actions which have *constituents,*" i.e., non-primitive actions; see "Volition and Action," *American Philosophical Quarterly* 25 (1988): 141.

[5] See, for example, Lawrence Davis, *Theory of Action* (Englewood Cliffs, N.J.: Prentice-Hall, 1979). For him a volition is "an event which is normally a cause of the agent's belief that he is acting in a certain way, *and* which normally causes such doing-related events [for example arm risings] as make it true that he *is* acting in that way" (p. 16). Further, "Volitions are attempts, and attempts—*tryings*—are doings" (p. 17). However, "the agent is not generally aware of the willing, the volition, in itself. . . . [I]t does not seem that there are any *intrinsic features* of the volition of which he can become aware"

If we ask what sort of mental event a volition is, we again find considerable diversity among volitionalists. Perhaps the most common view is that volition is some kind of *trying*. Brian O'Shaughnessy, for instance, says that "volitionalism, (Y), is correct in so far as it says: (y1) whenever we perform a voluntary act Φ of φ-making [say, an arm-raising, which entails making one's arm rise] there occurs a *sui generis* irreducible event V which is psychological, of the irreducible genus Will, and such that φ is causally explicable because of V,"[6] where willing is represented "in ordinary language" by the terms 'try' and 'strive': "Another name for this act of will is 'strive.' Another is 'try'."[7] D. M. Armstrong[8] and Raimo Tuomela[9] also seem to conceive volition as roughly equivalent to trying. Volition may also be conceived as a kind of decision.[10]

On the other hand, volition has been closely associated with *intending*. Mill, for instance, said, "Now what is an action? Not one thing, but a series of two things: the state of mind called a volition, followed by an effect. The volition or intention to produce the effect, is one thing: the effect produced in consequence of the intention, is another thing: the two together constitute the action."[11] For Wilfrid Sellars, volitions are "one variety of occurrent intention (state), as perceptual takings are but one variety of occurrent belief (state)";[12] and Myles Brand describes himself as following Sellars "in taking the proximate cause of action [which Sellars and others would call a

---

(p. 18). For some development of Davis's views, see his "What Is It Like to Be an Agent?" *Erkenntnis* 18 (1982), and W. R. Carter's commentary on that in the same issue. Cf. Bruce Aune, *Reason and Action* (Dordrecht: D. Reidel, 1977), pp. 69–71.

[6] See Brian O'Shaughnessy, *The Will* (Cambridge: Cambridge University Press, 1980), 2:269.

[7] Ibid., p. 264. For critical discussion of the attempt to understand trying as equivalent to volition, see Timothy Cleveland, "Trying without Willing," forthcoming in the *Autralasian Journal of Philosophy*.

[8] See D. M. Armstrong, "Acting and Trying," in his *The Nature of Mind and Other Essays* (St. Lucia: University of Queensland Press; Ithaca: Cornell University Press, 1980). He says that "all intentional action involves a mental event and that this event is a 'trying' or 'attempting' to do something. . . . Perhaps there is no term for this mental something in our ordinary discourse, and some term of art, such as 'volition', is required" (p. 70).

[9] See Raimo Tuomela, *Human Action and Its Explanation* (Dordrecht: Reidel, 1977), esp. chap. 6.

[10] For a development of this conception, see Michael J. Zimmerman, *An Essay on Human Action* (New York: Peter Lang, 1984), chap. 3.

[11] J. S. Mill, *Logic*, 1.3.5.

[12] Wilfrid Sellars, "Volitions Re-Affirmed," in Myles Brand and Douglas Walton, eds., *Action Theory* (Dordrecht: Reidel, 1976), para. 29.

volition] to be an intending to do something here and now. Let me call this 'immediate intention'."[13]

There are various other views of volition. For Alvin Goldman, occurrent (predominant) wanting is approximately equivalent to what has been commonly considered volition, where the relevant wants are occurrent in the same way as Sellarsian immediate intentions.[14] Castañeda at one point characterizes volitions as "episodes" of "the thinking of an intention about a present action, namely, the thinking which consists of deciding or intending to do something *right now*."[15] For him, as for Sellars and Brand, it is crucial to conceive the cognitive and volitional elements in question as events. If one regards intentions, wants, and other such psychological elements as dispositions rather than events, one must interpret *occurrent* intentions and (occurrent) wants as something like datable expressions of them in consciousness.

If volition is substantially like intending or wanting, one would expect its *content* to include action; one would, for example, expect the content of a volition directed toward raising one's hand to be *to raise one's hand*. But there are differences among volitional theorists regarding such content. While most conceive the content as actional, McCann construes it as referring to the *result* of the action, that is, to the movement intrinsic to the action in the way a hand's rising is intrinsic to one's raising it.[16] For Carl Ginet, on the other hand, "When I exert [my body] voluntarily . . . I will, not just exerting, but my exerting, exerting caused by me. The intentional object of my volition is not just my body's exertion but my voluntary control of its exertion. I will that my willing—this very willing of whose content we speak—cause the exertion."[17] Such voluntary exertion certainly appears to be a kind of action, however special its properties may otherwise be. Moreover, if we may think of John Searle's intentions-in-action as roughly equivalent to volitions construed as the proxi-

[13] Myles Brand, *Intending and Acting: Toward a Naturalized Action Theory* (Cambridge: MIT Press, 1984), p. 35. Brand is careful to distinguish his view from what he calls the "Oldtime Volition Theory," for example Mill's just cited.

[14] See Alvin I. Goldman, *A Theory of Human Action* (Englewood Cliffs, N.J.: Prentice-Hall, 1970), esp. pp. 86–99. For a more recent statement of Goldman's view, see his "The Volitional Theory Revisited," in Brand and Walton, *Action Theory*.

[15] Castañeda, *Thinking and Doing*, p. 309.

[16] McCann, "Volition and Basic Action," p. 467.

[17] Carl Ginet, "Voluntary Exertion of the Body: A Volitional Account," *Theory and Decision* 20 (1986): 234. For a later statement of Ginet's view see his *On Action* (Cambridge: Cambridge University Press, 1990), chap. 2.

mate mental causes of the results of actions, then his view, like Ginet's, puts intentional concepts into the content of volition. Searle
says, for example, that the "content of an immediate intention to raise
my arm is (my arm goes up as a result of this intention)."[18] In this,
he is not typical; but there are others, for example Gilbert Harman,
who have held that intentions of roughly this sort are self-
referential.[19]

Volitionalists also differ regarding the epistemic status of volition.
Since volitions are conceived as mental events, one would expect
them to be considered non-inferentially knowable by their subject.
But they are apparently not always so regarded. If, for instance, they
are functionally conceived, then the subject, S, might at times be able
to come to know their presence only by taking stock of certain other
mental phenomena. Lawrence Davis seems to suggest this.[20] Mc-
Cann, on the other hand, regards volition as "something the agent
must be immediately aware of, since it is thought. It is also the initia-
tion of the intended action, and has the content that the . . . result
occur. Thus a person who engages in volition can know directly that
he is acting, and what he is trying to do."[21] Given McCann's use of
'can know', we should perhaps take his view to be not that our engaging in volition is automatically known to us but (what seems more
plausible) that *if* we consider whether we are engaging in it, then if
we are, we directly know that we are.

Given the theoretical diversity just suggested, is there any hope of
framing a univocal conception of volition applicable to all the views
we have considered? If there is, it would be too general to constitute
an analysis. We could speak only of, for example, mental events which
(whether doings, or acts, or simply a kind of behavior) are, or are
crucial in, producing action—if not its immediate causes, then its
closest psychological causes. Perhaps there is a lesson in this. There

[18] John R. Searle, *Intentionality* (Cambridge: Cambridge University Press, 1983),
p. 93. This view and others cited may be usefully compared with those of Alan Donagan in *Choice: The Essential Element in Action* (London: Routledge and Kegan Paul, 1987),
esp. chaps. 5 and 6.
[19] See Gilbert Harman, "Practical Reasoning," *Review of Metaphysics* 29 (1976). The
idea is roughly that when S intends to A what he intends is to A as a result of that
very intention.
[20] That our access to our volitions is limited is suggested in the quotation from Davis,
Theory of Action, in n. 5.
[21] McCann, "Volition and Basic Action," p. 470. For a different account of volition
with much attention to epistemological aspects of volitionalism, see Odegard, "Volition
and Action."

may be no ordinary concept of volition, or willing, or even trying, which is being analyzed and used to understand action; there may simply be important problems about action which philosophers hope to solve by postulating a kind of mental event with the sorts of properties suggested above, and then explicating its connections with more familiar entities such as actions, movements, intentions, and desires. In any case, we can perhaps best appraise volitional theories if, instead of concentrating on one or two, we largely abstract from what differentiates one from the others and view them in relation to the sorts of problems they are intended to clarify or solve. We can do this without framing a univocal conception of volition or of volitionalism as a theory of action. For it turns out, I think, that the kinds of problems in question are all at least implicitly addressed by the theories mentioned above and others like them, and to a large extent their bearing on these problems does not depend on differences among the theories. This, anyway, is a hypothesis I shall explore. The first step is to formulate the problems, and that is the task of the next section.

II. Problems Motivating Volitional Theories of Action

Unless one accepts (as most philosophers do) a broadly causal theory of action, it is difficult to appreciate what motivates volitionalism. This may be one reason why Ryle, an apparently non-causal theorist who may have interpreted volitionalism mainly through his own caricatures, underestimated its resources. The first thing to note is this: granted that historically there has been deep disagreement among philosophers about whether actions are deterministically caused, the picture of actions as caused by such elements as the agent's desires, beliefs, and decisions has tended to dominate both philosophical and commonsense thinking about human action. Here, then, is one powerful reason to adopt a volitional theory: it supplies a causal factor which *genetically unifies* actions in terms of a common kind of origin, even if not necessarily its ultimate origin, in the psychology of the agent. Connected with this, volitionalism provides a conception of how actions arise from the welter of psychological elements internal to the agent. This second point is particularly important if one accepts the plausible view that, strictly speaking, (1) the causes of events are other events, and (2) events are changes.[22] For if this view is correct, then actions, which plainly are events, cannot be caused by dispositions, including desires and beliefs, since dispositions are not changes; and a causal theory of action must therefore indicate certain kinds of events as causes of action if the theory is to be clear regarding the genesis of action.

Neither of these points necessarily concerns the *analysis* of the concept of action: we have simply spoken of how a causal theory of action must be worked out. For with or without an analysis of that concept, such a view must say something about what actions are and how they are related to various other psychological and behavioral elements. Still, many philosophers who want to analyze the concept of action find volitionalism attractive. One may, for instance, plausibly analyze action as bodily (or mental) movement suitably caused by volition. Or, if one believes the concept of action to be irreducible, one can explicate it recursively by construing volitions as basic actions and characterizing all other actions in relation to them, for example either as performed *by* willing or as being identical with willing under a different description. When, for instance, my arm's rising is suitably caused by willing, my raising the arm might be either viewed as done *by* willing or even *identified* with my willing to raise it, under a different description, such as 'waving my hand'. Perhaps, as a Prichardian parody of Donald Davidson would have it, all we ever do is move our wills; the rest is up to nature.

Volitions have also promised to enable us to distinguish *voluntary actions* from others or at least from mere behavior.[23] Reflex "actions," such as the patellar reflex, are clearly not willed. On the other hand, we voluntarily do many things we do not do intentionally; for example, we regretfully but consentingly annoy people by opposing them, and we voluntarily but non-intentionally move our feet in coming

[22] These views need more explication than I can give here (and I must simply ignore the possibility that agents as such cause their actions). I do not take the mere passage of time to be a change in the relevant sense; but if it is, then such minimal temporal events are not the kind in question here. A further problem has been pointed out to me by Michael J. Zimmerman: standing at attention appears to be an action but not to entail change. If, however, it requires not just *standing in a physical attitude of attention,* but *attendingly standing,* then while there can be short uneventful *intervals* in an action, the occurrence of monitoring events, at least, seems essential to any *complete* performance of the action.

[23] See Goldman's "The Volitional Theory Revisited" for a conception of how volitions might help in distinguishing voluntary action from other behavior.

downstairs with only breakfast on our minds. In the former case we seem to act by permission of the will, in the latter by extension of the will. Its reach extends from its focal target—going to breakfast—to our customary means of hitting it.[24] Here it is plausible to suppose that some mental event or process produces the behavior and (perhaps together with other elements) plays a part in guiding it, particularly as data are received from any perceptual monitoring of the things one does, as in driving, and volition is directed toward the newly required adjustments. Why else do we exert force against an obstacle if we encounter one and, where achieving our objective requires skillful movement, adjust our behavior to the contours of the environment? Volitional events can apparently play a crucial initiating role and, to some extent, account for our adjustments of our movements in quest of our goals.

There are also powerful motivating factors analogous to the pressure to account for perceptual *illusion and hallucination,* although the counterpart problem in action theory has not been generally viewed in terms of this analogy. A widely familiar experience will suggest the relevant analogue of (non-delusive) perceptual illusion: you make the movements usual in opening a door but find to your surprise that someone on the other side is opening it just ahead of you; the door moves, but you have at best the illusion of moving it, rather as when you see an oar halfway in the water, you may have the illusion of its being bent. The same sort of thing can happen in relation to the arm itself: someone pulls it just as one is, as it seems, stretching it out, so that one realizes it moves, but lacks the sense of moving it. Hasn't one done something, say *tried* to move it? Indeed, don't we have what is left over when, in Wittgenstein's phrase, one subtracts the fact that one's arm moves from the fact that one moves one's arm? And is it not very natural to call that *willing?* Positing volition, then, promises to solve the subtraction problem.

The analogue of hallucination is even more favorable to volitionalism than the behavioral analogue of perceptual illusion. William James brought this out vividly: "Close the patient's eyes, hold his anaesthetic arm still, and tell him to raise his arm to his head; and when he opens his eyes he will be astonished to find that the move-

---

[24] These points are debatable but not without plausibility. There is also some question whether moving one's feet is an action here: moving one's feet is an action-*type,* but this instantiation might be a mere behavioral part of an action. A crucial question is what, if anything, the agent believes about the feet.

ment has not taken place. All reports of anaesthetic cases seem to mention this illusion."[25] Why is he astonished? A natural explanation is that he did whatever he usually does in raising his arm, except that the arm did not go up, just as, when Macbeth hallucinated a dagger, he apparently saw all one normally sees in viewing a dagger, except that there was no dagger before him. It is also natural to say that the patient willed, or tried, to raise his arm, for he surely followed—at least so far as he could—the doctor's order; he simply did not succeed in carrying it out. Surely he did something, and indeed something sufficiently action-like to make him think he raised his arm.

Still another set of problems which volitions promise to clarify or solve concerns the *dynamics of action.* Consider intentions: they do not execute themselves. Indeed, as dispositional states, they presumably do not cause anything except by virtue of some event suitably connected with them, such as their becoming occurrent, say as a person who intends to line up and pay a grocery bill has the thought, upon noticing a checkout counter with just one customer, that one should hurry there to get in line. As Castañeda puts it, "There must be an event to at least mobilize energy already available potentially."[26] Even if one does not think of intentions and other propositional attitudes as causal factors, one will want an account of their execution. Volitions can provide this account even if they are not conceived as events in virtue of which such dispositional states cause actions. But for any causal theory of action which construes these dispositional states as causal explainers, it is desirable—and indeed crucial if only events are, strictly speaking, causes—to find some event which more directly causes the action. One can then think of volitions as the psychological events that mediate between reasons and actions. They can also mediate between practical reasoning and action, for example between a practical judgment with which S concludes practical reasoning and S's acting accordingly. Here, as in other cases, volitions (or similar

[25] William James, *Principles of Psychology,* vol. 2 (1890; New York: Dover, 1950), p. 105.
[26] Hector-Neri Castañeda, "Conditional Intentions, Intentional Action and Aristotelian Practical Syllogisms," *Erkenntnis* 18 (1982): 253. But this event need not be a volition. Although he says that "a *volition* is an episode or event of intentional thinking, in which an agent thinks, in the appropriate causal framework and mood, to perform an act" (p. 240) and that the "intentionality of an action does seem to consist of some systematic causal connection between an agent's doing an action A and what he, determined to do A, thinks to do" (p. 239), i.e., between the doing and the associated volition, he also implies that volitions are not the only energizers, for example that (where Rosthal has the conditional intention to offer Rosenberg his best French wine if Rosenberg comes) "It is purely an empirical matter whether or not the event of

events) can help explain the possibility of weakness of will; for one way we can act against our better judgment is to fail to have the appropriate volition. If actions were geared directly to practical judgment, there would be less scope for weakness of will. Granted, they might be as closely geared to, say, decisions as to volitions, but this is not obvious; and if it is so, then decisions would be more like volitions than they appear, and the possibility of weakness of will would still be clarified along the lines suggested by volitional theories. From this point of view, volitions can be conceived as exertions, or at least expressions, of will power—of just the sort of thing whose absence can explain weakness of will; and Castañeda, for one, does at times conceive volitions as, in a distinctive way, inserting energy into the action system.[27]

If intentions do not simply execute themselves, then, except in the case of intentions to do something here and now, they also do not provide in themselves much indication of why they are carried out *when* they are; and the same applies to all the other action-explaining propositional attitudes.[28] This is an important point. For at least one kind of causation, namely, causation of one event by another, seems to be governed by what we might call a *principle of the differential temporality of causation:* in a generic form it says that there is an intimate relation between temporal properties of the cause and of the effect; and in a specific but still plausible form it asserts that the time at which the cause occurs explains why the effect occurs when it does.[29] Thus, if we want to know why a truck rolled down the hill when it did, one answer might be that it was at just that moment

---

perceiving Rosenberg can mobilize enough energy within Rosthal's body for him to rise up, go to his wine cellar. . . . His total intention covers holistically the whole sequence of movements" (p. 255).

[27] See Castañeda, *Thinking and Doing;* on p. 283, for example, Castañeda vividly expresses the energizing power of volitions when he says, "To think (4) [I shall jump at 3 p.m.] endorsingly is to have before one's mind the burst of the causality which the thinking of (4) exercises in the world," where such endorsing thinking is of the sort he considers volitional (p. 309).

[28] Perhaps, for example, one can explain why Beverly picked up her chalk when she did by noting that she intended to pick it up there and then. For a treatment of such proximal intentions and their role in doing some of the traditional work of volition, see Frederick Adams and Alfred R. Mele, "The Intention/Volition Debate," *Canadian Journal of Philosophy* 22, no. 3 (1992). That essay supports a number of points in this chapter. Note, however, that in order to do the required work, such intentions *may* have to be construed as events, in a sense in which intentions in general apparently are not events, and may perhaps have some of the properties that make volition problematic.

[29] This principle is introduced and discussed in chap. 6 of my *Practical Reasoning* (London: Routledge, 1989).

that someone dropped a heavy bale of hay into it. Similarly, we might suppose that we act when we do because of the occurrence of the appropriate volition (trying, immediate intending, or another form of willing).

We should also note that while *trying* is sometimes invoked in explicating volition, a volitional construal of trying might also enhance our understanding of what it is to try, which is a question of independent philosophical interest. Particularly in anesthetization cases like James's, where there is no overt action to count as trying, it may look as if the only way to conceive the trying which apparently occurs is as a kind of willing. What else could the patient have done, one may wonder, in order to raise his hand? Moreover, it often appears that one is trying to *A*, though there is no special exertion of effort with which to identify the trying. Armstrong, for example, says that even if "all I know is what his objective is and that he is pursuing it . . . will it not be linguistically legitimate for me to say that I know that [he] is at least attempting or trying to achieve whatever his objective is?"[30] If one is acting purposefully, one is at least trying to achieve some purpose.

Some writers have also suggested that we always know, non-observationally, what we are doing. Searle, for example, says that "at any point in a man's conscious life he knows without observation the answer to the question 'What are you now doing?' . . . Even in a case where a man is mistaken about what the results of his efforts are he still knows what he is *trying* to do."[31] Volitions conceived as tryings, or indeed in the various other ways that render them comparably accessible to awareness, yield an explanation of such non-observational knowledge. As mental events they are, on a venerable, traditional view, so luminous that *S* cannot help knowing of their presence; and even on a much weaker (I think more plausible) view, they are introspectable, or at least non-observationally knowable; they

---

[30] Armstrong, "Acting and Trying," p. 72. However, "The initial state, *i*, of an agent's intentional doing need not be caused to exist *directly* by the agent's volition to bring it into existence" (p. 313, emphasis mine). Cf. Ginet's view: "Volition is the initial part or stage of voluntary exertion (and thereby of any action that involves voluntary exertion" (*On Action*, p. 30).

[31] Searle, *Intentionality*, p. 90. For an earlier discussion of non-observational knowledge of one's actions, see G. E. M. Anscombe, *Intention*, 2d ed. (Ithaca: Cornell University Press, 1963); and for a quite different treatment, emphasizing the "spontaneity" of such knowledge, see David Velleman, *Practical Reflection* (Princeton: Princeton University Press, 1989).

can be, but need not be, non-inferentially (or otherwise) known. But their external behavioral effects, being subject, as we saw, to counterparts of illusion and hallucination, are not non-inferentially known.

My last point about what motivates volitionalism is much broader. It concerns the *unity* of one's philosophical outlook. Volitionalism parallels a major traditional position in epistemology. As Arthur Danto noted in the 1960s there is the same sort of reason to say that if we do anything at all, we do some things basically, as to say that if we know anything at all, we know some things basically.[32] This of course calls attention to the applicability of foundationalism in action theory as well as in epistemology. Let me develop the idea. In epistemology the idea implies that if there is any knowledge, then there is foundational knowledge, hence non-inferential knowledge and, in *that* sense, basic knowledge. Now suppose that one believes, with perhaps the majority of modern epistemologists writing before the middle of this century, that our basic empirical knowledge is roughly phenomenal, in a sense implying immunity to illusion and hallucination. There is *some* plausibility in this. For even if I should be hallucinating a dagger, surely I can still know that it *seems* to me that I see one. And should our *basic* empirical knowledge not be of this secure kind? We may take a similar approach in action theory: if our agency is to be on a firm foundation, should it not rest on something internal? If the external world does not cooperate, I may mistakenly think I raise my hand; but even then, surely I *will or try* to raise it, and know that I so will or that I try to raise it. On this view, agency, like knowledge, is rooted internally and thereby secured against the vagaries of the external world. *In foro interno,* if we are not omniscient and omnipotent, there are at least profound limits to our ignorance and our impotence. There is always much we can know, and much we can attempt; and what we do know, or attempt, in this domain, is the firm foundation on which knowledge of the world, and action upon the world, are built.

III. Action without Volition: An Alternative Treatment of the Motivating Problems

It should now be clear why volitional theories are philosophically attractive. There are in fact advantages of such theories

[32] Arthur C. Danto, "What We Can Do," *Journal of Philosophy* 60 (1963).

even beyond those pointed out above, but perhaps enough has been said to indicate the most important merits and to enable us to make some major points of appraisal. Let us simply proceed through the motivating ideas (except the appeal of volitionalism as a strategy for analyzing the concept of action, since this is best considered after examining the other ideas). In assessing how much these motivating ideas support volitionalism, I shall for convenience use the term 'volition' unless another, such as 'trying', is needed for specificity; but no particular conception of volition will be presupposed. I shall be thinking of volition as a mental event intended to play the sort of role which, in the light of the motivating considerations I have described, it *should* play in order to solve the problems from which those considerations derive.

Event Causes of Actions

Let us start with the question whether volitions can provide the sorts of event causes of action which a causal theory demands. Prima facie, they can. We must avoid, of course, postulating a one-one correspondence between volitions and actions. It is simply not plausible to suppose that for each action I perform there is a distinct volition. Consider fluent typing as a case in point. But as a number of defenders of volitional theories have pointed out, a single volition might govern a unified sequence of actions.[33] If I know a short Chopin prelude well enough, then, once having decided to play it, I may get lost in the music from start to finish. Moreover, there is no reason not to construe some complicated behavioral sequences (such as playing a musical passage) as, for people proficient enough, a single basic action performable at will.[34]

The first question to pursue here is what alternatives there are to volitions as the event causes of actions. There are at least six types

[33] See, for example, Goldman, "The Volitional Theory Revisited," and Castañeda, "Conditional Intentions," for discussion of how volitions may correspond to sets of related actions or to complicated basic ones.

[34] Not all volitional theorists would be hospitable to carrying this very far, however, particularly if volition is strongly associated with the sense of exertion. Ginet, for example, cautions that "volition is a fluid mental activity whose content is constantly changing; at each moment it is concerned only with bodily exertion in the immediate present. I can all at once decide to swim another length of the pool, but I cannot all at one time *will* the whole sequence of bodily exertions involved in swimming another length" (*On Action*, pp. 32–33).

of variables to be noted. Three are quite common. First, consider *perceptions*. Suppose that Ann intends to shoot a mad dog in the head as soon as it stands still. She tracks it in her sights, and when she first sees its head still in front of the bead, she fires. Her perception of the awaited opportunity causes the action. Second, *thoughts* about means (or apparent means) to some goal—such as the thought that in order to catch Joe before he leaves one must phone him right away—can be event causes of action. Third, decisions, choices, resolutions, and the like—what we might call *executive actions*—can apparently play the appropriate role. Resolving to decline alcohol at a party can cause one's declining, at that time, a drink one is offered; one might make the resolution at the very moment one is looking wishfully at the drink. A resolution can also be a *basis* on which, later, one's *noticing* Joe's offering one a drink causes one to reject it almost automatically.

Granted, decisions and the like are similar to volitions; but they are not equivalent to them. For one thing, they are not pervasive enough, since many actions, like impulsively picking a flower on a walk in the country, or steering around a bottle on the road, occur automatically or so spontaneously that they are not appropriately traceable to decisions. These actions are, however, intentional and should thus be considered to be under the control of volition. For another thing, unlike volitions, executive actions are very often comparative in a sense that entails *S*'s considering more than one option; and even when they are not explicitly comparative, they typically arise from considering a prospect or reflecting on what one is to do. In any event, if volitions ever *are* equated with any of these, the resulting theory should be accordingly renamed and then assessed in the light of the more familiar concept that shapes it.

This brings us to the remaining three kinds of non-volitional variable that can be an event cause of action. None is generally discussed, but each can straightforwardly cause action. The fourth kind is a *change in the balance of motivational forces*. Torn between roast beef and pastrami, one may look from one to the other and, through one's desire for the pastrami simply becoming the stronger of the two and tipping the motivational scale, order that. To be sure, one could just reach for the pastrami by an act of will intended to save one from the fate of Buridan's Ass. But no such intervention need occur in the kind of case in question, where one may be quite warranted in simply waiting for the stronger desire to prevail. The fifth case is the *overcoming of inertia*. Intending to rise upon hearing the alarm clock, one may still linger in bed. After a certain point is reached, presumably as one's motivation to get up, or one's realization that one has not done it, grows stronger relative to one's inertia, one may get up. Granted, inertia may arise from a conflicting desire to stay in bed, in which case we have a change in the balance of motivational forces, but conflicting desire *need* not be the source of such inertia. In the sixth case, an action simply strikes one as desirable, quite independently of its appearing to be a means to some goal. Looking ahead to a party, I might suddenly imagine a good conversation with Carl and invite him straightaway.

There may certainly be other kinds of events which, though not entailing volitions, cause actions, but the six kinds indicated cover a great variety of human actions. It must be granted that not all of these regularly provide much in the way of *explanation*. If, for example, one does not know why Ann shot the mad dog, it will not help to say that she saw its head standing still in front of the bead. However, the same applies to saying that, for example, she willed to shoot it. In both cases, explanation of the action seems to demand a *reason* for it. If we distinguish between the relations of *causing* and *causally explaining*, however, there is nothing disturbing in these points. Neither a volition to A nor, for example, perceiving an opportunity to A is supposed to provide a causal explanation of why S A-ed. But both are closely linked to prima facie causal explanations: the volition is presumably grounded in the reason(s) explaining the action, say wanting to rid the area of a dangerous pest and believing that shooting it is necessary to do so; and the perception is connected with the reason(s) by virtue of (for instance) generating a belief that now is a good time, or by indicating an opportunity to realize the relevant goal, such as ridding the area of a dangerous pest, and so on. Notice that by and large the non-volitional event causes seem to give us more information; for they apparently tell us something about why the action was appropriate in the circumstances. The occurrence of a volition, however, does not imply S's having a conception of a propitious occasion, or a change in the balance of motivation, or anything else that fits the action into a rational pattern. The work of volition seems to be done after these other elements are in place.

Voluntary and Involuntary Behavior

What about distinguishing voluntary actions from other behavior? This is very difficult on the basis of any currently available view.

Moreover, the notion of voluntary action is significantly vague. Mere reflexes are clearly ruled out; but what about more significant things done altogether unknowingly, such as waking a neighbor by letting one's phone ring too long, or things done accidentally, such as stepping on a toy? Are these latter, non-reflexual behaviors simply nonvoluntary *under* those descriptions? Whatever the answer, the intuitive idea, illustrated by the contrast between ordinary intentional action and mere reflex behavior, is surely that of being under the agent's control or, metaphorically, under the control of the will. Does that control require volition? It apparently need not. If, wanting to rid the area of a pest, Ann shoots the mad dog on sight, she can have perfect control of her shooting even if she is thinking about her work when the dog comes before her bead, and she just "automatically" fires. To be sure, she may have earlier decided to shoot the dog; but decision is surely not equivalent to volition, nor need it recur at or near the time of action, as volition is normally thought to do.

Suppose, however, that it could be shown that volition is necessary for voluntary action. Is its production of action *sufficient* for voluntariness? What if the volition is waywardly—or, as some say, deviantly— caused, for instance by a fortuitous electrical influence on the brain (or by the work of a demonic neurophysiologist), and produces an action for which S has no good reason, and from which S could not abstain by any amount of resistance? We thus have behavior S would not have willed spontaneously and cannot prevent or control (a kind of case discussed in detail in chapter 6). One might argue that a genuine volition cannot be waywardly caused; but even if that is not an ad hoc restriction, it will render the concept of a volition less clear and less readily usable in explicating action, since we shall need to understand wayward chains to distinguish volitions from waywardly caused mental events that seem to be volitions.

There is apparently still another way in which wayward chains can raise difficulties. We might start with a normally generated volition directed toward raising one's arm and imagine that it waywardly causes the behavior, as where the normal path between the volition and the arm muscles is blocked, but the volition happens to set off an impulse, which in turn activates a machine, which then gives off a current that, by good fortune, enters S's paralyzed arm and causes it to rise.[35] This would seem to be a mere bodily movement, particularly

---

[35] Davis, *Theory of Action*, contends that a movement caused by a volition is an action no matter how wayward the causal chain. But the closest he comes to arguing for this is to say that "[s]ince what led to the [for example, arm rising] was not just any doing

if (as might well be the case) its occurrence does not feel to the agent like the expected action, and probably even if it does. Supposing, however, that one's feeling as if one is moving one's arm is important for the question of whether one in fact is performing that action, this need not be owing to the role of volition in action: both the origin of this feeling and its importance for the notion of voluntariness could be explained on alternative theories. In the light of examples like this, it certainly looks as if volitional causation can explain voluntariness only in the context of conditions determining whether the agent controls the relevant behavior; and given an account of those conditions, it appears that one could also explain voluntariness without relying on volitions.

Behavioral Illusions and Hallucinations

We come now to the behavioral counterparts of illusion and hallucination. Let us begin with James's famous anesthetization case. Certainly S's surprise at discovering that his hand did not rise must be explained; and clearly volition, particularly conceived as trying, meets this need. For the agent would both be aware of the volition and expect it to be followed by the arm's rising. But there are other ways to explain S's surprise. It is agreed on all hands that he was in a general way following (or at least accepting) the doctor's orders. We may assume, then, that he formed the intention to raise his hand. Since he does not know his arm is anesthetized or held down, we may suppose that, at the time he intends to raise his hand, he also, as usual, *expects* to raise it.[36] And clearly a suddenly disappointed expectation tends to yield surprise.

Are we, however, to assume that S also has the impression that he *is* raising it (though having this impression might seem unlikely in the absence of the usual kinesthetic sensations)? If we do assume this, it is admittedly hard to explain on the basis of merely dispositional expectation that he will raise his arm. Volition might explain it, on the assumption that the sense of willing calls to mind here the sense of doing. But it may perfectly well be that if one forms the intention

---

but a volition, an event of the kind crucial to understanding action, we can say that the agent's doing an A was itself an action"; he adds that "it does not matter what the object of the volition is" (p. 21); thus, if my volition to move my arm moves my leg, I still act: I move my leg, though unintentionally.

[36] I argue that intending typically implies expectation in Chapter 2.

to raise one's hand now, and if one is normal except for the condition of one's arm, then one *occurrently* expects to raise it, for example one assentingly thinks of one's raising it. More important, brain or other neural events might occur which give one the sense of raising, or at least of beginning to raise or of being about to raise, one's arm. In either of these cases, discovering that one has not raised the arm would be surprising. These events certainly may not be assumed to be volitional; indeed, whatever can cause a volition can presumably also cause other such events: the latter events may not, then, be the effect of volition; rather, these events and the volition may all be common effects of the same causes. Moreover, the imagined brain events need not even be mental or have mental counterparts; they may be just impulses that travel from the motivational system to the behavioral system and produce a sense of acting. To insist that there must be a *volitional* intermediary between the intention and the surprise would simply beg the question.

Let us, however, grant Armstrong and others that there is an inclination to say at least that S tried to raise his arm (compare the inclination to say that Macbeth, in hallucinating a dagger, at least believed he saw one). It makes a great deal of difference how the case is described. For it is widely agreed and surely true that trying consists in doing something, or at least in the occurrence of something behavioral, and we must therefore be clear about just what it is that, in virtue of trying, takes place in S's consciousness. In James's example, it seems that the patient could simply hear the request and form the appropriate intention, in a way that normally would, with no further conscious occurrences, result in his raising the hand. Retrospectively, however, it is natural to think that he was being cooperative yet failed to do what cooperation required. And if he failed, he must have tried. But this is hasty: there is *failure as unsuccessfully trying*, and there is *failure as mere non-performance*, as where one does not appear at the dentist's office because the appointment wholly slipped one's mind. Similarly, in Armstrong's case of S's pursuing some unknown objective, the fact that S either accomplishes it or not does not entail that S is trying either successfully or unsuccessfully; for success may be constituted simply by accomplishing the thing in question, failure by simply not doing so. There is apparently both a weak and a strong sense of 'succeeding in A-ing': in the former, succeeding is just A-ing; in the latter, it is roughly A-ing on the basis of, or as the culmination of, trying to A. Failure has a parallel duality. In both cases equivoca-

tion is easy, particularly since it is often hard to tell in which sense
of 'succeed' an agent who A's is succeeding in A-ing.

Granted that, in James's example, the moment the man realizes his
plight, virtually anything he does which he thinks might get the arm
up, including tensing muscles that are actually irrelevant, *can* count
as trying to raise his arm. He can even "command" the arm to rise.
But, from the fact that virtually anything can count as trying to A
once S does it in hopes of A-ing, it simply does not follow that something or other that *does* happen in the patient's mind or body the first
time counts as trying, even if it normally is part of what causes the
arm to rise. To constitute trying, behavior must at least be conceived
by S in an appropriate way to be, as it were, aimed at producing the
desired result (this does not require linguistic conceptualization, but
is more than a mere tendency to *form* instrumental beliefs about the
behavior, for example when asked why one was so acting). This point
applies to an intriguing argument by Michael Gorr:

> Suppose that I attempt to raise my arm and fail . . . because someone
> else (much stronger than myself) is forcibly pinning my arm to the
> table. . . . I am able to tense and contract the muscles in my arm in
> the manner which, under normal circumstances, *would* result in my
> arm's moving . . . But, *ex hypothesi*, such truncation is due entirely to
> forces external to the agent, which in turn entails that he does exactly the
> same things, up to the point of truncation, both where he is successful in
> getting his body to move in the way intended and also where he is
> not.[37]

This passage is directed toward showing that all action involves trying
(conceived as moving muscles), not that all action involves volition;
but a parallel argument (based on paralyzing all the muscles) can be
used to show the pervasiveness of volitions. The argument's crucial
assumption is that S *does* the same things when successful as when
the action is "truncated." But when one effortlessly raises one's hand,
does one also perform an *action* of tensing the relevant muscles? I
doubt it. Certainly that is not entailed by the fact that one performs
such an action *when* exerting oneself against resistance; for there, one
both focuses on the muscles *and* hopes (or intends), by tensing them,
to move the arm. Neither this focus on a resistance nor the hope
made appropriate by that resistance are general features of action.

[37] Michael Gorr, "Willing, Trying, and Doing," *Australasian Journal of Philosophy* 57
(1979): 265.

The counterpart argument regarding volitions, as applied to James's case, is this: (1) *S* surely tries to raise the anesthetized arm (which seems plausible if one imagines his exerting himself as best he can after discovering the resistance, like the agent with an arm pinned down); (2) his trying is a volitional event; hence, (3) the same trying occurs where the hand is raised normally. One is reminded of the standard argument from perceptual hallucination, and this one is similarly flawed. Granting that Macbeth perceptually believes there is a dagger before him—or at least believes this on the basis of visual experience—to conclude that the explanation must be that he sees *something*, for example a dagger-appearance, is to beg the question in favor of a sense-datum theory over alternative explanations, such as that he only seems to see a dagger initially (as James's agent might only seem to raise his arm) and then postulates the existence of a dagger-appearance to explain why his physically empty visual field apparently contains a dagger (as James postulates a volition or trying in order to explain why the patient subjectively seems to have raised his stock-still arm).[38]

Another way of arguing for the ubiquity of volitional trying in human action is from contexts of moral responsibility. O'Shaughnessy presents a case in which, just as an actor is about to raise his arm on hearing his cue, antisocial scientists block the required nerve impulse, so that the arm remains still. "Suppose that by some quirk of fate scores of deaths resulted from his inaction and that he faces criminal charges. What can he say in his defense? Merely 'My arm did not move at t'? . . . *Must he not also say 'I tried?'* "[39] Surely the two correct points here, which make O'Shaughnessy's conclusion plausible, are, first, the actor could not have done better, or perhaps that he did all that could be expected; and second, that if he discovered that his arm did not move (as O'Shaughnessy apparently assumes he did), then he *should* have tried to move it. Usually, these points indicate that trying has occurred; but, like failing, which the actor also "does," they surely do not entail trying. Suppose, for instance, that the actor had been given an injection which put him to sleep and has thus failed to raise the arm. He would have an excuse without having tried to raise his arm.

---

[38] For an alternative treatment of paralysis cases which grants volitionalism considerably less than I do, see Richard Taylor, *Action and Purpose* (Englewood Cliffs, N.J.: Prentice-Hall, 1966), esp. pp. 79–85.

[39] O'Shaughnessy, *The Will*, p. 265.

There is more to say about paralysis and illusion in action, but perhaps I have shown enough to indicate why James's case and related ones are quite inconclusive. They are certainly plausible, however, and a fully developed theory of action should have a detailed account of them. It is a merit of volitionalism that its account of such examples is simple and prima facie compelling. The account is, however, far from conclusive.

The Execution of Intentions

The next major domain we must consider is that of the execution of intentions and, more generally, the behavioral realization of motivational states, for example where S chooses the pastrami over the roast beef. Let us grant that intentions do not execute themselves and that a theory of action should say something about how they are carried out. Surely the sorts of things cited above in explaining how actions can have non-volitional event causes can also explain the execution of intentions. If, plausibly enough, we think of intentions and other action-explaining motivational states, such as aims, purposes, and desires, as partly constituted by a tendency to do things believed necessary for realization of their objects,[40] it is to be expected that certain perceptions, thoughts, decisions, and changes in the balance of (aroused) motivational forces should be capable of accounting for the execution of intention and the realization of other motivational states. For Ann to intend to shoot the mad dog as soon as its head is still *is*, in part, for her to be such that, on perceiving, or in some other way coming to believe, that its head is still, she tends to shoot that dog. And to want something, say to call Joe, is, in part, to be such that if one has the thought that now is a good time to do so by using the phone before one, one tends to use it.

There are at least three important points here. First, such events as the perceptions and thoughts we have cited have the appropriate content to connect the action with the intention or other motivation that explains and, in a sense, rationalizes that action. Second, such events are among the eliciting conditions in terms of which one would

[40] For accounts of wanting and intending see Chapters 1 and 2. In the former, I argue that wants *are* in part tendencies to perform actions believed to contribute to achieving the thing wanted. In the latter I argue that intending implies wanting. If it does, then intending implies not only a tendency to perform the intended action, but a tendency to perform actions believed to be (say) necessary for doing so.

explicate the nature of the relevant dispositional states, and hence should be expected to figure in clarifying the manifestations of those states. Intentions, for example, are by their very nature manifested in *S*'s avowing and executing them; wants and beliefs are similarly manifested both in verbal behavior and in the intentional actions explainable in terms of them, such as pulling the trigger in order to rid the neighborhood of a pest; and, as illustrated above, these and other dispositions are realized by thoughts and perceptions, for instance the perception of opportunities. Third, there is no reason to think that the sorts of eliciting events in question are insufficiently pervasive to account for the execution of all the intentions whose execution needs explaining. Thought and perception, for instance, are ubiquitous in our lives.

The Timing of Actions

We are now in a good position to discuss the timing of actions. One merit of volitionalism is that it provides a natural way to explain why we execute our intentions when we do: if volitions cause such executions, it is to be expected that the latter occur when the former do, or at a definite interval afterwards. Notice, however, that since volitions themselves may occur when they do because of precipitating thoughts and perceptions of the kinds noted, volitionally explaining why we execute our intentions when we do is *compatible* with explaining it in the alternative way I have indicated. Actions *and* volitions might occur when they do because of perceptions, thoughts, and other events that trigger action. (Actions might also be overdetermined by both sorts of factors.)

These points about timing, however, suggest a problem for volitionalism: surely we often need to know why one wills to *A* when one does will this, as much as we need to know why one *A*'s when one does. Consider a man deliberately reaching out for a sweet, shortly after making a new year's resolution to abstain from sweets. Arresting his arm, his wife might remind him of the resolution, and he might say that the sweets looked so good he couldn't help wanting one, where this is a use of 'wanting' that in the context (where the want leads to an action) implies volition—or should, if volition plays the essential role in action it is supposed to play. Just as we may wish to know what made the time of action appropriate in *S*'s eyes, we may wish to know what, at that time, made willing it appropriate for

S. Granted, the occurrence, at time *t*, of a volition to *A*, for example to take a sweet, can explain why it was at *t* that *S A*-ed. But the explanation is not very deep; and if we wonder at all why *S A*-ed at *t*, we may also wonder why it was at *t* that *S* willed to do so. It is not clear, then, that volitions give us much understanding of the timing of action; and certainly we do not *need* to postulate them to understand it. Indeed, here it is the man's standing fondness for sweets, together with his espying an attractive dish of them, that seems to explain the timing of *both* his volition and his reaching toward the dish.

Volition and Trying

If we need not postulate volitions to account for the timing of actions, do we perhaps need them to understand trying? Given what has been said, we should perhaps wonder whether trying is not more helpful in clarifying volition than vice versa. Still, could we explicate trying without countenancing volition? This is a large question, and all I shall say here is that what counts as trying is at least largely a matter of what the agent does with something like a hope (even if ill-founded) of achieving some goal. Now if there are mental acts of willing, as there do seem to be, at least in cases of self-command aimed at moving oneself to do something difficult, then there is at least one kind of trying that we cannot account for without understanding volition, namely the kind consisting of willing, or commanding, or otherwise directing oneself toward, an action in order to get it accomplished. But it does not follow that the *concept* of volition must enter into any correct account of trying, and the deeper point here is that we must apparently conceive trying in terms of *action* performed under certain conditions; and if so, then except perhaps in the special case where volition *is* the action that constitutes trying, we may explicate trying without appeal to volition. This is not to claim that there is no plausible way to explicate trying in terms of volition; but there is no good reason to think it must be either explicated in that way or identified with volition.

Non-Observational Knowledge of One's Own Actions

If we now consider our pervasive non-observational knowledge of what we are doing, or at least of what we are trying to do, we can again see both why volitionalism is appealing and how the data can nonetheless be explained along other lines. Doubtless, if human action either *is* willing or is always grounded in volition or trying or, for that matter, immediate intending or occurrent wanting, it is to be expected that agents can non-observationally know what, under a volitional description, they are doing. For if, as all volitional theorists seem to hold, volitions are mental events, we should expect that, at least upon considering what I am doing, I can introspectively come to know that those events—presumably but perhaps not necessarily under a volitional description—are occurring in me, if they are. Volitions have this accessibility to introspection, however, because they are mental events, not specifically because they are volitions: the same applies, for example, to perceptual states, imagings, and free associations. Thus, if there are mental acts, whether they are volitions, tryings, or other intentional doings, any plausible theory of the mental can at least equally well account for such non-observational knowledge as we have of those events. The extent of that knowledge and whether some of it, though not observational, is *inferential* are important questions I cannot here pursue. My point is simply that on this score volitionalism seems to have no significant advantage over other plausible theories.

There is, however, one point that should help in indicating how the relevant kind of self-knowledge can be accounted for without positing volitions as essential to its grounds. There is good reason to believe that when one *intends* to A, one (to some degree) expects to do so; and more specifically, where an occasion arises in which one is, even if automatically, about to A, say to move one's hand to a directional signal before making a right turn, then one expects, or is disposed to expect, to A *then* and to experience whatever one strongly associates with doing so, say the movements of one's arm and the clicking of the signal. When these occur normally, one has a non-inferential acquaintance with them; and if they should be prevented, one is naturally surprised. Surprise is an almost inevitable response to a suddenly disappointed expectation; it is a natural response even when the agent is only disposed, in the way illustrated here, to expect to act.

The Structural Analogy between Action and Knowledge

In the light of the points that have now emerged, let us consider how well non-volitional theories can do justice to the analogy between the structure of action and that of knowledge. Assuming for the sake of argument that some sort of foundationalism holds in both domains, there is clearly something appealing about the volitionalist's internal, and in some ways rather Cartesian, grounding of our actions. But *must* our basic actions be mental at all (even if not irreducibly so), any more than our basic empirical knowledge must be mental—of our own psychological states, rather than of anything physical or external? I can see no cogent argument for this. There is, however, an interesting phenomenon in both domains, at least if a moderate foundationalism coupled with (a qualified) direct realism is correct. For on that view, while I may non-inferentially know, say through perception, facts about my external surroundings, still, should my perceptual beliefs be challenged, I may retreat inward to defend them. If I become convinced that I may be hallucinating a tree, I can form the beliefs that it seems to me that there is a tree before me and that, say, the best explanation of its seeming so is that there is a tree before me producing the arboreal appearance in me. What was a foundational belief is such no longer; it is now shored up from below by a new foundation. But this is permitted by moderate as opposed to Cartesian foundationalism, since the former view relativizes foundational status to time and circumstance—at any given time there must be some unmoved movers, but, for moderate foundationalism, unlike the better-known Cartesian kind, there need be no unmovable movers.[41]

Similar points hold in the domain of action. Ordinarily, my moving my hand seems basic; I do not do it by doing anything else. But if I encounter resistance, I can perform a supportive (and in *that* sense more fundamental) act of tensing muscles; and by doing this I may move the arm non-basically, just as I may come to know inferentially, and so non-basically, that there is a tree before me. I may, in any case, at least do something which is behaviorally more basic, possibly but not necessarily in the same way that phenomenal beliefs about appearances are epistemically more basic than physical object beliefs. It has not generally been noticed that there are at least two ways in which things may be basic: first, an element, such as a belief, may be basic in a *relative sense*, provided that there are actual or possible items in the same category which are candidate foundations for it, but it

---

[41] For a detailed discussion of moderate foundationalism and the extent to which it can accommodate points associated with coherentism, see my *Belief, Justification, and Knowledge* (Belmont, Calif.: Wadsworth, 1988), and Paul K. Moser, *Knowledge and Evidence* (Cambridge: Cambridge University Press, 1989).

does not rest on such a foundation, for example does not rest on a belief of a proposition that can justify it; second, an element may be basic in the *absolute sense* that it *could* not rest on such a foundation because there *are* no potential foundations in the category. Bodily actions seem capable of being basic in the relative sense, just as perceptual beliefs about physical objects apparently can be. But just as bodily actions are not basic in the absolute sense, neither are perceptual beliefs. Each may be grounded, in a similar way, in elements of the same kind: volitional action in the one case, phenomenal belief in the other. *Those* elements, however, have seemed to some to be basic in the absolute sense: roughly, to be such that there are no elements—of their kind—on which they can be based. Volitional action is intrinsically basic; phenomenal belief is intrinsically non-inferential.

A phenomenal belief can, to be sure, be at once foundational and based on an appearance, but that is not a belief; and volition can be at once foundational and based on a motivational state, but that is not an action. However, an "automatic" action apparently not arising from volition can also be based on a motivational state, for example a desire. Action can apparently bypass the intermediate foundation that volition provides. The analogy between action and knowledge, then, can be preserved without positing volitions as pervasive elements in action. On a plausible non-volitional view, volitions, or comparable mental acts, must simply be available in special cases, as phenomenal beliefs are available when physical object beliefs need support from below. Both support roles are important. We can acknowledge this, however, without postulating the (supposed) absolutely basic elements as foundations for every action or belief. A foundation may be genuine even when one can dig below it to yet firmer ground.

Volitionalism in the Analysis of the Concept of Action

In closing this section, I want to return to the question whether volitionalism might be our best hope in the analysis of the concept of action. I doubt this, since there is insufficient reason to posit volitions even in the generation of all action. Perhaps they can be shown to be pervasive enough to be candidates for the main element in an analysis of action; but I do not see cogent reason to think this, nor even to think that a volition is always at least part of what is left when we subtract an arm's rising from the agent's raising it. There are simply too many plausible alternative explanations of the data that motivate volitional theories. Perhaps, of course, I have neglected some important data. Certainly a powerful theory like volitionalism cannot be refuted by a study of this scope, if it can be refuted at all. But we have at least seen how one might begin to solve, in a less Cartesian way and with more modest postulations of mental events, the crucial problems motivating the position. We have also seen that a volitional analysis of action, like any causal analysis, must come to grips with the problem of wayward causal chains and the related problem of the sense in which agents must control their actions. We cannot simply suppose that *any* movement caused by a volition—not even any mental movement—is action, or even voluntary behavior; and even if volitional causation of an action momentarily grounds it in the will, the action can, because of interferences, immediately afterward cease to be under the control of the will in the way required for voluntary action. If a volitional analysis of action is to succeed, then, it must face some of the knotty problems plaguing other sorts of accounts; exemption from these problems cannot be considered one of its merits.

IV. Actions as Responses to Reasons

In this section, I want to outline a more positive view. Nothing said above implies that there are no volitions in any sense or even that volitions do not play a major role in action. Indeed, surely there are times when it is difficult to avoid positing acts of will of one or another kind. Consider Jan, focusing all her will power on remaining silent under torture: 'Don't talk!' might be her repeated injunction to herself, backed by all her resolve and accompanied by a determined attention to clenching her muscles. And there are times when, in building determination to do something difficult, one may reach a point at which one thinks something like '*now!*' and plows forward as if energized by the command. My thesis is not that action theory does not need volitions in some roles, but that neither a volitional theory of the nature of action nor a volitional analysis of the concept of action is adequately supported by the data.

Is any alternative theory more plausible? Let me suggest a conception of action which, supported by a number of the points made in Section III, seems preferable. In general terms, we might think of volitional theories as typically based largely on an *executive thrust model:* actions result when one, as it were, directedly moves oneself so that one's intentions or other motivational states are activated or energized by a volitional thrust. This model applies, I think, whether volitions are conceived as acts of will, tryings, here-and-now intendings, or in other ways, and whether actions *are* volitions under various descriptions or simply grounded *in* volitions. There are different kinds of thrusts, with different kinds of content; and different versions of the model allow differences in the complexity and temporal extent of the behavior traceable to a single volition. By contrast, we might adopt a *guidance and control model:* actions result when energy already present in the motivational structure is released in the appropriate direction by a suitable eliciting event, such as a thought or decision, or a perception of an opportunity to get what one wants, and guided in that direction by (above all) the agent's beliefs.

The chief difference between the models concerns the psychological origins of action; the models may tend to converge regarding ongoing actions, for example concerning how these actions are explainable by appeal to motivational factors and guided by beliefs. Still, there is a contrast of overall conception. The first model would have us understand action largely by looking inward for a thrust from below, from the foundations, one might say; and the Real Agent seems above all an inner executive. The second model would have us look, depending on the case, either inward or outward for the kind of event which, in the agent's situation, releases the energy: if I am sitting alone in silence with my eyes closed, we would expect the event to be internal; if I am playing tennis, we would expect it to be external, normally something I perceive.[42] In both cases, the cue is internally *registered,* but its origin may be external. The agent may exercise power in the interior arena; but this is not expected where the circumstances of action demand only that one engage the external world as its stimuli are sorted out, often automatically, when perception supplies them to the framework constituted by one's beliefs and motivational dispositions.

---

[42] I have developed the guidance and control model in some detail in Chapter 6. For a different account that does not require volition, see Alfred R. Mele, *Irrationality: An Essay on Akrasia, Self-Deception, and Self-Control* (New York: Oxford University Press, 1987), esp. chaps. 3–7.

On one version of the thrust model, the execution of intentions is somewhat like the firing of a rifle by pulling the trigger; the volition, the triggering, communicates energy which is then channeled in a definite behavioral direction according to the content of the volition, which in turn is expressed in the direction of the barrel. On the guidance and control model, the motivation underlying an action is more like a compressed spring; the energy of the spring is a function of the strength and number of relevant conative elements, such as intentions and desires, and its direction depends on the agent's belief(s) about how the relevant goal(s) may be achieved. Very little may be required to release the spring; or, if it is opposed by another one approximately as strong, will power may be needed, and may be exercised in an interior act. To be sure, a volitional model can treat volition more as a releaser of energy than a contributor of it; but this is not as common a conception. As an act of will or a trying, for example, volition is conceived as carrying considerable energy. In any case, because volition has intentional content, it is a more complex releaser than is required to understand the execution of intentions, given that the relevant intentions and other attitudes already have content sufficient to direct the action—in the context of the same perceptual guidance also required by any plausible volitional account.

One advantage of the guidance and control view is that it seems to do better justice to the *automaticity* of much of our action. To be sure, a single volition may control a whole sequence of related actions; but there are profound difficulties in determining just how much behavior can be controlled by a single volition. One difficulty is burgeoning of content in order to cover complex sequences; another is temporal preservation of the initial thrust, given how much time may be required for performance. Moreover, there are not only spontaneous and automatic actions that do not seem rooted in volition at all but also times when activity *changes* substantially without there being any reason to think a volitional event occurred. Consider, for example, someone who suddenly begins to talk about a different subject, and to a different person, at a party; this can happen almost instantaneously.

It is of course arguable that there is a single party-conversation mode of action which is under the control of a single volition; the behavior may be quite effectively "scripted."[43] But suppose that, by routinely accepting an invitation, one simply forms the intention to attend a party, and then, as one proceeds through the familiar experience of the party, one has the whole behavioral sequence of one's conversations guided by elements in one's standing motivation and by one's standing beliefs, in the light of one's perceptions and thoughts. Need one at any point have experienced something plausibly conceived as willing, for instance willing to attend the party? And if one does experience (or otherwise instantiate) a volition, what is its content? One wonders if it would not have to be very complex to achieve the required control of such complex behavior. By contrast, since intentions, wants, and beliefs are dispositional, they may be unmanifested at least most of the time during which they exist. They need not clutter consciousness; and since they are activated by perceptual and thought events that, on any plausible theory, are pervasive in human life, it is easier to understand how we can do so much so automatically, if we take the view that action is (for the most part) motivated, belief-guided behavior elicited by perceptions, thoughts, decisions, and changes in the patterns of motivational forces.

In addition to giving a better account than volitionalism of the automaticity of much of our action, the guidance and control model is also more economical. It explicates action in terms of concepts employed on all sides; and it does so by much more modest postulations of conscious events than those characteristic of volitional theories. The latter point is not to be underestimated. Mental events take up conscious space; only a limited number can occupy consciousness at a given time. Consciousness may be a stream, but it is not a river. This is especially so when the content of consciousness at a given time is actively produced by us, as in framing resolutions, and not passively received in the way external stimuli may be. It may be that,

---

[43] I take this term from Roger C. Schank and Robert P. Abelson, *Scripts, Plans, Goals, and Understanding* (Hillsdale, N.J.: Lawrence Earlbaum, 1977). It is an interesting empirical question how much behavior is controllable by a single volition, intention, or other psychological element—how full a script can be enacted by a single trigger. My view is neutral on this, as a plausible volitional view may be also—unless it puts too much detail into the content of volition, so that the limits of the scope of volition cannot go beyond those of the agent's ability to entertain the relevant details. When Ryle derisively asked how many volitions were required to recite "Little Miss Muffet" backwards, he was ignoring the point that *learning* may presumably put a rather long script under the control of a single volition.

normally, we can have more immediately before the mind when, like a sonata played for us, it is put there without our making any effort.

There is, moreover, surely some basis for the point, made by critics of volitionalism, that phenomenally we are not aware of what we should be aware of if mental events of volition, under any plausible description, are as pervasive in action as the theory seems to say. Granted that if I *focus* on what I am doing in say typing, I *become* aware of various feelings and can achieve a focal sense of agency, it does not follow that this awareness of agency was already there, subliminally or unnoticed—if such concepts even apply to awareness. Conscious attention may create, as well as discover, objects, and it may alter those it might seem merely to observe. Moreover, in producing or reproducing behavior in order to examine it phenomenologically for volitional content, we observe it artificially and may endow it with properties not necessary for its natural occurrence; volitional factors present in these cases should not be assumed to be elements in their natural unselfconscious counterparts. On the other hand, at a given time one can have indefinitely many intentional dispositions, and even a huge number of beliefs and intentions can causally affect one's behavior simultaneously. Their causal work can be done without their intentional objects being present in consciousness, and indeed without their manifesting themselves in consciousness at all. Thus, one's actions can be controlled by motivation and perception even when one's consciousness is almost wholly occupied with something else.

There is one powerful attraction of volitionalism that may set it apart from any other kind of account of action. It seems to root action directly in the will: we are agents acting on the world, or at least trying to; we do not merely *re*act to it. This picture is attractive. But if volition is not anchored in motivation and belief, then it is insufficiently connected with our character—our ideals, projects, convictions, and other attitudes. If it is so anchored, it can deservedly seem just as reactive as action conceived on the guidance and control model. Is there, then, anything creative about agency?

This is a large issue, and it leads to some of the questions about freedom I address in Chapters 7 and 10. I shall make just one point here: our beliefs and desires are not mere reactions to raw experience; they are mightily influenced by our thoughts. Thoughts can of course be affected, in turn, by our wants and beliefs; but although thinking is something we do, thoughts themselves are not in general actions. They play a double role: they can at once reflect truth, playing a passive role like that of belief, and communicate that truth to beliefs and judgments, playing an active role like that of speech. A thought that seems true may pass into a belief of the proposition felt to be credible. A thought may also yield a judgment bearing on action: the thought of how a gift would be received by a loved one can produce the judgment that it would be good to give it and, thereby, the desire to give it. Thoughts and judgments, then, can each produce beliefs, desires, and intentions. They can apparently also generate volition. Our creativity as agents is in part our creativity as thinkers. In its cognitive, productive, and monitoring role, thought guides our behavior. Even without appeal to volition, the guidance and control model can do justice to this pervasive and creative role of thought.

In the course of comparing volitional accounts of important problems in action theory with alternative accounts, we have seen that volitionalism can be adjusted to deal with various objections. As the adjustments are made, however, such volitional accounts come closer to what I call the guidance and control model of action. Perhaps a modified volitional theory will in the end emerge as our best route to understanding action. I have not tried to show that this cannot be so. But if volitionalism is taken to imply that all our actions are grounded in mental events which constitute willing, or trying, or anything similarly behavioral, then the view seems too strong, and the problems that motivate it can be better solved along more economical lines. Perhaps anything we do we might in principle have willed to do, just as, for any perceptual belief we have, we might in principle have had phenomenal beliefs on which it was based; and doubtless some things we do are produced by our willing them. But the availability of such internal foundations in the cognitive and behavioral orders does not entail that they are the only foundations sufficient to generate a structure of justified belief or successful action. Much of our action, like much of our perceptual belief, seems basic. Such action, above all moving our bodies, is not performed by, and in that sense is not based on, our performing some other action. Much of our action seems to be a spontaneous expression of our intentions, guided by our standing beliefs and habits, and unselfconsciously elicited by our thoughts and perceptions.

PART II

THE EXPLANATION
OF ACTION

Chapter 4

Intentionalistic
Explanations of Action

Many philosophers have maintained, using an argument which deserves close scrutiny, that what I shall call intentionalistic explanations of action cannot be "causal." By 'an intentionalistic explanation of action' I mean 'an explanation of action in terms of (by appeal to) one or more intentional dispositions of the agent'; for example, Ann donated money to Tom's campaign because she wanted to end the war and believed that donating money to his campaign would help to accomplish this. I cannot possibly undertake here to define the concept of an intentional disposition; but it should be of some help to say that wanting and believing are paradigms of such dispositions, and that the issue I am concerned with can be formulated without reference to any other intentional dispositions. Specifically, the issue is whether explanations of actions by appeal to the wants and beliefs of the agent can be nomological, that is, can be construed as implicitly subsuming the action explained under a lawlike generalization, either universal or non-universal. I shall make no attempt to define the problematic notion of a lawlike generalization; but the examples I discuss will be clear cases of such generalizations and will certainly satisfy two of the conditions usually agreed to be at least necessary for a proposition's being lawlike: namely, that it support counterfactuals and that it have at least some explanatory power.

I. The Logical Relation Thesis

Despite appearances, I believe my formulation of the question is not too narrow to capture the most important issues surrounding the view that intentionalistic explanations cannot be causal. First, such philosophers as R. S. Peters, A. I. Melden, and Charles Taylor, even if they are neither entirely clear nor entirely agreed among themselves on what constitutes a causal explanation, surely have suggested that the paradigm cases of scientific explanations of events are causal.[1] More important, even if they were to maintain that scientific explanations of events are not causal in their sense, this would be of limited help in defending their view that intentionalistic explanations of action cannot be causal; for the fundamental importance of their arguments for this view seems to be that these arguments appear to show the impossibility of explaining human actions scientifically.[2] Thirdly, although my formulation of the issue may appear too narrow because it seems to ignore a huge number of important cases, for example, those in which we explain actions as performed in *order* to achieve some end, I would suggest, without arguing the point here, that virtually all in-order-to explanations of action, as well as virtually all intentionalistic explanations which seem not to appeal to the agent's wants and beliefs, can be transformed into roughly equivalent explanations which do appeal to wants and beliefs. For example, 'Ann's purpose in sending money to Tom was to help end the war' is roughly equivalent to 'Ann sent money to Tom because she wanted to end the war and believed that giving money to him would help to accomplish this'.

We might call the thesis of Peters, Melden, Charles Taylor, and others 'the logical relation thesis regarding the connection between intentional entities and the actions they explain', or, for short, 'the

---

[1] R. S. Peters, *The Concept of Motivation* (London: Routledge and Kegan Paul; New York: Humanities Press, 1958); A. I. Melden, *Free Action* (London: Routledge and Kegan Paul, 1961); and Charles Taylor, *The Explanation of Behaviour* (London: Routledge and Kegan Paul; New York: Humanities Press, 1964).

[2] Except where they might be explained non-intentionalistically, which, for reasons which I shall be unable to mention, they also think impossible.

logical relation thesis'; for all these writers agree that this connection is some kind of logical one incompatible with any causal or lawlike one. A number of philosophers[3] have advanced cogent arguments against this thesis; but I shall be discussing a statement of the thesis different from and more recent than the statement of it which they have attacked, and I hope to add some important points. Specifically, I hope to show why a particular kind of argument which philosophers have often used, and which seems very widely accepted, is unsound.

As Charles Taylor states the thesis, intentionalistic explanations differ from "causal" ones in that the latter, but not the former, appeal to causal laws. With the former

> we are not explaining the behaviour by the 'law,' other things being equal, intending X is followed by doing X, for this is part of what we mean by 'intending X', that, in the absence of interfering factors, it is followed by doing X. I could not be said to intend X if, even with no obstacles or other countervailing factors, I still didn't do it. Thus, my intention is not a causal antecedent of my behaviour.[4]

Malcolm has drawn a quite similar conclusion from a very similar premise:

> A typical form of purposive principle would be the following: if a person desires G and believes that behavior B is required for G, he will do B unless there are interfering factors. This connection between desire and behavior is part of what we mean by "desiring" or "wanting" G. By virtue of this connection of meaning, purposive principles are *a priori*.[5]

Regarding Taylor's position, as Malcolm points out, we can more plausibly represent Taylor if, when he speaks of explaining an action in terms of the intention *to* perform it, we take him to mean explaining an action in terms of the intention *with* which it was performed.

---

[3] Perhaps most notably, William P. Alston, "Wants, Actions, and Causal Explanation," in Hector-Neri Castañeda, ed., *Intentionality, Minds, and Perception* (Detroit: Wayne State University Press, 1966); Donald Davidson, "Actions, Reasons, and Causes," *Journal of Philosophy* 60 (1963); and Alvin I. Goldman, *A Theory of Human Action* (Englewood Cliffs, N.J.: Prentice-Hall, 1970).

[4] Taylor, *The Explanation of Behaviour*, p. 33.

[5] Norman Malcolm, "Explaining Behavior," *Philosophical Review* 76 (1967), 102.

Thus, we can probably conclude that he is for the most part implicitly talking about what Malcolm is explicitly talking about, namely, explaining actions in terms of wants (which I shall regard as including desires) and beliefs. And Taylor does say, for example in comparing desiring with having an intention, that "desiring something is also noncontingently linked with doing it."[6] Thus if we explain someone's *A*-ing by saying that she had a desire for *G*, or that she wanted *G*, or that she *A*-ed with the intention of getting *G*, Taylor would deny that we are subsuming the action under any "law."

II. The Logical Connection Argument

It seems, then, that Taylor and Malcolm are arguing for the logical relation thesis as follows:

1. A purposive principle (or at least the kind we are concerned with) is true by virtue of a connection of meaning, specifically, because part of what we mean by saying that its antecedent is satisfied is that, in the absence of interfering factors, its consequent will also be satisfied. Hence
2. Purposive principles are true a priori.
3. A proposition cannot be both a priori and contingent. Hence, by 2 and 3,
4. Purposive principles are non-contingent. Therefore
5. Purposive principles cannot be ("causal") laws.

The first thing we should try to get clear about is the meaning of 'a priori'. Taylor's and Malcolm's use of the phrase, 'part of what we mean', and Malcolm's speaking of our purposive principles as true by virtue of a "connection of meaning," suggest that what they here mean by 'a priori' is 'analytic', where an analytic proposition in this sense is one true by virtue of the meanings of the terms in which it is expressed. Now I believe that the purposive principle which Malcolm cites is extremely important, since something at least quite similar seems to be tacitly invoked by a great many explanations of action by appeal to wants and beliefs. But leaving aside for a moment the difficulties surrounding the notion of analyticity, I think this purpos-

---

[6] Taylor, *The Explanation of Behaviour,* p. 49.

ive principle is not obviously analytic in the above sense and not analytic at all in the stricter sense in which analytic prepositions are, in addition to being true by virtue of meanings, reducible to logical truths by putting synonyms for synonyms. But I do not wish to argue at any length that Malcolm's purposive principle is not analytic in the strict sense. I prefer to concentrate on the sort of connection of meaning on the basis of which Taylor, Malcolm, and others claim purposive principles to be a priori; I want to see whether, if there is such a connection—and I shall assume that there is *some* meaning connection—this justifies the conclusion that purposive principles have any logical status incompatible with their being nomological (lawlike).

The notion which I think we should attend to first is that expressed by 'part of what we mean by "x" is "y"', where 'x' and 'y' are expressions in a natural language. Perhaps this could most plausibly be claimed to mean that if asked what we mean by 'x', one of the things which we would, or at least should, say is 'y'; for example, part of what we mean by 'bachelor' is 'unmarried man'. The idea here is that the meaning of, and hence what we mean by, 'bachelor', is something like 'adult unmarried man who has never been married', and 'unmarried man' is part of this. Now given this interpretation of 'part of what we mean by "x" is "y",' it is not obvious that part of what we mean by 'S wants G and believes A-ing necessary to getting G' is that in the absence of interfering factors S will A. Certainly ordinary people, if asked to explain what we mean by saying things of the form, 'S wants G and believes A-ing necessary to getting it', would probably be very puzzled—in a way in which they would probably not be puzzled if asked what we mean by 'bachelor'. Possibly, on reflection, or helped along by the questioner, they could produce something containing at least a rough approximation of S will A in the absence of interfering factors'. But this is not at all obvious. It is well known that the ability to use terms correctly and comprehendingly does not imply an ability to define them or explain their meaning; and in this case there is the added difficulty that a great deal seems to be packed into the rather technical notion of an interfering factor.

To be sure, from the fact that people cannot articulate what they mean by 'x' without such aids as leading questions, it does not follow that 'y' is not part of what they mean by 'x'; but what does seem to follow is that 'If x then y' cannot be regarded as analytic in the rather clear-cut way in which 'If S is a bachelor, then S is an unmarried man' perhaps can be, nor does there appear to be any other clear-cut way in which conditionals that are at all like our purposive principles can be analytic. By substituting, for 'bachelor', 'adult unmarried man', which is (let us assume) what we mean by 'bachelor', we can reduce 'All bachelors are unmarried' to the logical truth that all unmarried men are unmarried; but what do we mean by expressions of the form, '*S* wants *G* and believes *A*-ing necessary to getting *G'*, such that by making a similar substitution in Malcolm's purposive principle we can produce a logical truth? It seems quite unlikely that such a substitution is possible. If I am correct in these points, then first, proponents of the logical relation thesis cannot simply claim, as they do, that part of what we mean by *S* wants *G* and believes *A*-ing necessary to getting *G'* is that in the absence of interfering factors *S* will *A*; they must argue for this. Second, and more important, since Malcolm's purposive principle certainly does not appear analytic in the strict sense, Taylor and Malcolm must argue for their thesis that this proposition's being a priori in their sense—true by virtue of meaning—entails that it could not be nomological.

But Taylor and Malcolm have not argued for this latter thesis; they appear simply to assume that it is true. I believe that it is false. I want to grant that Malcolm's purposive principle may plausibly be held to express part of what we mean by '*S* wants *G* and believes *A*-ing necessary to *G'* and is in *this* sense true by virtue of meaning. But I shall argue that it could still be nomological. This becomes apparent if we consider certain nomological propositions which can also be reasonably regarded as each expressing part of what we mean by the concept(s) figuring in its antecedent. Consider first the predicate 'is magnetic' construed as a term of electromagnetic theory. Suppose the question is raised of what it means to say that some object is magnetic. Surely it might be plausibly replied that part of what is meant (part of what we mean in the context of electromagnetic theory) is that (if nothing interferes) the object will exert a force on iron brought into contact with it. It might also be said that (provided nothing interferes) if the object is passed throught a closed wire loop, it will induce a current in the wire; and there are other generalizations which could plausibly be said to express part of what is meant by 'magnetic'. Note that in these cases, ignorance of the generalities would give us very good reason for saying that, from the point of view of electromagnetic theory, one does not understand, or at least does not fully understand, the term 'magnetic'. Suppose, for example, that though S says that M is magnetic, when someone asks her why it exerts no force on some iron filings placed against it, she thinks the question irrelevant. It would be another thing for her to say that M is extremely weak, or to point to an interfering factor; but if she failed to see the relevance of the question, this would give us good reason to say, not just that she is ignorant of a well-known fact about magnets, but that she fails to understand (at least part of) what is meant by 'magnetic'.

It seems to be part of the very concept of a magnet that it is the sort of thing which, unless something interferes, exerts a force on iron brought near. If this requirement were dropped, our concept of a magnet would have changed. Yet 'magnetic' is a term of electromagnetic theory with a significant role in physical science, and the generality just mentioned, far from being strictly analytic, is testable when taken together with at least one other proposition that gives us a logically independent and reliable way of identifying an object as magnetic. Why, then, are purposive principles incapable of having the same kind of logical status as the lawlike principle relating being magnetic to exerting a force on iron? Why does it not have as good a claim to being a priori in Taylor's and Malcolm's sense as do our purposive principles?

I believe these points also apply, though to a considerably lesser extent, to the less familiar law that if an object is magnetic, then it induces a current in a closed wire loop through which it is passed. To be sure, for the everyday concept of a magnetic object, the tendency to exert a force on iron may essentially exhaust the concept; but it is crucial to my point here to treat the predicate 'is magnetic' as a term of electromagnetic theory. One might still suppose—and some philosophers may be tempted to suppose—that there is one "operational" test, or at least one distinguishing feature, in terms of which a scientific concept is defined, whereas the lawlike propositions in which the concept figures express merely contingent facts about it. A full discussion of the issues this view raises would require a great deal of space,[7] and here I shall have to be content with simply consid-

---

[7] For detailed discussions of the shortcomings of operationalism, see Carl G. Hempel's *Aspects of Scientific Explanation* (New York: Free Press, 1965), pt. 2; and his *Philosophy of Natural Science* (Englewood Cliffs, N.J.: Prentice-Hall, 1966), chap. 7, in which he argues that concept formation and theory formation go hand in hand. Also valuable on the issues discussed in this and the next two paragraphs are Hilary Putnam, "The Analytic and the Synthetic," in Herbert Feigl and Grover Maxwell, eds., *Minnesota Studies in the Philosophy of Science*, vol. 3 (Minneapolis: University of Minnesota Press,

ering some further examples which may serve better than the above to discredit the view.

Let us consider briefly the term 'electron'. One might offer as a theoretical definition something like 'small particle having a unit negative electric charge equal to $(4.80294 \pm 0.00008) \times 10^{-10}$ absolute electrostatic units; a mass equal to $\frac{1}{1837}$ of that of the hydrogen nucleus, and a diameter of about 10^{-12} cm.[8] But can this be regarded as a synonymous definition—or any other kind of definition that can ground strictly analytic propositions about electrons, for example that their charge is $(4.80294 \pm 0.00008) \times 10^{-10}$ electrostatic units? Surely not. This figure is experimentally determined and, as the mention of allowable error indicates, open to revision. This implies that even though certain propositions express part of what is meant by 'electron', they are revisable in the light of experiment. This removes an important bar to construing them as lawlike. Indeed, there are propositions not entailed by this definition which might also be plausibly held to express part of what we mean by 'electron', in the sense that ignorance of one of them would give us good grounds for holding that one did not fully understand 'electron'. Consider, for example, the Pauli Exclusion Principle, which states that no two electrons can occupy the same quantum state. There are certainly great difficulties in ascertaining the *degree* to which a given lawlike proposition expresses part of the meaning of a concept; but it seems quite clear that some lawlike propositions express some part of what is meant by certain of the concepts figuring in them.

III. The Testability of Purposive Principles

At this point Taylor or Malcolm might reply that even if I have been correct in what I have said about the lawlike propositions I have mentioned, there is still a crucial difference between them and

---

1962); Peter Achinstein, *Concepts of Science* (Baltimore: Johns Hopkins University Press, 1968), esp. chaps. 2 and 3; and Rudolf Carnap, "The Methodological Character of Theoretical Concepts," in Herbert Feigl and Michael Scriven, eds., *Minnesota Studies in the Philosophy of Science*, vol. 1 (Minneapolis: University of Minnesota Press, 1956).

[8] This is essentially what is offered as a definition of 'electron' in the *Handbook of Chemistry and Physics* for 1965–66. It is relevant to my point to note that at least one of the figures represents a revision of a fairly recent entry: the 1958–59 edition reports the charge as $(4.8023 \pm 0.00007) \times 10^{-10}$.

our purposive principles: the former can, and the latter cannot, be disconfirmed and thus revised in the light of experiment; the latter can at most be shown inapplicable to the world,[9] in which case we would have to grant that people do not have, say, wants. Thus, the sentences now expressing our purposive principles might come to express different propositions, but the principles are not disconfirmable: we might adopt a different concept of wanting, but given our present concepts, our purposive principles cannot be revised. This objection assumes an unrealistically sharp distinction between disconfirmation of certain of the propositions in which a concept figures and, on the other hand, revising the concept. But leaving this point aside, I believe the arguments presented in Section II suggest that it is most implausible to hold that the lawlike propositions I have mentioned could be drastically revised or totally rejected without any accompanying change in our concepts of electrons and magnetic objects. Surely this is part of the force of saying that such propositions express "part of what is meant by" 'electron' and 'magnetic'. I am not implying that all revisions of these propositions, however minor, would justify us in speaking of conceptual change; but I reject as false the contrast expressed in the view that all lawlike ("scientific") propositions, but no purposive principles, can be revised without requiring us to acknowledge a change in one or more of the constituent concepts.

The falsity of this contrast between purposive principles and lawlike propositions should also be evident if we consider what a great many scientists will normally say when asked what their concept of a *T* is, where '*T*' is some theoretical term[10] with which they are well acquainted. Do they put forward one or more strictly analytic propositions which tell us what '*T*' "really" means, and leave aside as merely contingent truths the main lawlike propositions in which the concept of *T* figures? Not at all. As I have suggested, it is not even clear what the analyticities might be. As most students of even fairly elementary physical science know, a common reply, to anyone presumed to have some acquaintance with the relevant theory or group

---

[9] This way of putting the point is suggested by Malcolm's statement that "if mechanism is true, the a priori principles of action do not apply to the world"; see his "The Conceivability of Mechanism," *Philosophical Review* 67 (1968), 63.

[10] It is notoriously difficult to say what a theoretical term is. For helpful discussions of the notion of a theoretical term, see Hempel, *Aspects of Scientific Explanation* and *Philosophy of Natural Science;* Carnap, "The Methodological Character"; and Achinstein, *Concepts of Science.*

of theories, would consist at least in part in citing at least some of the main lawlike propositions, though it is not always easy to decide what propositions are the main, as opposed to the subsidiary, ones. We might be told, for example, that magnetic objects are those having (among other things) the properties attributed to them in the propositions mentioned earlier. Similarly, there are other propositions, quite different from Malcolm's purposive principle, which also seem to express part of what we mean by, say, 'want'[11]

If the main lawlike propositions in which a theoretical concept figures are essential to its explication, or at least to its full explication, it follows that if we totally rejected, as opposed to having merely revised, one or more of these, then it would be reasonable to say that we had adopted a new concept, even if it were sufficiently similar to our original concept to warrant our calling it a concept of "the same thing," for example, an electron. If this is so, then it again appears that intentional concepts do not differ from all scientific concepts in the way proponents of the logical relation thesis say they do. Specifically, while it is probably true that our present concept of certain intentional dispositions such as wanting, requires us to hold that when people have these they will in the absence of interfering factors do certain things, it is *false* that our present concepts of theoretical entities can be retained unaltered even if we come to hold that these entities may not produce, even when nothing interferes, the effects attributed to them by the main lawlike propositions in which they figure.

But are my examples of magnetic objects and electrons bad ones? It could be argued that, for example, in order for a magnet (or an electron) to produce the sort of event which its presence can explain, for example, a movement of a piece of iron, an antecedent condition must be fulfilled, such as namely, the coming together of the magnet and the iron, whereas no analogous condition must be fulfilled in order for wanting and believing to produce the action which their presence can explain. It is not at all clear whether this disanalogy would have important implications if it were genuine, since our concern is with the logical status of lawlike and purposive propositions, not with the details of the explanations in which they figure. But the disanalogy is probably not genuine: we must not allow broad phrases

---

[11] For a discussion of some of these, see Chapter 1 and Alston, "Wants, Actions, and Causal Explanation." Here Alston also brings forward powerful considerations against taking purposive principles like Malcolm's as strictly analytic.

like 'in the absence of interfering factors' to cloak the fact that even given, say, a want for G and a belief that A-ing is necessary to getting it, the person will not A until certain antecedent conditions are satisfied, such as the arising and noticing of an opportunity and the acquisition of realization of an ability. Just as a magnet cannot move a piece of iron until they are brought (sufficiently) near one another, so one cannot A until the opportunity arises, and will not do it until one realizes, notices, decides, or the like that the right time, or a good time, has come.

This is not to deny that there are important differences between intentionalistic explanations of action and typical scientific explanations of events. Indeed, I do not hold that the former are causal, though the notion of causal explanation seems to me sufficiently vague to leave unclear just what is being denied when intentionalistic explanations are held to be non-causal. If what is denied is that they can be nomological—and Taylor and Malcolm seem to be denying at least this—then I believe that, even if the denial can be sustained by arguments not now in the literature, the argument examined here is unsuccessful.

The difference between the logical status of purposive principles and that of lawlike propositions, the difference which proponents of the logical relation thesis seem most concerned to establish, appears not to exist, and certainly not to be demonstrated by the arguments of Taylor and Malcolm. Indeed, it may well be that intentionalistic explanations of action are in some important respects similar to certain scientific explanations. It could be argued that in both cases the event to be explained is subsumed, explicitly or implicitly, under a lawlike generality. This is a possibility which I cannot examine now; it is sufficient if I have shown, and to some extent explained, that from the fact that part of what is meant by 'x' is 'y', we cannot validly infer that generalizations of the form 'If anything is an x then, if nothing interferes, it is a y' cannot be lawlike propositions.[12]

---

[12] This chapter was read, in a much earlier version, at the Western Division Meetings of the American Philosophical Association in 1968; and I am grateful to my commentator, S. Marc Cohen, and to Robert Causey and Philip Hugly, for helpful comments.

Chapter 5

Wants and Intentions in
the Explanation of Action

In everyday life we frequently explain our own actions or those of others. In doing this we may say, 'Because I wanted . . .', 'Because I believed . . .', 'In order to . . .', 'He did it with the intention of . . .', 'She did it for the purpose of . . .', or any of an enormous number of things which appeal, directly or indirectly, to what we might call an intentional state of the agent.[1] How are such common-sense explanations to be understood? Philosophers have been vigorously debating this issue for over two decades. An increasing number of psychologists have also examined the logic of these commonsense explanations.[2] Like philosophers, psychologists disagree both about

[1] We may of course appeal to sets of such states, for example to one's wanting to achieve something and one's believing, of the action to be explained, that it will achieve this. The notion of an intentional state is notoriously difficult to explicate, but for our purposes it will suffice to say that intentional states are, roughly, those psychological states whose content is expressible in a clause having propositional content. The clause may be indicative, for example 'that A-ing will achieve the goal'; infinitive, for example 'to A'; or subjunctive, for example 'that she be the winner'. This leaves open whether, as some have held, all psychological states are intentional.

[2] See, for instance, Alan Gauld and John Shotter, *Human Action and Its Psychological Investigation* (Oxford: Basil Blackwell, 1977); Willard F. Day, "Contemporary Behaviorism and the Concept of Intention," in James K. Cole and William J. Arnold, eds., *Nebraska Symposium on Motivation*, vol. 23 (Lincoln: University of Nebraska Press, 1976); C. Daniel Batson, "Linguistic Analyses and Psychological Explanations of the Mental," *Journal for the Theory of Social Behaviour* 2 (1972); Martin Fishbein, "A Theory of Reasoned Action: Some Applications and Implications," *Nebraska Symposium on Motivation*, vol. 27 (Lincoln: University of Nebraska Press, 1979); and D. Rubenstein (a sociologist),

how the explanations are to be construed and about how much understanding of human behavior they can provide. Moreover, in both cases the sharpest division, though by no means the only division, is between causalist accounts of the explanations in question, such as the theories of Davidson and Goldman, and hermeneutic accounts of these explanations, such as those of von Wright and Gauld and Shotter.[3] This essay is written with the conviction that some of the disagreement can be resolved by careful analysis and that an intermediate theory may be superior to both causalist and hermeneutic positions. In Section I, I will introduce what I call an intentionalistic nomological theory of action. In Section II, I will defend a related theory of wanting against some representative hermenuetic criticisms, particularly from the Wittgensteinian side of the hermeneutic tradition, the side that has been most influential in the English-speaking world. In Section III, I will defend a nomological construal of the role of intentions in explaining actions. In Section IV, I will argue that the nomological theory may be useful to psychologists, including those in the hermeneutic tradition.

I. The Nomological Theory of Action

Philosophers and psychologists alike have generally taken commonsense explanations of action to depend on an appeal, often tacit, to at least one belief of the agent *(S)*. It has often been argued that *S*'s wants play a similar and at least equally important role in commonsense explanations of action, but this view is highly controversial. Commonsense explanations of action have also been held to depend on an appeal to at least one of *S*'s intentions. This view is controversial as well, though less so than its counterpart concerning wants. Other explanatory elements have been thought to play a crucial role in commonsense explanations of action; but beliefs, wants, and intentions have dominated the field in recent decades, and they will be my main concern.

"The Concept of Action in Social Sciences," *Journal for the Theory of Social Behaviour* 7 (1977). Many other psychologists and other social scientists could be cited.

[3] Donald Davidson, "Actions, Reasons, and Causes," *Journal of Philosophy* 60 (1963); Alvin I. Goldman, *A Theory of Human Action* (Englewood Cliffs, N.J.: Prentice-Hall, 1970); G. H. von Wright, *Explanation and Understanding* (Ithaca: Cornell University Press, 1971); and Gauld and Shotter, *Human Action and Its Psychological Investigation.*

Most commonsense explanations of action represent the action in question as explainable in terms of one or more reasons *S* had for performing it. Beliefs, wants, intentions, and other psychological elements plausibly held to play a similar role in such explanations are generally agreed to constitute (or at least to express in their propositional content) reasons for acting. There has been much disagreement, however, about how these elements are related to the actions they apparently explain. It has been argued that reasons, most notably wants and beliefs, *cause* the actions they explain;[4] and it has been argued that reasons bear to the actions they explain a *logical* relation of a kind incompatible with reasons' being causes.[5]

The notion of a cause seems as elusive as it is important. The special kind of logical relation just mentioned is perhaps even more elusive, and a considerable amount of the explication it has received seems to have failed to distinguish it from causal relations.[6] In part for these reasons, it may be preferable to cast at least part of the main issue dividing causalist and hermeneutic theorists in terms of the question of how significantly commonsense explanations of action are like or unlike scientific explanations. This way of viewing the matter can help us in a number of ways. Philosophers and psychologists alike are interested in the extent to which human agents are part of 'nature'. This question bears on the free will controversy, among others. For if, as some apparently believe, reasons are not causes and human actions are explainable *only* in terms of reasons, then our actions would seem to be neither 'determined' nor purely

[4] See, for example, Davidson, "Actions, Reasons, and Causes"; Goldman, *A Theory of Human Action;* and Raimo Tuomela, *Human Action and Its Explanation* (Dordrecht: Reidel, 1977). William P. Alston in "Wants, Actions, and Causal Explanations," in Hector-Neri Castañeda, ed., *Intentionality, Minds, and Perception* (Detroit: Wayne State University Press, 1966), and "Motives and Motivation," in *The Encyclopedia of Philosophy* (New York: Macmillan, 1967) provides much explication of this causal view, though without endorsing it.

[5] The logical relation thesis is held by many philosophers influenced by Wittgenstein, but it is not clear that he was committed to it, at least in any of the well known forms. For some of them, see A. I. Melden, *Free Action* (London: Routledge and Kegan Paul, 1961); R. S. Peters, *The Concept of Motivation* (London: Routledge and Kegan Paul, 1958); Charles Taylor, *The Explanation of Behaviour* (London: Routledge and Kegan Paul, 1964); Norman M. Malcolm, "Explaining Behavior," *Philosophical Review* 26 (1967); and von Wright, *Explanation and Understanding.*

[6] This is argued in, for example, Davidson, "Actions, Reasons, and Causes," Alston, "Wants, Actions, and Causal Explanation," and my Chapter 4, this volume, particularly with respect to the claim that there is a connection by virtue of meaning which reasons have to the actions they explain, and causes cannot have to their effects.

natural phenomena. There is also much interest in whether any single conception of explanation can account for all explanations of empirical phenomena, or at least for both scientific explanations and the most important kinds of commonsense explanations of action. Third, there is the question of whether history and those social sciences which attempt to understand the behavior of agents as governed by reasons provide a kind of understanding radically different from the kind provided by the natural sciences.

One difficulty with the approach I am suggesting is that there is much controversy over whether, in principle, any single theory of explanation can even account for all scientific explanations. Worse still, many people would argue that because the social sciences are not, say, 'quantitative', they really should not be considered sciences. Others, whether or not they hold that the social sciences ought not to be considered sciences, believe that it would be insignificant to discover that commonsense explanations are very much like explanations in the *social* sciences, because the latter explanations are parasitic on, or even disguised forms of, commonsense explanations anyway.[7]

A reasonable response to this is to try to locate commonsense explanations of action in relation to the following models: (1) a *covering-law model* of action-explanation, including, as do many proponents of the covering-law theory of scientific explanation, non-deductive covering-law explanations;[8] (2) a *hermeneutic model* of action-explanations, according to which their central feature is, roughly, their expressing the meaning, for the agent, of the action explained; and (3) an *Aristotelian model* of action-explanations, according to which their explanatory power resides in an appeal to final causes and to a conception of the agent as efficient cause. I shall be especially concerned with the first model, in part because I believe that its ability to account for action-explanations has often been underestimated and in part because I think that, rightly understood, it is closer in substance to the other models than is generally realized.

Some philosophers have argued that, despite appearances, com-

---

[7] I have argued this (as have others) regarding Skinner in "B. F. Skinner on Freedom, Dignity, and the Explanation of Behavior," *Behaviorism* 4 (1976).

[8] Even Carl G. Hempel has liberalized his covering-law theory in this way. See, for example, his *Aspects of Scientific Explanation* (New York: Macmillan, 1965), and Wesley C. Salmon, ed., *Statistical Explanation and Statistical Relevance* (Pittsburgh: University of Pittsburgh Press, 1971).

monsense explanations of action are covering-law explanations.[9] I have elsewhere developed a highly qualified version of this view,[10] arguing that at least a very important subset of such explanations can be plausibly considered (elliptical) *inductive* covering-law explanations. My contention has been that this view does not commit one to calling them causal explanations, in part because the explaining factors are not events. The view may be a plausible interpretation of what some causal theorists have meant in calling them causal, and doubtless the view is a bit closer to the causalist theory than to the hermeneutic position. I want to stress, however, that in setting out my account of commonsense explanations of action I have tried to show that it does justice to some of the important insights underlying the 'logical relation view' central to the hermeneutic theory. The account is developed in a number of my essays, including one defending a theoretical construct explication of wanting and another arguing that intending is analyzable in terms of believing and wanting, and, by implication, that an action explainable in terms of the agent's intentions could be explained by appeal to her beliefs and wants.[11]

These last two essays have been criticized in detail, and from a hermeneutical point of view, by Gauld and Shotter.[12] Their criticisms are highly representative of the objections hermeneutical philosohers and psychologists would bring (or, in some cases, have brought) against the nomological theory of action. Moreover, their book has the advantage of combining a professional knowledge of psychology with a wide-ranging grasp of much recent philosophical literature on action. For these reasons and for the sake of brevity, I shall defend the

---

[9] This view is suggested by R. B. Brandt and Jaegwon Kim in "Wants as Explanations of Actions," *Journal of Philosophy* 60 (1963), and argued in detail by Paul M. Churchland in "The Logical Character of Action-Explanations," *Philosophical Review* 79 (1970), and by me in Chapter 1, this volume.

[10] In a number of my essays: "The Concept of Believing," *Personalist* 53 (1972); "On the Conception and Measurement of Attitudes in Contemporary Anglo-American Psychology," *Journal for the Theory of Social Behaviour* 2 (1972); "Psychoanalytic Explanation and the Concept of Rational Action," *Monist* 65 (1972); Chapter 1, this volume; and "Inductive-Nomological Explanations and Psychological Laws," *Theory and Decision* 13 (1981).

[11] Chapters 1 and 2, this volume.

[12] Gauld and Shotter, *Human Action and Its Psychological Investigation.*

nomological theory against hermeneutic objections primarily with reference to their critique.

II. A Hermeneutic Critique of the Theoretical Construct Account of Wanting

The idea underlying the account of wanting which Gauld and Shotter criticize is that the concept of wanting is like theoretical concepts in science in at least one crucial respect: the concept is to be understood in terms of the main lawlike propositions in which it figures. These are, as it were, constitutive of its 'meaning', and they can be regarded as licensing the patterns of inference such that to have the concept is (at least largely) to have an adequate mastery of these patterns. In Chapter 1, I offer seven lawlike propositions as the 'explicative set' for wanting. They exhibit important relations between wanting and overt action, patterns of thought and discourse, avowals of wants, and certain affective reactions. The propositions are said to be constitutive of the concept of wanting in part because they exhibit relations of which those who have the concept must be at least implicitly aware.

From the point of view of understanding commonsense explanations of action, the crucial proposition constitutive of wanting is this:

> *S* wants *p* if and only if: for any action or activity *A* which *S* has the ability and the opportunity to perform, if *S* believes either (1) that his *A*-ing is necessary to *p*, or (2) that his *A*-ing would have at least some considerable probability of leading to *p*, or (3) that his *A*-ing would have at least some considerable probability of constituting an attainment of *p*, then *S* has a tendency to *A*.[13]

Regarding this and the other explicative propositions, I have argued that (1) they are in principle testable, hence non-trivial; (2) they have explanatory and even some predictive power; and (3) they figure in

---

[13] This is W_4 of Chapter 1, "The Concept of Wanting."

our discourse about wanting in such a way that it is plausible to regard them as constitutive of the concept of wanting.[14]

Gauld and Shotter do not explicitly dispute any of these theses. But they do argue that the concept of wanting is not theoretical in the required sense and that my account commits me to a false view of one's knowledge of one's own wants. The relevant passage is worth quoting. They argue that wanting cannot be a theoretical construct, since

> the essence of such 'constructs' as electrons and magnetic fields is that electrons and magnetic fields are assigned properties from which the truth of certain law-like propositions can be seen to follow. W_1–W_7 [the explicative propositions] cannot be derived from any unitary set of properties assigned to 'wants': they are a (far from satisfactory) list of the ways in which someone who already knows about wanting (whatever it is) might say it commonly manifests itself. Furthermore, this person's notion of wanting cannot possibly have been acquired in the way in which scientists acquire theoretical constructs such as 'electron' or 'magnetic field'. The give-away here is Audi's W_7—x wants p if and only if he has a tendency to avow that he wants it. How does x know that he wants p? Does he observe his own behaviour, note features of his own mental activities and *infer* that he has a certain want? (P. 141)

Let us first ask what Gauld and Shotter mean by *assigning* to theoretical constructs properties from which the truth of certain lawlike propositions can be seen to follow. They surely do not refer to sheer stipulative assignment of properties; for then they could not plausibly account for the explanatory power of such constructs. They appear to have in mind the familiar and apparently sound point that theories and the constructs in terms of which they explain are *postulated to explain* certain regularities. In any case, it is strange that they should think W_1–W_7 ought to be derivable from a "unitary set of properties assigned to 'wants'." For it is *these* propositions that are the basic principles of the want-belief explanatory framework; and they express the chief known properties of wanting in *terms* of which certain regularities involving wants, beliefs, and behavior can be explained. In-

[14] Another constitutive proposition would be this (discussed in Chapter 1): if S wants p, then (1) S tends to think (reflect, muse, or the like) or daydream about p at least occasionally, and especially in idle moments; and (2) in free conversation S tends to talk at least occasionally about p and subjects she believes to be connected with p. Other members of the explicative set will be considered below.

deed, I specified some regularities of this sort in the essay they are discussing (Chapter 1, Section III). On this point, then, they have simply misconstrued my analogy.

It is more difficult to assess the contention that someone who has the concept of wanting cannot have acquired it "in the way in which scientists acquire theoretical concepts such as 'electron'." It is not clear what this way is, if there is just one way; and Gauld and Shotter offer no sketch of it. But it will help us considerably if we distinguish between

    I. the way(s) in which a linguistic community (such as physicists) acquires a concept

and

    II. the way(s) in which a person in a linguistic community acquires a concept which that community already *has.*

It is also essential to distinguish between

    III. propositions about I or II

and

    IV. propositions about the *logic* of the concept.

III may help us understand IV, but there are few if any straightforward entailments between facts about how a concept is acquired and facts about its proper analysis.

With these distinctions in mind, I think we can agree that the way one ordinarily acquires the concept of wanting is radically different from the way scientists acquire theoretical concepts. My analogy does not require denying this. What it suggests (but does not entail) is that a linguistic community which acquires, from scratch, as it were, the concept of wanting does so in a way significantly similar to the way (some) scientists acquire (or develop) theoretical concepts. Is this obviously false? Our distant ancestors may be supposed to have noticed food-seeking and eating behavior following long periods without food. One way to explain this is to attribute it to a combination of inner states of wanting (caused by the deprivation) and believing (arising from, among other things) features of the environment which come within S's perceptual field. They may also have been expected to notice elation upon the discovery of certain things (a source of fresh water, for example) and disappointment upon the discovery of others (say the food's being gone upon returning from an outing).[15]

Our linguistic history is of course far more complicated than that. But the central idea is that certain explanatory concepts may have arisen—in interrelated sets, to be sure—largely through the postulation of unobservable states or processes to explain certain observable phenomena. Is this 'scientizing' commonsense and ordinary language? I believe not. For one thing, surely it is reasonable to regard science as having evolved from commonsense thinking about the world. My suggestion would help to account for that evolution. In any case, even if it is wrong to portray certain commonsense explanations as arising from a kind of rudimentary science, that view is not strictly required by my analogy between the *logic* of the concepts of wanting and that of certain theoretical concepts in science. Let us explore that analogy for a moment.

Gauld and Shotter seem to think there is a crucial disanalogy. For they suggest (in the last three of the sentences quoted) that whereas one cannot non-inferentially know, of something, that it instantiates C, where C is a theoretical concept, one can know non-inferentially what one wants. I quite agree that one can have non-inferential knowledge of what it is one wants. Moreover, nothing in my account of wanting implies that one cannot have such knowledge (indeed, I am inclined to believe that typically this is the kind of knowledge we have of what it is we want). Gauld and Shotter are apparently overlooking an important distinction between

> V. the idea that a concept cannot be analyzed except by appeal to events and states whose occurrence is evidence for its application

and

> VI. the idea that a concept of that sort can be *known* to be instantiated in a given case only on the basis of evidence.

[15] Wilfrid Sellars, in "Empiricism and the Philosophy of Mind," in Herbert Feigl and Grover Maxwell, eds., *Minnesota Studies in the Philosophy of Science*, vol. 1. (Minneapolis: University of Minnesota Press, 1956), has developed the sort of idea I am suggesting in this paragraph and has defended a similar use of it.

If V entailed VI, *no* dispositional concept could be non-inferentially known to be instantiated in any given case.

How our non-inferential self-knowledge is to be explained is not obvious. But my account leaves room for what seems a plausible answer regarding wants and beliefs: since they are both inner 'states' and knowledge is in some way a matter of belief, there can be neuro-physiological connections such that normally when, for example, S wants *p*, they 'directly' cause S to believe that he wants it.

Another important distinction is called to mind by Gauld and Shotter's objection that if my account of wanting is correct, "then transient wants, sudden yearnings would not be wants, and looking forward to something would be equivalent to wanting it" (p. 142). The objection is not explained. I imagine that they are assuming that since the constitutive manifestations of wanting I cite—such as finding it pleasant to daydream about the object—take time, wanting itself cannot be momentary. This reasoning has some plausibility. But surely

VII. that the manifestations of a dispositional property, *P*, are non-momentary events or states

does not entail

VIII. *P* cannot be momentarily instantiated.

A thing's stretching under pressure and then resuming its shape takes time. Yet surely a thing can momentarily enter an elastic state (say in the course of temperature change). I might add that in any case the manifestations of wanting that figure in my account can be *as* 'momentary' as wanting.

Regarding the second part of the objection, it is not obvious that looking forward to *x* completely satisfies my account of wanting. But if one thinks of a case of looking foward to something *as* satisfying the account, I am inclined to believe, however, that looking forward to *x* entails wanting it, but not conversely. Note that 'I am looking forward to hearing her sing, but I don't want to' sounds rather like a contradiction. If it does embody a contradiction, that has some importance. For *S*'s looking forward to something can provide an explanation of his action, in terms of a reason. Thus, if the entailment holds, it can be argued that it is the wanting involved in looking forward to which carries the explanatory power; and one more ostensibly distinct kind of action-explanation can be regarded as a species of explanation by appeal to S's wants and beliefs.

One other objection posed by Gauld and Shotter deserves comment: that feeling obligated to A does not entail wanting to. Much has been written on this issue, and I cannot even review here my own account of it.[16] However, Gauld and Shotter do not meet my arguments. They simply contend that feeling obligated does not satisfy any of my explicative propositions except W_4. But since the first three give only *sufficient* conditions for wanting, there is no need for feeling obligated to satisfy them (though I think it might often satisfy at least two of them); and I believe it does minimally satisfy the rest.

A clarification may help here: I do not take a want to be equivalent to a *desire*, as Gauld and Shotter apparently do (p. 140). The distinction[17] is easily overlooked because in many contexts interchanging the terms seems to make only a stylistic difference. But consider an example. Asked if she wants to hear one of her beginning voice students perform tonight, Margaret might say, 'I want to hear her sing, but I'm really not looking forward to it.' Is this not a kind of case in which one has a want but no *desire*? And is it not quite obviously the sort of case in which one might, in *another* context, have said— consistently with the previous remark—that one is going to hear her not because one wants to but out of a sense of obligation? Distinguishing wanting from desiring (which seems to be a species of wanting) enables us to account for the otherwise puzzling compatibility of such remarks.

III. Intending, Believing, and Wanting

In Section I it was suggested that intentions are among the elements most widely accepted as explaining actions. It will now be obvious why a proponent of the sort of view I defended in Section

[16] In, e.g., Chapter 2, this volume; "Goldman on Ability, Excuses, and Constraint," *Journal of Value Inquiry* 8 (1974); and "Weakness of Will and Practical Judgment," *Nous* 13 (1979).

[17] In "Goldman on Ability, Excuses, and Constraint," I have discussed this distinction and suggested why overlooking it makes it natural to deny that feeling obligated (at least on the assumption that it involves motivation) entails wanting.

II would be concerned to show that their role in explaining action is at least consistent with the thesis that commonsense explanations of action are a kind of covering-law explanation. In Chapter 2, I argued that intending is analyzable in terms of believing and wanting, and, by implication, that "intention explanations" may be plausibly construed as fitting the want-belief model of explanation developed in Chapter 1.

Gauld and Shotter raise some interesting objections to my account of intending, some of which are representative of hermeneutic criticism of the nomological theory of action. They first argue that intending to do something does not entail believing one will:

> For in ordinary circumstances the question of whether or not one will do what one intends to do simply does not arise for one. One does not believe that one will or that one will not. One does not consider the matter at all. One just gets on with the job. (P. 143)

The assumption here is apparently that one comes to believe a proposition only if one considers either it or some appropriately related matter. This is surely a mistake. Consider perception. When one enters a room one sees that a number of things are so even when one does not consider them or related matters; for example, one sees that a window is open. If it were replied that this is knowledge without belief, I would not try to argue this here. Consider instead one's memory of the room later, when one is no longer certain what one saw. It might not then be appropriate to say one remembers that the window was open. One might still sincerely say, however, that one believes this. It would not follow either that one had considered the matter at some time or that, say, one *now* considers one's memory impressions and, by consulting them, forms the belief.

I would speculate that Gauld and Shotter may be taking

IX. It would be 'odd' for *S* to say that *p* in circumstances *C*

to entail

X. *S* does not, in *C*, *believe* that *p*.

But while this is a natural move, it would surely be a mistake. It would be odd for me to say, on what seems an ordinary weekday, 'I believe I'll go to my office', when I intend as usual to go there. But suppose I discover to my surprise that I cannot go there because the university is closed. It would be at best difficult to explain my surprise on any other assumption than that I believed I would go; and, before I discovered the closing, a colleague who saw my lecture notes in my hand and said, 'Where do you think (believe) you're going?', would not be inaccurate, however firm my intention.

Gauld and Shotter also argue that the combination of believing and wanting by which I have analyzed intending fails to provide a sufficient condition. The want component of an intention, say to A, is, roughly, a want that is neither temporarily forgotten nor overridden by an equally strong or stronger want, for example to abstain from A-ing. The other main component is a belief that one will (or that one probably will) A (see Chapter 2 for the full account). In Gauld and Shotter's case, S believes S will do A 'because he is pretty sure that whether he likes it or not Svengali, the evil hypnotist, will work upon him to that effect'. Then, even if S wants to A, he does not intend to (p. 144). Unfortunately, the example is highly indeterminate. Does the agent want to A *more* than anything he believes incompatible with doing it? The way the example is worded, one is inclined to believe that, though he wants to A, he would prefer that the hypnotist not bring it about that he A and believes that he cannot both A and have the hypnotist not bring about his A-ing (for example, because he believes that apart from the hypnotist's work, his own competing wants would prevail). In that case, however, my conditions are not met, since the agent does not want *on balance* to A.

Suppose, on the other hand, that the agent does want to A more than anything he believes incompatible with that, for example fulfilling a moral obligation, or B-ing, which would also achieve his overall goal in the situation, or avoiding having Svengali determine what he is to do. Imagine, moreover, that A is, say, voting for Carter. Assume too that what S believes is *not* that Svengali will cause his hand to mark the appropriate ballot against S's will. For then S does not believe he will *do* the deed, but rather something to the effect that his body will be caused to make movements which would be A-ing if they were appropriately brought about by S. We now have a situation in which (1) S believes he will vote for Carter and (2) S either does not want to do anything to alter this, such as try to prevent Svengali's giving him the post-hypnotic suggestion, or S wants to alter it *less* than he wants to vote for Carter. If we now ask S whether he intends to vote for Carter, may he truly say 'no'?

Granted, S expects not to A in a normal way. But surely we need to distinguish between

   XI. intending to A (simpliciter)

and

   XII. intending to A in a particular way (under particular conditions, as a result of wanting to, etc.).

We individuate intentions in terms of their content; the contents of XI and XII differ, and XI apparently does not entail XII. Even if the entailment does hold, it would not follow that XI is inconsistent with believing one will A in a strange way.

It is worth pointing out that my conception of intending accounts in good part for what Gauld and Shotter see as central to intending: "When one commits oneself to something one comes to regard the relevant actions as having a gerundive or imperative quality for one. And this is surely the central feature of intending" (148). On my view, wanting on balance to A and believing that one will do it is, as it were, to be *motivationally committed* to doing it. To be sure, one's want, though not outweighed by an equally strong or stronger incompatible want, may be weak. Moreover, the paradigms of motivational commitment embody wants arising from deliberations, decisions, resolutions, plans, and so on. But not all intentions arise this way, as I have argued in Chapter 2. Some arise almost 'automatically' in the course of ordinary activities. Nor are all intentions *firm*.

More troublesome than a case of hypnotic influence as imagined above would be one in which S meets my conditions for intending, yet *unconsciously* wants to A. I am inclined to say that if one countenances unconscious wants, one will countenance unconscious intentions. If intentions can be unconscious, then such cases as I am imagining require no qualification of my account. The issue is too large to take up here, particularly since only minor qualification of the account would be needed in case unconscious intentions are not possible. Suppose, on the other hand, that S consciously wants on balance to A, yet mistakenly believes she wants something incompatible with it more. In our voting example, S would, under these conditions, likely deny that she intends to vote for Carter and probably say that she will do so only under compulsion. Perhaps this would be correct. On the other hand, it seems clear to me that people can be mistaken about what they intend. Showing this would not require postulating unconscious intentions. Wishful thinkers sometimes falsely believe they have certain intentions. Moreover, conceptual errors about what intending entails may lead one to disavow an intention one has. If, for example, one thought intending to A required being certain one would A, one might falsely deny that one intends to A, thinking one only hopes to. I believe, then, that S might intend to A even when she mistakenly believes she has a stronger want for something incompatible with it. In any event, if this is a mistake, rectifying it would require only minor revision of the account and would leave it equally much an account in terms of the wants and beliefs of the agent.

This response to Gauld and Shotter's example suggests a significant distinction. There are important differences among even simple intentions to A. Where S believes she will be caused by an external force to do A, her intention might be called *passive*. For one thing, it does not, or is at least unlikely to, give rise to subsidiary intentions, such as the intention to try to take steps to A, since S believes these inappropriate. Still, S's overall motivation *favors* A-ing and if she does not take steps to bring it about, she is so disposed that she *would* if her beliefs changed appropriately, for example, if she ceased to believe Svengali would bring about her A-ing.

The past few paragraphs give only a sketch of a case for countenancing what I call passive intentions. If, however, it should turn out that it is best not to call these intentions at all, I believe minor modifications of my account would take care of the problem. Indeed, one possible revision of the account is suggested in Chapter 2, namely, that S not believe either that she will not A intentionally, or anything to the effect that she will A only by virtue of being physically or psychologically overpowered.

I shall have to be briefer in treating some other interesting objections Gauld and Shotter raise: (1) that the concept of wanting cannot be analyzed without appeal to that of intending, so that a want-belief account of intending is ultimately circular; (2) that since intending to A entails having decided to do it, yet wanting to A, together with believing that one will, does not, my account of intending is too broad; and (3) that since intentions are "indefinitely various," we cannot hope for "any unitary account of what it is to possess an intention" (pp. 145–46).

The ground for (1) is apparently that "wants are pregnant with possible lines of action, possible intentions." But surely this *supports* my account: part of my aim was to suggest that under appropriate conditions—very roughly, when a want becomes dominant and *S* beleives she will realize it—an intention is formed. I not only agree that wants are pregnant with intentions; I offer the basic conditions for gestation and birth. Regarding the circularity objection, Gauld and Shotter are apparently thinking that

XIII. It is a conceptual truth about *F*s that they tend to generate *G*s

entails

XIV. *F*s cannot be analyzed without appeal to *G*s.

But this entailment does not hold. A good analysis requires a set of conceptually necessary and sufficient conditions that are in some way illuminating. This does not require appealing to *every* conceptually necessary condition. Indeed, to achieve unification and simplicity it may be best *not* to appeal to notions—such as intending—that can be explicated in terms of others—for instance wanting and believing—which seem absolutely indispensable in the overall enterprise—such as the analysis of action-explanations. This has been my strategy.

Concerning (2), I am surprised that Gauld and Shotter do not take up my counterexamples to the view that intending to *A* entails having decided to *A* (Chapter 2). To be sure, 'I haven't decided' may in some contexts be rightly understood to imply a negative answer to 'Do you intend to *A*?' But typically these contexts involve *considering* whether to *A*. Perhaps one cannot form the intention to *A* in the usual way one does in the course of considering whether to do it, unless it is by deciding to. But to say that intending to *A* requires having decided to *A* seems to me to be mistaken for much the same sorts of reasons it is a mistake to suppose that coming to believe a proposition entails considering whether it is true.

Objection (3) is surprising: after all, wants are "indefinitely various" in the same way intentions are; for they share the same enormous range of contents. It looks as if Gauld and Shotter think that because intentions have this feature, we cannot construct a "unitary account" of them. But this seems to conflate an account of the content of intentions with an account of what it is to have them. Doubtless we cannot give a "unitary account" of the contents of intentions—or wants. It does not follow that we cannot give such an account of *having* an intention (i.e. intending). Museums, too, have indefinitely various contents. It does not follow that we cannot give a unitary account of what it is to be a museum.

IV. Nomological and Hermeneutic Theories of Action: Toward Reconciliation

In this section, I want to set out several ideas which bear on both the philosophical and the psychological study of the explanation of human action. My point of departure will be a hermeneutic thesis which I believe Gauld and Shotter, among others, take to be as important for psychology as for philosophy. My aim will be to show how readily the very theory they criticize can accommodate many of their own views and to offer some reasons for psychologists to give the want-belief theory more attention.

Speaking of what is among the most important kinds of common-sense explanation of action, Gauld and Shotter say this:

> To ask for the 'meaning' of an action is to ask for this sort of explanation [one in terms of the agent's 'intention or purpose']. It is to ask what envisaged scheme of things the agent hoped to further by initiating that action. It is, in short, to ask what was the agent's intention in acting as he did when he did. (p. 49)

Let me suggest that if we put 'want' for 'hope' here, nothing significant is lost, and something important is gained. For surely hoping entails wanting in the widest sense of 'wanting', which is the one I take to be crucial in understanding most action-explanations. Consider 'I hope to see him, but I don't want to'. If this is ever permissible, it is where 'want' is used to mean something like 'desire'; and not desiring something is quite consistent with one's wanting it. One thing gained by my proposal is the elimination of an error: sometimes we *A* in order to realize an end, where we are *certain* we will succeed. In that case, we do not *hope* to realize the end by *A*-ing. But it remains true that we want to realize it by *A*-ing.

If we make the move I sugg;est, how are intentions to be regarded in the explanation of action? Here it is essential to grasp that analyzing them in terms of other concepts does not in the least divest them of explanatory power. Indeed, I have been at pains to give an account of their explanatory power.[18] Nor have I tried to 'reduce' or to analyze *away* the concept of intending, if that means providing, through my account, a synonymous expression. At most, I take an analysis to require providing an *equivalent* concept.

This brings me to a further point. Not only intentions but many other concepts used similarly in commonsense explanations of action seem analyzable in terms of wanting and believing. This may indeed apply to all the intentional concepts so used. I have argued elsewhere that it holds for attitudes,[19] and similar considerations suggest that it may apply to hopes, purposes, aims, goals, plans, and so on. This is not in the least to suggest that there are no important differences among these elements. There are. But far from ignoring them, analyses in terms of wants and beliefs can use the enormous diversity of these two concepts to explain differences among the other elements. If I am right about the pervasiveness of wanting and believing and the analyzability of other concepts in terms of them, one may wonder why our language has apparently been so uneconomical. Why so many terms for what are simply various combinations of wants and beliefs? I have heard it said that because of the importance of snow to the Eskimos, they have about twenty terms for it, each designating a distinct variety. I do not know whether this is true, but I see no reason why a similar hypothesis could not at least partially explain the richness of our action-explaining terminology consistently with the view that the crucial explanatory elements are wants and beliefs.

Notice also that this approach offers a plausible way of accounting for the huge range of everyday explanations of action in which all

---

[18] I have argued, however, that *A*-ing intentionally does not entail having intended (as opposed to hoping) to do it (see Chapter 2, Section 3). If that view is correct, then the explanatory power of intentions is apparently not as broad as Gauld and Shotter seem to think; for not all intentional actions would be explainable by appeal to *S*'s intentions.

[19] In "A Cognitive-Motivational Theory of Attitudes," *Southwestern Journal of Philosophy* 5 (1974) and "On the Conception and Measurement of Attitudes"; the latter develops the significance of this account of attitudes for explanation in psychology.

that is cited is a fact. One might, for example, explain why *S* jammed her brakes by saying that a dog ran into her path. Are we to give up providing a well-unified theory of action explanation because such fact-citing explanations may be indefinitely various? Surely not. Why not say that in the context it is implied that *S* believed she would hit the dog if she did not jam her brakes and wanted to avoid hitting the dog? If we suppose she did not believe this or did not want that, we would reject the explanation. That is good reason to think these elements play a crucial role. Why, then, is there any mention of the *external* fact that the dog ran across the path? The answer is surely that it gives us an explanation of why the belief arose (we would expect the want to arise, given the belief). For we assume the driver *sees* such things in her path, thereby coming to believe (and know) they are there. Thus, like the hermeneutic approach used by Gauld and Shotter, this way of viewing intentional action enables us to understand such action in terms of its 'meaning' for the agent; and the want-belief model I have developed can very readily do this even when what is to be understood is how citing an external fact can explain an intentional action.

If my account of commonsense action-explanations enables us both to unify them in a systematic framework and to account for their differences, it also enables us to regard commonsense explanation as continuous with scientific explanation in ways one would expect from the history of science and from its evolution, in part, from common-sense thinking. A kind of theoretical understanding of observable regularities seems to characterize commonsense thinking; and as one would expect from this, a kind of nomological explanation seems to be highly pervasive in ordinary discourse. One may or may not con-nect these explanations with the idea that our intentional actions manifest powers rooted in our nature.[20] Similarly, one may or may not connect them with causal generalities; but if one does, it can be with due regard for the differences between reasons as causes and non-intentional phenomena as causes. Moreover, this approach does not force us to deny the quasi-analytic character of some action-ex-

[20] As this suggests, my position seems to allow us to construe intentions and certain wants as a kind of *power* in the sense explicated by Rom Harré and Paul F. Secord, *The Explanation of Social Behaviour* (Oxford: Basil Blackwell, 1972), chap. 12. There is certainly some reason to think of an intention or a want on balance as in part "a likelihood to behave in a certain way in virtue of the nature or state of a thing" (p. 241), in this case the agent. If so, then the nomological theory of action may have an important connec-tion with the conception of action-explanation Harré and Secord have developed.

plaining principles: on the contrary, we can find a quite similar phenomenon in certain scientific contexts.[21]

At this point it may be objected that there remains an underlying
issue which has been neglected both by me and by Gauld and Shotter.
The issue is whether the intentionalistic explanations under discussion are or are not Aristotelian, where this implies that their explanatory power depends not only on an appeal to final causes, but also
on a conception of the agent as efficient cause in the sense expressed
by Aristotle in, for example, *Metaphysics* (Delta, 1013a–b). On the sort
of Aristotelian view in question, I, as *agent,* not my wants or beliefs,
cause my actions; I, not they, am their source. My wants and beliefs express the final cause(s) of my action, rather than constituting
its efficient cause.

If this view requires postulating a kind of causation wholly different
from any kind exhibited when one event causes another—*agent causation,* as it is sometimes called—then the view seems rather unclear. It
is certainly proper to speak of persons or objects, as well as events,
as causing things. But how are we to understand a person's or object's
causing something? For Goldman, to say that an *object, O,* is a cause
of *x,* "presupposes that there is a *state of O* or an *event involving O*
that caused, or was a partial cause, of *x*"; and agent causation "is
simply a special case of object-causation, since an agent is simpy a
particular kind of object or substance."[22] Indeed, for Goldman,
"agent-causation is *explicable* in terms of want-and-belief causation"
(p. 83). In my view, wants and beliefs need not be considered causes,
and I generally prefer not to call them that. On the other hand, my
position is like Goldman's in construing a *person's* (intentionally) causing something as a special case of doing something explainable inten-
tionalistically. The difference may not appear major, but I believe that
it enables my view to accommodate the central points of the Aristotelian conception of intentionalistic explanations just sketched. Let me
indicate why this is so.

The first point to be made is that I do not construe wants or beliefs
as events or as Aristotelian efficient causes of any kind. They are not

---

[21] I have argued for this in "Psychoanalytic Explanation." A similar idea is discussed
in Hilary Putnam, "The Analytic and the Synthetic," in Herbert Feigl and Grover
Maxwell, eds., *Minnesota Studies in the Philosophy of Science*, vol. 3 (Minneapolis: University of Minnesota Press, 1961), and Sellars, "Empiricism and the Philosophy of
Mind."

[22] Goldman, *A Theory of Human Action*, p. 81.

agents, nor inner thrusts, nor anything of the sort. This is one reason we need not take them to compete with the agent as producer of the action. I may be regarded as the source of my actions and may truly say that *I* cause them. But surely this does not require postulating agent-causation in any sense incompatible with the explainability of the actions by appeal to my wants and beliefs. More positively, one's wants and beliefs may be regarded as, in part, that *through* which one's agency is expressed. *I* produce my actions; but I do so *for* reasons, that is, by acting, in the light of my beliefs, *in order to* realize certain of my wants.

A second important point is that the explanatory power of intentionalistic explanations of actions is, in my view, in part a function of the *content* of the explaining factors. Take, for example, a case in which S's A-ing is explainable by his wanting ϕ and believing that A-ing is necessary to realize ϕ. Given the content of the want and belief, the action is exhibited as reasonable from S's point of view (at least on the assumption that the want and belief are not irrational for S). This enables us to see the action as part of a pattern of goal-seeking activity, and often it will also enable us to see the agent as following some kind of rule. From an Aristotelian point of view, by virtue of their content the explaining want(s), and belief(s) enable us to see the (or an) *end* for which the action is performed; this we may take to be its final cause.

It may appear that this way of conceiving of intentionalistic explanations conflicts with the nomological conception of such explanations defended above. But it does not. Certainly intentionalistic explanations differ from the typical nomological explanations in appealing to explanatory factors that have content; and I take the intentionality of ordinary action-explanations to be every bit as important as their nomic character. By virtue of the content of their explaining factors, these explanations exhibit the action explained as *reasonable* from the agent's point of view; and by virtue of a nomic relation between the existence of the relevant wants and beliefs and the occurrence of the action they explain, the explanations exhibit the action as *expectable* given the character of the agent. This nomic expectability in the light of S's wants and beliefs does not require construing them as causes, but it is consistent both with the view that the agent causes the action and with the view that there are events which cause actions.

On the other hand, though my position is, on these counts, consistent with various causal theories of action, I do not regard it as a causal theory. One might think that a nomological theory of action must be causal. But if I am right, a nomic relation can not only be intentional, but also hold between other things than causes and their effects. One may, like Davidson and Goldman,[23] call wants and beliefs causes of action, but I am not committed to this. Perhaps the existence of a nomic relation between wants and beliefs and, on the other hand, actions, entails that there is *some* causal relation between (i) something (for example the agent) involving the wants and beliefs and (ii) the actions as effects. One might, for instance, construe wants and beliefs as, in part, that through which agents exercise causal power in a sense of 'causal power' close to that employed by Harré and Secord.[24] But this is quite different from saying that these and other reasons are themselves causes.

We are now in a position to view the logical relation thesis in a new light. Suppose that we take it, not as a claim about the relation between the *existence* of the explaining reasons and that of the action explained, but as a claim about the relation between the *content* of those reasons and the performance of the action. Then the relation will quite obviously not be causal; and if we think of the content of the want as expressing a state of affairs desirable for the agent and of the content of the belief as the proposition that the action will (or may) realize this state of affairs, we can view the relation between these contents and the performance of the action as a kind of logical one: a rationalizing or (subjectively) justificatory one. By virtue of the relation, the action is exhibited as the (or a) reasonable thing for S to do. Moreover, complex sets of wants and beliefs may interact with each other in such a way that (1) the content of a number of them can rationalize a single action, and (2) the existence of the set can render the action more likely to occur than the existence of any one potentially explaining want-belief subset. The intentionalistic nomological theory I have been developing is thus able to account for the *systematic* way in which an agent's reasons interact to produce—and rationalize—his actions. The theory does not specify the dynamics underlying actions so conceived; but it leads us to expect that there is a complex underlying dynamics, and it is consistent with a wide variety of philosophical and psychological accounts of the underlying dynamics.

A further implication of the theory I have developed is this. If it

---

[23] Davidson, "Action, Reasons, and Causes," and Goldman, *A Theory of Human Action.*

[24] Harré and Secord, *The Explanation of Social Behaviour.*

should turn out that the social sciences do rely on ordinary action-explaining concepts, such as wanting and intending, or indeed must rely on them to provide an understanding of *action* rather than mere human movements, my account of commonsense action-explanations would at least enable us to argue plausibly that the social sciences deserve the name 'science'. If their explanations using intentional concepts, however refined these explanations become, are non-deductive, they are at least nomological; and the relevant explanatory propositions are testable, capable of providing some form of covering-law explanation of observed regularities, and couched in theoretical concepts having kind of systematic interconnections often held to be distinctive of a theoretical framework in the physical sciences.[25]

The concepts of wanting and believing have an additional advantage for both philosophers of mind and psychologists. These notions are central in understanding rational action;[26] they appear capable of explaining actions even when the relevant want or belief is unconscious,[27] so that a wider spectrum of behavior may be explained than on many other theories of action; and the notions have been extensively used in game theory and economics, so that their use in psychology might enhance communication between psychologists and other social scientists. To be sure, psychologists would then be in part—but only in part—extending common sense. But if that is not a lofty mission, it is at least preferable to abandoning the parlance of common sense, only to rely in the end on its concepts disguised in scientific jargon.[28]

V. Conclusion

If the position I have been developing is correct, where does it leave the hermeneutical thesis that, as Gauld and Shotter put it,

[25] I have argued for the analogy in "Psychoanalytic Explanation," and Chapter 1, this volume. For some supporting discussion of theoretical concepts, see Peter Achinstein *Concepts of Science* (Baltimore: Johns Hopkins University Press, 1968), and Hempel, *Aspects of Scientific Explanation*.

[26] I have illustrated this in "Psychoanalytic Explanation." See also R. B. Brandt, "Rational Desires," *Proceedings and Addresses of the American Philosophical Association* 42 (1969).

[27] I defend this in "The Concept of Believing," and suggest its application to self-deception in "Epistemic Disavowals and Self-Deception," *Personalist* 51 (1976).

[28] Skinner appears guilty of this, as I have argued in "B. F. Skinner."

hermeneutic explanations of human actions are ineradicable and irreducible. . . . And since the 'meaning' of actions for the agents who execute them are given by those agents' intentions, hopes, fears, beliefs, anticipations, desires, plots, plans, reasonings, schemes and immediate perceptions, it is these everyday, yet systematically related, psychological concepts that must constitute our initial, though not necessarily our final, framework of thought.

We propose, then, that . . . the conceptual framework of the psychology of human action must, therefore, be that of the everyday notions—action, agent, intention, purpose, desire, belief, hope, fear, reason, plan and so on and so on—within which such explanation [hermeneutic explanation] has its being. (P. 77)

The nomological theory I have defended is consistent with, though it does not entail, all of these points, provided that what Gauld and Shotter call 'hermeneutic explanations' can be neutrally characterized as those intentionalistic explanations of action we give in ordinary life, rather than identified with those explanations *as* construed by Gauld and Shotter and others who hold what I call the logical relation thesis. Indeed, even if the explanations are also said to be non-mechanistic in roughly Gauld and Shotter's sense (chap. 2), I see no reason why they cannot be nomological in the sense I have indicated. To be sure, I have argued that all ordinary intentionalistic explanations of action depend, in the ways I have sketched, on an appeal to the concepts of wanting and believing. But this is not to say that hermeneutic explanations—which I prefer to call intentionalistic explanations—are dispensable or reducible. Rather, there are two hermeneutic concepts which, at least from the point of view of explaining actions, are fundamental to the hermeneutic conceptual framework. If the hermeneutic explanations of action other than those expressed in terms of the agent's wants and beliefs can in some sense be reduced to the latter, it would not follow that the latter could be reduced to *non*-hermeneutic explanations.

It may be that Gauld and Shotter have tended to take my effort to achieve explanatory unification within the intentional domain as an attempt to pave the way for a reduction of intentionalistic explanations to 'mechanistic' explanations. My aim has been more nearly to consolidate their own forces. Moreover, in doing so, I have tried to give an account of hermeneutic explanation that makes it "scientifically respectable." If I have succeeded, then it seems more reasonable than on Gauld and Shotter's view to suppose, as they do, that at least our initial framework of thought for the psychology of human action must be that of our everyday intentional notions.

The theory of action-explanation I have proposed does a great deal of unification and puts considerable weight on the concepts of believing and wanting. Anyone sensitive to ordinary language is apt to feel that there must be some oversimplification. Perhaps there is, but I do not think that this has been established. Far from theorizing with too little attention to the data, or nourishing myself on too few examples, in Wittgenstein's phrase, I have tried to unify only where the data permit. And the concepts I take as fundamental are surely rich enough to do justice, in the ways I have sketched, to phenomena of indefinite variety. If they cannot, I believe that is yet to be shown.[29]

[29] For helpful comments on an earlier version of this chapter I want to thank Rom Harré, Robert M. Gordon, Michael S. Moore, and anonymous readers for the *Journal for the Theory of Social Behaviour.*

Chapter 6

Acting for Reasons

If we do not know for what reasons a person acts, we do not fully understand that person. If we do not know any reason for which an agent does something, we cannot adequately assess whether, in doing it, that agent is acting rationally. And if Kant is right, unless we know the reason(s) for which an action is performed, we do not know its moral worth. But what is it to act for a reason? Clearly, acting for a reason is closely related to acting intentionally, to acting rationally, and to acting on the basis of practical reasoning. An action for a reason apparently must be intentional; an action based on practical reasoning must be performed for a reason; and at least the paradigms of rational action must be intentional. Whether there are some equivalences among these notions will be discussed below. Let us begin by laying out some guiding assumptions.

I. Actions, Reasons, and Practical Reasoning

Consider an ordinary case in which a representative agent, S (Sue, let us say), acts for a reason. In the course of mailing impersonal invitations to a conference Sue has organized, she puts John's aside. Her reason: to delay it until after she sends him a condolence letter (his mother has died). If this case is *typical* of action for a reason, we may say the following. (1) Her action is explainable by appeal to her reason; for example, she put the invitation aside in order to delay it until after she sends condolences. (2) She believes something to the effect that her putting it aside will delay it. (3) If asked why she is putting it aside, she will tend to answer by appeal to her reason. (4) Her action is, in some way, a response to, and occurs because of, her reasons. For instance, if she ceased to have the reason because she decided to send no condolences, then (assuming she had no other reason for the action) she would no longer put the invitation aside. (5) In putting it aside, she has a sense of what her reason for doing this is and of her action as a response to the reason. She may, for example, be aware of wanting to delay the invitation and of her action as delaying it. (6) She knows or believes that she is putting it aside, and knows why. (7) The action is, *relative to* her reason for it and her belief that the action will delay the invitation, prima facie rational. And (8) she controls whether she carries the action out and, to some degree, how. It is up to her, for example, that she flips the invitation aside with her fingers rather than her pen. Generalizations of (1)–(8) do not apply to all actions for a reason; but they hold in paradigm cases, and an account of acting for a reason should both unify and refine them. The account I shall give will do this by exhibiting action for a reason as explainable by motivation embodying that reason, and as guided by S's beliefs, reflected in S's cognitive dispositions, and, in a special way, under S's control.

There are many kinds of reasons. My focus is reasons *for which* one acts. It should be uncontroversial that if S A's for a reason, her A-ing is motivated. For convenience, I also assume that if S A's for a reason, she A's because she wants something, in a very broad sense of 'want'.[1] Thus, a reason, r, for which one acts, can be expressed by an infinitive clause giving the content of the relevant want. Where A is, for example, phoning, S's reason might be to say that she is late, and the relevant want—to say that she is late—is what motivates her phoning. This is not to identify motives with wants; I simply assume that wants are pervasive motivating elements in action. Let us say that a reason for which S A's is, in part, a state of affairs, r, which (i) expresses something she wants, and (ii) is connected with her A-ing through an appropriate belief, for example that her A-ing will achieve

---

[1] That 'want' has a sufficiently broad use I argue in Chapter 2, this volume. Other terms might suffice, however.

r. Thus, *S* wants to say she is late, believes phoning will achieve this, and phones for that reason, that is, to say she is late.[2] These assumptions may well be neutral regarding a plausible internalism which says that certain judgments, for instance that one ought to *A*, can provide a sufficient reason for which one *A*'s (and can explain one's *A*-ing); for such judgments may perhaps imply wanting in the broad sense. If they do not, then an internalist reading of the account of acting for a reason to be developed may simply replace wanting by the relevant judgments or by other motivating elements, for example attitudes or intentions.

We sometimes refer to people's wants, beliefs, fears, and other states as reasons for which they act. *S*'s wanting wine might be cited as her reason for leaving just before dinner. Such states express reasons as described above and might be called *reason states*. It is reason states, and not reasons proper, that I take to have causal power, though for convenience I shall sometimes speak of the latter in causal terms. Facts may also be cited as reasons: the fact that Tom has a fine record might be the reason for which *S* asks him to speak. But while many kinds of things are cited as reasons for which an agent acts, the context normally provides enough information for infinitival expression of the agent's reason.

It is important to distinguish reasons for which *S* *A*'s from other kinds. *Reasons to A* are normative and impersonal. There can be reasons to keep one's promises, even if nobody wants to keep promises. *Reasons for S to A* are personal and normative. That *A*-ing would fulfill *S*'s yen to visit China might be a reason for *her* to *A*. A *reason S has for A-ing* is personal, but need not be normative; it is also potentially motivating, whereas a reason there is for her to *A* need not be. Thus, if she *believes* *A*-ing will fulfill her yen, she *has* a reason for *A*-ing. A *reason for which S A's*, however, must be a reason she has *and* must actually motivate her *A*-ing, in a sense implying that it is a *reason why she A's*, that is, one that at least partly explains her *A*-ing. But a reason why she *A*'s need not be one for which she does so; the action could be simply due to drugs. When *S A*'s for a good reason, for example writes a recommendation to keep a promise, all five kinds of reasons are involved: keeping her promise is a reason to write; a reason for her to do so; a reason she has to do so; a reason why she writes; and

[2] It may seem that some reasons for action are not expressible infinitivally. Consider *A*-ing because one wants *that* Sam benefit. I believe that the reason here is (say) to *contribute* to his welfare, but no major point below turns on this issue.

a reason for which she writes. Even *A*-ing for a bad reason involves at least the last four kinds of reason.

In construing reasons for which one acts as the contents of motivating wants, I am not denying that beliefs are also crucial. Indeed, a reason for which one acts can be conveyed by citing a belief—such as that by phoning one can say one is late—as effectively as by appeal to the motivating want. Intuitively, the want—or intention, judgment, or whatever plays the motivational role in our account—*moves* one to act; the belief *guides* one in acting. One's reason, through its relation to one's motivating want, is that for the sake of which, and on account of which, one acts; but given different beliefs one would not (other things equal) do what one does do. For these and other reasons, beliefs are as important as wants in the account to be developed.

Acting for a reason may seem equivalent to action based on practical reasoning.[3] Such action occurs when, for example, one considers one's goal, say to visit China, sees a way to realize it, decides on that way, and acts accordingly. Certainly (1)–(8) apply to actions based on practical reasoning, and one might think that *S A*'s for a reason if *and* only if her *A*-ing is based on such reasoning. But not all actions for a reason are so based.[4] Moreover, even assuming we understand practical reasoning, it is very hard to explicate an action's being *based on* it.

There is, however, a correspondence between acting for a reason and acting on the basis of practical reasoning. If *S A*'s for a reason, for example buys a ticket in order to visit China, we may construct a practical argument which represents, in its major premise, *S*'s motivating want (to visit China) and, in its minor, *S*'s guiding belief (that she must buy a ticket). The correspondence holds whether or not *S* actually reasoned from these premises to a conclusion. Indeed, we may construe acting for a reason as a concrete *realization* of such a practical argument. The point is not simply that *S instantiates* the argument, that is, has the want and belief expressed in its premises and does the thing indicated by the conclusion. There are at least four other factors. First, the premises represent the *structure* of the causal and explanatory basis of the action, namely the relevant want and belief. Second, the explanatory relation which that want and belief bear to the action mirrors a kind of support (or prima facie

---

[3] This has been held or implied by a number of writers. I have cited some and discussed the rationale for the view in "A Theory of Practical Reasoning," *American Philosophical Quarterly* 19 (1982).

[4] I have defended this in "A Theory of Practical Reasoning."

justificatory) relation which the premises of the argument bear to its conclusion. Third, *S* is at the time disposed to appeal to the argument if asked to explain or justify her *A*-ing, rather in the way one appeals to a rule or practice one has been automatically following. If, for example, *S* is asked why she *A*-ed, she is disposed to say things like, 'Because I wanted to *r* and believed *A*-ing would enable me to *r'*. Fourth, where *S*'s *A*-ing is a realization of a practical argument, then even if the action is not based on practical reasoning, the explanatory relation between her reason and action is just what it would have been if (other things equal) she had *A*-ed on the basis of actual reasoning from its premises to its conclusion; she would, for example, have *A*-ed for the *same* reason, though perhaps more deliberately for it.

When *S* simply infers the conclusion of a practical argument from its premises, I call the argument *inferentially realized.* My point here is that it may also be at once noninferentially and *behaviorally realized,* through a spontaneous action that expresses *S*'s motivating want and is guided by a belief which *S* need not entertain. Practical reasoning can also occur *without S*'s acting on it.[5] There the practical argument is only partly realized, whereas its full realization implies *S*'s doing what its conclusion favors. Thus, while acting for a reason is not equivalent to acting on the basis of practical reasoning, we may take as a guiding idea—which will help us interpret (1)–(8)—the view that action for a reason is a realization of a practical argument. Granted, this idea presupposes some understanding of practical reasoning, but the idea is clear enough to help explicate acting for a reason.

II. The Basic Elements of Action for a Reason

In the light of the examples and guiding ideas set out above, we can begin to clarify acting for a reason. Initially, our focus will be on quite simple actions, and for the present we may ignore acting for more than one reason.

Explainability

Clearly, if *S A*'s for a reason, *r*, she must act *on account of r,* and her wanting to *r* must move her to *A*. Thus, the motivating want, the

[5] An important case of such failure to act is weakness of will. In "Weakness of Will and Practical Judgment," *Nous* 13 (1979), I have argued that the relevant kind of weak-willed action is possible.

want to *r*, plays a causal role in a sense implying that *S* *A*-ed at least partly because she wanted to *r*, where 'because' has explanatory import. This suggests an *explanatory condition*: if *S* *A*'s for *r*, then her wanting to *r* is part of what explains why she *A*'s. This in turn normally implies that *S* *also* *A*-ed partly because she believed an appropriate relation to hold between her *A*-ing and *r*. But neither the want nor the belief need be a necessary condition: *S* can *A* for a reason even if something other than the relevant want and belief (such as an alternative goal) is sufficient to her *A*-ing. The relevant want and belief, must, however, be important enough, for her *A*-ing, to have the appropriate explanatory power.[6] Moreover, if *A*-ing is temporally extended, they must *sustain* it and have comparable explanatory power: while *A*-ing is in progress, citing them must be adequate to explain why *S* *is* *A*-ing, in the same way it might explain why *S* did something that was instantaneous. For instance, assuming there is no other reason for her *A*-ing, then just as, in the latter case, *S* would not have *A*-ed if, other things equal, she *had* not wanted to *r*, so, in the former case, *S* would not *continue* to *A* if, other things equal, she did not *still* want to *r*.[7]

Acting for a reason, however, takes far more than satisfying the explanatory sustaining condition. Imagine that *S* wants to wake Jan, a guest, and believes that a way to do it is just to open her bedroom door. Now suppose this want and belief evoke the thought of waking her, and that this thought makes *S* nervous. Her nervousness might cause her to drop the breakfast tray, and by dropping the tray against the door she might open it. It would then be (indirectly) because of *S*'s want and belief that *S* opens the door. Yet *S* does not do so for a reason. She does it *because of a reason* (strictly, because of a reason state), not for one. Her *A*-ing is an *effect* of her want, but not a *response* to it. To see these contrasts better, let us explore the role of beliefs.

Connecting Beliefs

The example just given suggests the importance of belief in guiding an action for a reason to its goal. Suppose *S* had believed instead that

---

[6] An action for a reason may be *overdetermined* in at least two ways: (1) there may be other reason states, *or* non-mental factors, that *would* have made *S* *A* if her want and belief had not; (2) other factors may, at the very same time also *partly* cause her *A*-ing.

[7] In referring to *A*-ing as temporally extended I presuppose an intuitive notion of *performative extension*: reading a letter takes time in a way touching a button does not.

dropping the breakfast tray was the best way to wake Jan, and had dropped it in order to wake her. Then *S* would have acted for, not merely because of, a reason. What has been added? When a *connecting belief*, together with a motivating want, brings about the action (in a suitable way), *S* acts not just because of but *in the light of* a reason. Such beliefs make *A* relevant, for *S*, to her reason. In the first case, it just happens that *S*'s opening Jan's door is an action for which she has a reason. But when *S A*'s for a reason, it is to be expected that *A* in some sense match her reason. This is largely due to the guiding role of connecting beliefs. Suppose *S* wants to saw a plank at right angles, pencils in a line, and carefully saws. She is guided by her belief that sawing straight down will yield a square cut. Thus, if she realizes she is cutting leftward, she pressures the saw to the right. Her motivation sets her goal; her connecting belief guides her to it. The guidance may involve other beliefs, say, that she is sawing left (and elements, such as perceptual data, besides beliefs). Corrective adjustment may also be automatic, in the sense that the guiding is done without explicit awareness. And where the action is so routine that no guidance need be exercised, guidance may be simply a matter of readiness to adjust. Here the action itself is in a way automatic. In all three cases, what counts, for *S*, as a correction depends on her connecting belief; and that belief is essential to what we might call the *discriminative* character of action for a reason.

If acting for a reason implies acting in the light of it, must *S believe* she has a reason for *A*-ing, or believe the reason for which she *A*'s to *be* a reason for which she *A*'s? Often, acting for a reason satisfies these conditions. But it need not. Just as one can see a face in the light of a lamp, without believing that there is lamplight on it, or believing, of this lamp, that it lights the face, one can *A* for a reason, without believing that one has a reason to *A* or believing, of this reason, that it is a reason for which one *A*'s. Moreover, presumably a child can act for a reason before acquiring the concept of a reason, and thus before acquiring beliefs like these, which entail having that concept.

The lighting example can mislead, however. For while *S* need not

---

But suppose *S*'s touching a button causes, days later, a boiler explosion. Then *S*'s exploding the boiler would exhibit *generational extension*. Even if the bodily action at its base—*S*'s performative contribution to exploding the boiler—is instantaneous, her exploding the boiler is—arguably—not completed until the explosion that her bodily action causes. Performative extension is my concern here. I leave open the possibility that generational extension is only a matter of the effects of action.

believe a lamp to bear some relation to an object she sees in the light of it, she must believe some appropriate relation to hold between her reason and any action she performs for it. For instance, S might believe her A-ing to be a means to r. Since a connecting belief may be *de re*, it does not require S's having the concept of a reason, or that of any specific connecting relation, such as causal sufficiency, nor, I think, any concepts beyond the grasp of the least conceptually advanced creatures that can act for a reason. Such relations might be called *conduciveness relations;* for example, if S's reason for opening the door is to wake Jan, S may simply believe her opening the door to be a way to wake Jan. S's connecting belief may also be *de dicto*, say, that opening it is the best way to wake Jan, or that if she opens it she will probably wake Jan, though in these cases S must perhaps also believe, of some appropriate bodily action (like grasping), that *it* is opening the door.[8] As these cases suggest, it may be impossible to specify the connecting belief or motivating want simply by using S's name and the relevant action-description, for example by speaking of Sue's opening the door. For what S wants is often self-referential, say, that *she* open the door; and S need not conceptualize or have beliefs about her goal in terms of either her own name or any particular true description of herself.[9] It is hard to specify S's reason precisely, but no major thesis of this paper turns on how this problem is solved.

Our second requirement, then, is the *connecting belief condition: S A*'s for a reason, r, only if there is some connecting relation, C, such that (i) S believes C to hold between her A-ing and r, or believes something to the effect that C holds between her A-ing and r, and (ii) this belief (or set of beliefs) guides, and partly explains, S's A-ing. Like S's motivating want, a particular connecting belief may not be a

---

[8] For a plausible, less inclusive view of how one must conceive one's reasons, see Stephen L. Darwall, *Impartial Reason* (Ithaca: Cornell University Press, 1983); he says, "What distinguishes the agent's reasons [for acting] . . . is that they are considerations she took to be reasons *for* her *to* have acted, considerations that, in her view, were grounds for a positive rational appraisal of the act" (p. 205). Cf. pp. 206–7. Apparently, then, if S A's for r, she takes r to be a reason for her to A. I prefer a weaker view, but the cases Darwall describes are common and important.

[9] Hector-Neri Castañeda has developed this point. See, e.g., "Philosophical Method and Direct Awareness of the Self," in Ernest Sosa, ed., *Essays on the Philosophy of Roderick M. Chisholm* (Amsterdam: Rodopi, 1979), esp. pp. 29–35. Also relevant is Lynne Rudder Baker, "*De Re* Belief in Action," *Philosophical Review* 19 (1982). For criticism of Castañeda see Steven E. Boër and William Lycan, "Who, Me?" *Philosophical Review* 89 (1980). For a reply by Castañeda, see his "Self-Profile," sec. 4, in James Tomberlin, ed., *Hector-Neri Castañeda* (Dordrecht: Random House, 1985).

necessary condition for *S*'s *A*-ing, but some connecting belief must play an actual part in producing or sustaining the action.

Attribution

The explanatory sustaining condition and the connecting belief condition are not all we need. Consider a variant of the guest example. Suppose that *S*'s wanting to wake Jan, *together with S*'s believing this to be best done by rattling the breakfast tray, makes *S* nervous, and that this nervousness, by making her rush, causes her to rattle the tray unintentionally. Our first two conditions could apparently hold, yet she does not rattle the tray for a reason. One might tackle the problem by requiring that the relevant want and belief produce *A directly*. But consider Ken, an aphasiac accident victim who habitually grunts when he wants food and believes grunting will get the nurse to bring it. Suppose he now takes a deep breath, get ready to grunt, and then unexpectedly grunts at a pitch and loudness that surprise him and in a way that feels involuntary. The grunting might be a "direct" result of the relevant want and belief, yet fail to be action for a reason.

We can understand such cases better by reflecting on how Ken might explain his grunt if his awakened roommate asks why he grunted. Given that Ken realized he grunted unintentionally, he presumably would not think he did it because he wanted to call the nurse, nor anything else suggesting he did it for a reason. To be sure, if he is embarrassed and wants to rationalize doing it, he might cite the reason he *had* to grunt. But a natural answer would be something like "I don't know—I suddenly found myself grunting automatically." Yet when one *A*'s for a reason, one quite naturally cites the reason if asked why one *A*-ed. Indeed, the reason tends to occur to one without inference or observation, and so readily that even if one disapproves of it, self-deception or repression may be needed to block one's becoming conscious of it when asked why one *A*-ed. We have at least this much privileged access to the reasons for which we act. In acting for a reason one normally has a sense of one's agency; this sense, in turn, tends to give one knowledge or potential knowledge of the action (or of one's attempt at it) as casually grounded in the motivating want and the connecting belief(s). The beliefs constituting such knowledge are among the characteristic marks of acting for a reason. Ken lacks both the sense of agency and beliefs of this sort.

In the light of these points, one might think that in acting for a reason S *must* have a sense of acting in response to it, and that we should adopt some such phenomenal condition. Perhaps we should. There is surely some way one's A-ing for a reason is cognitively reflected. But suppose one A's for a reason with one's mind wholly on something else. On a walk one may be buried in thought, yet wave at a passing friend in order to greet him. It is not clear that one need have a sense of agency in so waving. I suggest a related thesis weaker than but consistent with the phenomenal condition: that if S A's for a reason, then, quite *independently* of seeking reasons she had or might have had for A-ing, she is disposed, *non-inferentially*, to attribute her A-ing to the motivating want and connecting belief(s). This disposition *may* be based on a sense of agency; it certainly seems rooted partly in the way A-ing for a reason is *belief-guided*. Indeed, it might be a kind of impression made by the action even is S lacked a sense of agency, as in absent-mindedly waving. That sense and this disposition could both be due to the same elements underlying the action, that is, to processes involved in its generation by the motivating want and connecting belief. By contrast, if Ken has any disposition to attribute his grunting to the reason he had for it, it is *derivative*; it depends on his seeking a reason (say, to rationalize his odd behavior). Nor does his attribution seem non-inferential: he very likely infers that his wanting food must have produced the grunt "by itself."

The sort of disposition in question is often not manifested, particularly in behavior; only at certain times do we tend, for example, to explain our actions. But the disposition is especially likely to be manifested should S try to explain or to justify her A-ing. This is indeed part of the force of the idea that action for a reason is a realization of a practical argument: since the explaining want and belief—of whose causal efficacy S normally has a sense—correspond to the premises of the argument, it is natural that S be disposed (in effect) to invoke the argument if she tries to explain or to justify her A-ing. If, however, an action for a reason arises, as I assume it may, from wants or beliefs that are in some sense unconscious, the disposition may be *inhibited*, perhaps by whatever keeps S from being conscious that she has those wants or beliefs. But apart from, say, self-deception or repression, we expect people who are acting for a reason to be able to tell, non-inferentially and very reliably—though by no means infallibly—for what reason they are acting.

To capture some of what has emerged I propose an *attribution condition*: if *S A*'s for a reason, *r*, then, independently of seeking reasons she had or might have had for *A*-ing, she is non-inferentially disposed to attribute her *A*-ing to her wanting to *r* and her believing some connecting relation to hold between her *A*-ing and *r*. (Connecting beliefs may also be *de dicto*, and the disposition normally persists after *S A*'s; but we may ignore these complications.) This disposition can be manifested not only in overt behavior, for example speech or writing, but also in thinking or even belief. If one has the thought that one *A*-ed because one wanted revenge, this may suffice for attribution of the action to that want. Suppose, however, one is acting routinely and simply forms the belief that one *A*-ed for revenge. I take such belief formation to be a minimal case of attribution, though I do not consider it (or belief) something one does. We do say things like, "If you believe that, you are attributing ignoble motives to him." Either attribution need not be behavior, or believing is sometimes sufficiently behavioral to count as attribution.

We might call the kind of attribution just illustrated *causal,* since *S* conceives the want for revenge as causing her action. Similarly, attribution may be *explanatory.* Our case might also illustrate that; for *S* might take her wanting revenge to explain her *A*-ing (though one could regard a want or belief as causative but not consider it explanatory, or vice versa). There are at least two other kinds of attribution. Suppose Tom is removing labels. We ask why. "I'm recycling envelopes." Call this kind of attribution *redescriptive,* since he attributes his action to his (connecting) belief that he is recycling, and implicitly to his wanting to recycle. He also explains both what he is doing and why (though redescription is possible without explanation, and explaining action is possible without redescription). Since I assume that attribution may be manifested in beliefs, and that knowing entails believing, I regard the attribution disposition as manifested in the (extremely common) case of *knowing what one is doing,* understood to imply believing (or at least taking) one's action to be, as in Tom's case, a realization of (or contribution toward) one's goal. The attribution here may be redescriptive; but we should not assume that a linguistic description must figure in attributive beliefs. We might thus call such attribution *cognitive.*

Cognitive attribution is conceptually elementary enough to occur in tiny children. Imagine Amy, who has just learned to talk, stretching toward a cookie and saying, "Want cookie!" In the context, she expresses her wanting the cookie and her believing that (for example) reaching for it will get it. Moreover, she in some sense *sees* her stretching as getting (or trying to get) it. If so, she may be viewed as manifesting a disposition to attribute the action, cognitively, to the relevant belief and want. This disposition does *not* entail a further disposition to explain or justify the action in terms of them. (She might only partially grasp the concepts of wanting and believing.) To be sure, since the attribution may be *de re*, even if it is causal she need only to be taken to attribute, to the want and belief on one side, and to the stretching, on the other, an appropriate relation, such as making happen. I leave open whether she may be so described. I suggest only that she may believe her stretching to have a property—say, getting the cookie—appropriate to connect it with her guiding belief and motivating want. Perhaps even prelingual children and some animals may have such beliefs. I see no need to deny that. If they may, then they can act for reasons in the sense of our account. Some philosophers are inclined to say that for prelingual children and animals, talk of acting for reasons is metaphoric: while they may *have* reasons for acting—given suitable wants and beliefs—and while there surely are reasons, perhaps including wants and beliefs, *why* they act, they do not full-bloodedly act for reasons. Other philosophers think it obvious that such creatures act for reasons. I suspect these cases are borderline; if they are, it is appropriate that the account does not decisively include or exclude them. Moreover, any account of acting for a reason will encounter borderline cases at *some* point on the evolutionary ladder, and it may be a merit of the proposed account that borderline cases arise for it where reflective intuitions differ, and that the materials of which it is built—for example the different sorts of reasons sketched in Section I—may be so arrayed that they are progressively acquired in the development of an agent. Perhaps the development of human agents mirrors the evolution from mentally lower to higher creatures, and any account that does justice to acting for a reason as applied to normal adults will encounter hard cases as we go back into infant and animal behavior.

Preliminary Account

The three conditions so far proposed account for most of the eight points set out in Section I. If *S*'s putting the invitation aside satisfies the explanatory, connecting belief, and attribution conditions, then clearly her doing so is explainable by appeal to her reason, she has an appropriate belief connecting her reason with her action, and she is non-inferentially disposed to attribute her action to her connecting belief and motivating want. Moreover, her action is a *response* to her reason. Not only does she act because of the corresponding want and the connecting belief; her putting the invitation aside is also sustained by them: if, for example, she ceased to have them, then (if she has no other reason for the action), she would stop putting it aside. The action is, then, subject to alterability due to change of reason. So much for points (1)–(4).

The three proposed conditions also accommodate (5)–(7). First, if S satisfies them, then typically she has an awareness both of the reason for which she is acting (delaying the invitation) and of acting in response to it (strictly, to the want expressing the reason). That awareness, in turn, indicates both why it is natural to explain one's action by redescribing it in terms of the reason for which one is act-ing, and why agents have a special authority regarding what they are doing. Secondly, the conditions enable us to see why, in typical cases of acting for a reason, S knows she is doing (or at least that she is trying to do) the thing in question. Thirdly, they suggest why, at least normally, an action for a reason is prima facie rational relative to S's motivating want and connecting belief(s). It in some sense serves her (motivating) reason: her *A*-ing is aimed at realizing a want (purpose, goal, etc.) of hers. S may overlook a conflicting want more important to her, but her *A*-ing may still be prima facie rational.

The three conditions can also deal with a number of problematic examples introduced in the literature, for example by Chisholm, Goldman, and Davidson.[10] In Chisholm's case, a nephew accidentally runs over his uncle as an indirect result of nervousness produced by the motivating want (to inherit a fortune) and connecting belief (that by killing his uncle he would inherit it). The want and belief may not even sustain the action, since the nervousness has its own momen-tum; but clearly the agent has no sense of acting for a reason and is not non-inferentially disposed to attribute the action to them. Gold-

[10] See Roderick M. Chisholm, "Freedom in Action," in Keith Lehrer, ed., *Freedom and Determinism* (New York: Random House, 1966), pp. 19–20; Alvin I. Goldman, *A Theory of Human Action* (Englewood Cliffs, N.J.: Prentice-Hall, 1970), p. 54; and Donald Davidson, "Freedom to Act," in Ted Honderich, ed., *Essays on Freedom of Action* (London: Routledge and Kegan Paul, 1973). For critical discussion of these cases as challenges to a causal account of action, see Irving Thalberg, "Do Our Intentions Cause Intentional Actions?" *American Philosophical Quarterly* 21 (1984).

man's agent wants to offend his host and believes that grimacing, upon tasting the soup, will do it; but he grimaces unintentionally because, as a result of (discovering) his want and belief, a friend befouls his soup. Here the want and belief do not sustain the grimace; and given the way it is involuntary and unexpected, he would doubtless be disposed to attribute it to something strange in the soup, not to his own motivation. Davidson's case of a climber whose want and belief unnerve him so that he loosens his hold on a dangling companion is similar to Chisholm's: it turns on an intermediary with its own momentum, and it does not satisfy all of our first three conditions.

So far, then, our conditions account for many important points about acting for a reason and show why so acting is not simply behavior caused by appropriate wants and beliefs. The conception embodied in the conditions is roughly this: an action for a reason is a discriminative response to that reason, performed in the light of it, and such that one is non-inferentially disposed to attribute it to that reason. Let me elaborate. Because an action for a reason is grounded in a guiding belief and a motivating want (normally one stronger than competitors—else one would not normally act on it), it expresses both one's intellect and one's will. This is in part why it is a response and not a mere effect. Because an action for a reason is performed in the light of a reason, it tends to change with alterations in that light: if one ceases to have the reason, one tends to cease doing the thing which expresses it; and if one senses that one is not acting in accord with one's guiding belief, one tends to make corrective adjustments, for example pressuring the saw to the right to get a square cut. Action for a reason thus expresses one's present make-up, not merely one's motivational history. And because we are disposed as we are to attribute our actions for a reason to that very reason, we tend to know non-inferentially what we are about: our sense of agency is not just a consciousness of movement, but a (normally automatic) cognitive grasp of the direction—at least the psychological direction—of our behavior. This is partly why, as agents, we are not merely well-placed spectators of our own actions. The attribution condition helps to capture this cognitive grasp that we tend to have of our own agency: without the self-knowledge it provides for, we would be cut off from what we do; it could, to be sure, be rather like acting for a reason, but if there is no such non-inferential disposition at all, as opposed to one that is overridden by self-deception or undermined by error, then the behavior falls short of acting for a reason. It might be a patterned result of our reasons, but not fully action for a reason.

Accidentality

We must now explore how an action for a reason is controlled. We might begin with an idea that emerged in discussing attribution: normally, if S A's for r, then either she knows she A-ed for r, or at least is in a position to know this by virtue of her sense of her own agency. S *need* not know why she A-ed; she might have another reason for A-ing which, while she hopes not to be influenced by it, may still have motivated her. S may also not know she *is* A-ing, as where she calls a warning to distant swimmers, but cannot tell if they hear her. Even then, however, she knows for what reason she is calling out, and for what reason she is warning them *if* she is.

Consider, by contrast, a case where, unbeknownst to S, her right arm has become paralyzed. She might still want to greet Jan and believe that waving is the way to do so. Now imagine that there happens to be a brain-affecting machine nearby so adjusted that her want and belief cause it to emit rare radiations; these just happen to affect her brain in the right way to overcome the paralysis, so that (indirectly) the want and belief produce her waving, after which the paralysis recurs. Imagine that the machine also induces in her a non-inferential disposition to attribute the waving to the want and belief that caused it. Has she waved for a reason—to greet Jan? There is much to be said. Even assuming that the attribution condition can be satisfied in this way, the accidental genesis of the waving prevents S from knowing that she waved in order to greet her friend. For it is simply a lucky accident that the relevant want and belief (through the machine) produced the action; and if she believed that she waved *because* of them (taking the connection between them and her action to be normal), she would be mistaken, and her attribution of her action to the reason would not yield knowledge. We should also consider the observer's viewpoint: whereas we can normally know certain things about S's motivation from her behavior, here our likely inference would not yield knowledge, but only justified (accidentally) true belief. The action is not an *expression* of her reason for it. That, in turn, helps to differentiate this case from acting for one of two competing reasons, say, one selfish and one unselfish, yet not knowing which is responsible for the action: there the connection between the explaining reason and the action is not accidental and the action *is* an expression of that reason.

If an action for a reason cannot be one produced by the reason (state) accidentally, how should we conceive non-accidentality? May we say that the relevant want and belief(s) *reliably* produce the action? Consider an analogy. Suppose that, from a distance, Ann sees Joe in a shop window and believes him to be a man. Imagine that the figures usually in such windows are manikins. Being myopic, Ann would have taken one to be a man if she saw it instead. Her vision is unreliable, and even if she justifiably believes Joe to be a man, she does not know him to be one.[11] Compare the greeting: S would have believed she waved because she wanted to greet her friend, even if her wanting to do so had not activated the machine and thereby her arm, but instead the machine had similarly raised her arm by itself. Observers, moreover, would form the same beliefs about her motivation whether it was efficacious or not. Such facts suggest that if S A's for a reason, the reason produces the action reliably: otherwise, neither S nor observers can know what they normally can about her motivation or belief. The action is a mere product, not an expression, of her reason.

Compare this case, however, with one in which Tom sinks a putt, yet, being a very poor golfer, succeeds only by great luck. Has he sunk it for a reason, say, to win? We are pulled in two directions. If we conceive sinking the putt as the same action—under another description—as hitting the ball, we tend to say yes, since clearly he hits the ball for a reason. If we conceptually isolate his sinking the putt and view it as a different action that he can bring off only by lucky accident, we tend to say that it is not for a reason. Notice, moreover, that if Tom is so inept that he is lucky even to hit the ball, we are much less inclined to say he sank the putt for a reason. For though there is something causally significant he does for a reason, namely, swinging *at* the ball, we do not view his sinking the putt *as* this (wild) swinging, under another description, for example 'hitting it'.

Let us explore reliability and accident through another case, Russian Roulette. Zed puts one bullet in a nine-chambered revolver, spins the magazine, and, hoping to kill himself, fires. If he shoots himself,

<hr />

[11] For discussion of similar cases see Goldman, "Discrimination and Perceptual Knowledge," *Journal of Philosophy* 73 (1976).

is it for a reason? Again, there are conflicting inclinations; but his shooting himself is plausibly identified with his pulling the trigger, and one is inclined to say that he has shot himself for a reason: to kill himself. Now imagine a firearm with 2,000 chambers. Should we say the same? I think so, for given the actual causal route from the triggering, which is produced by his reason states reliably and in the usual way, to the shooting, the latter may be described *as* triggering; and this description of the shooting anchors it to his reason. By contrast, suppose Tom had missed the ball and hit it on his backswing, whereupon it struck a tree, bounced off a golf cart, and then rolled into the hole. It is doubtful that he sinks it for a reason, if only because it is not clear *what* action for a reason to view as his sinking it. The contrast indicates a further point: the issue is not mainly a matter of the probability with which, given what S clearly does do for a reason, the final outcome will occur, for example the putt's sinking. The probability of the shooting might well be even lower than that of the sinking, without the former's ceasing to be an action for a reason or the latter's becoming one. Low probability does not entail accidentality. Nor does *luck:* if I seek you in a crowd of 50,000, my finding you could be good luck yet non-accidental. Perhaps where S contemplates an action of hers (say searching) as a possible way to achieve something, then, apart from untoward intervention, we tend not to call her succeeding accidental even when her chance is very slim. This case, too, suggests that even if normally an action for a reason has a description under which it is probable, or at least not highly improbable, given S's reason states together with her abilities and circumstances, we cannot specify a cutoff or even a precise range of acceptable probabilities. Whether or not we may say that the relevant connections are reliable, they are at least non-accidental.

One point we can add to clarify the relevant non-accidental connections is that *for* S the causal link between her A-ing and any intermediaries there may be between them and her want to r must not be abnormal, for example run in certain ways outside her body, especially through others' actions. But imagine that, to overcome paralysis, a brain aid is attached to S's head and regularly produces appropriate intermediaries between her wants and beliefs and her actions: here there need be no unreliable connection or inadmissible intermediary, that is, intermediary that prevents S's A-ing from being performed for a reason. The case also shows that an admissible intermediary need never have occurred: S can act for a reason the first time such a device aids her. Once properly installed, it becomes normal *for her*. Compare the effect, on our manikin viewer, of donning corrective glasses. Straightaway, she may know the man she sees to be one. As some of our examples suggest, the concept of acting for a reason is consistent with the existence of various sorts of intermediaries. What it rules out is that a crucial intermediary be only accidentally produced by the relevant want and belief, or only accidentally produce the action.[12]

Accident can intrude at yet another place: in causing the disposition to attribute the action to the motivating want and connecting belief(s). When S A's for a reason, this disposition seems partly due to these same factors. That might explain why S has the disposition independently of seeking reasons she had for A-ing. *Must* the disposition be non-accidentally produced by the relevant wants and beliefs? It seems so produced in paradigm cases of action for a reason, and the sorts of things one imagines accidentally producing the disposition from those wants and beliefs (for example stray radiations) suggest that an action they also produce is not for a reason. I am inclined to think that where S acts for a reason the disposition is non-accidentally produced. In any case, so far as one considers it accidentally produced, one is less inclined to regard the associated action as performed for a reason.

What emerges in this subsection, then, is a *non-accidentality condition: S A's for a reason, r, only if her A-ing is non-accidentally produced by her motivating want and connecting belief(s). Perhaps* non-accidentality of the relevant sort, though a prima facie weaker notion than reliability, is equivalent to reliable generation of the kind that some actions for a reason exhibit. More could certainly be said about accidentality and reliability; but our examples go some way toward

[12] Such examples may suggest that A-ing for a reason is governed by a law to the effect that, given the relevant want, belief, *and* intermediary (say, the functioning of the brain aid) S A's. But suppose Ken's wiggling his ears is hard for him, and he sometimes tries and fails. It might still be an action for a reason when they do produce it. This suggests that the strongest nomic connection plausibly affirmed here is something like this: if S's wanting to r and believing her A-ing to bear a connecting relation C to r bring about her A-ing, via an intermediary, there is a law to the effect that a person in whom a want and belief of these types produce an intermediary of that kind *tends* to A. (This formulation leaves open whether the tendency generalization can be replaced by a universal one, perhaps formulated using quite different concepts.) But there may not even be a tendency (or probabilistic) connection here, unless—as is by no means clear—it is implied by our point that A must have a possible description under which it is non-accidentally connected with reason states.

clarifying the notions and seem to show that, sometimes, where it is doubtful whether *S A*'s for a reason, it is also doubtful, apparently for similar reasons, whether the connection between the relevant want and belief and her *A*-ing is non-accidental, or reliable. We may at least conclude, then, that by clarifying these notions we can better understand acting for a reason.

Intermediaries

The non-accidentality condition brings us closer to explaining the eight points set out in Section I, but we must clarify further how actions for a reason are controlled. One difficulty is wayward causal chains. It is no surprise that such chains plague an account of acting for a reason, since that entails acting intentionally and they are a well-known obstacle to explicating intentional action.[13] Consider again a brain-affecting machine. Imagine that Tom wants to shorten a conversation with Joe and believes that he can do so by looking at his watch. The machine might so affect this want and belief that they produce both his looking at his watch and a non-inferential disposition to attribute his looking at it to them, yet do so just before Tom would have looked at it, so that he now looks at it abruptly. (The timing might surprise him without eliminating his disposition to attribute his action to this belief and want.) Imagine, too, that the machine regularly accompanies his doings, that its timing usually coincides with his, and that it systematically takes account of his wants and beliefs so as to produce his action from them non-accidentally. Has he looked at his watch for a reason? This is not quite clear. That *may* indicate that our first four conditions come close to providing an account of acting for a reason. Perhaps the machine only affects *when* Tom acts for a reason, and one can *A* for a reason even if the timing

---

[13] Davidson suggests, in "Freedom to Act," that philosophical reflection cannot solve the problem of wayward chains. Tuomela and Armstrong have proposed at least partial solutions. See esp. Raimo Tuomela, *Human Action and Its Explanation* (Dordrecht: Reidel, 1977), esp. pp. 256–58; and D. M. Armstrong, "Acting and Trying," in his *The Nature of the Mind* (Ithaca and London: Cornell University Press, 1981). In "Tuomela on the Explanation of Action," *Synthese* 44 (1980), I have assessed Tuomela's proposal (making some points applicable to Armstrong's as well). For criticism of Armstrong's view, see Harry G. Frankfurt, "The Problem of Action," *American Philosophical Quarterly* 15 (1978). For valuable recent discussions, see Myles Brand, *Intending and Acting* (Cambridge: MIT Press, 1984), esp. chap. 1; Christopher Peacocke, *Holistic Explanation* (Oxford: Clarendon Press, 1979); and Michael J. Zimmerman, *An Essay on Human Action* (New York: Peter Lang, 1984), esp. chap. 6.

of one's doing so is not based on that reason, or on any reason. It is not obvious, then, that cases like this undercut the first four conditions.

If, however, the proposed conditions do rule out wayward chains, more should be said about one's control over what one does for a reason. Perhaps the appropriate connection between reason and action may be undermined by intermediaries *apart from* the circuitous patterns we naturally call wayward chains (though we may simply use 'wayward' to mean 'of a kind incompatible with acting for a reason'). Suppose we alter our last example so that Tom's wanting to shorten his conversation and believing his looking at his watch would do this had caused Ann, who likes to think she is making people do things they would do anyway, to use the machine to cause him to look at his watch in just the way he intends and at the appropriate time. The action would then seem normal to him. But this is not mere overdetermination, as where one *A*'s for two reasons but would have *A*-ed for either alone. Ann uninvitedly exercises agency parallel to Tom's and in a way that seems to undermine his: he did what he wanted, but only *through* her action, and by a kind of short circuit. A guiding idea here is that actions one performs for a reason are *one's own*. From that point of view, Ann is a preemptive or at least diluting influence. It is not entirely clear that the dilution is sufficient to make her an *alien* intermediary: one that prevents *S*'s *A*-ing from being for a reason. If it is sufficient, then our four conditions may not rule out enough.

It is quite otherwise when someone is one's *instrument*, as where *S* uses Tom, on whom Ken is falling, as a means to support Ken. But there are intermediate cases. Recall *S*'s temporary inability to raise her arm, and suppose that Ron turns on a machine which counteracts the inability, so that *S* then raises the arm normally in order to greet Jan. Ron is not *S*'s instrument for *A*-ing, yet Ron's intervention seems friendly. Ron removes an obstacle; he *enables S* to *A*, but does not cause her *A*'ing. The distinction is difficult to explicate, and I shall not elaborate. But we may at least say that if the relevant want and belief bring about *S*'s *A*-ing via another agent's producing, rather than simply enabling, her *A*-ing, then *S* does not *A* for a reason. We have, then, one rough sufficient condition for an alien intermediary.

Another sufficient condition may be implicit in the idea that an action for a reason is *voluntary*, in the sense that, unlike reflex behavior, it is under the control of one's motivational system. Even compelled action may be voluntary in this sense. Acting for a reason seems possible only if S can have opposing reasons that pull her in another direction. The notion of acting for a reason is, I suggest, *contrastive*. This is not to say (what is surely false) that S must have chosen A-ing from among alternatives. On one interpretation, the idea is that S's A-ing is under the control of her *will* and is thus *reversible*. Let me illustrate. Imagine a drug that acts like a motivational step-up transformer: it is so affected by the want and belief that produce S's A-ing that it strengthens her tendency to A, for example raises her resistance to dissuasion. It does not, however, do so independently of the reason states: its operation is sustained by them, though it increases their power. Now suppose the increase is so great that even if S had had an opposing want as strong as she is capable of, say to avoid causing nuclear war, she would still have A-ed.[14] Then her action is somewhat like a runaway car which, though one's foot is stuck on the accelerator, punctually stops where one wants it to go. The action seems not to be controlled by S's motivational system, and hence not appropriately under *her* control. This idea may partly underlie the inclination to connect the voluntariness exhibited by action for a reason with freedom, and thus to consider any action for a reason free to *some* extent: degrees of freedom are largely a matter of what sorts of reasons would have led S to do otherwise, and actions reversible by *any* opposing reasons are not wholly unfree. Threat of death, for example, normally reduces freedom drastically; yet one might prefer death to lying, and hence even acting to save one's life may be believed not wholly unfree. (One is reminded of Aristotle's idea, in *Nicomachean Ethics* 1110a, regarding an agent compelled to jettison cargo: "[W]hen the origin of the actions is in him, it is also up to him whether to do them or not to do them.") On this view, then, acting for a reason implis that minimal degree of freedom possessed by voluntary actions, conceived as those reversible by opposing reasons.

Arguably, then, action for a reason must be voluntary in a sense

[14] It is not clear that the notion of maximal motivational strength applies to persons. Even if S could not want any one thing more than, say, to avoid causing nuclear war, surely she could acquire a belief linking that to something else she wants to avoid, for example breaking a promise. Could she not then want to avoid the conjunction of these more than to avoid causing nuclear war by itself? How could the aversive conjunct add no motivation? In any case, the sense that motivation can always be greater as S acquires further reasons is part of what makes the reversibility condition plausible: if she A's for reasons, she might have abstained given sufficient counterreasons.

implying that the causal power of an intermediary may not exceed the causal power of S's motivational system: roughly, that if S would have done it no matter what else she wanted, she did not do it in order to get what she wanted. But does voluntariness require reversibility? Imagine that A-ing is something S deeply believes in, for example preventing nuclear war, and S would be *glad* to be compelled to do this if that would help her to A. If she then irreversibly A's because the transformer intervenes on the side of this deepest of all her desires, might she not do so for the relevant reason? This is perhaps not a clear case of acting for a reason, but it seems more like acting for a reason with a vengeance than like merely acting because of one.

There is, however, another way to view the contrastive aspect of acting for a reason. Suppose that instead of focusing on reversibility, we ask whether opposing reasons can reduce the strength of S's tendency to A. Assuming that S wants more than anything to avoid causing nuclear war, would her tendency to act accordingly be reduced by her opposing reasons, such as its vanquishing the wicked? Imagine an intermediary that, while sustained by the relevant want and belief, *isolates* her reason for A-ing from the influence of opposing reasons so that they do not reduce *at all* her tendency to A. If S now acts because of the want to avoid causing nuclear war, her action is disconnected from opposing reasons, no longer seems suitably under her control, and is quite arguably not performed for a reason. On this view, voluntariness requires *integration* into one's motivational system, and thus susceptibility to counterinfluence.

Let us explore the relevant kind of voluntariness further. Perhaps if an action is performed *for* a reason, it must be under the control *of* reason, in the sense that it is appropriately responsive to the agent's reasons. This might explain why an action for a reason must at least normally be reversible should S develop a counterreason with motivational strength as great as is within her capacity. But the reversibility and integration views of voluntariness differ importantly in where they locate the contrastiveness of acting for a reason: on the former, action for a reason implies the possibility of *alternative action;* on the latter, it implies the possible influence of *alternative reasons*. The first view, we might say, emphasizes being under the control of the will, the second, being under the control of reason. Thus, the reversibility view makes a kind of *freedom*, however unlikely its exercise, necessary for acting for a reason. The integration view makes a kind of *autonomy* necessary: if, in virtue of one's reasons—for example by bringing information about the bad effects of A-ing to bear to produce opposing motivation—one cannot even influence the motivation on which one acts, one's capacity to govern one's conduct is undermined, and one cannot act for a reason. One is reduced to a spectator: one can experience one's reason states' causing one's A-ing, but cannot bring reasons to bear in self-direction. Integration is the better candidate for a necessary condition on acting for a reason. If the strongest opposing reasons which S can have would not even weaken her tendency to A, then A-ing is presumably not under the control of her reason, nor appropriately integrated into her motivational system. In any event, autonomy and freedom must be distinguished; and when they are, it may turn out that the inclination to think that freedom persists to the point of irreversibility is based on the perception that a measure of autonomy, in the form of a capacity to marshal a degree of resistance to compulsion, can survive even when irreversibility is reached.

A second sufficient condition for an alien intermediary, then, is undermining the kind of voluntariness characteristic of acting for a reason. But does motivational integration (or even reversibility) belong to the concept of such voluntariness, and in a philosophical account of acting for a reason, or have we been just articulating psychologically important truths? Surely this distinction, if ultimately real, is not sharp. Perhaps acting for a reason should not be taken to include only actions subject to the influence of opposing reasons. But if not, such integration surely is implicit in a concept of acting for a reason very close to the non-technical one we are explicating.

There is a further aspect of control of one's actions for reasons. Normally, we control, within limits, not only *what* we do, but the *way* we do it.[15] We do not merely wave; we do it with a certain style, speed, and accent. Now suppose an intermediary causes S to wave with her elbow, and she is astonished. Actions for reasons typically occur against the background of one's beliefs about how one will (or can) act. An action that deviates enough from these is probably not under one's control. But how should we regard such deviations? Must A be carried out in a way S intends, or at least expects, to carry it

---

[15] I assume here that A-ing in a particular way is not performing a different action, B; but if that is false my point could be re-expressed.

out?[16] One might think so. When *S* waves with her elbow, she will
tend to answer in the negative "Did you intend or expect to wave
that way?" We must not infer, however, that *S* intended or expected
to wave in a particular way, as where she means to flap her handker-
chief. For her *not* intending or expecting to wave as she did does not
imply her *having* an intention or expectation to wave in any specific,
other way.

The parallel point holds for beliefs: even if, before waving, *S* would
have assented to, for example, "Do you believe you will wave in the
usual way?" it does not follow that she believed she would (or intended to) do so, *before* being asked.[17] Moreover, supposing she did
have the postulated intentions and beliefs before waving, there are
problems for this approach. First, these intentions and beliefs could
be waywardly caused (say, by accidental influences from outer space).
Must a waywardly caused intention to wave with fingers together
prevent *S*'s normal spread-fingered wave from being an action for
a reason? That seems doubtful. Second, even where the postulated
intentions are normal, the action need not match them to be performed for a reason. *S* may pleasantly surprise herself by the elegant
way she recites a line of poetry she had intended simply to read
unerringly. The elegant recitation may still be an action for a reason
(even if its elegance is not due to a reason). Perhaps some way in
which an action for a reason is carried out must be intended, but not
every significant way need be intended, or even expected. Acting for
a reason occurs in a (usually rich) field of expectations, purposes,
and habits; but the extent to which it must follow a preexisting plan
or pattern—if indeed every action for a reason must follow such a
plan or pattern—should not be exaggerated. The *control model* we are
developing seems to give a better account of these points than the
preconception model which, in one form, we are criticizing as too narrow. Creativity can come not only in what we do for reasons, but in
the sometimes surprising ways we do it.

Even though the control appropriate to *S*'s *A*-ing for a reason does
not entail *S*'s intending the specific ways in which she *A*'s, perhaps

[16] This is suggested by Goldman in *A Theory of Human Action*, e.g., on p. 59, where
he cites Chisholm as holding a similar view. A view of this sort is also suggested by
Tuomela, "Human Action and Its Explanation," pp. 256f. Cf. John R. Searle, *Intentionality* (Cambridge: Cambridge University Press, 1983), esp. chap. 3.

[17] I have argued for this in my paper "Tuomela on the Explanation of Action," pp.
301–2. Related supporting arguments are given in my "Believing and Affirming," *Mind*
91 (1982).

the manner of her *A*-ing must still have *some* correspondence with her intentions, beliefs, habits, or the like. But when might a departure from such elements warrant calling an intermediary that causes that departure alien? It is very difficult to capture the sense of 'control' appropriate to the *way* one acts for a reason. Perhaps we can extend the idea that an action for a reason is a belief-guided response to it. It may be that if *S A*'s for a reason, the way *S A*'s, for instance saws, is *alterable* by her (at least up to a certain time) should she try to alter it—and thus has a kind of reversibility of manner. It is partly this kind of control that we miss in some standard cases of waywardly caused behavior. But there may be exceptions. After an accident, *S* might be able to move her hand in only one direction, for just one distance, and at just one speed. Even here, however, there would be a measure of integration: opposing reasons could weaken her tendency to move it in the relevant way.

We have now noted a number of necessary conditions for *S*'s controlling the way she *A*'s. An intermediary that undermines one of these is plausibly called alien. Notice that what is crucial is *S*'s *exercising control*. Ann, with her brain machine, might *have control* over what *S* does: yet if Ann does not exercise supplantive control, we have at most a potential threat, not actual compulsion. May we now conclude, then, that an intermediary is alien if and only if it undermines *S*'s appropriately controlling either her *A*-ing or the way she *A*'s, that is, roughly, if *and* only if it (i) renders accidental the connection between the explaining want and belief(s) and the action; (ii) embodies supplantive action by another agent; (iii) undermines the voluntariness of *S*'s *A*-ing; or (iv) produces a way of *A*-ing that *S* cannot suitably alter? This condition, taken with the four proposed above, seems to deal with both problematic intermediaries discussed in the literature and the examples used in this subsection. But the notion of an alien intermediary is elusive; (i)–(iv) provide a good sense of the notion, but they may not be strictly necessary and sufficient conditions.

To rule out alien intermediaries, then, I propose a *normal intermediaries condition*: *S A*'s for a reason only if her motivating want and connecting belief(s) do not bring about or sustain her *A*-ing, via an alien intermediary, understood as just sketched. If (as I am inclined to think) voluntariness requires the integration of the explaining reason into *S*'s motivational system, then we must construe alien intermediaries as including factors that *precede* formation of, or are somehow embodied in, the motivating want, and affect it so as to destroy integration. These might be considered intermediaries by virtue of intervening between *S*'s motivational history and the want motivating *A* or *A* itself. Even with these qualifications, borderline cases persist. But those remaining seem to be just the sort one would expect given the points at which the notion of acting for a reason is itself vague.

If an action for a reason is conceived as proposed above, our account, with temporal variables added (and '*S*' representing any agent), would be this:

> I. *S*'s *A*-ing is an action for a reason, *r*, at *t*, if and only if, at *t*, *S A*'s, and there is a connecting relation, *C*, such that (1) *S* wants to *r* and believes *C* to hold between her *A*-ing and *r*, or believes something to the effect that *C* holds between her *A*-ing and *r*; (2) *S*'s *A*-ing is at least in part explained by this motivating want and at least one connecting belief, and is guided by the belief(s); (3) *S* is non-inferentially disposed, independently of seeking reasons she has had, or might have had, at or before *t*, for *A*-ing, to attribute her *A*-ing to the want and (explaining) belief(s); (4) *S*'s *A*-ing is non-accidentally produced by the want and (explaining) belief(s); and (5) the want and (explaining) belief(s) do not bring about (or sustain) *S*'s *A*-ing via an alien intermediary.

Condition (1) expresses a reason *S has* to *A*, (2) a (guiding) reason *why* she *A*'s, and (3)–(5) a reason *for which S A*'s. One further point in order before we proceed is that while the account may seem to use the notion being explicated, it does not. It refers to reasons *S* had; but the kind of reason being explicated is one *for which S* acts, and this is not presupposed in explaining the conditions. Above all, (3) is explicated not by appeal to the notion of attributing an action to a reason for which it is performed, but in terms of attributing one's *A*-ing to the relevant reason *states*, and none of the kinds of attribution distinguished presupposes the concept of acting for a reason.

III. Non-Basic Action, Multiple Reasons, and Partial Explainers

So far, we have invoked no distinction between basic and non-basic actions. Consider an example. Suppose Joe shoots wildly in the air and the bullet, which would normally miss Tom by 5,000 meters, is deflected by an airplane propeller so that it strikes his head and kills him. Does Joe kill Tom? *If* he does, it is doubtful that he does so for a reason, even if he shot because, in anger, he wanted to kill him and impulsively believed that somehow shooting in the air might do it. For one thing, the reason states seem to cause the death accidentally. At best Joe kills Tom *by* bouncing the bullet at him. But that is not an action for a reason either. There is a plausible principle here: if *S* *A*'s for a reason, then either (i) *A*-ing is basic—roughly, it is not performed *by* performing any other action—and has its status as being for a reason directly, that is, other than through an action by (or in) which it is performed, or (ii) it *inherits* this status from a basic action *by* (or in) which *S* performs it. The distinction between basic and non-basic action (tokens) is controversial and need not be presupposed. We can put much the same point in terms of descriptions (or properties): if *S*'s *A*-ing is, under that description, performed for a reason, then either it has the status of being for a reason directly, that is, simply as an *A*-ing, or it derives that status from fitting some description '*B*-ing', and thus is an *A*-ing because it is a *B*-ing.

Perhaps we may generalize: if *A* is a non-basic action for a reason, then no intervening agent not appropriately under *S*'s control brings about the essential constituent in *A*, here, the victim's death. With von Wright, let us call this the (entailed) result of the action.[18] For moving a hand, it is the hand's moving; for pulling a trigger, the trigger's moving back; and so on. Now if the propeller is an intervening agent, it is plainly not under Joe's control. For one thing, the connection between his shooting and Tom's death is accidental. But consider a different case. Suppose *S* delivers a gift to Ken through her son. It may be delivered for a reason even though her son brings about the result: Ken's receiving it from her. But now imagine that the boy is rebellious and throws the gift in a trash can, unaware that the can belongs to Ken's mother. If Ken now gets the gift, it would be wrong to say that *S* delivered it. Granted, he received it, but not *from her.* Not only does she lack appropriate control of the boy; her reasons only accidentally lead to Ken's receiving it.

We can further clarify the relevant kind of control by another contrast. In the first case, the boy is *S*'s *means* of delivering the gift. In

---

[18] See G. H. von Wright, *Explanation and Understanding* (Ithaca: Cornell University Press, 1971), pp. 66–67, 75, and 88.

the second, S fails to deliver it by means of her son. Similarly, it seems wrong to say, in the shooting case, that Joe kills Tom by means of bouncing the bullet off an airplane propeller (at least where Joe is not even hoping to do so in that way). Doing one thing by means of another is closely associated with having or exercising appropriate control over an intermediary. Perhaps exercising this kind of control is typically a matter of being so related to the intermediary that one A's by means of it, or, at least, it is the (or a) means by which one A's. Typically, where S has no control of an intermediary agent or event, then even if it helps her A, it is not a means by which she A's; and if it is a means by which she A's, then even if she does not intentionally use it she typically has some control over it. Moreover, where we doubt whether one of these notions applies to an intermediary, we often doubt whether the other does, and whether the relevant action is performed for a reason.

If we presuppose the distinction between basic and non-basic actions, non-basically acting for a reason may be construed as follows:

> II. *S A's* non-basically, for a reason, at *t*, if and only if, at *t*, there is some action *B* such that (1) *B* is basic and is an action for a reason in the sense specified in I; (2) *S A's* by (or in) *B*-ing; (3) *A* satisfies the first four conditions of I; and (4) if *S's B*-ing generates her *A*-ing via an intermediary that causes the result of *A*-ing, then (i) *S* appropriately controls any such intermediary, and (ii) *S's B*-ing *also* causes, or is a cause of, this result.[19]

An action *for* a reason must be suitably under the control *of* reason; and when its status as an action for a reason is derivative, whether owing to transmission across the by-relation or to its fitting certain descriptions, that control must be preserved. We have seen how the notion of a means can help to clarify (i). This notion itself needs further study, and both (i) and (ii) need more explication; but some of the points made in Section II indicate various lines of inquiry which may clarify the notion of control.

There are other problems in action theory that can now be clarified. One is how to understand acting for a number of reasons. Another is how to conceive the extent of a reason's influence in producing

---

[19] II does not specify for *what* reason *S A's*. It need not be the same reason for which she *B's*, but what it is can be determined using I. II can be reformulated, moreover, in the terminology of action under a description.

or sustaining an action—a matter of much importance in evaluating people. Let us consider these problems.

We have not so far captured the idea of acting (wholly) for a single reason, only that of acting for at least one. But surely to act for one reason is to have just one reason with the properties specified in I. What we must add is an *explanatory uniqueness condition:* if S has any other reason, r_1, for A-ing, then the previous conditions do not hold with r_1 in place of r. Hence her A-ing cannot be (correctly) explained as performed in order to r_1. But where S acts for two or more reasons, an in-order-to explanation can cite any of them, though it might be misleading to omit any, at least if they are of equal weight.

To capture the notion of acting for multiple reasons, I suggest this:

III. S A's at t for reasons $r_1, r_2, \ldots , r_n,$ if and only if, at t, S A's, and (i) each r_i satisfies (1)–(5) of I, and (ii) for each r_i, her wanting to realize it explains (adequately) why she A's, and explains it in such a way that it would be correct to say that she A-ed, for one thing, in order to realize it (or because, for one thing, she wanted it).

This implies that each motivating want is important in bringing about A-ing; but each is important, since each expresses (unqualifiedly) a reason *for* which S A's. Moreover, while each want, together with the appropriate belief(s), is only *part of what explains* S's A-ing, it is not a merely *partial explainer* of that. For, together with the belief(s), it *adequately* explains it. Indeed, in a sense it fully explains it; for it enables one to understand why S A-ed. Yet the want is only part of what explains the action because other wants *also* adequately explain it.

There are many problems concerning the *importance* of a reason in producing an action. Our account can clarify this notion. First, consider reasons S has for A-ing which *contribute* to producing her A-ing, yet are not main reasons for which she A's. Call these *partially explaining reasons* for which she A's, to contrast them with fully (in the sense of 'adequately') explaining reasons:

IV. A reason r, which S has, at t, for A-ing is a (merely) partially explaining reason for which she A's, at t, if and only if, at t, (i) r satisfies clauses (1), (4), and (5) of I; (ii) the relevant want and belief(s) *contribute* to bringing about S's A-ing; (iii) S has the disposition specified in (3) of I, except that normally she is disposed to attribute her A-ing only in part to the relevant want and belief(s); and (iv) it is not the case that S's A-ing is explainable by appeal to her wanting to r, or that she A's because she wants to r.

A number of partially explaining reasons working *together* can fully explain S's A-ing: each want can partially explain it, and jointly they would adequately explain it. They might even be the only reasons that explain it. This can be so even if no one of them is necessary for A (none could be sufficient, even together with S's beliefs, or it would not be just a partially explaining reason).

Both partially explaining reasons *and* "main" reasons may differ in *motivational influence:* in how much they contribute to producing or sustaining the action. Thus,

> V. Where r_1 and r_2 are reasons for which, at t, S A's, r_1 is more influential than r_2, at t, and relative to S's A-ing, if and only if, at t, S's wanting to r_1, together with the associated connecting belief(s), contributes more to bringing about or sustaining her A-ing than does her wanting to r_2 together with the connecting belief(s) associated with r_2.

The relevant contribution is in some sense causal, and the key idea is giving a more nearly adequate explanation of A-ing, or, for two fully explaining reasons, a more nearly complete explanation. A related "measure" is how much a reason contributes to the strength of S's tendency to A. Such strength is difficult to explicate, but a central element is how hard S would try, say how much work she would do, to overcome obstacles to A-ing. Clearly, then, the strength of S's motivating want(s) is crucial for how much influence her reason(s) have on her A-ing. But beliefs are also important: if S wants r_1 as much as r_2, yet believes A-ing is far more likely to realize r_2 than r_1, then other things equal r_2 gives her both a better reason to A and one that, if she A's, will be more influential in her doing so.

IV. Action for Reasons, Intentionality, and Intrinsic Motivation

How is acting for a reason, conceived as proposed, related to intentional action? Certainly intentional actions that are not intrinsically motivated, that is, are performed in order to realize a *further* end, are actions for a reason. If *S A*'s in order to *r*, say, strolls to get fresh air, where *r* is not equivalent to *A*-ing, *S A*'s for a reason. But suppose realizing *r* is logically equivalent, but not identical, to *A*-ing. Does *S A* for a further end? I shall assume so, at least if *S* does not believe the equivalence holds. If *S* does believe this, the issue may turn on whether she conceives realizing *r* as distinct from *A*-ing.

It is not clear whether intrinsically motivated intentional actions— roughly, actions performed just for their own sake—are actions for a reason.[20] Suppose Tom strolls simply because he feels like strolling. Asked his reason, he might say, "No reason, I just feel like it." However, he might have said, "I just feel like strolling; I'm not avoiding you." Thus, just feeling like it—roughly, wanting it for its own sake— can be offered as a reason. Tom might also have said, "No particular reason, I just want to." Here just wanting to is given as a reason, though not a "particular" one. Perhaps the key contrast is not between intentional actions that are, and those that are not, for a reason, but between those for a *further* reason and those that are intrinsically motivated, for example performed because one wants to. If this is so, then Tom's "No reason" may be a denial of a further reason for strolling. Since further reasons are far more common—and much more often the kind we have in mind in asking someone's reason for an action—there can easily be a point to Tom's saying this even if he is aware of acting for an intrinsic reason.

There is, then, some ground for taking intrinsically motivated intentional actions to be actions for a reason. But what is the connecting belief? *S* surely does not believe her *A*-ing is a *means* of realizing *r*, for example that her strolling is a means of strolling. Perhaps she believes strolling to have some desirable characteristic, such as being enjoyable. This view might explain the 'for' in 'for its own sake': one does want it for something, but not something extrinsic to it. Note, too, that there is a corresponding kind of practical argument: from premises expressing one's wanting to stroll for some intrinsic property of it, and one's believing strolling would have that property, to a conclusion that favors strolling. The connecting belief, despite non-instrumental content, would *function* like an instrumental belief. But

---

[20] This question has received too little attention, considering how often intentional actions have been conceived as actions for reasons. See, e.g., G. E. M. Anscombe, *Intention*, 2d ed. (Ithaca: Cornell University Press, 1963), p. 9; Davidson, "How Is Weakness of the Will Possible?" in Joel Feinberg, ed., *Moral Concepts* (London: Oxford University Press, 1969), esp. p. 110; and Goldman, *A Theory of Human Action*, pp. 76–79.

must there be connecting beliefs for intrinsically motivated actions? If we distinguish strolling intentionally from doing so merely voluntarily, as where one just meanders along, it is arguable that the strolling is intentional only if *guided* by a belief connecting it to a motivating want. Believing the strolling to be enjoyable can guide *S*, even if she does not conceive the action as a *means* to enjoyment. It would seem, in fact, that wanting to stroll for its own sake would cease to sustain strolling unless *S* took the strolling to be, for example, pleasurable.

This problem is important in part because, if intrinsically motivated actions are actions for reasons, then intentional action is equivalent to action for a reason. If it is, our account of acting for a reason should serve as an account of intentional action. I am not quite prepared to affirm the equivalence. But except possibly in cases of intrinsic motivation the account apparently applies as well to intentional action as to action for a reason. Granted, if intrinsically motivated actions are actions for a reason yet do not require a connecting belief, the account must be qualified. It is not clear, however, that the account does not apply to intrinsically motivated actions; and if it does, it applies to all intentional actions. This in itself would be an important result. But it might also lead to an account of action in general. Perhaps (as some philosophers hold) action may be viewed as behavior, in the sense of what one *does*, that is intentional under some description. This is not obvious; but if it is so, we may well be able to understand action in general as behavior which, under some description, is acting for a reason.

We can now better understand the relation of action for a reason and action performed on the basis of practical reasoning. If our account is correct, then apparently an action for a reason need not arise from, or be preceded or accompanied by, practical reasoning. For except on an implausibly weak account of practical reasoning, *S* could *A* for a reason, yet not have engaged in such reasoning about *A*-ing. This point is best seen by distinguishing action for a reason from *reasoned action*. The former does not entail the latter. Reasoned actions, however, are all actions for a reason, and actions based on practical reasoning are all in a sense reasoned. If so, we can clarify the relation between a piece of practical reasoning and an action *based* on it. Minimally, it is an action for one or more reasons that figure in the premises. Thus, given the motivating want and connecting belief(s) expressed in the premises, the account can partially explicate how the action is based on the reasoning. It will be *for* the reason(s) expressed in the major premise.[21] It should be noted that similar points may hold for the relation of actions for a reason to actions arising from *volition*. For instance, an action arising from a volition might be performed for a reason underlying (or in some other way closely associated with) the volition, as where wanting to greet Tom may generate, when S sees him, her volition to raise her arm. Our account allows that at least a great many actions for a reason arise from volition, though it also allows that an action for a reason *need* not stem from a volition conceived as, say, a phenomenal event of trying. However, every action for a reason is such that a volition *could* produce it and S could be aware of the relevant mental event.

An action for a reason is one that is, in a special way, under the control of reason. It is a response to, not a mere effect of, a reason. It is non-accidentally produced or sustained by a motivating want and a connecting belief. It is guided by these, and thereby discriminative; it is explainable by appeal to them, associated with a non-inferential disposition to attribute the action to them, and, in a certain way, voluntary. In the light of this conception, actions for a reason, though they need not arise from a process of practical reasoning, may be viewed as realizations of practical arguments. Actions for a reason are intentional, and the converse holds except possibly for intrinsically motivated actions. Thus, our account of acting for a reason constitutes at least a partial account of intentional action, and it applies unrestrictedly to most of its varieties. The account unifies and, in some cases, explains, many of the distinctive features of action for a reason; it helps us to explicate the sense in which an action may be based on practical reasoning; and it clarifies both acting for multiple reasons and a number of ways in which reasons for which one acts may be more or less important for understanding the action. Some of the concepts we have used to explicate acting for a reason need further clarification, but we have at least laid out what appear to be the major constituents of acting for a reason. If these need further explication, they are nonetheless conceptual materials well worth the effort of scrutiny. They are both intrinsically interesting

---

[21] I have discussed how the major and minor premises are to be construed, and examined a number of relevant works on practical reasoning, in "A Theory of Practical Reasoning," cited in note 3. A full account of an action's being based on practical reasoning must anchor *A*-ing to the reasoning process of S's from which it suitably arises. Only some of the crucial materials for such an account are provided in this essay.

and important for a number of topics in the philosophy of mind. If the account of acting for a reason is at points incomplete, it at least provides a structure within which further inquiry might progress.[22]

[22] This chapter was originally written for presentation at the University of Helsinki, and I am grateful for that occasion and for a National Endowment for the Humanities Fellowship which supported part of my work. For detailed and very helpful comments, I thank William P. Alston, John G. Bennett, Michael Bratman, Hugh J. McCann, and readers for the *Philosophical Review*. I have also benefited from comments by Malcolm Acock, Albert Casullo, David Alan Johnson, John L. Longeway, Alfred R. Mele, Allison Nespor, John Tienson, Mark C. Timmons, Raimo Tuomela, and Michael J. Zimmerman. Earlier versions were given to a number of audiences and in an NEH Summer Seminar which I directed in 1981, and I profited from all of those discussions.

FREEDOM, RESPONSIBILITY, AND THE CAUSATION OF ACTION

Chapter 7

Moral Responsibility, Freedom, and Compulsion

Philosophers have very often held that one can be morally responsible for having done something only if one did it freely.[1] I shall argue that this view is false; but it will be clear that the notion of free action is still quite important for moral philosophy. A great deal has been written on the free will problem; yet until very recently most writers on the problem have been chiefly concerned with the issue of whether determinism, most often vaguely construed as the thesis that every event has a cause, is compatible with the existence of free action. In the English-speaking world, at least, philosophers have increasingly tended to defend the compatibility of de-

---

[1] For instance, A. C. Ewing maintains that "responsibility requires freedom either in the indeterminist sense or at least in the determinist sense" in his *Ethics* (London: English Universities Press; New York: Macmillan, 1953), p. 145. The view that being morally responsible for an action entails (or presupposes) performing it freely is also held by many others: Kant in his *Foundations of the Metaphysics of Morals*, trans. by Lewis White Beck (New York: Macmillan, 1959), p. 80; C. A. Campbell, for example in "Is 'Freewill' a Pseudo-Problem?" *Mind* 60 (1951), reprinted in Bernard Berofsky, ed., *Free Will and Determinism* (New York: Harper and Row, 1966), p. 129; S. I. Benn and R. S. Peters, *The Principles of Political Thought* (London: Allen and Unwin, 1959), pp. 229 and 241; Harry G. Frankfurt, "Freedom of the Will and the Concept of a Person" *Journal of Philosophy* 68 (1971): 19; P. H. Nowell-Smith (see the citation by Maurice Cranston) in *Freedom: A New Analysis* (London: Longmans, Green, 1953), p. 92; and Moritz Schlick, who speaks of freedom as "the presupposition of moral responsibility," in his "When Is a Man Responsible?" from *The Problems of Ethics* (New York: Prentice-Hall, 1939) and reprinted in Berofsky, *Free Will and Determinism*, p. 59. Cf. D. J. O'Connor, *Free Will* (New York: Anchor Books, 1971), p. 30.

terminism and free action. Some of them have accepted a kind of compatibilism on the ground that even if determinism is true, actions are immanently caused by the agent and hence need not be determined ultimately by events beyond the agent's control;[2] other writers have held that even if all events are determined, actions are not mere events and are not caused;[3] and still other writers have argued that actions may be free even though they are events caused by other events.[4] But despite the extensive literature on freedom and determinism, too few writers have tried to construct a detailed account of free action itself.[5]

My principal aim will be to give an account of free action and its relation to moral responsibility. There is a technical use of "free action," but we do sometimes ask whether an agent did a particular thing freely, or (meaning approximately the same thing) of the agent's own free will. These are the main uses of "free" I shall try to explicate. Surprising as it may seem, this task does not require discussion of what it is for the will to be free. One can, as Frankfurt does,[6] make sense of "free will," but this notion is only indirectly connected with that of free action. I shall devote little space to arguing directly that free actions may be "determined." But if my account is correct, it will serve as an indirect argument; for on my account an action's being free entails neither that it is nor that it is not determined.

My first question will be this: if a person *S*—Susan, let us say—is morally responsible for having performed some action, *A*, at a given time, *t*, does it follow that *S A*-ed freely at *t*? I shall then consider the notion of doing something freely, and finally the relation between moral responsibility and free action. I hope to enhance our understanding of freedom as contrasted with compulsion and to show,

[2] See, for example, Roderick M. Chisholm, "Freedom and Action," in Keith Lehrer, ed., *Freedom and Determinism* (New York: Random House, 1966), pp. 11 and 17.

[3] For discussion of this view, see O'Connor, *Free Will*, pp. 99–111. A leading proponent of it is A. I. Melden, *Free Action* (London: Routledge and Kegan Paul, 1961).

[4] For a good statement of this view, see Alvin I. Goldman, *A Theory of Human Action* (Englewood Cliffs, N.J.: Prentice-Hall, 1970), esp. chap. 6. Another vigorous defense of compatibilism is offered by Adolf Grünbaum in "Free Will and the Laws of Human Behavior," *American Philosophical Quarterly* 8 (1971).

[5] Cranston, *Freedom: A New Analysis*; Gerald Dworkin, "Acting Freely," *Noûs* 4 (1970); and Felix E. Oppenheim, *Dimensions of Freedom* (New York: St. Martin's Press, 1961) are among those who have proposed helpful accounts of free action. But none of these accounts seems to me fully satisfactory or adequately detailed.

[6] See Frankfurt, "Freedom of the Will."

through an account of both, how we can defeat certain popular but unwarranted disclaimers of moral responsibility.

I. Moral Responsibility, Free Action, and Avoidability

We should first note some of the important kinds of moral responsibility. When sentences of the form 'S is morally responsible for A-ing' have future reference, they are usually used to attribute to S an obligation to A. Typically such obligations are of the kind Hart calls role responsibilities.[7] Our concern, however, is with cases in which the reference of 'S is morally responsible for A-ing' is past. In these cases, there seems to be both a weak and strong sense of "moral responsibility." The weak and less common sense I shall call the accountability sense.[8] To say that S is morally responsible in this sense for A-ing is to say that it would be appropriate to ask her to give a moral justification of his having A-ed. ("Just remember that you will be morally responsible for what you do about this.") In the stronger sense, which I shall call the liability sense,[9] to say that S is morally responsible for A-ing is to say that she is prima facie liable to moral blame for doing it. It is chiefly, perhaps only, moral responsibility in this sense that is implicit in *holding* someone morally responsible. ("He has every right to hold S morally responsible for having done that.")

There is often, though not always, a further implication, in ascriptions of liability responsibility, that S ought (morally) to be punished, or at least to pay compensation, for A-ing. Perhaps in part because we rarely speak of people as morally responsible for having A-ed unless we think they may be blameworthy for doing it, some philosophers seem to have thought that being morally responsible for an

---

[7] H. L. A. Hart, "Responsibility and Retribution," in Hart's *Punishment and Responsibility* (Oxford: Clarendon Press, 1968), pp. 212–14.

[8] My use of "accountability" differs slightly from Kurt Baier's in his very useful study, "Responsibility and Action," in Myles Brand, ed., *The Nature of Human Action* (Glenview, Ill.: Scott, Foresman, 1970). See esp. pp. 103–8.

[9] My notion of liability responsibility is suggested by, but not equivalent to, Hart's notion of liability responsibility. See Hart, "Responsibility and Retribution," pp. 225–27.

action entails being blameworthy for it.[10] But this is surely a mistake. One may be morally responsible, without being blameworthy, for breaking certain promises and for giving one's twelve-year-old child permission to go on a potentially dangerous camping trip. Indeed, as these cases suggest, 'S is morally responsible for having A-ed at t' is compatible with A's being praiseworthy. There is a fairly common philosophical use of this statement in which it means roughly. "If A is wrong S is blameworthy for it, and if A is right S's A-ing is praiseworthy (or worthy of approval)." I shall not discuss this technical notion, but much of what emerges concerning moral responsibility will apply to the notion.

Both responsibility in the liability sense and responsibility in the accountability sense figure in contexts in which there is a question whether S was morally responsible *over* a given period. Hart calls this kind of responsibility capacity responsibility.[11] We should also note what might be called *dispositional responsibility:* this is our concern when we ask whether S is a morally responsible person. This paper should provide much of the basis for an account of capacity and dispositional responsibility, since both can be partially analyzed in terms of notions I shall be explicating. But I shall concentrate on liability responsibility, though my main points about this will also apply to responsibility in the weaker, accountability sense. Liability responsibility admits of degrees, but for our purposes it will be adequate simply to explore some important conditions for x's bearing at least some degree of liability responsibility for doing A.

Let us first ask whether 'S is morally responsible for having A-ed at t' entails 'S freely A-ed at t'. Certainly in most cases in which S is morally responsible for having A-ed she A-ed freely. But suppose S fails to notice a flashing sign that says "Children Crossing," proceeds at substantially above the speed limit, and hits a child who is crossing. Even if S hit the child by accident, it is clear that she would be morally and legally responsible for hitting him. Yet it would be wrong to say either that she hit him freely or that her hitting him was a free action. One may object that S is responsible primarily for reckless-

[10] For instance, Mill says, "What is meant by moral responsibility? Responsibility means punishment"; see his *An Examination of Sir William Hamilton's Philosophy* (New York: Holt, 1874), vol. 2, excerpted by Berofsky, *Free Will and Determinism*, p. 171. Cf. Schlick, "When Is a Man Responsible?": "The question of who is responsible . . . is a matter only of knowing who is to be punished or rewarded," p. 61.
[11] Hart, "Responsibility and Retribution," pp. 227-30.

ness. But that is compatible with her also being morally responsible for hitting the child. It is also compatible with the possibility that her hitting the child is a consequence of her recklessness. For we are morally responsible for many of the consequences of our actions, and some of these are other actions of ours. Moreover, if S were not morally responsible for hitting the child, it would be wrong to determine her blame and punishment in part according to what she recklessly *does*. Nor would there be any difference, in respect of responsibility, blameworthiness, and (moral) punishability, between S and someone who drove through a moment before with equal but inconsequential recklessness. (It is very difficult to say what this difference is, but there surely is one.) Note also that it is correct to say such things as that S must bear responsibility for crippling a child and deserves the condemnation she has gotten for scarring the child's life. The most— perhaps the only—plausible interpretation of these remarks presupposes that S is morally responsible for hitting the child.

The point that 'S is morally responsible for having A-ed at t' does not entail 'S freely A-ed at t' also holds for intentional actions. Imagine a man whose job is to guard a missile launcher. Suppose he realizes that both the duties of his office and his ordinary moral obligations require that he give his life rather than reveal the combination of the launching mechanism to unauthorized persons. Assume that as a precaution he has readily available a poison which he need only touch to commit suicide instantly. Let us also assume that his physical endurance is high. Now suppose that for two hours he is threatened with death by gunmen, severely slapped by them, and punched several times in the stomach. If, as a result, he then (intentionally) gives the combination, knowing that many thousands will probably be killed, he would surely be morally responsible, even blameworthy, for giving it. He ought to have taken the poison or held out longer. Yet it would be wrong to say that he gave the combination freely, or that his giving it was a free action. It was extracted from him only through threats and sustained force: "beaten out of him."

Granted, if the beating were more severe, or went on for ten hours, the action would be even further from being free. There may also be a point at which the torture would be so severe that we could no longer consider the man morally responsible for giving the combination at the time he did, though he might still be morally responsible for not touching the poison before his assailants took hold of him and made this impossible. But where he simply fails to endure the threats and physical abuse for two hours, we cannot reasonably say either that he freely gives the combination (or gives it of his own free will), or that he bears no moral responsibility for giving it. To be sure, if, like many philosophers, one assumes that "moral responsibility presupposes freedom," one may insist that the combination is given freely. But surely this is not plausible independently of the above doctrine: if one had no interest in protecting it, one would not say that the frightened, pained, and bleeding guard freely gave the combination.

The case of the guard is doubly interesting because it shows that even when S does not A freely it may be true that she could have done otherwise. The guard could and in fact should have given up his life rather than reveal the combination. Another reason for denying that free actions are those one could have done otherwise than perform is that "could have done otherwise" does not admit of degrees, whereas freedom in the relevant sense does. If Jack joins the Army because he wants a military career and Jill joins only because the Army offers her a better job than anyone else, then other things being equal he joins more freely than she. It may be true that, very often, when an action is such that one could not have done otherwise, or, as I shall sometimes say, *unavoidable*, it is as far as possible from being free. But this does not imply that 'S freely A-ed at t' is equivalent to 'S could have done otherwise than A at t.' It is in part because these notions have been mistakenly equated that freedom has been thought necessary for moral responsibility.[12]

An important question that now arises is whether 'S is morally responsible for having A-ed at t' entails that S could have done otherwise than A. We should first make explicit that 'could have done otherwise' needs to be completed by the specification of two temporal variables: one designating the time of action, the other the time of avoidability, that is, the time at which S could have done otherwise than A. Our case of the reckless driver shows that 'S is morally responsible for having A-ed at t' does not entail that *at t* (the time of action) S could have avoided A-ing. But it does seem to entail that either at t or at *some* time prior to t S could have done otherwise than A. This in turn raises the question of the conditions for such

[12] See, for example, Campbell, "Is 'Freewill' a Pseudo-Problem?" pp. 118–19 and 133; and P. H. Nowell-Smith, "Psychoanalysis and Moral Language," reprinted in May Broadbeck, ed., *Readings in the Philosophy of the Social Sciences* (New York: Macmillan, 1968), p. 712.

avoidability. For one thing, there must be (or at least must have been) some other action which S had the ability and the opportunity to perform. As in the case of the reckless driver, either there must be some alternative action(s) which at *t*, she had the ability and opportunity to perform, or at some earlier time at which she could reasonably be expected to believe that she would (might) *A*, there must have been some other action(s) which she had the ability and opportunity to perform *and* could reasonably be expected to see would (might) prevent her *A*-ing. The chief point of this last restriction is to make clear that, when there is a question whether S is morally responsible for having *A*-ed at *t*, it is not sufficient for 'she could have done otherwise' that at some time before *t* there was some action which she had the ability and opportunity to perform and which would (might) *in fact* have prevented *A*. If this were sufficient, we would have to say that a man who is unexpectedly held up at gunpoint on a street he knows is normally safe could have done otherwise than give up his money, because he had the ability and opportunity to take a different route home. The sense in which he could have avoided giving up his money by taking another route is not the sense of "avoidability" presupposed by moral responsibility.

This is not the place to discuss ability.[13] What needs to be said now is that what S could have done, insofar as it is relevant to her moral responsibility, is not definable simply in terms of what is physically and psychologically possible for S, nor even definable in more complex non-normative terms. As the missile case suggests, where there is a question of whether S is morally responsible for having *A*-ed at *t*, what S could have done is in part determined by what a morally sound person in the situation in question might reasonably have been expected to do. There is of course disagreement over what constitutes a morally sound person. But in schematic terms, which are all our purposes require here, a morally sound person is one who holds "the right" moral principles, has "the right" moral intuitions, and, with minor exceptions, does the "right things."

Let me illustrate further how the notion of a morally sound person figures in the concept of avoidability. Suppose that kidnappers who threaten the life of my daughter force me to give up my life's savings. If asked whether somehow I could have kept the money, I could

---

[13] For a very good account of this notion, see Goldman, *A Theory of Human Action*, esp. chap. 7.

reasonably reply that I could not have done otherwise. My point would normally not be that I was physically or psychologically unable to do otherwise (nor was I, presumably), but that it would have been wrong (or unreasonable) to do so. It is also true here that I do not freely give the money. This suggests that if one could not have done otherwise than *A*, then one *A*-ed *un*freely. But suppose that because of a solemn promise one helps a sick person with some legal problems. Upon being thanked for one's help, one might say "I couldn't have done otherwise." This is the kind of unavoidability Kant called *moral compulsion*. Granted that here one implies one was not *free to* to do otherwise, does one also imply that one did not do the service freely? It seems so, though one could argue that the only sense of 'free' in which the action is not free is the sense in which it means 'spontaneous'. But we do not, at least not outside discussions of free will, speak of morally compelled actions as free in any other sense, or as done of one's own free will; we speak instead of being compelled by, say, duty, to do them. To be sure, since moral compulsion is unlike most other compulsions because, at least normally, it constitutes a justification and it is never merely an excuse, one might want to call it compulsion in a different sense. But since we do treat it as a kind of unavoidability and can easily distinguish it from other compulsions, it seems more reasonable to resist bringing in a different sense of 'compulsion'. We can thus seek a unified account of its various uses and avoid multiplying concepts of compulsion beyond necessity.

May we, then, say that '*S* is morally responsible for having *A*-ed at *t*' entails that at or at least before *t*, *S* could have done otherwise than *A*? Frankfurt has ingeniously attacked this view through two examples.[14] First, suppose I decide to do *A*, but am then ordered under threat to do it. If I now do it purely for the reasons I have independently of the threat, I am morally responsible for doing it, yet, because of the threat could not have done otherwise. Secondly, suppose that Zack has a way of knowing whether I have decided to *A* and, if he finds that I have not decided to do it, can and will do whatever would justify ascribing 'could not have done otherwise than *A*' to me. Now if I, in utter ignorance of Zack's power, *A* for my own reasons, I would then be morally responsible for *A*-ing, even though I could not have done otherwise.

[14] Harry G. Frankfurt, "Alternate Possibilities and Moral Responsibility," *Journal of Philosophy* 66 (1969), esp. pp. 832–36.

Are these genuine counterexamples to avoidability as a necessary condition for moral responsibility? Take the first case. Suppose *A* is a murder. Surely if I could commit it for my own reasons and without regard to the threat, then I could have abstained from it for moral reasons and without regard to the threat. If my personal reasons for *A*-ing can overshadow the threat, moral reasons for not *A*-ing should be able to do so also. The kind of person in whom moral reasons for abstaining from *A* cannot outweigh personal reasons for *A*-ing is certainly one sort we wish to—and do—hold morally responsible for *A*-ing. Thus, surely I could have done otherwise.

Frankfurt's second case is more complicated. It does show that *S* may be morally responsible for *A*-ing even if, during *some* small time interval following *t* (the time *S A*'s), *S* would not have been able to do otherwise. But I hold only the restricted view that '*S* is morally responsible for having *A*-ed at *t*' entails that *at t* (or in some cases before *t*) *S* could have done otherwise than *A* at *t*. Now suppose that, in Frankfurt's second case, I pleaded, as an excuse for *A*, that I could not have done otherwise. This would not do: my own decision surely did not compel me, and Zack's *potential* compulsion was not operative. The general point here, which Frankfurt's argument overlooks, is this. If *S A*'s at *t* for reasons of a kind that make her morally responsible for doing it, the fact that if she had not had those reasons and did not intend to do *A*, she *would* have been compelled to do it (whether at or after *t*) for *other* reasons, does not entail that she could not have done otherwise at *t*. Frankfurt does not show that there is any possible set of reasons why *S A*'s at *t* which makes it plausible to say that *S* is morally responsible for having *A*-ed at *t and S* could not have done otherwise than *A* at *t*. To be sure, in his second example it may be causally necessary, *given* the power of Zack, that I *A*; but Frankfurt does not argue, nor does he seem to assume, that *this* entails that the agent could not have done otherwise. That in fact no such entailment does hold will be supported by a number of arguments in this essay.

If Frankfurt's examples can be dealt with as I have suggested and if *I* am right about 'could have done otherwise,' then '*S* is morally responsible for having *A*-ed at *t*' does entail that at (or before) *t*, *S* could have done otherwise than *A* at *t*. The converse, however, is false. Suppose that an art student asks 'Did he *have* to put that yellow patch there?' One might reply 'No, he could have used a soft blue.' In contexts like this the assessment is not moral; and if the fact that

S could not have done otherwise absolves her of any kind of respon-sibility, it is not moral responsibility.

In most contexts, however, both questions of whether S could have done otherwise than A and questions of whether she freely A-ed are meant at least in part to ascertain whether S is morally responsible for having A-ed at t. My main concern is to give an account of the notion of free action embedded in these contexts and to determine its relation to the notion of moral responsibility. I shall assume that we can best understand acting freely by considering contrasts to it. For I take it that normally sentences of the form 'S A-ed freely' have the precise content they do by virtue of what, in the context, they are intended to rule out.[15]

II. Acting under Compulsion

I shall assume that the most general contrast to the notion of acting freely is that of acting under compulsion. I shall also assume that S A's under compulsion at t if and only if S is compelled to A at t, though these expressions differ in nuance. Various locutions are used in affirming that a person acted under compulsion. I have al-ready discussed 'could not have done otherwise.' Consider also 'I was forced to open the safe'; 'He could not help using too much water, because of his obsession with cleanliness'; 'She couldn't refrain from hiding her face on the bridge, because of her acrophobia'; and 'He seized his dancing partner out of an irresistible impulse'. Being com-pelled often results from being forced, coerced, pressured, or driven, but these are not mutually equivalent. Compulsions may be external or internal. The former include such things as blackmail and various threats, most notably that of death; the latter include things like ad-dictions and certain obsessions, phobias, and unconscious desires. I shall not consider whether the subclasses are mutually exclusive. The classification is simply for convenience.

Some of my examples raise the question whether compelled actions must be intentional. Typically, this is so. One might think that where S is compelled *not* to A, for example, not to appear in court, A may

[15] For a good discussion of this idea, see Cranston, *Freedom: A New Analysis*, esp. pp. 3–47.

not be intentional. She might be locked up and thus physically unable to appear. It would then be false to say that she intentionally fails to appear. But here her failure to appear is not an action at all: we must distinguish between an act of omission and the mere non-performance of an action. If *S* were blackmailed into not appearing, yet was physically and psychologically able to do so, then she intentionally abstained from appearing, though under compulsion. But where her failure to appear is due solely to the physical impossibility of her appearing, this failure is surely not an action. A more problematic case would be one in which, under threat of death, Mike, who is a clerk, hands over the money in the safe and in doing so bankrupts the firm, which, unbeknown to him, is not insured. If Mike has no idea that he may be bankrupting the firm and thus does not do so intentionally, can we say he did so under compulsion? One might say that he bankrupts the firm only as a *result* of compulsion. A distinction between what we do under compulsion and what we do as a result of it is certainly worth drawing; but it does not follow that the clerk's bankrupting the firm is not done under compulsion. Indeed, if he were blamed by an unsympathetic stockholder for bankrupting the firm, he might reasonably protest that he couldn't help it, or even that he did so under compulsion.

One may object that since he bankrupts the firm non-intentionally he does not do so unwillingly, and that if *S* is compelled to *A* at *t*, then *S* must *A* unwillingly. This holds for the typical cases of compulsion. But imagine a peculiar clerk who has no disposition to abstain from giving away the money in the register and no disposition to do so either. Still, if he has the normal desire to live, and, at gunpoint, gives the money to save his life, he is compelled to give it. Or, suppose a man is told under hypnosis that when a certain topic comes up during a lecture he is to attend, he will stand up and then reseat himself. If, when the topic comes up, he feels an irresistible urge to stand up and thus suddenly does so, he may or may not do so unwillingly. To be sure, the standing cannot be so automatic that it qualifies only as bodily movement. Mine is a case in which he is surprised that he stands up and immediately sits down in embarrassment. He would doubtless say that he did not know why he stood; and in some such cases he could be said both not to have stood up intentionally and to have been compelled to stand. Actions performed under compulsion, then, need be neither intentional nor performed unwillingly.

We can now work more positively toward an account of compulsion. To begin with, it seems that if S is compelled to A at t, then no motive of personal gain is an important part of what motivates S to A. I shall assume that, except in cases of overdetermination, in which there are two or more independent sets of sufficient conditions, a motivational factor is an important part of what motivates S to A, if and only if it is at least necessary for S's A-ing. If a motive of personal gain is an important part of what motivates S to A, then surely, one wants to say, she sees herself as getting too much out of it. Perhaps Zack has no desire to promote Jim; still, if a threat, say to expose relations with the underworld, is not sufficient to make him promote Jim without his believing that it will yield him extra income, which he wants, then Zack did not make the promotion under compulsion.

One difficulty with the suggestion that motives of personal gain cannot be important parts of what motivates compelled actions is that 'motive of personal gain' is vague. But the following points will indicate roughly how it is being taken. First, very often, an intrinsic want to A is a motive of personal gain. Roughly, to say that S's want for something is (purely) intrinsic is to say that she wants it for its own sake; hence, her want for it is such that, if she has any reason for wanting it, no part of this reason is a belief that satisfying the want is necessary to (will, may) realize anything else that she wants, nor is any such belief a necessary condition for her retaining the want. If, for example, threats of a drubbing would not have led the clerk to give up the money if he had not been motivated by an intrinsic want to wreak vengeance on the store's owner, he does not give it under compulsion. Motives of revenge should, for our purposes, be counted motives of personal gain. By contrast, if S has an intrinsic want to do her duty, or to preserve her life, the want is clearly not a motive of personal gain; indeed, surely no want to do what one thinks morally obligatory is a motive of personal gain. A second class of motives of personal gain consists of the typical desires for more property, power, influence, or prestige than one has. When such an increase is wanted for friends or for certain relatives, this want is also a motive of personal gain—unless S wants the increase because she thinks she is morally obligated to realize it. Nor should a desire to avoid blackmail count as a motive of personal gain, even if S has an obligation to reveal what his would-be blackmailer threatens to expose. But it is difficult to be precise about personal gain, though at least the vast majority of such motives seem to be of the above sorts.[16]

Another important point is that if S is compelled to A at t, then clearly there must be someone or something which compels her. In what I shall call the standard cases, there must be some action(s) of one or more other persons, or some condition(s) (for example, the unavailability of food, or a psychological condition such as an irresistible desire or even a paranoiac delusion), or some event(s) (such as a hail storm), which impose on S her predominant motivation for A-ing. One may think that, at least in cases of compulsion by another person, S must disapprove of the compelling action(s). But this is not necessary, nor is S's disapproving of her A-ing at t: Mike might think it would be good for Ann, his too lenient employer, to threaten him with dismissal to compel him to finish an important project; and if she does so, he might not disapprove of it, or of his doing the project.

We need a further condition to distinguish compulsion both from persuasion and from mere influence. We need to capture the idea that, in the standard cases, if S is compelled she feels she "has no choice." What I suggest is that, at least by t, S must believe that there is some state of affairs on account of which her not A-ing would (might) have very bad consequences, and as a result of this belief she must also believe either (or both) (i) that her A-ing is so substantially preferable to her not doing it that it would be very unreasonable for her not to do it, or (ii) that from the point of view of her own welfare, or the welfare of someone (or something) she wants to protect, her not A-ing would (might) have very bad consequences. Clearly, we must put some restriction on *what* consequences are relevant. Not just any consequences S believes her not A-ing would have, and considers very bad, would justify her saying she was compelled to A. Our interest is mainly in contexts in which there is a question whether S

[16] Perhaps we should require here only that a motive of personal gain not be one of S's *main* reasons for A-ing. For some uses of "compel" *appear* to violate my requirement. Mike might say that his family compelled him to take an extra job because they wanted more money. But it seems to me that if he would not have taken the job unless he believed he stood to gain *more* than what his family and he needed (or what he was obligated to provide for them), he is using 'compel' in an extended sense—or deceitfully. If one takes compulsion this broadly, then when questions of moral responsibility arise, compulsion might scarcely even count as an extenuating circumstance. Possibly we should recognize more than one sense of 'compulsion'; but I am not convinced of this. Indeed, often the point of the use of 'compel' just illustrated is to give the impression that one was *not* in part motivated by a motive of personal gain.

is morally responsible for A-ing, and at least in these S must believe that the very bad consequences of her not A-ing are of the following sorts, or at least as serious from the point of view of human welfare, or the welfare of other sentient beings: first, death, or serious physical harm, or serious psychological harm, or crippling loss, to S or to some person(s), or social entity (such as a nation) with whose welfare she is concerned (where personal loss, for example financial loss, excludes mere lack of personal gain); secondly, the destruction or serious damaging of important property; and thirdly, a serious immorality (this accommodates moral compulsion and could be omitted if we found it best to construe moral compulsion as compulsion in an extended sense).

The idea here is that, for the standard cases of compulsion, one cannot be compelled to A unless one believes that it is in some way "too costly" not to do it. One may object that this would not account for such things as compulsive handwashing. But we must distinguish what is *compulsive* from what is *compelled*. Not all actions representing compulsive behavior are performed under compulsion; and typically the compulsive handwasher is at worst compelled to wash very frequently: not to wash *on* precisely the occasions when the washing occurs. Unfortunately, it is impossible to be precise about what envisaged consequences can sustain a claim that S is compelled to A at t. But this is to be expected if we are to analyze, rather than replace, the notion of compulsion. For often the question whether S is compelled to A at t turns on whether what she believed would occur if she did not do it qualifies as "unacceptably bad" and thus as leaving her no choice. Suppose a messenger, Tim, gives up a briefcase which he knows contains important documents, because he is threatened by a man much bigger than he, who says he will catch Tim on his way home some night and make a punching bag out of him. Was Tim compelled to give up the briefcase, or just cowardly? The main reason the answer is not clear is that there is some question whether the indefinite risk of such a beating is the kind of very bad consequence Tim must envisage to justify the claim that he was compelled to A. I shall return to this problem.

One might think that if S is compelled to A at t, she must have some reason for her belief(s) to the effect that her not A-ing would be too costly. But suppose that on a crowded street, and in clear view of two policemen whom she can see, a jovial, harmless-looking drunk with his hands in his coat pockets asks her for a dollar. If she thinks she is being threatened with a gun, she might give the money in trepidation and later say (to someone who asks her why she gave away her last dollar) that she was compelled to. One may say that she was merely duped. Perhaps she is duped, and certainly the drunk does not compel her. But it is quite reasonable to say that S's fear of death does compel her, though one could also treat the case as one in which she merely thinks she is compelled. Indeed, she does merely think that the drunk is compelling her; but 'S is compelled to A at t' does not entail that some *person* compels her to A, not even a person she thinks is compelling her. I am not attempting to analyze the special case in which a person compels S to A; most compulsions of this sort are *coercions*, though there may be coercions that are not compulsions. Similarly, suppose S believes, but has no reason to believe, that her not A-ing would be a serious immorality and A's for this reason. Is this a case of *moral* compulsion? I think not, though it would be not unreasonable to say yes, provided one kept in mind that then not all moral compulsions would be cases of unavoidability. But even if S cannot A under *moral* compulsion unless she has reason to believe that her not A-ing would be a serious immorality, we may still treat the above case as a kind of (quasi-moral) compulsion. The compelling factor is S's conviction that she must A to avoid committing a serious immorality; and because this is the compelling factor, she could plead extenuating, though not necessarily excusing, circumstances.

The conditions so far specified only partially capture the idea that in standard cases of compulsion S feels she has no choice. We need to add that, regarding the very bad consequences we have specified, S strongly wants to avoid them and indeed wants to avoid them substantially more than she wants to avoid A-ing, or to avoid any bad consequences she believes her A-ing would (might) have. Must S also regard her A-ing as so substantially preferable to her not A-ing that it would be unreasonable for her not to A? This is usually so for standard cases of compulsion, but our missile case shows that it need not be. The guard might believe that the reasonable thing is to abstain from A-ing, but fail to muster the motivation required to act in accordance with his better judgment.

We have still said nothing which entails that S actually A's, nor have we ruled out her A-ing for some reason that would preclude its being compelled. I suggest we say that the wants just specified, together with the above-cited beliefs concerning the consequences of not A-ing, constitute at least the main reason *why S A's*. To say that a set of S's wants and beliefs are the *main* reason why S A's at t, is, in large part, to say that if S had been forced at t to choose between (i) acting, on the belief(s), solely to satisfy the want(s), and (ii) acting, on the remaining belief(s) motivating her doing A, solely to satisfy the remaining want(s) motivating her A-ing, then, other things equal, she would normally have chosen (i). If, for example, the main reason why S A's is to avoid being beaten, but part of her reason is to spare her husband anxiety, then normally, if forced to choose between performing A_1, solely because she believes it would avoid the beating, and performing A_2, solely because she believes it would spare her husband the anxiety, she would do A_1.

If the conditions so far discussed are the only ones necessary, as I believe they are for the standard cases of compulsion, then we may say that for these cases S is compelled to A at t if and only if, at t (and for (2)–(4) usually before t as well)

(1) it is not the case that a motive of personal gain is an important part of what motivates S to A;

(2) S believes that there is some state of affairs on account of which her not A-ing would (might) have very bad consequences (where these are restricted as above);

(3) because of the belief specified in (2), S believes either (or both) (i) that her A-ing is so substantially preferable to her not A-ing that it would be very unreasonable for her not to A, or (ii) that, from the point of view of her own welfare or the welfare of someone (or something) she wants to protect, her not A-ing would (might) have the sorts of consequences specified in (2);

(4) S strongly wants to avoid not A-ing (or what she believes are the consequences of her not doing it), and this want is substantially stronger than any want(s) she may have to avoid A-ing or to avoid any bad consequences which she believes her A-ing would (might) have; and

(5) the beliefs and wants specified in (2)–(4) constitute at least the main reason why S A's.

There are vague expressions in (1)–(5), most conspicuously 'motive of personal gain' and 'very bad consequences'. But 'compulsion' is itself vague; and as I have tried to show, often in borderline cases our hesitation in applying it results from doubt about whether the consequences S believes her not A-ing would have are very bad in the sense sketched above. This confirms my view that these notions figure in the concept of compulsion in the way I have specified.

There remains a more serious difficulty than the vagueness of some elements in (1)–(5). The conditions do not encompass certain compulsions we might call non-standard. These include at least cases in which *A* is not intentional or, if intentional, performed without *S*'s having the beliefs specified in (2) and (3). An example of the first sort would be her standing up during the lecture because of a posthypnotic suggestion. An example of the second kind would be my being compelled to drink ale, which I abhor, because, due to posthypnotic suggestion, I suddenly feel an overpowering thirst. Here I might drink intentionally, yet not satisfy (1)–(5). Similar possibilities are implicit in certain uses of things like drugs or implanted electrodes to control behavior, whether "directly" or through inducing sufficient motivation. I believe that such cases can be accounted for mainly in terms of the materials of the account of the standard cases of compulsion, by disjoining the following to (1)–(5):

(6) either (1) or, if a motive of personal gain is an important part of what motivates *S* to *A*, it is, without her consent, induced in her by some interference with her normal functioning, such as hypnosis, implanted electrodes, drugs, or surgery;

(7) either (2) or there is some state of affairs which produces in *S* either simply a powerful (and possibly unconscious) desire to *A*, or a non-motivational tendency to *A* *in order to* realize any extrinsic or intrinsic want;

(8) even if, at *t*, (i) *S* should believe (as she may or may not) that her *A*-ing would have a consequence of the sort specified in (2), and (ii) *S* was as strongly motivated to avoid *A*-ing as would be appropriate to this belief, she would still *A*;

(9) either the non-motivational tendency specified in (7), or a set of wants and beliefs of the sort cited in (2)–(4), or one or more desires of the kinds cited in (6) and (7), constitute at least the main reason why *S* *A*'s.

We could simplify (8), which is meant to guarantee that the compelling force is sufficient to justify saying *S* is compelled to *A* at *t*, by requiring that no amount of motivation possible for *S* at *t* would prevent her *A*-ing. But this would be too strong. Suppose that, in our lecture case, if *S* knew her life depended on remaining seated she would have resisted standing. Does this imply that she was not compelled to stand? I think not. For if S had tried as hard not to stand as was appropriate in the light of what she had reason to think was at stake, for example, damaging her reputation, we could plausibly say she was compelled to stand. But suppose that she was warned of the posthypnotic suggestion and that we had good reason to think it was insufficient to outweigh the appropriate degree of motivation to abstain. Here her claim to have been compelled to stand would be disallowed.

If my main points are correct, we can say that S is compelled to A at t if and only if either (1)–(5) or (6)–(9), or both. The standard cases seem to be those satisfying the former set, or both sets; compulsions satisfying only (6)–(9) seem non-standard. But it might be reasonable to call some compulsions fitting only (1)–(5) non-standard and some fitting only (6)–(9) standard. My suggested distinction between standard and non-standard cases is not of major importance. It does, however, help with some puzzles.

Suppose Zack compels Mike to rob Ann's store, which is the local heroin center, though neither Mike nor Zack has any inkling of this. Is Mike also compelled to rob the local heroin center, assuming this is a distinct action? We are puled in both directions. No, because neither Mike nor Zack had any idea Mike was doing this. Yes, because Mike "couldn't help" robbing the local heroin center. The way out, I think, is to note that Mike's robbing Ann's store is a standard case of compulsion and his robbing the local heroin center is not. If we conceive both actions in terms of (1)–(5), which is natural since the paradigms of compulsion satisfy (1)–(5), we cannot account for the intuition that (because Mike couldn't help it) he was compelled to rob the local heroin center; for (1)–(5) require that one realize that one is (or at least might be) A-ing. However, assuming Zack's threat is severe enough, Mike's robbing the local heroin center *would* satisfy (6)–(9).

One can see this last point by considering how the two sets of conditions are related. Note first that typically, if S is compelled to A at t in the sense of (1)–(5), S is compelled to A at t in the sense of (6)–(9): she would obviously satisfy (6), (7), and (9); and she would typically satisfy (8) because if S satisfies (1)–(5) typically her motivation to avoid the consequences of *not* A-ing would be stronger than the minimum motivation to *avoid* A-ing specified by (8). Hence, typically if S satisfies (1)–(5) she would A even if she believed it had *some* consequence of the kind specified in (8) and she were as highly motivated to abstain as (8) requires. Secondly, for the same sorts of reasons, if S is compelled to A at t in the sense of (1)–(5), and either *by* or *in* A-ing she must, at least in fact, A_1, then in most cases she is also compelled to A_1, at least in the sense of (6)–(9). For instance, if S is compelled to A at t in the sense of (1)–(5) then normally her motivational tendency to A will create a (possibly non-motivational) tendency to do whatever she must do in (or by) A-ing, and the latter tendency will normally have sufficient strength to make S satisfy (8). It is the in-relation that holds between Mike's robbing Ann's store and Mike's robbing the local heroin center. But suppose Mike is compelled to fire a gun and by doing so he creates a smell of sulphur. Is he also compelled to create a smell of sulphur? Again we may be pulled in two directions; for his creating a smell of sulphur may not be intentional, and typically the actions we speak of as compelled are. Nevertheless, actions that satisfy (6)–(9) are surely compelled, and this accounts for our tendency to regard as compelled most actions that are performed in (or by) performing one that is compelled in the sense of (1)–(5). What I am saying implies that when S is compelled to A at t she is also compelled to do indefinitely many other things. But typically few if any of these concomitant actions are worth mentioning (which largely accounts for the peculiarity of saying, of such actions, that S is compelled to perform them); and though they must not be overlooked, they pose no special problem here.

In closing this section I want to make a general point about compulsion. Where we take S's A-ing to be morally wrong, the more seriously wrong we take it to be, the more stringently we tend to interpret the conditions; for example, the more evidence we require to be convinced that S is compelled to A at t. This is not surprising, since we allow compulsion to count as an extenuating circumstance even when it does not absolve S of moral responsibility. There is, then, a normative element in many important uses of 'compel'. The above account of compulsion—and probably any realistic account of it, or of free action construed as its opposite—should be interpreted in the light of this, despite the complexity it adds. If S's A-ing is a mere peccadillo, it would be unreasonable to interpret the conditions stringently, disallowing, say, that the psychological drubbing she believed she would get from her husband was "unacceptably" bad; and if S's A-ing is a grave wrong, such as a murder of a competitor, it would be unreasonable to allow S's anticipated loss of a good client to count as a very bad consequence of the relevant kind.

III. Acting Freely and Its Relation to Moral Responsibility

If it is true that the most general contrast to 'acting freely' is 'acting under compulsion' and that to say that S A-ed freely is to rule out some kind of compulsion indicated in the context, then perhaps we can understand free action as (intentional) action that is not compelled.[17] One difficulty is that even where A is intentional, 'free' and 'not compelled' may seem to be contraries, not contradictories. When one (intentionally) turns the page of a book one is reading, must one do this either freely or under compulsion? To say one does it freely would suggest the possibility of compulsions whose presence here is ordinarily out of the question. This is the sort of consideration that led Austin to say, "No modification without aberration."[18] But if, where A is intentional, 'S freely A-ed at t' is equivalent to 'It is not the case that S is compelled to A at t' would seem that we must say one freely turned the page. For such actions are both intentional and uncompelled.

The simplest way to deal with this objection is to distinguish what is true and what there is point in saying. It is true that this paper is white, but there would ordinarily be no point in saying this and it would thus be odd to say it in an ordinary situation. So with 'free'. A more cautious reply would be this. *Given* that it is appropriate to ask whether S A-ed freely—and I take this question to presuppose that A was intentional—she A-ed freely if and only if she was not compelled to do it. The plausibility of this suggestion is confirmed by the fact that questions of whether S was compelled to A are appropriate and inappropriate in roughly the same cases in which 'Did S A freely?' is appropriate and inappropriate. Indeed normally 'I was

[17] Schlick held that "freedom means the opposite of compulsion" (Berofsky, *Free Will and Determinism*, p. 59). Hume and others have held a very similar view. What I have tried to do is, in part, to fill the gap other compatibilitists have left in our understanding of compulsion.

[18] J. L. Austin, "A Plea for Excuses," reprinted in Herbert Morris, ed., *Freedom and Responsibility* (Stanford: Stanford University Press, 1961), p. 12.

not compelled to turn this page' would have the same sort of oddity as 'I freely turned this page,' and for the same reason: that in the context there is no hint of what compulsion is being ruled out and hence no point in making the statement. Apparently, then, we can meet the above objection to construing free actions as uncompelled intentional actions.

Another objection to this proposed equivalence is that whereas there are degrees of freedom with which one can A, there are no degrees of compulsion. We can meet this objection as follows. Perhaps 'degrees of compulsion' does not have a common use; but since there are degrees of compelling force, that is, the force used to compel S, we can give 'degrees of compulsion' a clear use, and indeed it is a merit of the above account of compulsion that it enables us to make clear sense of this comparative notion. Thus, we can suppose both that S freely A's when it is intentional and uncompelled, and that she does so more freely in inverse proportion to the number and intensity of the elements present which, when they are all present in the appropriate degree, render the action compelled. We can also say that when S is compelled to A at t, the greater the degree of force used beyond the minimum required for the compulsion, the further S is from A-ing with any degree of freedom and the greater the degree of the compulsion. Thus, for the standard cases of compulsion, other things being equal: (i) the more S intrinsically wants to A or believes she will gain in some other way from A-ing, the lower the degree of her compulsion (the less unfree she is) in doing it; (ii) the less her motivation to A is "pathologic" or externally imposed, the lower the degree of her compulsion in A-ing; (iii) the worse she believes the consequences of her not A-ing to be, the *higher* the degree of her compulsion (the less free she is) in A-ing; (iv) the more she wants to avoid these consequences, the higher the degree of her compulsion in A-ing; and (v) the worse she believes her least objectionable alternative, the higher the degree of her compulsion in doing A. For non-standard cases of compulsion, other things being equal, the greater the motivation that would be required for S to resist doing A, or the further her resisting it is from the strongest motivation to resist she is capable of, the higher the degree of her compulsion in doing A.

Can the account of compulsion also help to explain the relation between free action and moral responsibility? I think it can. Recall that S can be morally responsible for A-ing even if she did not A freely, but not if, in addition, her A-ing unavoidable.

Our missile guard acts under compulsion, but the action is not unavoidable, since he could have done otherwise even at the time he gave the combination. Admittedly, it is slightly odd to say that though S is compelled to A at t S could have done otherwise; but I believe this is because the vast majority—and the paradigms—of compulsion are also cases of unavoidability. But when is an action unavoidable? And under what conditions does an action that is compelled—and thus also unfree—but not unavoidable, absolve one of moral responsibility?

Part of the answer to the first question has already been foreshadowed. We normally do not (and we surely should not) accept a claim that S could not have done otherwise if we believe a morally sound person in the relevant circumstances could reasonably have been expected to do otherwise. Taking this point together with the account of compulsion, we have the materials for an approximate non-hypothetical account of 'could not have done otherwise' in the sense relevant to moral responsibility. Roughly, S could not have done otherwise than A at t if and only if S is compelled to A at t and it is not the case either (i) that S could reasonably have been expected to avoid (or try to avoid) the situation in which A occurred, or (ii) that a morally sound person in the relevant situation could reasonably have been expected to do otherwise. To be sure, if a psychotic uses up the water during a shortage, because of an obsession with cleanliness, we might grant that this action was unavoidable. But such cases do not violate (ii), since surely a morally sound person could not have been in this situation: here a purely personal desire outweighs a clear moral obligation. There is no simple way, of course, to unpack the notion of what a morally sound person could reasonably be expected to do; but here I simply want to show what would be required for a detailed analysis of unavoidability.

Our question about the relation between moral responsibility and free action is more difficult. Part of the answer is implicit in the discussion of unavoidability: this sort of compulsion is sufficient to absolve S of moral responsibility. But where an action is compelled and hence unfree, yet not unavoidable, how do we (and should we) decide whether the compulsion is sufficient to absolve S of moral responsibility?

One consideration has already been suggested by our reflections: the moral gravity of the action in the situation. Suppose that, because she is beaten and threatened with the destruction of her store, Ann reveals the whereabouts of a person she knows her threateners will then murder. Her doing so under compulsion would not absolve her of moral responsibility for this action. But if, under the same threat, she gives them the $75 in the cash register, then normally she would not be morally responsible. Clearly in the first case the action is of greater moral gravity than in the second, where the moral gravity of an action, *A*, in a given situation, is primarily a function of (i) the degree of harm to sentient beings which a reasonable person would, in the relevant circumstances, believe it would (or might) do, and (ii) the strength of the obligation one would normally have (apart from the compulsion) to abstain from *A* in the situation in question; (ii) in turn is a function of such things as the number and kinds of rights *A* violates.

These remarks suggest a second consideration: the degree of compelling force that brings *A* about. Suppose Mike is threatened with death by two gunmen if he does not immediately hand them the purse of a woman he is accompanying. Normally, he would not be morally responsible for doing this. But if a ten-year-old boy with a small pocket knife made the same threat, then normally an able-bodied man who made no attempt to resist would be morally responsible for handing over the purse, even if he were ultimately excused. I have suggested some ways of measuring degree of compelling force, though in practice this is difficult, especially for internal compulsions. Regarding these, I shall say only that we can get an idea of the degree of compelling force by combining our knowledge of some of *S*'s behavior with general considerations about her psychological (or physical) makeup.

With external compulsions we can judge their degree partly on the basis of how much harm *S* believes her not *A*-ing will (may) cause her or others; how much pain or fear she withstands before *A*-ing; and the degree to which she attempts to escape performing the action: such attempts not only suggest that more force was used than would have been had *S* *A*-ed at the first opportunity; they also have independent extenuating import because they show that *S* tried to avoid *A*-ing. There are other factors as well, though none of them admits of precise measurement. Perhaps the best we can hope for is a way of rationally deciding, for some cases of compulsion, whether there was more force used than in some other cases. But even this is significant in assigning moral responsibility, particularly since we can make sense of *inter*personal as well as *intra*personal comparisons.

A third consideration concerns how much reason S has for the beliefs and wants motivating the compelled action. Suppose S is occasionally paranoiac and believes, without reason, that if she does not dismiss an employee under her (whom S's boss dislikes) her boss will dismiss her. In some such cases she might be compelled, by her own delusion, to dismiss the person. But other things being equal, the less reason S has for the motivating beliefs and wants (the wants and beliefs of the forms specified in (2)–(4)), the less her being compelled to A extenuates her moral responsibility for it. One may object that if S—and her motivating beliefs and wants—are psychotically irrational, then far from being more responsible, S is so disturbed that she bears no moral responsibility for A. But when this is so it will usually turn out that S could not have done otherwise, and then we are no longer talking about an action which is compelled but not unavoidable. But even supposing S could have done otherwise, it does not follow that S is morally responsible for having A-ed at t. As I have shown, avoidability is only a necessary, not a sufficient, condition for moral responsibility.

Sometimes utilitarian considerations also do and should enter into determining when a person is morally responsible for an action which is compelled yet not unavoidable. This applies more to legal than to moral responsibility. But sometimes it is relevant to ask what would be the effect, on the welfare of the victim and others, of considering him morally responsible in such a case, and what would be the effect on the welfare of people in general of adopting a policy of considering persons morally responsible under the conditions in question. Suppose that Zack, who is a good deal bigger than Mike, threatens Mike with a beating if he does not give Zack Ann's car, where Mike, who has borrowed the car, knows Ann will be seriously inconvenienced by this, even though she has the car insured. We might well allow that Mike was compelled to give up Ann's car, yet be uncertain whether to consider Mike morally responsible for doing so. Granted that the sorts of utilitarian considerations I have mentioned are relevant to deciding whether to *hold* Mike morally responsible, for example, whether to demand that he defend his action, are they relevant to deciding whether he *is* morally responsible? I believe they may be. For people usually do not like to be considered morally responsible (prima facie blameworthy), even if they believe they will be excused; and if we adopt a policy of considering them morally responsible in cases like the above, this may well increase their tendency to resort to violence to avoid the actions in question. That might be undesirable on balance and might warrant us in deciding that, in such borderline cases, *S* is not morally responsible. But whether utilitarian considerations are even the reason we consider *S* morally responsible in *non*-borderline cases is a large question, and I shall not try to answer it here.

IV. Avoidability, Compatibilism, and Disclaimers of Moral Responsibility

Let me now draw out some implications of my main points. I have argued that being morally responsible for an action does not entail performing it freely, though it does entail that there was at least some time at which the agent could have done otherwise. One reason this negative thesis is important is that philosophers have commonly assumed, and to my knowledge not seriously questioned, that in clarifying the idea of acting freely we are clarifying a necessary condition for moral responsibility. I do not deny that often *S*'s *A*-ing under compulsion, and therefore unfreely, absolves her of moral responsibility for it; and I have tried to sketch an account of the conditions under which compulsion does absolve. But only an action's being unavoidable—and therefore unfree in a very strong sense— automatically absolves *S* of moral responsibility.

One may protest that I have merely shown that many philosophers do not use 'free' in the ordinary sense. I doubt whether many of them use it as a technical term *in* the contexts that chiefly concern us, those in which there is a question of someone's moral responsibility for an action. But if 'free' is being used as a technical term in important contexts, and this is not generally recognized, there is a danger of confusion. Moreover, if, in actual moral discourse, we distinguish the concepts of free action, unavoidable action, and action for which the agent bears moral responsibility, then conflating these, as a good many philosophers have, not only invites confusion but reduces the descriptive power of our system of moral concepts. But let me indicate more important consequences of my conclusions.

The first is that the notion of avoidability is in part a moral notion. It is not, for example, definable simply in terms of physical and psychological ability, or absence of causal determination. For at least very often, to ascertain whether S could have done otherwise, we must determine, or assume we know, whether a morally sound person could reasonably be expected to do otherwise in the relevant situation. Moreover, where considerations of the freedom of an action bear on whether S was morally responsible for it, here too certain moral notions are inescapable. We must consider, for example, the moral gravity of his action in the situation. Some philosophers, especially those who have equated 'S is morally responsible for having A-ed at t' and 'S freely A-ed at t', have hoped to explicate in non-moral terms at least the notion of avoidability,[19] which is generally taken to be necessary and sometimes also sufficient for moral responsibility. But neither this notion, nor the conditions under which acting unfreely absolves one of moral responsibility, can be explicated without the burden of employing moral terms, nor justifiably applied in practice without the onus of making, or having to assume, certain moral judgments. It is true that an action's being compelled is always an extenuating circumstance. Yet even the degree of extenuation is in part a function of moral considerations.

A second general consequence of my position can be brought out by contrasting it with the incompatibilist claim that S freely A-ed at t only if there is no set of laws of nature which, together with certain antecedent condition statements true of S at least by t, entails that S A's at t. On my view, 'S freely A-ed at t' is compatible with, though it does not entail, the existence of such a set of laws and antecedent condition statements. This gives compatibilism a clear advantage. For on an incompatibilist view, to know, or even to have good reason to believe, that S freely A-ed at t, one must know, or at least have good reason to believe, the sweeping negative existential claim that there is no set of laws and true antecedent condition statements of the specified kind. But surely we are never in a position to know, or even have good reason to believe, such a claim about our actions.

Consider also the positive account provided by incompatibilism. On one kind of incompatibilism, to say that S freely A-ed at t is simply, or primarily, to rule out A's being determined; whereas on my account free action can be understood in contrast to the diverse compulsions encompassed, and unified, by the necessary and sufficient conditions for 'S is compelled to A at t.' On a more sophisticated incompatibilist

---

[19] See, for example, Robert J. Richman, "Responsibility and the Causation of Actions," *American Philosophical Quarterly* 6 (1969): 195.

account, 'S freely A-ed at t' might be understood as ruling out 'S is compelled to A at t' but cases in which S's A-ing is entailed by a set of laws and true antecedent conditions statements would be treated as cases of compulsion, or at least of unavoidability. But if I am even roughly correct about the notion of compulsion, to treat all such cases thus would be wrong. Moreover, there are surely some who understand the notions of compulsion and unavoidability without even being aware that actions might be determined, since they lack the relevant concept of nomic determination; and of those who are aware that actions might be determined, certainly no one other than an incompatibilist (or even incompatibilists in their everyday affairs) would automatically regard such cases as instances of compulsion. Whether an action is compelled and whether it is avoidable both depend, as I have tried to show, on the *kind* of thing that "brings it about," not on *whether* the action is brought about according to deterministic laws.[20]

A third consequence of my position has some general significance beyond its purely philosophical implications. If 'S is compelled to A at t' is compatible with 'S is morally responsible for having A-ed at t', then we may reassess the impact of recent psychological discoveries—and claims—suggesting that a great many of our actions, far more than we usually suppose, are compelled and thus unfree. Broadly speaking, I refer to "neurotic" and apparently normal behavior, not to "psychotic" behavior, though no doubt many exaggerate the extent to which anything that can plausibly be called mental illness renders the actions said to result from it compelled. This century has seen a tendency on the part of the educated to regard fewer and fewer of our everyday actions as free, and to attribute many of the allegedly vitiating compulsions to irrational (often unconscious) psychological forces, or to pervasive social pressures. The tendency has probably been strengthened by a widespread incompatibilist construal of the progress, or purported progress, of psychology in discovering the springs of human action. We may certainly dispute whether this tendency to diminish the domain of free action is justified. In the light of my account of compulsion, I suspect that the

---

[20] It is worth noting that one reason many philosophers have resisted compatibilism may be that it has been defended mainly by writers in the empiricist tradition, most of whom have been utilitarians of some kind. But compatibilism does not entail any particular moral theory; hence objections to utilitarianism are not necessarily objections to compatibilism.

extent to which the actions of normal persons are compelled by psychological forces or social conditions is often exaggerated, though my account makes clear why it is often natural to make unwarranted extensions of the notion of compulsion, and corresponding unwarranted encroachments upon the notion of freedom. But however that may be, compulsion simpliciter does not defeat moral responsibility; and it is a moral question, not a psychological question, under what conditions an action's being compelled and hence unfree absolves the agent of moral responsibility for it. Insofar as one deplores the widespread tendency to try to avoid moral responsibility by vague appeals to compulsion, or facile claims of impaired freedom of action, this should be a welcome conclusion.[21]

[21] For helpful comments on an earlier version of this chapter, I want to thank Bernard Berofsky, John Exdell, David Gerber, Norman C. Gillespie, Hardy E. Jones, Martin Perlmutter, and H. Van R. Wilson.

Chapter 8

Self-Deception and
Practical Reasoning

Self-deception is commonly viewed as a condition that bespeaks irrationality. This chapter challenges that view. I focus specifically on the connection between self-deception and practical reasoning, an area which, despite its importance for understanding self-deception, has not been systematically explored. I examine both how self-deception influences practical reasoning and how this influence affects the rationality of actions produced by practical reasoning. But what *is* self-deception? There are many accounts,[1] yet there is probably none sufficiently well known and compelling to serve as an adequate background given my purposes. Hence, I shall briefly present my own account of self-deception and, on that basis, explore its connections with practical reasoning and rational action.

I. Sketch of an Account of Self-Deception

For all the disagreement over what self-deception is, there is consensus on *one* challenge it poses: how to resolve the dilemma

[1] For an indication of the diversity of approaches in philosophy and psychology, see Alfred R. Mele, "Recent Work on Self-Deception," *American Philosophical Quarterly* 24 (1987); Mike W. Martin, ed., *Self-Deception and Self-Understanding* (Lawrence: University of Kansas Press, 1985); and Brian McLaughlin and Amelie O. Rorty, eds., *Philosophical Perspectives on Self-Deception* (Berkeley: University of California Press, 1988).

that arises as soon as one reflects on the term. Taken literally, self-deception seems to imply that a self-deceiver both believes and disbelieves the same proposition: disbelieving it as agent of the deception, believing it as victim. Writers on the topic have taken many approaches. *Literalists* hold that one can believe and disbelieve the same proposition. Some contend that this is irreducibly paradoxical and self-deception is thus impossible; but, arguably, construing the term literally does not require a complete analogy with other-person deception, and if this is so, the paradox can be avoided. *Non-literalists* have sometimes given accounts of self-deception, sometimes characterizing it without offering an account, and sometimes arguing that since no interesting set of necessary and sufficient conditions is to be found, we cannot give an account, and should be content with clarifying the various cases.

My view takes self-deception literally, though not precisely on the model of one person's deceiving another. I also consider the notion sufficiently determinate to make a philosophical account possible. Granted, 'self-deception' is vague. It is also liable to distortion because people may want to mold it to their needs for excuses, for understanding strange behavior, and for a criticism of others that has the special advantage of being muted by its suggestion that they were victims as well as perpetrators. Given the vagueness of the term, then, and the biases affecting its use, even a plausible account may not cover all its uses.

Let me introduce my account of self-deception in relation to some theoretical divisions that distinguish the major approaches. The question of *paradoxicality* has already been stressed: for some accounts it is real, for others apparent. Second, the *ontological category* a view ascribes to self-deception is important. Is it an act, or at least behavioral? Is it a state? Or does it straddle both categories? A third issue is *conceptual priority*. If (as I hold) there are both acts and states of self-deception, should we conceive the state in terms of the act or vice versa? In either case, there is the question of the *constitutive materials* of self-deception: are cognitive concepts, such as belief and knowledge, basic, or should we rely more on volitional notions, such as focusing attention and selecting sources of evidence? A fifth issue concerns the *conscious-unconscious dimension:* do unconscious elements play a role, say because one can believe and disbelieve the same proposition if one of the beliefs is unconscious?

Described in the theoretical terms just suggested, my account of self-deception is *non-paradoxical* (since I deny that it entails believing and disbelieving the same proposition); it is *dispositional* rather than behavioral, in that, ontologically, it construes self-deception as a state and, conceptually, it takes the state of self-deception as primary and interprets acts of self-deception as properly so-called by virtue of their relation to the state; it is *cognitive*, using cognitive concepts, such as that of unconscious belief, as its main building blocks (though it connects them with motivation and action); and it is *stratified*, since it appeals to levels of consciousness. The core of the account is this:

A person, S, is in self-deception, with respect to a proposition, p, at time t, if and only if, at t:

(1) S unconsciously knows that not-p (or has reason to believe, and unconsciously and truly believes, that not-p);

(2) S sincerely avows, or is disposed to avow sincerely, that p; and

(3) S has at least one want which (non-waywardly) explains, in part, both why S's belief that not-p is unconscious and why S is disposed to avow that p, even when presented with what S sees is evidence against p.[2]

Here unconscious belief is understood in a non-technical and quite unmysterious sense. It is roughly belief which S cannot, without special self-scrutiny or outside help, come to know or believe S has; it is not buried in a realm which only far-reaching methods, such as psychotherapy, can fathom. While this concept is akin to Freudian notions of unconscious elements, no special Freudian assumptions are presupposed.[3] In every other respect, for example, in directing behavior and guiding inferences, the belief can be almost entirely like any other; the often thin and delicate veil between it and unaided

[2] I have developed this account in several directions (and defended aspects of it) in "Self-Deception, Action, and Will," *Erkenntnis* 18 (1982), and "Self-Deception, Rationalization, and Reasons for Acting," in McLaughlin and Rorty, pp. 92–120. I have added 'non-waywardly' in (3) to rule out cases in which, for example, wanting to have one's brain manipulated leads a neuropsychologist to produce in one beliefs of the sort specified in (1) and (2). Perhaps we would now have artifically induced self-deception; but at least normally a want that is part of the psychic economy non-waywardly explains the factors in question.

[3] Unconscious belief is discussed in some detail in my essays cited in n. 2. Also relevant to my conception of it is the account of believing in "The Concept of Believing," *Personalist* 57 (1972). Cf. Eddy Zemach, "Unconscious Mind or Conscious Minds?" *Midwest Studies in Philosophy* 10 (1986).

consciousness may affect it little. Moreover, while *typically* self-deception has a certain kind of history, my account is *non-historical:* roughly,
I take self-deception to supervene on S's psychological properties in
such a way that (logically) S could be *created* as an adult in self-deception. S would thereby *tend* to act in certain ways, but cannot have
done so already. This is a good way to see both how it is possible to
be in self-deception without having performed acts of deceiving oneself and why the state is plausibly held to be conceptually more fundamental than the acts.

Clearly this view of self-deception presupposes a degree of dissoci-
ation. But it does not imply—as *homuncularism* would—that self-deception is the work of interacting subpersonal agents. My view does
not even imply *compartmentalism*, which accounts for self-deception
by appeal to partly autonomous subsystems, each capable of action,
belief, or both. Certainly there is a notion of a subsystem for which
it is plausible to suppose that such systems may figure in self-deception; but their work surely does not require agency or belief, as opposed to psychological processes simply going on in S. It is not as if
we must explain how S could believe obviously incompatible propositions and so must posit two believers constituting one person. For as
important as sincere avowal normally is in indicating belief, it does
not entail belief.[4] The mechanisms of self-deception might be clarified
by neuropsychological research, of course, and it may turn out that
cases of self-deception differ in ways that invite talk of somewhat
autonomous subsystems capable of belief. Some split-brain studies
may suggest such talk.[5] But the clear cases of self-deception are best
accounted for by postulating interferences with the usual level of self-
understanding, and in any event we should try to understand
self-deception without multiplying either subsystems, or senses of
'belief', or other cognitive or volitional concepts, beyond necessity.

Consider an example. Sara dislikes and is jealous of her sister-in-
law, Janet. But Sara is also a person of good character and is deeply
committed to maintaining harmonious family relations. At an anni-
versary party for her brother and Janet, Sara toasts the couple. But

[4] Thus, 'conscious belief' is misleading. I also doubt we need a weaker cognitive
attitude than belief here; but for some reasons to think we do, see Georges Rey, "Akrasia, Self-Deception, and the Promise of Practical Reasoning," in McLaughlin and Rorty,
pp. 92–120.
[5] See, for example, Michael S. Gazanniga, "The Social Brain," *Psychology Today* (No-
vember 1985), for a split-brain case in which (as he seems to see it) we have two centers
of belief.

in doing so she raves about her brother and, almost as an after-thought, adds something perfunctorily positive about Janet at the end. When her husband points this out to her, Sara minimizes the perfunctory element and says that Janet tends to be embarrassed by praise. In saying this, however, Sara is uncomfortable, and later she goes to artificial lengths to be courteous to Janet. All this *can* be explained by appeal to hypocrisy toward Janet; but if certain other elements are present, self-deception may emerge as a more likely explanation. Let us add some details that suggest this.

Suppose we discover that Sara knew Janet was concerned about how Sara felt toward her, that Sara is articulate and generally percep-tive, and that they were looking right at each other during the relevant part of the toast, with Janet visibly uncomfortable on hearing Sara's compliments. This would confirm that Sara had reason to think she was slighting Janet. On the other hand, if Sara is scrupulously honest and has a self-image to which being honest and kind are central, it might be unreasonable to conclude that she is simply lying in ex-plaining her toast as appropriate to Janet's tendency to be embar-rassed by praise. This would be even less reasonable if, as is quite possible, Sara voluntarily does a number of things for Janet, such as errands, canvassing for political candidates they both support, and lending Janet clothes. That very pattern, however, might be marked by strain on Sara's part, particularly when the contact is personal, say in lending clothes as opposed to canvassing. Given all this, self-deception is a plausible explanation of parts of Sara's pattern of conduct.

There are many propositions with respect to which Sara might be self-deceived. Consider two related ones—that she likes Janet and that her toast was positive. We have seen, on one side, evidence that Sara (i) in some way realizes her toast was slighting and (ii) did not really try to please Janet in making it. But we also have evidence that Sara is not simply lying when she tells her husband—rationalizing—that Janet tends to be embarrassed by praise. Similarly, Sara expresses affection for Janet when people tactfully ask her if she likes her, yet has much reason to believe she does not like Janet: from her own behavior—what she does not do as well as what she does—and from her thoughts and emotional reactions, such as a sense of strain in lending Janet clothes.

Describing the case in the language of my account of self-deception, when Sara says she likes Janet, she is *deceiving* herself because she knows, unconsciously, that she does not like her; but she is also *deceived*, because, in saying this, she is both avowing something false and yet not lying, at least not in the usual sense implying something like an attempt to get us to believe something false: at the level of her avowals about her emotions and of her surface conventional behavior, she is taken in. But she does not quite believe what she says. As an intelligent person aware of her own behavior and feelings, actually believing what she avows is further than her cognitive system will go in response to what it seems natural to call her ego defenses; and this is why we do not expect the full range of behavior one would expect from genuine belief, including planning for a long vacation trip together (though in a well-developed case, even such planning might be self-deceptively done). Yet her sincere avowal of the proposition is *like* an expression of belief; normally, in fact, sincerely avowing that p implies believing it. We have, then, both knowledge that not-p and the satisfaction of a major criterion for believing p. The criterion is not a logically sufficient condition, but it is strong enough to make its satisfaction in avowing a false proposition seem like being deceived in so speaking.

The motivational condition on self-deception is also illustrated here. If Sara is jealous of and dislikes Janet, it is not surprising that Sara tries to slight her in making the toast. However, if she does indeed (unconsciously) know that she has hurt her, as we might expect both from her intentionally doing so and from her acuity about people, then given her honesty and general uprightness, we should expect both some compensatory behavior, such as artificial warmth toward Janet, and avowals of affection toward her. If the honesty is firm enough, and her need to see herself as upright deep enough, these avowals can be at once sincere, mistaken, and incompatible with what, deep down, she knows to be true. Here, then, is a sketch of how self-deception as I conceive it might look.

Using the suggested account of the state of self-deception, we can understand other aspects of self-deception and distinguish it from notions with which it may be confused.

First, consider *acts of self-deception:* roughly, those that manifest a state of it. Sara's rationalizing her toast, when her husband asks about it, is an act of self-deception. She manifests self-deception in her sincere but misguided attempt to rationalize the offense. If there are acts of deceiving others by a mere utterance, are there also instantaneous acts of deceiving oneself? Not if an act of self-deception must

manifest self-deception already present; but there could be instantaneous acts of *causing* oneself to be self-deceived: *genetically*, as opposed to *manifestationally*, self-deceptive acts. Still, the limited analogy
to other-person deception does not imply this. In self-deception,
there is only one person, and normally the dynamics of self-deception require a gradual onset. Nor is self-deception ever identical with
an act: we apply the term to patterns of behavior, but one should not
infer that self-deception is ever constituted by an act. We also use
'generosity' to designate patterns of behavior, and we talk of acts
of generosity; but it does not follow that generosity itself is ever an
act.

We should also distinguish self-deception from *being deceiving toward oneself*: a kind of behavior through which, usually by degrees,
one gets into self-deception, for example putting evidence out of
mind, focusing often or onesidedly on an unreasonably favorable
view of oneself, and so on. Being deceiving toward oneself does not
entail self-deception. It may simply produce *delusion*: Sara might
really come to believe she likes Janet, without the veiled realization
that this is false, required by self-deception. Granted, someone genuinely deluded might first have been self-deceived. But it need not be
so. Tom might simply become deceived in believing that *p*, as a *result*
of being deceiving with himself, yet not enter self-deception, because
he is too wholehearted and there is nothing of the perpetrator about
him. This is not self-deception; it is *self-caused deception.*

Self-deception must also be distinguished from self-manipulation,
with or without resulting self-deception or delusion, from putting
evidence out of mind, and from wishful thinking, construed
(roughly) as belief produced, non-evidentially, by a desire that the
proposition in question be true. My account can help us make these
distinctions, but I cannot pursue them further nor defend the account. I believe, however, that most of what I say about self-deception
in relation to practical reasoning and rational action can be seen
(though perhaps less easily) from the perspective of quite different
accounts of self-deception.

II. Practical Reasoning

Using the account of self-deception just outlined, I want
to consider the interaction between self-deception and practical rea-

soning. I cannot simply presuppose consensus on what practical reasoning is, and I shall thus lay out, very briefly, a conception of practical reasoning that can sharpen the issue.

As I conceive practical reasoning, it is reasoning undertaken to decide what to do. We can best understand it if we distinguish among (1) practical arguments, construed as structures of propositions; (2) episodes (or at least processes) of reasoning constituting inferential realizations of such structures; and (3) actions, decisions, intentions, and other motivational elements based on such reasoning. We can think of the conclusion of a practical argument as the *answer* to a practical question, such as 'What should I do to celebrate my niece's graduation?'; of *S*'s drawing that conclusion as a *response to S*'s asking a practical question; and of *S*'s doing the thing favored by the conclusion as—subjectively, at least—a *solution* to the problem motivating the question.[6] My special concern here is not with practical arguments, for example with the issue of their cogency, but with the process of practical reasoning and its effects, chiefly the actions it produces. Before we consider how self-deception affects these things, however, we should focus on the major elements that figure in practical reasoning.

If one wants to be fine-grained, one can distinguish a vast variety of kinds of reasoning undertaken in deciding what to do. But in the tradition handed down from Aristotle it has been common to regard as fundamental, in everyday practical reasoning, a motivational premise, a cognitive premise, and a conclusion conceived either as a practical judgment in favor of an action or as an action or practical attitude, such as decision or intention. For my purposes, we may take as fundamental the case in which the motivational premise expresses a want of *S*, the cognitive premise expresses a belief of *S*, and the conclusion is *S*'s practical judgment to the effect that *S* should *A*, where *A*-ing is an action *S* sees as realizing the want.[7] The action may occur straightaway on *S*'s concluding the reasoning, as where *S* wants to save a friend writing a publisher for a book, believes that calling to say it has just come in the mail will accomplish this, and directly picks up

---

[6] Here and in the next few paragraphs I draw on my essay "A Theory of Practical Reasoning," *American Philosophical Quarterly* 19 (1982).

[7] The sense of 'express' does not require *having* the relevant propositional attitude, in part because we should allow practical reasoning that is in some way suppositional. My "Theory of Practical Reasoning" defends and qualifies the suggested conception of practical reasoning.

the phone. Thus, some writers *identify* the action with the conclusion. On my view, this assimilates the conclusion of the reasoning to its behavioral upshot. Moreover, I want to allow for failure to act on one's practical reasoning, as where one suffers weakness of will; and this is at best difficult if a piece of completed practical reasoning *contains* the action as its conclusion.

This last point brings me to an important distinction. In selecting options and in long-range planning, we do practical reasoning in an *exploratory* way, quite aware that we are not resolved to act on our conclusion. Thus, if one is deciding where to vacation for rest and stimulation, one may go through a series of practical reasonings to see what instrumental actions, such as expenditures, are required by each attractive option. It is true that one might instead simply reason theoretically about means-end relations, for example about which resort has the best entertainment; but sometimes imaginative rehearsal of a plan, with hypothetical judgments and visualized actions, plays a different role in facilitating decision. A tentative practical judgment favoring a prospect represents it quite differently from merely entertaining (say) the proposition that it is most desirable; the former provisionally commits one to an overall valuation of an action projected for oneself, the latter merely represents an alternative as most valuable. The notion of exploratory practical reasoning turns out to help in understanding how self-deception affects both practical reasoning and actions related to that reasoning.

It may appear that the suggested sketch of practical reasoning precludes the underlying motivation or belief from being unconscious in the sense appropriate to a belief central in self-deception. For it may seem that if a want, say to do something one would be ashamed of, figures in one's reasoning leading to a judgment that one should *A*, surely one must realize that one *does* want that to which one believes *A*-ing will contribute. But this need not be so. I might suppose I am only *imagining* what it would be like to realize that state of affairs. Moreover, just as one can present a theoretical argument enthymematically, one can do practical reasoning without entertaining *all* of its constituent propositions. Even the conclusion might not be consciously confronted.[8] One can also acquire the belief expressing the minor premise later than the want figuring in the major, and then complete the reasoning when, although the want is not manifest in

---

[8] Enthymemes are discussed in my "Theory of Practical Reasoning."

consciousness, it still motivates one's drawing the conclusion—judging that one should *A*. The most common case of this occurs when we notice a means to an already existing end we have and judge we should do the thing in question. (I shall return to such cases.)

I should add that I do *not* take practical reasoning to be so pervasive that for every intentional action there is a piece of practical reasoning from which it arises. But there is a truth underlying this view: to each intentional action (or at least to each performed for a further end) there *is* a corresponding practical argument, whether the agent instantiates it in an actual reasoning process or not. Indeed, intentional actions are *realizations* of practical arguments conceived as abstract structures.[9] But it would be a mistake to consider actual practical reasoning the basis of all intentional action and to view the influence of self-deception on practical reasoning as doing that would require. Still, practical reasoning is very common in the genesis of actions; and if in some way it does underlie all intentional action, that would only broaden the application of my points about how self-deception affects it.

III. Self-Deception as an Influence
on Practical Reasoning

If I am roughly right about what self-deception and practical reasoning are, there are many ways in which the former may affect the latter. Among the most interesting possibilities are these: self-deception might (1) supply a cognitive premise; (2) contribute a motivational premise; (3) lead to practical reasoning one would not otherwise have done; (4) produce a self-deceptive practical judgment as conclusion; (5) alter the course of practical reasoning already in process; (6) lead to weakness of will; (7) produce a practical judgment incongruous with one's overall desires; (8) obscure factors that might otherwise lead *S* to undertake conflicting practical reasoning, or at least might affect reasoning *S* does do; and (9) generate rationalizational practical reasoning. This section considers these possibilities in turn.

1. Since self-deception embodies belief, we should expect that a

---

[9] In Chapter 6, this volume, I have characterized such realizations in some detail.

self-deceiver can perform practical reasoning whose minor premise represents a belief produced by, or intimately connected with, self-deception. Imagine that as part of her self-deception with respect to her feelings about Janet, Sara has an unconscious desire (hence unconsciously wants) to hurt Janet. This may lead her to notice ways of doing that, even if she does not seek them. Thus, if she discovers from a mutual friend that Janet would like to know of Sara's pregnancy *from* Sara and before it is generally known, she may form the belief that if she does not mention it to Janet, Janet will be hurt. This belief can provide a minor premise for her practical reasoning as follows. At some point when the question whether to tell Janet comes up, Sara might judge that she should not mention the pregnancy. This judgment could be the concluding element in practical reasoning whose major premise, expressing the unconscious want, does not enter consciousness. That is quite possible even if the minor—that not mentioning it to Janet will hurt—does enter consciousness; for Sara might have a rationalization which protects her from realizing what her real reason for not mentioning the pregnancy is. She might, for instance, say to her husband, who is suggesting she tell Janet about the baby, that though she realizes this will hurt Janet slightly, she must not hurt her own cousin, who is Janet's friend, by telling Janet first, and she hasn't yet had a chance to tell her cousin.

2. The same example illustrates how self-deception may supply a motivating want which underlies the major: here, the want to hurt Janet. It is in the light of the major, namely that she wants to hurt Janet, that Sara's judging that not mentioning the pregnancy will accomplish this *leads* to her actually judging she should not mention it. Here, then, Sara exhibits *self-deceptive practical reasoning*. First, one of her premises, the motivational one, expresses an element in the associated self-deception, in this case the unconscious want to hurt Janet. Second, the belief corresponding to the minor premise arises in part because of the self-deception, and on that ground the reasoning is even more closely connected with self-deception than it would be if only the want were involved. There are, then, degrees to which practical reasoning may be self-deceptive. I offer no definitional account of self-deceptive practical reasoning, but we may say at least this: the greater the number of elements in the reasoning that are embodied in, or (non-waywardly) produced by, self-deception, the more self-deceptive it is, where the former elements count more than the latter.

3. In addition to producing self-deceptive practical reasoning, self-deception can simply lead one to do practical reasoning one would not otherwise have done. An especially interesting case of this is practical reasoning that *serves*, but does not *embody*, self-deception. We have assumed that Sara, as a nice person who realizes that Janet is a perfectly good sister-in-law, *wants* to like her, wants to believe she does, and wants others to believe she does. Given these desires, Sara might keenly want to do something which manifests good feeling toward Janet. She might consider various options, notice that sending Janet grapefruit for Thanksgiving would manifest good feeling, and, wanting to manifest such feeling, conclude that she should send it. Here we have motivation which is related to the self-deception—perhaps *occasioned* by it, though not produced by it—yielding perfectly ordinary practical reasoning. The self-deception leads Sara to seek a way of showing good feeling; doing this is self-preservational for that deception, since doing it supports both the content and the sincerity of Sara's avowals to the effect that she likes Janet. Yet the reasoning she does in the service of her wanting to show good feeling is not self-deceptive, at least not if we take that to require a more direct causal connection or, especially, to imply that the reasoning embodies a constituent in the deception itself.

4. The same example can be varied, however, so as to yield what is a case of self-deceptive practical reasoning and has a self-deceptive practical judgment as conclusion. Suppose that at the time of the reasoning Sara *also* wants to avoid warm gestures toward Janet and believes that sending grapefruit would be one. If she wants this more than to manifest good feeling, then, while she might still engage in the reasoning just described, she might not be wholehearted in judging that she ought to send grapefruit. It is possible, in fact, that in making that judgment she is deceiving herself, just as she is deceiving herself in protesting, to her husband, that she really does like Janet. If she then does not actually send the fruit, we could explain it as due in part to her not having *assentingly* judged she should. However, the practical reasoning is still genuine; she still *draws* a practical conclusion and *makes* the appropriate practical judgment. Nor is she lying to her husband in making it; she is self-deceptively insincere, and so lying only to herself. We could rule that this is not really practical reasoning; but it is artificial to do so, and if we countenance exploratory practical reasoning, whose conclusion need

not be assentingly drawn, then so ruling would unwarrantedly narrow our conception of practical reasoning.

5. So far, I have concentrated on cases in which self-deception influences what practical reasoning one does, as opposed to affecting practical reasoning already taking place: roughly, I have stressed the *productive* as opposed to *interventional* role of self-deception. But if we imagine a person deliberating about options, we can see how self-deception may intervene, either in the reasoning process or between it and the action in favor of which it concludes. Consider Steve, a terminal cancer patient in self-deception about the seriousness of his illness. He is deliberating about what to give his daughter for her birthday. Feeling expansive, he asks her what she might like—an airline ticket to romantic places, jewelry, clothing, and so on. She leaves him free to choose, but expresses a slight preference for the ticket. As he thinks the matter through, with wanting to make her happy as his main goal, he tentatively concludes in favor of the ticket, then pauses. In a flash he realizes that there is some chance he will fall ill while she is away and spoil her trip. In this context, he finds it pleasant to think of the permanence of jewelry as a reminder of him. It then occurs to him that he wants to give her lasting happiness, and he judges that the jewelry would be best. In such a case, his unconscious knowledge that he is soon to die leads him to have the related thought—which he *can* bear to entertain—that there is a chance he will fall ill. This in turn enables his desire to give her something permanent to override his desire to make her happy now. The practical reasoning which was about to produce action is outweighed by elements of his self-deception, and a new practical inference carries his conviction.

6. Weakness of will—*incontinence* or *akrasia* in some terminologies— is another phenomenon with diverse connections to self-deception. There are several ways self-deception can be linked with weakness of will in relation to practical reasoning. It might seem that one way has already been illustrated: if Sara does not act on her (overall) judgment that she should send Janet grapefruit, she may appear to be exhibiting a weak-willed failure to act on her practical reasoning. But recall that she did not assentingly make this judgment. Hence, it is unclear that weakness of will occurs. To be sure, if the judgment is sound, then she does make an *error* in not acting on it. But, at least if she has a conflicting practical judgment aligned with her motivation—say, to avoid drawing closer to Janet—the error should not be considered

weakness of will.[10] On the other hand, if she had assentingly made the judgment, but simply could not bring herself to give the fruit because of her entrenched unconscious desire to keep Janet at a distance, then she would exhibit—what I suspect is common—weakness of will that is induced by self-deception through a strong want which that deception embodies.

7. There is still another case: instead of self-deception's causing weak-willed action by virtue of a desire involved in the former outweighing a sound practical judgment, self-deception may produce a practical judgment incongruous with one's overall desires. An especially interesting case is such a judgment that is also unsound and deserves to be *motivationally outweighed* by desires not involved in the self-deception, that is, to have them prevent its producing action. Let us imagine Steve differently. Because he wants to maintain the appearance of recovering, he also wants to go with his daughter on part of the vacation trip. His practical reasoning leads him to judge that he should buy two tickets. He is about to order them when he realizes that he does not feel well, nor will his presence in his state be an unmixed blessing to his daughter. His rational desire to treat his illness seriously and to let her have an unfettered vacation, simply outweighs his stubborn judgment that he should order the ticket, and he puts the phone down, with mingled shame and relief. These same elements could of course change his *judgment;* but that is a different case, and where self-deception partly underlies a practical judgment, we should expect that judgment to exhibit some resistance to being motivationally outweighed. On the other hand, precisely because Steve's judgment deserves to be outweighed and *is* overridden by a rational desire, we have an especially interesting case not generally recognized: one in which, although an action is prima facie irrational as contravening one's 'better judgment' and thereby incontinent, it is, on balance, rational.

8. The next case to be examined is that in which self-deception, by limiting what S considers or is influenced by, obscures otherwise relevant factors and affects what reasoning S undertakes or S's practical judgment or action in response to it. Self-deceivers tend to put certain things out of mind, or to manipulate evidence bearing on

[10] There is a problem here, however: suppose she has a second-order judgment that she should act to change her desires toward Janet. *If* that judgment is not aligned with a want on balance, then she might perhaps instantiate weakness of will by virtue of implicitly acting against that judgment.

their self-deception. Recall Steve. Imagine that if he were not self-deceived about his impending death, he would not be even considering sending his daughter away on vacation; he contemplates this oonly because he wants to exhibit confidence in recovery. Moreover, because he unconsciously knows his case is terminal, he does not consider sending his other daughter with the first, since he cannot bring himself to face the near future with both of them gone. Yet he might know that a trip for the two together might be the best birthday present he can give. His self-deception, then, tends to have contrasting effects: first, by obscuring relevant factors it narrows the field of his practical reasoning so far as that might satisfy his underlying desires, such as to have his family near at the end and to seem confident at the same time; and second, it broadens that field so far as doing this accords with his motives that serve to camouflage his self-deception, such as his wanting to appear confident that he will recover by the time of his daughter's return. This is the *selective* influence of self-deception *on* practical reasoning, as opposed to its substantive influence *in* practical reasoning that actually occurs.

9. The connections between self-deception and practical reasoning may involve rationalization.[11] We have already noted how rationalization can help to screen self-deception from consciousness, as where Sara rationalizes her not informing Janet about the baby by appeal to her wanting to avoid hurting her own cousin's feelings. That example can be adapted to show how self-deception may lead to practical reasoning that is itself rationalizational. I want to sketch two cases and close the section with some general points.

One kind of rationalizational practical reasoning serves to rationalize a practical judgment; the other kind I am concerned with rationalizes an action. Suppose that instead of simply *citing* a reason Sara had, but did not act on, for not informing Janet about the pregnancy, Sara had actually reasoned, in the course of deciding how to handle Janet, from her wanting not to hurt her cousin to the conclusion that she should not inform Janet now. If this judgment is not *based* at least in part on that want and her believing something to the effect that not telling Janet would realize the want, then even though the judgment is *warranted* by the premises of her reasoning, her making it is not *explained* by the motivation and belief they express, and the rea-

[11] I have discussed self-deception specifically in relation to rationalization in "Self-Deception, Rationalization, and Reasons for Acting."

soning is a rationalization, rather than a real explaining ground, of the judgment. Now suppose she does abstain from informing Janet about the pregnancy. The same reasoning is then a rationalization, and not a real explaining ground, of that action. This holds whether the reasoning is used retrospectively—and thus not as practical reasoning—in attempted justification, or considered as a possible explanation of the action.

To be sure, there are times when either *S*'s making a practical judgment or *S*'s performing an action are explainable *in part* by appeal to one factor and in part in terms of another. If the rationalizing elements are a partial explanation, but not sufficient to explain the relevant item, we have a partial rationalization. If they are indispensable elements in a correct explanation of it, they may be as much an explanation as a rationalization.[12] Explanatory and rationalizing elements can be mixed in a variety of ways, and some cases defy easy classification.

Self-deception can affect practical reasoning to differing degrees along the explanatory spectrum; and like other practical reasoning, the rationalizational kinds of self-deceptive practical reasoning may be more or less self-deceptive depending on many factors, particularly the extent to which self-deception determines (i) what *does* explain the concluding judgment or the action rationalized by the reasoning, and (ii) what want(s) and belief(s) are crucial in the reasoning itself. For instance, if, in making the judgment with which the reasoning concludes, one is deceiving oneself, then the reasoning is less typical, and more self-deceptive, than where one assents to the practical judgment.

It should be stressed that practical reasoning can also rationalize without being self-deceptive. When it rationalizes an action, practical reasoning need have no constituents produced by self-deception. To be sure, if such reasoning occurs in rationalizing an action done from self-deception, we may call the reasoning self-deceptive in a weak sense. Thus, there may be nothing intrinsically self-deceptive about Sara's reasoning, from her wanting to save money and her believing that not going on a trip with Janet would do this, to the conclusion that she should not go. But if her declining was really due to her desire to avoid intimacy with Janet, the reasoning is self-deceptive at

<hr>

[12] In "Rationalization and Rationality," *Synthese* 65 (1986), I consider various kinds of rationalization and their relation to justification.

least in being at once a rationalization of an action performed from self-deception and part of Sara's global avoidance strategy with respect to the object of her self-deception: above all, her unconscious desire to hurt Janet.

IV. Self-Deceptive Practical Reasoning and Rational Action

Self-deception is very commonly associated with irrationality, and it may seem that actions based on self-deceptive practical reasoning cannot be rational.[13] On my view of self-deception, while it is clear how it can manifest irrationality, it is also evident how it may occur in a rational person, perhaps even as a rational—though non-intentional—response to a subjectively intolerable situation. It does, after all, typically embody knowledge; and even apart from that, it is an *evidence-sensitive* state. Nor are the typical underlying desires, normally expressing deep-seated psychic needs, generally irrational. With this perspective in mind, let us explore the rationality of actions based on self-deceptive practical reasoning, that is, roughly, reasoning in the doing of which one is deceiving oneself, or otherwise manifesting self-deception in a significant way (such as the ways I have illustrated). Typically, the significant manifestations are the kinds I have cited in relation to the judgment with which one concludes, or the want motivating the reasoning, or the belief determining its minor premise.

Suppose that Steve unconsciously wants to avoid facing his approaching death. This leads him to consider various ways to brighten his days, since he believes (perhaps also unconsciously) that doing this will help him avoid that thought. As he begins to plan, it occurs to him that going to a spa will brighten his days, and he concludes that he should go. The reasoning may be considered self-deceptive because the motivating want, to brighten his days, is grounded directly in his unconscious want to avoid facing his impending death, which is in turn part of his self-deception with respect to that death. If Steve now goes to the spa, on the basis of this reasoning, for example

---

[13] It is very difficult to specify what it is for an action to be *based on* practical reasoning. A partial account is suggested in Chapter 6.

acting in accord with its conclusion and on the basis of the motivation and cognition expressed in its premises, is there any reason to believe he acts irrationally? I think not. Granted, if Steve's self-deception causes him to overlook a better alternative, or if his wanting his days to be cheerful is itself irrational, that is another matter. For while rationality may not require choosing what, from one's own perspective at least, is optimal, some deficiency in rationality is suggested by doing something one would readily take to be, on balance, inferior to an option easily obtained, such as a much shorter route to a destination; and it is arguable that there can be desires so grossly irrational as to preclude *rational* action in their service (the second of these points, at least, is controversial, nor am I trying to be precise given my limited illustrative purpose). But if we assume that going to the spa is Steve's best way to make his days cheerful and that he rationally wants that, why not suppose his action is rational? It is true that his wanting to avoid thinking of his approaching death underlies his wanting to make his days cheerful; but that want is not irrational, it is simply unpleasant to entertain. Moreover, there are other factors that make it reasonable to want one's days cheerful: factors affecting any sick person. So here, I think, we have a case where self-deception is not the tail that wags the dog, and seems to serve a useful, rational purpose in *S*'s psychology.

Compare Steve's case with that of Bill, who does the same thing for precisely parallel reasons, but wholly without self-deception or unconscious reasons. Would Bill be acting *more* rationally? There is an inclination to say so. Yet that may be due to Bill's apparently greater rationality as an *agent*. He would *have* more to say for his action; but that does not imply that there *is* more to be said for it. Other things equal, Bill can *justify* his action better, since, unlike Steve, he can readily trace it to its real basis in his hierarchy of rational desires. But it does not follow that the action itself is more rational, any more than if Ann (or anyone else) can explain why her painting is a good one better than Betty can explain why *hers* is, it follows that Ann's *is* better.

A major ground for my doubting that Steve's action is less rational than Bill's is this: I construe rationality both holistically and causally— as a matter of the overall pattern of reasons that actually explain the action in relation to *S*'s overall situation. A central element in this pattern is the action's having the appropriate *plasticity*, as manifested, say, in *S*'s readiness to change course if new information favors it. In this, action seems like belief: the rationality of a belief appears to be normally a matter of factors in which it is grounded, and of how they enable the agent to respond to relevant considerations, not of S's ability to marshal such factors in defending it. Such elements as unconscious perceptual cues, which one cannot, without special knowledge, know one is using, may ground rational belief even if one is no more able to appeal to them in justifying the belief than Steve is to invoke his underlying desire in justifying his going to the spa.

Consider a different kind of self-deceptive practical reasoning, in which the unconscious knowledge constituent (indirectly) yields the minor premise. If Sara unconsciously knows that she wants to hurt Janet, she may as a result believe (whether consciously or not) that she is disposed to hurt Janet and that *if* she hurts her by excluding her from a family gathering, she will appear to people to want to hurt Janet. When the gathering comes up, Sara may reason from her wanting to avoid this appearance, together with this conditional proposition, to the conclusion that she should invite Janet. If she then does so, her action helps to hide her self-deception from herself as well as to conceal her ignoble want from others. Surely self-deception often yields this sort of behavior; indeed, if it could not camouflage itself, it would not be so resilient. Now granted that inviting Janet as her sister-in-law is a *rational thing for her to do,* is Sara also rational *in doing it?* In Kantian terms, does her action merely conform with reason or is it rational? One mark against it is that it does not accord with her underlying desire to hurt Janet. Still, Sara's desire to avoid appearing to hate Janet may be as strong a desire as that; and more important, it is rational given the wide basis it has in Sara's generally rational, civilized body of desires. Hence, though she is in some way criticizable for harboring an irrational desire, and perhaps for being self-deceived, the action emerging from her self-deceptive practical reasoning can be perfectly rational.

Things may of course be otherwise; perhaps most actions produced by self-deception are not rational. Suppose that it produces practical reasoning with an irrational motivating want or irrational means-end belief, or both. Surely, there is no better reason to think that acting on the basis of this reasoning is rational than in the case of non-self-deceptive practical reasoning with comparably flawed constituents. It might be objected that the view I am defending wrongly stresses explanatory considerations, that, for example, the rationality of the action depends wholly on the quality of the practical argument that concludes in favor of that action, and what matters is *that* S do what a good argument supports, not *why* S does this. But I do not think this line any more plausible here than in epistemological cases. It is widely (though not universally) agreed that a belief *based* on an irrationally held premise—say, on a blind acceptance of what a discredited "authority" has said—is not rational (at least not on the basis of that premise), even if the belief is in *accord* with an argument S abstractly accepts, as where S considers an argument by a hated authority cogent, but is not influenced by it, and uses it, or is disposed to use it, only as a rationalization.

This is not to deny that the quality of reasoning that underlies an action is *also* relevant to the rationality of the action. Suppose that I produce two pieces of practical reasoning, one self-deceptive, one not, and reach conflicting conclusions. If the better justified conclusion is that of the latter argument, but I act on the former argument, then presumably I am not acting *as* rationally as I would have in acting on the better justified conclusion, and I may be acting irrationally. Thus, imagine that Steve self-deceptively reasons to the conclusion that the air ticket is his best gift, then reconsiders and non-self-deceptively reasons to the better justified conclusion that the jewelry is preferable. If, from fear of seeming afraid to part with his daughter for two months, he decides on the ticket, then he is acting irrationally, in terms of the total pattern of his relevant desires and beliefs. But the explanatory role of practical reasoning, as well as its quality as argumentation, is also crucial for the rationality of an action it favors. Thus, Steve's action would be no more rational—though it would be more readily rationalizable—if he could cite, but did not act on, a third, plausible, piece of practical reasoning he did, to the effect that since she will worry too much about him if he does not go, he should buy a ticket, too. This reasoning *would* give him something to say for buying the ticket, as an abstract option. But to cite it in defending the rationality of *his* buying it, as a concrete action, is like defending one's character by noting the good effect of something one did for a selfish reason.

V. Conclusion

I have characterized self-deception by appeal to the notion of unconscious knowledge and explained how, as embodying such knowledge yet giving rise to at least dispositions to avow incompatible propositions, it can affect various dimensions of human life. In exploring the interaction between self-deception and practical reasoning, I have construed such reasoning as an inferential process in which, on the basis of premises expressing motivation and cognition, an agent makes a practical judgment. It turns out that self-deception can affect practical reasoning in many ways. It may supply, or at least contribute to the agent's adopting, one or even both premises; it may produce practical reasoning one would not otherwise have done; it may lead the agent to draw a self-deceptive conclusion; it may camouflage practical reasoning from the agent or redirect its course after it begins; it may cause weakness of will, thereby preventing the agent's acting on the reasoning; it may produce a practical judgment incongruous with one's overall desires, with resulting conflict between avowed intention and preponderant motivation; it may narrow—or sometimes broaden—the field from which one selects materials for practical reasoning; it may obscure considerations that would lead one to do conflicting practical reasoning; and it may produce practical reasoning that serves, whether wholly or in part, as a rationalization.

Self-deception does not, however, always impair either the agent in general or practical reasoning in particular. Neither the wants, nor the beliefs, nor the concluding judgments, figuring in self-deceptive practical reasoning need be irrational; and as this suggests, actions based on practical reasoning need not be irrational either. They are to be assessed holistically, in terms of the same kind of pattern of elements relevant to the appraisal of actions based on ordinary practical reasoning. Self-deception may certainly impair the agent's ability to explain or justify the action influenced by it, but that action is not thereby rendered less rational.

One further implication of my points deserves mention. While I have not denied that both beliefs and desires can be produced by non-rational processes in a way that renders them irrational, my account of self-deception tends to minimize the need to posit irrational beliefs and desires, and it dispenses altogether with postulation of inconsistent beliefs to ground the apparent paradox of self-deception. There is paradox enough without them, particularly if we do not insist on a complete analogy with other-person deception. As I see it, self-deception is more a defect in our self-knowledge (or at least conscious self-knowledge) than in our psychological constitution, though our liability to it may be a kind of constitutional deficiency in itself. In the main, then, self-deception does not force us to recognize beliefs so irrational as to violate the normal presupposition of minimal rationality we make in attributing beliefs.[14] If it is true that beliefs and desires can arise, or be artificially induced, in such a way that they are utterly irrational, and if people themselves can act irrationally, it remains the case that only creatures with a significant degree of rationality and complexity are even candidates for self-deception. That by its very nature it readily intertwines itself with practical reasoning confirms this. For all the existence of self-deception shows, we are, however imperfectly, rational animals.[15]

[14] This, I take it, is one thing Donald Davidson worries about in "Paradoxes of Irrationality," in R. Wollheim and J. Hopkins, eds., *Philosophical Essays on Freud* (Cambridge: Cambridge University Press, 1982), pp. 289–305.

[15] An earlier version of this essay was given in a symposium on self-deception at the 1986 meeting of the Society for Philosophy and Psychology. I especially want to thank my commentator, Brian McLaughlin. I have also benefited from comments by Reinaldo Elugardo, Laurence Thomas, and readers for the *Canadian Journal of Philosophy*, as well as from discussion with Béla Szabados, with my co-symposiasts, Kenneth Gergen and Georges Rey, and, less recently, with John King-Farlow, whose repeated attacks on stereotypes about self-deception contributed to my efforts to place it in the context of the overall rationality of the human agent.

Chapter 9

Responsible Action
and Virtuous Character

Much of the literature on moral responsibility is dominated by the question of whether moral responsibility is compatible with determinism. Indeed, sometimes philosophers assume that actions for which we bear moral responsibility are equivalent to free actions, and they often say little about moral responsibility beyond illustrating the equivalence claim and discussing the relation between free action and determinism. There is, however, much about moral responsibility that needs clarification; and even when we understand what moral responsibility is, questions about its scope persist. My aim is to clarify both its nature and its scope, and particularly to explore our responsibility for our character. In doing this I shall partially assess the Aristotelian idea that our character traits are under our voluntary control.[1]

I. The Conceptual Territory

There are various kinds of responsibility. One is *causal responsibility*. The pressure of a tree can be responsible for the crook-

---

[1] See, for example, *Nicomachean Ethics*, bk. 1, in which Aristotle says that moral virtue is formed by habit (1103a), and that we are praised and blamed for virtues and vices (1106a). Compare his remarks, in bk. 3, that our character is determined by our choos-

edness of a trellis. Similarly, an agent can be responsible for a fire simply by virtue of causing it, though to be sure we do not usually attribute even causal responsibility to agents unless we think they might bear some other kind of responsibility. In sharp contrast is *role responsibility*, as illustrated by a teacher's responsibility to present course materials competently. Whereas causal responsibility for something presupposes its having occurred, role responsibility for it does not: the latter need not be fulfilled. The former is usually attributed retrospectively, the latter usually prospectively, though it makes sense to say that by being careless someone will be responsible (a causal attribution) for a forest fire, or that a teacher was responsible for grading one hundred papers by Monday (a role attribution) and did it.

Philosophical discussions of responsibility have focused mainly on a third kind, illustrated by the notion of an agent's moral responsibility for giving up a military secret or—as a result of being kidnapped—not being morally responsible for failing to keep a promise. Our widest term for this might be *normative responsibility,* which is above all a type of eligibility for normative assessment regarding an action.[2] The most common kind of assessment appropriate to normative responsibility is moral; but one could be normatively responsible in another way, say aesthetically or prudentially. Perhaps the central idea is that responsible action, that is, action for which one is normatively responsible, is an appropriate partial basis for assessment of one's character and indeed of an agent overall, insofar as such global assessment is different from assessment of character. For instance, responsible action that fulfills a duty counts positively in the appraisal of character; responsible action that wrongs someone counts negatively; and so forth. On the other hand, normative responsibility should not be assumed to apply only to action. One may be responsible for one's students' failing to know a certain technique, and that failure is not an action. Arguably, this responsibility must be owing to, say, one's deciding not to teach the technique; but even if that is so, the responsibility is still truly predicable of something other than action. Is re-

---

ing good or evil (1112a), and that the virtues "are in our power and voluntary" (1114b).

[2] This is at least roughly equivalent to what Michael J. Zimmerman calls appraisability; see *An Essay on Moral Responsibility* (Totowa, N.J.: Rowan and Littlefield, 1988), esp. chap. 1.

sponsibility for non-actions derivative, then, from responsibility for actions? This is among the questions to be addressed shortly.

One of the most important distinctions we must observe in discussing responsibility (of any sort) is between direct and indirect kinds. Consider Jack, who is responsible for a forest fire. He threw a lighted cigarette into dry leaves and walked on. He is indirectly responsible for the fire by virtue of doing something that caused it. He is, on the other hand, directly responsible for the causative act—discarding the lighted cigarette in dry leaves, or at least for some basic act by which he did this, such as throwing his hand out and releasing his fingers (presumably knowing that the cigarette would remain lighted). Plainly, if we are responsible for anything, we are directly responsible for something. It is not reasonable to posit either an infinite regress or a circle here.[3]

Must all normative responsibility ultimately rest on responsibility for basic acts, understood roughly as those we do not perform by performing any other act(s)? The answer is apparently yes, provided we are talking about responsibility for acts. Call this view, that all normative responsibility rests on responsibility for basic acts, the *traceability thesis.* To be sure, we commonly attribute responsibility for non-basic acts without either having a sense of inaccurate ascription or making any specific assumptions about the underlying basic act(s). But even here we take it that there is some basic act to which the responsibility can be traced. Suppose, however, that the issue is responsibility for an *omission.* Not all omissions are acts. Some are *abstensions.* These are acts. But others are mere *failures,* mere non-performances. These are not acts. The teacher who abstains from introducing a technique may thereby be responsible for the students' ignorance of it, whereas mere failure to introduce it need not trace to responsible conduct. I am not now taking a cruise; but I have not considered or had occasion to consider doing so, and my non-action is neither an abstension nor traceable to any responsible conduct.

What should be said, however, about a happy-go-lucky couple who unthinkingly fail to provide for their children's future? They do not squander their earnings in gambling or abstain from saving for the children or even reject a suggestion that they save. It is possible that there is simply a series of non-performances which, together with

---

[3] On some views basic action is equivalent to volition. I leave that possibility open; the point here is that there apparently must be a behavioral locus of responsibility for action. The kind of behavior in question is a largely independent matter.

the couple's pattern of normal expenditures, accounts for the absence of savings for the children's future. Must there be actions on which one might hang their responsibility for this deficiency in savings?

Such a case presents two main options. The theoretically most appealing is to say that by spending money as they do, for example on many non-necessities, they culpably preclude saving for the children and so irresponsibly use their resources. The other main option is to say that while they should do something to save, the lack of savings is only preventable by what they might have done, and not indirectly attributable to deeds they actually have done. The former solution seems preferable. For one thing, if they really are responsible for the state of affairs in question—the absence of savings for their children— by virtue of what they can be expected to have done, surely we may describe what they have done as a case of culpably—or at least responsibly—precluding or supplanting what they ought to have done. If they could have saved and did not, and if they are responsible for not saving, presumably they must have done something instead, such as lavishly entertain friends, that resulted in the absence of savings and for which they bear responsibility.

Where the agent is responsible and praiseworthy (a case in which 'responsibility for the action' and similar terms are not commonly predicated of the agent), there is less reason to doubt the traceability thesis. Perhaps this is because we tend not to attribute such positive responsibility unless it seems clear to us that the agent did something causally responsible for the good outcome in question. If Maria is responsible for the discovery of the missing manuscript, it seems clear that (ultimately) she must have found it because she decided to search for it, or, perhaps, simply began to search for it, as a basic action in response to the author's perceptible distress.

Considerations like those cited provide some reason to conclude, then, that all (normative) responsibility traces to acts and ultimately to basic acts. If one is responsible for a non-act, such as a fire or the children's lack of future resources, it is by virtue of some act or omission; and for that, in turn, there will be some basic act for which one is responsible—say a careless movement of the hand, or the purchase of an expensive car. Such responsibility seems ultimately traceable to the making of certain bodily movements or to uttering certain words or to some other basic act.

Supposing, however, that the traceability thesis is false and that there is responsibility not traceable to acts, it will be understandable in terms of acts. For surely if I am (criticizably) responsible for a state of affairs' having occurred which I did not bring about by something I did, there must have been some option that I should have taken and did not (I omit the case of responsibility for something praiseworthy, since that seems not to threaten the traceability view).[4] The concept of responsible action, then, is central to responsibility even if not all normative responsibility rests on some actual deed. Even if traceability to a basic act is not necessary to normative responsibility for some state of affairs, intelligibility in terms of such acts is necessary.

II. Responsibility for Character

With this framework in mind, we can explore the extent of our responsibility for our character. Sometimes 'character' is used broadly, to encompass personality. But my main concern is moral character, which must be distinguished from personality.[5] Two people can be radically different in personality, yet very much alike in moral character. Strong personality, moreover, is compatible with weak character, and charming personality can go hand in hand with execrable character. Moral character is largely an interconnected set of traits, such as honesty, fairness, and fidelity, which, in turn, are largely deep-seated dispositions to do certain things for an appropriate range

[4] This needs qualification to take account of the kinds of cases Harry Frankfurt has introduced in which, though I act (or do not act) without interference, were things to be different so that I *would* do otherwise, a demon would then compel the very action (or non-action) in question. Can we say that I should have picked up a lighted match I discarded, even where, had I so much as gone into a motivational state inclining me to do so, a demon would have compelled my abstention? Must we not say that I "could not have done otherwise" than leave the match where it lay? It is not clear to me that the sense of 'could not have done otherwise' here is the one crucial for moral responsibility (as perhaps Frankfurt might grant). I have explicated that sense, and briefly discussed cases of this sort, in Chapter 7. We might, of course, say that what Frankfurt's cases show is that there is a sense of 'could' in which 'ought' does not imply 'could' (or 'can'). This suggestion is pursued in Chapter 10.

[5] For valuable discussions of personality and character see William P. Alston, "Toward a Logical Geography of Personality," in *Mind, Science, and History*, ed. Howard Kiefer and Milton Munitz (Albany: State University of New York Press, 1970); Richard B. Brandt, "Traits of Character: A Conceptual Analysis," *American Philosophical Quarterly* 7 (1970); and Laurence Thomas, *Living Morally: A Psychology of Moral Character* (Philadelphia: Temple University Press, 1989).

of reasons. (I cannot now give an account of moral character, but much can still be determined about the extent of our responsibility for our character.)

A trait of character, unlike an action, is not an event; it is, like a state of being, something that both persists over time and does not entail change, at least not in the way the occurrence of events does. A trait need not be unchanging or static, however; one can, for instance, become more fair, or more judiciously fair. Because a trait is not an action, responsibility for a trait cannot be direct (assuming the trace-ability thesis is correct). Instead, it will be a matter of something one does which appropriately affects one's character. One might, for example, practice polite acts in an effort to become a polite person.

It is essential to distinguish among three kinds of normative responsibility, none of which implies the others. As applied to traits, there is *generative responsibility*, which is responsibility for having produced the trait in question (a kind of genetic responsibility); *retentional responsibility*, which is responsibility for retaining the trait, whether for retaining it now or for having done so; and *prospective responsibility*, which is responsibility for taking on the trait—as where one promises to develop patience—and normally also for retaining it thenceforth. There are other cases as well, for example responsibility for altering the trait and responsibility for making it more influential in one's conduct, say by reducing the strength of competing traits. But if we can adequately understand just two major cases—generative and retentional responsibility—that will serve our purposes well. Let us consider these in that order.

It might seem that we cannot be wholly responsible for producing our traits of moral character, since one must have a character in order to do the things necessary to affect character. But this reasoning will not do, particularly if we distinguish character and personality. For one might have a personality antecedently to having a moral character, and might then, as a result of sheer personal preferences, choose a character by, say, arranging for appropriate brain manipulations to produce it in oneself. Even apart from this, one might choose a new character, whether by psychosurgery or by adopting a regimen that gradually yields the result; then one might be generatively responsible for one's present character, though not one's initial character. In everyday life, however, few if any agents set out to produce a wholly new moral character.

A normal goal of such moral self-reconstruction as there is, is to retain some trait, say benevolence, and seek to strengthen it and to subordinate certain new traits to it. This subordination is largely a matter of becoming such that one does not tend to act from the subordinate traits unless the actions in question are consonant with maintaining the governing trait. Such subordination would be required for successful, morally motivated moral self-reconstruction (at least first-order self-reconstruction, whose aim is to acquire or alter a trait, as opposed to becoming a different kind of person overall); it would be expected as a factor in any successful self-reconstruction. Second-order moral self-reconstruction, the kind aimed at becoming a moral person overall, is also possible. A non-moral person might simply want, for reasons of self-interest, to become a moral one (and moral agents who falsely believe they are not moral persons could also seek to become such). But this second-order reconstruction is a very different case; and since it implies no antecedent moral commitments, unqualifiedly calling it moral reconstruction would be misleading: its target is moral, but its grounds and at least its initial execution are not.

Ascriptions of generative responsibility imply that, by appeal to the agent's own deeds, there is an answer to "How did you get like that?" But this historical question is by and large of less moral importance than "Why are you like that?" If I am responsible for becoming a certain way, but can now do nothing to alter it, my retaining the trait is not a blameworthy condition, nor can I be expected to reform.[6] I am thus not eligible for the kind of assessment pertinent to moral responsibility for retaining the trait now. And if I can reform now, but became as I am unavoidably and through no deeds of my own, then I am now eligible for assessment on the basis of retaining the trait and can be both blamed for staying in my present condition and expected to reform. From the point of view of ethics, then, the central question here is the extent to which we bear retentional responsibility for our character.

Consider Jean, who is dishonest, but has the decency to feel guilty about it. Some of her values go against dishonesty, and she wants to reform. Perhaps she became dishonest because honesty was not stressed to her as a child and in her childhood environment she found lying a defense against certain frightening prospects. It is consistent with such a story that she not bear generative responsibility for her

---

[6] The qualifications expressed in n. 4 above are also needed here.

dishonesty. This does not imply that she is not responsible for dishonest acts or that she cannot, at least gradually, change her character so as to become solidly honest. Thus, the crucial question of what one should do now and in the future can remain open even if one could not help getting to where one now morally is. Virtue is not a precondition for its own development, any more than it is necessarily self-sustaining; it can arise from the ashes of vice as well as from sound moral education.

It is an interesting question whether responsibility for an act that expresses a trait of character depends on one's ability to change that trait: certainly if Jean can become honest, then, other things being equal, she is responsible for dishonest acts. But could she be incapable of becoming an honest person, yet still be responsible for an individual act of dishonesty? I think so. For even when an action manifests an inextirpable trait, it need not be such that one could not have done otherwise, nor need it be in any lesser way compelled. We can expect people to do better on individual occasions even if we cannot expect them to change their initial dispositions. The ineradicability of a trait does not imply the inevitability of actions that manifest it. A major point that emerges here, then, is this: even if responsibility for traits of character always traces to acts for which one bears responsibility, the converse does not hold. Responsibility for an act—even one that expresses a vicious trait—need not trace to or imply responsibility (of any relevant kind) for that trait. The agent need not be generatively or retentionally responsible for the trait and may be quite unable to uproot it.[7] Similar points hold for emotions in relation to action. Acts done from passion, for instance, need not be excusable even if the causative emotion is both strong and unavoidable.

In pursuing the extent of our responsibility for our moral character, it is useful to think of the relevant traits as constituted by fairly stable and normally long-standing wants and beliefs—or at least by beliefs provided they carry sufficient motivation.[8] Consider fairness. If it is

---

[7] To be sure, it is always logically possible for an agent to change a trait (unless it is essential to the agent's identity); for it is possible that some machine be devised such that the agent's pressing a certain button, even unintentionally, produces the change in question. But the text concerns people's actual capacities.

[8] Two points are in order here. First, this formulation is intentionally vague, but should serve our purposes adequately. Second, I do not think beliefs can carry all the motivation required; but for this essay, as opposed to a full-scale analysis of traits, what is essential to the point is only that traits require both a cognitive and a motivational dimension. It is at least more perspicuous to separate these as I do in the text.

a trait, it must have a measure of stability; if Jean's fairness can be slept off, or she can be dissuaded from it by a mere suggestion, then it is at best a disposition of hers, not part of her character.[9] Moreover, normally a trait must be long-standing. One can imagine a massive (for example, surgical) change making someone immediately fair, in the deep-seated way characteristic of a person with the trait of fairness, but then being reversed shortly afterward by similar changes in the opposite direction. But if this is the only kind of trait one has, it is unclear that one has a character at all. Regarding the makeup of fairness, surely it requires appropriate wants, such as to treat people equally, and certain beliefs, say the belief that providing the same opportunities and rewards for people in the same circumstances is morally required. The more self-consciously fair an agent is, the greater the moral content of the appropriate wants and beliefs, or at least the greater the tendency for the agent to entertain the relevant content; but even being spontaneously fair is more than a matter of simply doing the relevant kinds of deeds. They must be appropriately aimed, in terms of what the agent wants and believes, or they are not moral but merely consistent with morality. If I give my seminar students the same grade only because I like them equally well, then even if they all deserve that grade I am not exhibiting fairness in my grading; the fairness of my results is quite coincidental.

Once we conceive traits as cognitively and motivationally constituted, we can explore responsibility for them through our knowledge of our responsibility for our wants and beliefs. Again, it is useful to consider generative and retentional responsibility separately.

Normal agents are not directly responsible for producing either their beliefs or their wants. We can produce them by doing certain things, but normally we cannot produce them except through indirect and often tedious means. This does not imply, however, that we are not indirectly responsible, generatively, for having produced certain of our traits. A selfish person who, as a result of the selfishness, is unfair but wants to reform, can, through repeated self-discipline, become unselfish and fair. In this way one could become, to a large extent at least, morally self-made.

---

[9] That a trait must be stable is plausible independently of the idea that traits are constituted by fairly stable wants and beliefs. Indeed, if one's wants or beliefs changed often but within a suitably restricted range, a changing set of them might still constitute a trait. Moreover, in distinguishing traits from mere dispositions of a person I am not implying that the former are not dispositional, as opposed to occurrent, properties.

In categorizing the techniques by which one can produce a trait, it is useful to note the dynamics of a related, trait-like phenomenon: self-deception.[10] One way I may get into self-deception, say about the seriousness of my cancer, is to seek appropriate *social support*, for instance to associate with people who express the desired view (say, that recovery is in the offing). I can put out of mind evidence against that view; this is *evidential denial*. I might dwell on any evidence I can find for the view—*evidential magnification*. I can do things that support the view, for example play sports whose practice suggests one is in good health; call this *consonant behavior*. And I can reward and punish myself at strategic times, say when I do something, such as play good tennis, consonant with the view, or succumb to the temptation to do something that tends to undermine it, say acting sickly; this is a strategy of *selective reinforcement*.

Similar points hold for altering one's moral character (though there are also important differences). Suppose Jean wants to reform by developing fairness. She can associate with people who behave fairly and support fair conduct; here again is a strategy of seeking social support. She can put out of mind the considerations that lead to cheating people; call this *banishing temptation*. She can dwell on the extrinsic rewards of acting fairly—a kind of *instrumental goading*—or simply focus on any intrinsically pleasant or attractive features she can think of that belong to so acting—a kind of *self-encouragement by association*. She can make a point of rehearsing reasons for being fair, and of acting fairly where it will bring appreciation—a *magnification of incentive*. And she can reward herself with desired purchases upon finding that she has been fair despite temptation, while denying herself pleasures if she slides into the old ways; here again is selective reinforcement.

The same kinds of techniques that can induce a trait can generally be used to uproot it, especially where doing so is in part a matter of developing a competing trait, say fairness in place of injustice. Many of these techniques involve sheer self-discipline, for example reminding oneself what is right and exercising will power to do it. Certainly enough is known about how one can improve one's character to make it reasonable for us to expect people to engage in a certain

---

[10] Some of these are discussed in essays (by me among others) in Mike W. Martin, ed., *Self-Deception and Self-Understanding* (Lawrence: University Press of Kansas, 1985), and Brian McLaughlin and Amélie O. Rorty, eds., *Perspectives on Self-Deception* (Berkeley: University of California Press, 1988).

amount of moral self-monitoring and, when they find themselves deficient, to take appropriate action. If Jean is a psychologically normal person with no special excuse for being dishonest, she should disapprove of her own dishonest behavior and take appropriate action to change both that behavior and the trait underlying it.

Notice that the responsibility in question is largely fulfilled when Jean becomes a person who, in virtue of sufficiently deep wants and beliefs with the right content, can be counted on in respect of honesty. She need not become a person who is never or scarcely ever tempted to lie or deceive. Moreover, the distinction between obligation and supererogation applies to traits, as it does to actions (or at least to appropriate actions affecting traits, such as maintaining one by self-discipline). We are responsible for being honest, where this implies meeting—for the right reasons—a certain standard of conduct. To rise above that standard, say by maintaining a highly scrupulous honesty, is to go beyond fulfilling our responsibility. The applicability of supererogation to traits confirms the point that responsibility for them is traceable to responsibility for the (responsible) actions of ours that produced them, sustain them, or might alter them.

While my focus has been on responsibility for traits of character, I have not meant to imply that one cannot be responsible for other traits. Much depends on the extent of our (indirect) control of our constitution. Certainly we can construe aspects of personality involving prudence as somewhat parallel to the moral aspects. And if Gary has an unpleasant but not morally criticizable personality trait, say loquacity, he can be responsible for the trait, especially retentionally. But imagine that Gary has become anxious through growing up in a war zone and under abusive parents. In practice, it might not be possible to alter his anxiety, and in that case he is not appropriately criticized for retaining it. It should be emphasized again, however, that even an inextirpable trait is not an excuse for doing any given thing among those it might incline one to do. For incurable anxiety, Gary may not be responsible, but this would not excuse his making others miserable to console himself.

III. Responsibility and Control

Our discussion has presupposed that one is not (normatively) responsible for something over which one has no control.

Whereof one has no control, thereof one is not responsible—at least not directly. If at present I have no control over the extent of my honesty, then I am not (retentionally) responsible for the degree of that trait characteristic of me, nor can I be prospectively responsible for acquiring a trait if I do not have (at least indirect) control of variables that might instill it. On the other hand, if I did something over which I had control in order to prevent my now having control over the degree of my honesty, then I may be indirectly responsible for the extent to which I now have the trait. In fact I do have a measure of control over the traits constituting my moral character: even if I have not contributed much to creating this character, I can affect it and I may be expected to monitor it in ways that will lead to my trying to reform it if the need becomes evident, or to buttress it under conditions of impending erosion. The control I have over my traits derives from my control over my actions, which in turn affect my acquisition or retention of traits. This raises the question whether, in order to control, or be able to control, my actions, I must control, or be able to control, the variables underlying those actions, notably my wants and beliefs.[11]

The answer is surely that I can have or even exercise control over my actions even if I do not have or exercise control over their underlying wants and beliefs. Indeed, if I had to satisfy this condition, would it not be through other actions? And then I would need to have or exercise control over the variables underlying them, which would be further wants and beliefs. We would have a vicious regress or a vicious circle.

Why, however, should we want in general to control our wants and beliefs? Our wants are often natural and such that we approve of them and enjoy fulfilling them,[12] and our beliefs, we suppose, reflect reality and often show us how to satisfy our wants. We should certainly not seek unrestricted control of our beliefs; if we had it, it

---

[11] That wants and beliefs do underlie actions was apparently held by Aristotle and probably Plato, among many later great philosophers, and is at this point scarcely controversial. I have given an account of how they do, with a partial explication of the relevant notion of our control of our actions, in Chapter 6.

[12] Approval of, and other propositional attitudes toward, our wants, especially those we act on, are important for understanding both our freedom and our autonomy. For detailed discussion of the relation between second-order attitudes, including wants, and, on the other hand, freedom and autonomy, see Gerald Dworkin, "Acting Freely," *Noûs* 4 (1970), and *The Theory and Practice of Autonomy* (Cambridge: Cambridge University Press, 1988), esp. pt. 1.

would undermine the presumption that they are under the control of the facts external to them which we like to think they reflect.[13] So, if we do not control the cognitive-motivational basis of every action, we need not feel that alien forces produce our conduct. Moreover, we have a reflective capacity whereby we can single out any particular want or belief for scrutiny and potential elimination so long as we have some want and belief as a basis for the reflective process. This applies even to our foundational wants and beliefs (roughly, those not based on others), such as wants to be liked by peers and beliefs grounded in memory. I think, then, that no paradox underlies the notion of control which I have used in setting out an account of our responsibility for our traits. Our normal wants and beliefs are not alien determinants of action which we must control in order to control it; they are that by virtue of which our actions express our reasons and, in some sense, our nature. Hence, they are essential to our control of the actions they underlie.

It must be granted, however, that we should want to have control of our desires at least to this extent: we should, as rational beings, want our desires to conform with our values in roughly the following sense. We should want that if we rationally believe that a state of affairs is on balance desirable, this will tend to bring about, or enable us to bring about, our wanting on balance to realize it, that is, wanting to realize it more than to realize anything we believe incompatible with our doing so. After all, it is rational to want that, within certain limits, our faculty of reason, of which valuational beliefs should presumably be a manifestation, control our desires and thereby our conduct. This is largely what our control comes to, and the idea indeed expresses one concept of autonomy.[14] Reason indicates what is good for me and how to get it; desire conforms to reason by motivating the appropriate action.

If we pursue this picture of autonomy in relation to responsibility, it takes us in an unexpected direction. The picture makes it natural to hold motivational internalism—roughly, the view that beliefs—and, especially, judgings—to the effect that one ought on balance to A

---

[13] This is in part why skepticism is not plausible: intuitively, that our beliefs tend to reflect reality correctly is a better explanation of our having the ones we do have—given that they are not produced by our will—than any skeptical explanation.

[14] I have developed this conception and compared it with an instrumentalist conception of autonomy, in "Autonomy, Reason, and Desire," *Pacific Philosophical Quarterly* 72 (1991).

imply motivation to *A*. After all, how can reason exercise control over conduct without having its own motivating power? The question for us, then, is whether responsibility requires internalism. In particular, does my having control over my action depend on certain of my beliefs or judgments about the action themselves implying motivation to act accordingly? Suppose I judge that I must become more fair. If this judgment does not produce any motivation to change my character in the relevant ways, then unless I am fortunate enough to have the appropriate motivation from another source, how can I have any control over the trait, or be responsible for remaining unfair? On the face of it, responsibility implies motivational internalism.

This reasoning is plausible, but not conclusive. Notice that even if the relevant practical judgments—those to the effect that on balance one should *A*—do not imply motivation, there is no reason to think that their purely cognitive status would interfere with the existence of such motivation. That motivation might come from an independent source such as a general desire to do what on balance one ought to do, or from desire for the sort of thing to be obtained by the action—whether it is moral, say achieving justice—or non-moral, say restoration of health. Prospective responsibility requires that one can do the crucial thing, for example act to change one's character; it does not require that one must do it, or must be motivated to. Granted, in a fully rational person the implication in question presumably holds, since in fully rational people there is a good integration between cognition and motivation. But we need an account of responsibility for persons in general, who are seldom if ever fully rational. The only internalism implied by a correct account of responsibility, then, is at most a weak form asserting (1) that practical judgments (and perhaps certain beliefs with similar content) tend to produce motivation to act accordingly—call this *inclinational internalism*—and (2) that by virtue of the principle that *ought* implies *can* their truth entails a capacity to act accordingly and so implies the possibility of any motivation such action requires—call this *capacity internalism*.[15]

If an account of responsibility leads us to see how natural a view motivational internalism is, we must also remember that motivational internalism—in a form strong enough to guarantee that agents will

---

[15] For something like this weak version, see Christine M. Korsgaard, "Skepticism about Practical Reason," *Journal of Philosophy* 83 (1986). It should be added that the principle that *ought* implies *can* is problematic and is plausible only in carefully qualified forms.

act on their practical judgments if they can—has its own liabilities. One is the difficulty of accounting for weakness of will, construed as implying (uncompelled) action one takes to be against one's better judgment. Another is the problem—at least for cognitivism about normative judgments—of accounting for how a cognitive faculty can be intrinsically motivational. As already stressed, however, it may well be that in a fully rational person, a strong motivational internalism holds, and certainly most of us have desires regarding our own good that can supply the motivation needed to move us to act on most of our practical judgments. For most of these judgments are such that we see acting on them as conducing in some way to our good, broadly conceived, and so, often, as involving realization of moral ideals.

The control required by responsibility, even prospective responsibility, does not, then, entail motivational internalism. Having such control does require that certain options be open. It is natural to want to guarantee that we will take them if we judge we should, so that responsibility depends only on reason; but it is more realistic to suppose that responsibility depends in part on our motivational makeup. If we *could* not have the wants needed to produce responsible action, for example because it is causally or psychologically impossible, we would not be responsible agents. But there is surely no reason for any such pessimism, and rejecting motivational internalism would do nothing to support it.

IV. The Internality of Responsibility

Motivational internalism is not the only kind. There is also what I shall call *normative internalism*, of which internalism in epistemology is a special case. For normative internalism, normative judgments of a person, such as an attribution of justified belief or of responsibility for an action, are true (or false) in virtue of the presence (or the absence) of certain facts, states, or events whose obtaining or occurring is either accessible to that person by reflection, including introspective reflection, or producible by the person at will.[16] Episte-

[16] Four comments are in order here. First, this is not meant as an analysis of responsibility and leaves much unspecified. For instance, the formulation leaves open just what aspects of the facts, states, or events are relevant, and how. Second, as before, I leave open whether volition is required to account for the relevant notion. Third, while

mic internalism as applied to justification is quite plausible. What justifies my belief that there is paper before me, for instance, is apparently my visual experience of white, which is accessible to me in the strong sense that it is actually present in my awareness.[17] Similarly, what makes me responsible for having started a fire is, ultimately, something like this: my having been able (i) to abstain, at will, from the crucial careless act, and (ii) to realize, by reflection on what I already knew, that if I did not abstain I might start such a fire. In this section I want to explore the possibility that responsibility for both actions and traits is internal.

To begin with, let us continue to assume that the fundamental bearers of (normative) responsibility are acts, in the sense that it traces to them. On the assumption that this traceability thesis is true, normative internalism as applied to action would be roughly the view that one is eligible for the relevant assessment, say as responsible for remaining dishonest, precisely in virtue of types of acts that are (or were) internally available to one and such that, by reflection, say reflection on one's moral obligations, one can (or could) see that one should perform them. There are thus three main cases in relation to responsibility for traits: those of genetic, retentional, and prospective responsibility. On the internalist view in question, genetic responsibility for, say, being aggressive might trace to, and rest on, a decision to undergo assertiveness training and to various decisional and deliberative acts of reinforcing the decision. Responsibility for retaining it might also trace to, and rest on, similar reinforcing acts, together with such things as an awareness of resentment and hurt feelings in others and, in the teeth of that awareness, abstention from efforts to change. Prospective responsibility is different in that there need be no antecedent act to which it traces—except insofar as all our moral responsibilities are behaviorally incurred, for example by

---

it is odd to speak of facts as producible where this does not mean just 'citable', the point is simply that one can bring about, at will, states of affairs, such as the extinguishing of a cigarette, in virtue of which the corresponding fact holds, for example that the cigarette is out. Fourth, if excusability judgments are (plausibly) taken as normative, then some of them seem exceptions to internalism: I may be excusable for not A-ing because, owing to manipulation of my brain I had no inkling of (and have no internal access to), I was made to forget to A.

[17] For discussion of internalism in epistemology and references to relevant literature, see Paul K. Moser, *Knowledge and Evidence* (Cambridge: Cambridge University Press, 1989), and my "Causalist Internalism," *American Philosophical Quarterly* 26 (1989), reprinted, with related essays, in my *The Structure of Justification* (Cambridge: Cambridge University Press, 1993).

promises or other actions that bind us to others.[18] Here the internalist view would be something like this: because of my awareness of others' responses to me, or at least because I can by reflection become aware of them, I should (given my obligations, which are also accessible to my reflection) seek to reform.

Perhaps the clearest form of the internalist position on responsibility would embody a volitionalist view on which our basic acts are willings or tryings (if they are different from willings), combined with a Kantian moral view on which reflection can tell us our general obligations.[19] Ultimately, it is by trying to change my character—or by trying to do something constituting a special case of that—that I do so; and if I do try, say by undertaking to improve my relations with others, yet circumstances prevent me from succeeding, I am still behaving properly and am fulfilling my responsibility to change myself as well as I can.

The central point here is that we assess people by their most fundamental deeds, not—except contingently—by those which, like delivering a book across the country, they do only through the cooperation of circumstances that they cannot, by their fundamental deeds, control. One reason for the plausibility of the view is that what we do basically, and especially internally, we tend to see most clearly. A related point is that we tend to have better control over such deeds than over what we can accomplish only with the help of external circumstances. A third is that these deeds best indicate the deepest projects we harbor or pursue. We are judged not by how well nature cooperates with our projects, but by our volitional nature.

It is important to see that while volitionalism perhaps enables us to give the clearest expression of normative internalism about responsibility, it is not the only theory of the foundations of action available to internalism. One might deny that all basic action is volitional or even internal, while still holding that agents are responsible only

---

[18] Suppose, however, I simply see someone fall and get hurt, where it is obvious that I am the only one who can help. I here acquire a responsibility simply through what I become aware of. The behavioral incursion view would require arguing that the general obligation of beneficence which underlies my special obligation here is acquired by acts of mine. This view is consistent with both internalism and the traceability thesis, but cannot be assessed here.

[19] For accounts of trying and volition, see Hugh J. McCann, "Volition and Basic Action," *Philosophical Review* 83 (1974); Raimo Tuomela, *Human Action and Its Explanation* (Dordrecht: Reidel, 1975); Brian O'Shaughnessy, *The Will* (Cambridge: Cambridge University Press, 1980); and David Armstrong, *The Nature of Mind* (Ithaca: Cornell University Press, 1984).

when, in their purview, and so accessible to them, are considerations in the light of which they act, can act, or could have acted, in a relevant way. Thus, Jack might be responsible for the physical act of flipping his hand, but only because he could have reflected on what he was doing and thereby at least tried to do otherwise, say by stepping on the discarded cigarette, thus preventing a fire. He is responsible because of what is internally accessible and producible; but the responsibility need not trace, causally, to an internal act. On the other hand, we need not deny that there are tryings or that they can be bearers of responsibility; if, for example, his brain had been so wired that when he tried to put out the cigarette he still threw it away lighted, we might then say that he nevertheless behaved responsibly by virtue of trying to do otherwise. Responsibility depends on what is internally accessible to us and on what we can do internally, but it need not require that we actually do something internal which serves as its ultimate bearer. My responsibility can depend on what act types are internally accessible to me—roughly on those I am aware of as options or by reflection could become aware of and try to perform—without tracing to what, if anything, I actually do internally. The culpable basic action need not be an act of will, even if my responsibility for it depends on my internal access to a countervailing act of will. Neither internalism nor the traceability thesis entails volitionalism.

The internalist account of responsibility may sound plausible enough to leave one wondering what would count as an externalist view of normative responsibility. That there should be a contrasting view might be expected from the Kantian character of the internalist view suggested, at least if the difference between the Kantian and consequentialist perspectives is as pervasive as I think it is. To see how the contrast applies to responsibility, suppose that, as a hedonistic utilitarian might hold, agents are—normatively as opposed to causally—responsible for an action provided so construing the action is, say, optimific. One cannot tell whether an action has this property by reflection (since inductive grounds are needed to determine the hedonic consequences of an action), whereas, on the internalist view, one can tell by reflection (at least given certain factual assumptions) whether an action is one's obligation. Thus, whether I am responsible for changing my character depends on whether people's taking me to be responsible for it, and perhaps acting accordingly, has the appropriate consequences. Now I might have no way of grasping, by reflection, that my character needs changing; thus, by internalist lights, I might not be responsible. But if my changing would have better consequences, externalists might, by their principles, properly regard me as responsible and goad me accordingly. And suppose that by accident I make an optimific change. It might then be appropriate to consider me responsible and praise me, since one might want to reinforce the behavior that produced the change.

This externalist view seems unsound. It is too weak, since I might only think I freely and responsibly A-ed, when I was in fact compelled to A. Taking me to be responsible and praising me might still have optimific consequences, but surely I would not have been responsible. This view apparently confuses being praiseworthy with being, by the relevant consequentialist standard, worth praising. The view is also too strong. If I am an unregenerate malefactor, it might be fruitless to consider me responsible, yet I surely might be responsible, having freely and intentionally done evil. Responsibility is more a matter of what I deserve in virtue of my acts than of what I might produce by being considered responsible.[20]

This issue over whether responsibility is ultimately an internal or external notion cannot be settled here. I simply want to bring it to the fore. Some of the materials for resolving it are developed above; but others require ethical and metaphysical arguments not appropriate to this essay. That responsibility ultimately traces to acts, and that we are nonetheless (indirectly) responsible for aspects of our moral character, are points which can stand on either an internalist or an externalist view.

If action is central to responsibility in the way I have indicated, there is one further question we must ask. Is responsibility ultimately an incompatibilist notion, that is, does the existence of normative responsibility presuppose that determinism is false? I cannot see that it does and have elsewhere offered a compatibilist account of freedom

[20] Michael J. Zimmerman has pointed out (in correspondence) that there is no incompatibility between an internalist theory of responsibility and an externalist theory of obligation. True; but at least on the assumption that the consequences to be sought by moral agents are not in general intrinsic to the actions at which they should aim, as on a hedonistic view the crucial consequences are often not, then actions' having the normative status of responsibility will not in general be a matter of internally accessible factors—or at least our attributions of responsibility will be justifiable only on the basis of their total consequences. If the truth conditions of these attributions of responsibility are explicated along internalist lines, that would yield a theory with what seems an objectionable disparity between the (internal) truth conditions and the (external) justification conditions for one of its key notions.

and of the possibility of alternative action—an account meant to be free of the difficulties besetting conditional accounts.[21]

It is true, however, that incompatibilism is natural from the deliberative perspective, that in which we are considering what to do.[22] To decide meaningfully what to do, we must see ourselves as having options, in the sense of alternatives each of which we can, in some appropriate sense, perform. Similarly, to consider ourselves responsible we must take it that we had or have options. This allows us to think of ourselves as causes of our action, but sits ill with thinking of those actions as caused by anything else. The reason for the latter point may be twofold. First, we may not realize that we cause our actions by virtue of their being caused in a suitable way by certain elements in us with which we do or can "identify"; and second, we tend to think of what is caused as necessitated, when actually it is necessary only relative to its cause: generalizations are the bearers of causal necessity, not singular events. Suppose, for example, that it is causally necessary that all Fs are Gs. Even if it is true that *a* is *F*, it does not follow that it is necessary that *a* is *G*; that would follow if it were causally necessary that *a* is *F*, but there is no reason to think, nor does determinism entail, that the occurrence of any singular event is causally necessary.[23] Perhaps it is partly because of a realization of

[21] See Chapter 7. The difficulties I refer to concern accounts of 'could have done otherwise' that take it to be equivalent to propositions of the form of 'if S had . . . then S would have _____'. Peter van Inwagen skillfully brings out difficulties for such accounts in *An Essay on Free Will* (Oxford: Oxford University Press, 1983).

[22] Tomis Kapitan, in a number of essays, has given detailed expression to a view rather like this; he holds that deliberating agents view prospective actions they are considering as contingent relative to the world as they see it, but need not take what they will do as undetermined relative to the entire past. See, e.g., his "Doxastic Freedom: A Compatibilist Alternative," *American Philosophical Quarterly* 26 (1989).

[23] Incompatibilists who, like Carl Ginet, seem well aware of this nevertheless speak of events, under determinism, as "*nomically necessitated* by the antecedent state of the world and the laws of nature," without noting the importance of the distinction I am drawing here (and develop in Chapter 10). See chapter 6 of his *On Action* (Cambridge: Cambridge University Press, 1990). Compare William L. Rowe's reference to causally necessitated action, in "Causing and Being Responsible for What Is Inevitable," *American Philosophical Quarterly* 26 (1989). Compatibilists, too, sometimes speak as if what is nomically (causally) determined is necessary. Daniel Dennett, e.g., says at one point: "Suppose . . . he could *not* have done otherwise. *That is,* given Jones' microstate at *t* and the complete microstate of Jones' environment . . . no other Jones trajectory was possible. . . . If Jones were put back into exactly that state again, in exactly that circumstance, he would pull the trigger again" (second set of italics added; see *Elbow Room* [Cambridge: MIT Press 1985], p. 137). A compatibilist should be unwilling to accept the equivalence claim; as the second sentence implies, Jones would pull the trigger

something like this point that we only tend to think of what is caused as necessitated; for instance, we sometimes think of others as causing us to take action and do not see ourselves as necessitated or unfree in choosing our response.

Whatever we conclude about compatibilism, we may say that (normative) responsibility for an actual deed or other event entails whatever causal connection with it is implied in an explainability relation. For surely if an act is in no way explainable owing to how it is rooted in my character, or due to elements in me, or if an event is in no way explainable in terms of my doings, I am not responsible for it. I am not responsible for others' (past) actions unless I had an appropriate role in producing (or at least enabling) them, nor even for my non-intentional actions if they are not, say, negligent and hence in some way reflective of my character. Even if I merely should have abstained from a deed, or prevented an action, there must be some act of mine because of which (at least in part) the deed or action occurred. This suggests that, whether determinism is true or not, a measure of causal power must issue from something in the agent—presumably from wants and beliefs or something essentially connected with them—as a condition of responsibility. An action or event that is accidental so far as my wants and beliefs are concerned may be rationalizable by me so long as I had appropriate reasons for it, though I did not act from those reasons; and I may even *take* responsibility for it, say in claiming credit or agreeing to make amends. But if it does not trace to me by an appropriate causal line, I am not responsible for it.

We have explored the nature and scope of moral responsibility. It may be direct or indirect; it may be applicable to events or states of being or character; and, particularly as applied to traits, it may be generative, retentional, or prospective, depending on whether one's responsibility is for producing the trait, retaining it, or acquiring or altering it. But responsibility for actual deeds seems always to trace to at least one act, and it presupposes the agent's having control over the relevant foundational behavior. By virtue of our capacity to affect our traits, our responsibility extends to our character; but one can be

---

again, but his act is not considered such that he "could not do otherwise." The relevant modal notions are explored in some detail in Chapter 10.

responsible for an action that expresses a trait of one's character, such as dishonesty, even if one neither produced, nor sought to retain, nor is able to change, that trait itself. I have stressed that such responsibility may be generative or, more often, retentional or prospective. It is sometimes fulfilled in part through the influence that our practical judgments or normative beliefs exercise upon our actions, but responsibility for character does not presuppose any strong version of motivational internalism. The basis of responsibility seems to be internal, though that basis need not always lie in inner acts, such as volitions; but even if the basis of responsibility is not internal, its scope extends to the future and reaches beyond the category of action. Agency, and thereby moral responsibility, indirectly extends to how we are constituted and not just to what we do.[24]

[24] This chapter has benefited from discussion at the University of North Carolina at Greensboro Symposium in which it was given in 1990, and particularly from remarks by my commentator, Gerald Dworkin, and by Jeffrey Poland, Ferdinand Schoeman, Robert Schopp, and Michael J. Zimmerman.

Chapter 10

Modalities of
Knowledge and Freedom

The problem of free will has been widely and ably discussed by generations of philosophers. No one knows the entire literature on the problem, and few have mastered even the multitude of major contributions to the subject. Significant points about free will or—what is often treated equivalently—free action also occur in works not mainly addressed to these notions. What may seem an original point on the free will problem, then, can easily turn out to have been made before.[1] Despite these sobering facts I am going to try to contribute something. There are, I believe, some important epistemological analogies that have been insufficiently appreciated. Moreover, the account of free action I give in Chapter 7 can be fruitfully

[1] I naturally hope that at least some of the points to emerge here have not been made; doubtless similar points may have been expressed in one or another place, but I cannot survey the relevant literature. There is in any event something to be said for trying to make a case in a perspicuous and distinctive way, even if specialists reflecting on the issues might have collectively anticipated most of its elements. I will refer to a number of major works published since Chapter 7 was written, but I presuppose that chapter and its references as background. Apart from the works cited there and below I would mention at least the following books as developing distinctive views: Daniel Dennett, *Elbow Room* (Cambridge: MIT Press, 1984); Robert Kane, *Free Will and Values* (Albany: State University of New York Press, 1985); Bernard Berofsky, *Freedom from Necessity: The Metaphysical Basis of Responsibility* (London: Routledge and Kegan Paul, 1987); Alan Donagan, *Choice* (London: Routledge and Kegan Paul, 1987); Michael J. Zimmerman, *An Essay on Moral Responsibility* (Totowa, N.J.: Rowman and Littlefield, 1988); and Susan Wolf, *Freedom within Reason* (Oxford: Oxford University Press, 1990).

extended. My first task will be to approach the free will problem, construed as a controversy about freedom of action, in relation to an epistemic analogy: specifically, from the point of view of an account of a major element that can lead to skepticism. With that account laid out, I shall proceed to my second main task: to extend the positive characterization of free action presented in Chapter 7. The first task concerns the question whether action can be at once free and *nomically caused*, in the strong sense that it is produced by factors which, by virtue of natural law, invariably yield an action of the same type in the same circumstances. The second task concerns the question of how to understand free action, on the assumption that it can be nomically caused.

I. The Analogy between Skepticism and Incompatibilism

There are at least two major routes to skepticism. One of them proceeds through modal arguments about knowledge, clustering around the claim that if you know, you can't be wrong, and concluding that at best we have far less knowledge than we usually suppose. Call this the *modal route*. The other route proceeds, less abstractly, from considerations of the possibility of error, say through misremembering what one thinks one witnessed, to the same skeptical conclusion. Call this the *defeasibility route*. Let us take these in turn, first in relation to knowledge and then in connection with action.

If a proposition, *p*, is false, we cannot know it to be true. This and similar truisms make it natural to think that if you know, you can't be wrong; that is, if you know that *p*, then you can't be wrong (incorrect) in the belief that *p*. But consider the things we believe. How many are such that we *cannot* be wrong in holding them? One liability is that our memories can deceive us; indeed, on many of the occasions when we take ourselves to perceive ordinary physical objects, we could be hallucinating. And whenever we believe something on the basis of premises, if the premises do not entail the proposition believed on the basis of them, they leave open the possibility of its falsehood. Thus, if the conclusion is not itself necessarily true—

which is usually the status of propositions inferentially believed on non-entailing grounds—then, even if we know our premises, we do not know our conclusion through them.[2] By contrast, the skeptic may continue, if our known premises do entail our conclusion, then it cannot be otherwise and we can know it on the basis of them.

If we focus on free action in relation to causation, we can formulate a claim analogous to the principle just articulated—that a proposition which is not itself necessary is knowable on the basis of known premises that entail it. Notice first that causality is commonly (though not invariably) understood in terms of modality; certainly this holds insofar as the causation of actions is taken to undermine their freedom. Consider a physical example: it is very natural to say that if I release my pen in midair, then it must fall. The necessity apparently expressed by the 'must' is nomic: it is that of the law of gravitation. Nomic necessity is structurally parallel to the logical necessity that figures in the skeptical claim. We might say, then, that given this law, and given my releasing the pen—which is the (main) cause of its falling—it *must* fall. Now, from a metaphysical point of view, action seems no different from other kinds of events: if our actions are events caused in a sense implying that there are laws linking the relevant causal factors to the actions they produce, then, given the causes of our actions—certain desires, let us imagine—the actions must occur. If, for instance, I want (sufficiently strongly) to drink some hot coffee and I have (and know that I have) the ability and opportunity to drink it, surely I must drink. But what I must, of causal necessity do, I do not freely do. Hence, if all my actions are nomically caused, they are all necessitated and hence unfree. Moreover, anyone who knows the causes and the law(s) linking them to my action can know what I must, of necessity, do, even before I do it.

The defeasibility route to skepticism can be pursued independently of the modal route, though the two are often traveled together and are sometimes not distinguished. Even if one does not hold that if we know, we can't be wrong, one may be aware of many ways in which defeaters can prevent a belief from constituting knowledge. We know that we sometimes confuse items in memory, or even take

[2] I say "commonly" rather than "always" for two reasons: people sometimes believe necessary truths on the basis of invalid arguments that they would reject upon reflection; and there might be some who (following Mill, perhaps) believe them on the basis of inductive grounds which they reflectively think yield sufficient evidence.

a merely imagined event to be genuinely remembered. We know that our evidence is often inconclusive, as where we take a number of individually fallible indications, such as track records, to imply—what we may think we know—that a plane will not crash in a storm. If we so much as believe that these indications are fallible, or accept the limited reliability of memory, can we know the things which, unreflectively, we think we do? It may seem that we cannot; certainly skeptics tend to believe that the pervasiveness of these defeaters of knowledge implies that there is far less knowledge than commonly supposed.

With free action, we may also distinguish a defeasibility route from the modal line of argument just articulated. There are defeaters of freedom somewhat similar to defeaters of (would-be) knowledge. Even if determinism, construed as the view that every event is (strongly) nomically caused, is false, one might fail to act freely because of a compulsion one is unaware of. Unconscious mental elements are the best-known candidates for such an undermining role.[3] As an unnoticed lapse in memory can defeat what appears to be knowledge, an unconscious force can compel an action that appears to be free. Ignorance and prejudice, neither of which need be unconscious, can also compel us without our realizing it; hence, there are even more potential defeaters of freedom than those residing among unconscious elements. For instance, those who avoid the company of certain other people because (they believe) they "do not enjoy it," may, owing to deep prejudice or strong fear, be unable to endure their company and hence not genuinely free in avoiding it.

So far, I have tried to make plausible both some skeptical arguments regarding knowledge and their counterparts regarding freedom. But I do not think that any of these arguments is sound, and I want to assess the skeptical arguments in a way that should help us appraise the behavioral arguments. I begin with a task of disambiguation.

At least three things might be meant by the seemingly innocent skeptical aphorism, 'If you know, you can't be wrong'. One is that it is necessary that (it cannot be false that) if you know that p, then p. Call this the *verity principle*; it simply says that knowledge must be of truths. (The specific nature of the modality need not concern us, but I take it to imply truth in all possible worlds.) A second interpretation

---

[3] See, e.g., John Hospers's widely read, "What Means This Freedom?" in Sidney Hook, ed., *Determinism and Freedom in the Age of Modern Science* (New York: New York University Press, 1958).

is that if you know that *p*, then *it* can't be wrong, that is, *p* cannot be false (it is necessarily true). We might call this the *necessity principle*, since it says that knowledge must be of necessary truths. The third interpretation I want to suggest is that if you know that *p*, then your *belief* can't be wrong; that is, beliefs constituting knowledge cannot be false. Call this the *infallibility principle*. It differs from the necessity principle in permitting knowledge of contingent truths. Consider, for example, my belief that I exist, or that I have a belief. These beliefs cannot be false despite its being a contingent matter that I exist and that I have such a belief.[4] For I cannot believe I exist unless I do, and my believing that I have a belief entails that I do.[5] Here it is not the content of my beliefs, as in the case of believing a necessary truth, but something about my *having* these beliefs, that entails their truth. Their possession is fully sufficient for their truth. This makes it natural to say that these particular beliefs cannot be false.

The distinction between the verity and necessity principles parallels one applicable to the problem of free will. Recall the claim that if my action (*A*-ing, let us say) is caused, then it must (of causal, as opposed to logical, necessity) occur. Call this the *causal necessitation principle*, since it apparently implies that causes (at least causes of actions) necessitate their effects. The formulation of the principle just given could mean that (1) it is causally necessary that if the causes of my *A*-ing do in fact occur, then I do in fact *A*—which we might dub the *causal determination principle*—or (2) that if those causes do in fact occur, then it is (causally) *necessary* that I *A*—the *causal necessity principle*. In the first case, the following conditional proposition holds, as a matter of causal law: *if* the causes occur, then the effect does. In the second case, the conditional asserted is not said to be a matter of causal law but is taken to be true (at least) as a matter of fact: if the causes occur, then as a matter of causal law the effect does also.[6] Here

---

[4] This paragraph draws on chap. 9 of my *Belief, Justification, and Knowledge* (Belmont, Calif.: Wadsworth, 1988), which also contains further discussion of skepticism.

[5] I might have in mind some other belief than this second-order one, the one whose possession is entailed in the original description; and if I could lack any belief of the kind I have in mind, my *ground* for believing I have a belief could be defective in a way that prevents my knowing I have one. But that shows only that an infallible contingent belief need not be knowledge, not that there are no such beliefs.

[6] I make no claim that this and highly similar distinctions have not been made. Something close to the central contrast here may go back at least as far as Aristotle's *On Interpretation.* See 9, 19a23–31.

it is the consequent of the conditional—that the effect occurs—which is said to hold as a matter of causal law.

It might seem that from the point of view of the problem of free action there is no behavioral analogue of the infallibility principle, but there is at least this possibility: that the mere presence of causes of an action constitutes a compulsion, even if causation is not conceived nomically in the way illustrated so far, that is, in terms of laws true as a matter of some kind of natural necessity. Thus, someone might think that if my action is caused at all—at least by anything besides me as agent—then it is not free. Call this the *causal compulsion principle*, since it takes causation (other than "immanent causation" by the agent) to imply compulsion, even where the causal factors are neither necessitated by antecedents nor nomically imply the action. This view may not in the end be plausible apart from the notion of causes as nomically necessitating, but it is conceptually distinct from the others, and, just as a belief of a contingent proposition may be infallible, a causal factor might contingently produce the action, yet still compel it.[7]

It should now be apparent how the analogy between skeptical theses about knowledge and causal theses about action can clarify a range of arguments for incompatibilism, construed as the position that the existence of free action is incompatible with determinism (or even as the weaker position that if an action is [strongly] nomically caused, hence subsumable under a covering law of *universal* form, then it is not free). Just as a belief of a proposition that can be false is not knowledge, an action that cannot be otherwise, that is, whose agent cannot do otherwise, is not free. In the one instance, the necessity is desirable but (in the case of empirical beliefs) missing; in the other case it is undesirable but (with caused actions) present. Should we, however, be moved by either the skeptical argument from the

[7] Perhaps it is felt that *any* event cause of an action preempts its rightful causation by the agent. Agent causation is a major topic, and neither it nor the approach to freedom it supports will be discussed, in part because if the approach of this book is successful there is no need to make out a notion of agent causation as an alternative to event causation, which is the more common (and on some views only) alternative. Thomas Reid is a major proponent of the conception. William L. Rowe has explicated the Reidian view in "Responsibility, Agent-Causation, and Freedom: An Eighteenth-Century View," *Ethics* 101, no. 2 (1991). Roderick Chisholm is another source for the view; see, e.g., his "Freedom and Action," in Keith Lehrer, ed., *Freedom and Determinism* (New York: Random House, 1966). For a recent sketch of how agent causation might be construed, see Randolph Clarke, "Toward a Credible Agent-Causal Account of Free Will," *Noûs* 27 (1993).

necessity principle or the incompatibilist argument from the causal necessity principle?

In answering this, it is crucial to distinguish between theses that differ in the way the verity principle and the necessity principle do. The verity principle is surely sound: knowledge must be of truths. But the necessity principle does not follow from it and is not plausible given the obviousness of one's knowing at least such contingent propositions as that one exists. To see that the necessity principle does not follow, consider a statement commonly used in explaining deductive validity to students: if all humans are mortal and Socrates is human, then he must be mortal. I doubt that any philosopher reflectively believes that the antecedent (all humans are mortal and Socrates is human) implies that it is *necessary* that Socrates is mortal. The proposition in question, that Socrates is mortal, which is what I take to be the consequent of the if-then statement rightly understood, is contingent. English idiom simply makes it natural to express the modality of the entire conditional—if all humans are mortal and Socrates is human, then he is mortal—by placing a 'must' before the consequent. Nor is that placement mysterious given that the relation between antecedent and consequent is *not* contingent; it is a necessary relation of entailment, in the sense, roughly, that propositions standing in this relation absolutely could not fail to be so related.

Apart, then, from arguments that I believe skeptics cannot provide, we should not take 'If you know, you can't be wrong'—as asserted in contexts in which it is plausible—to be an expression of the necessity principle. Similarly, I see no reason to take the plausible-sounding claim that, given the cause of something, it must occur, to imply the causal necessity principle. The causal *relation* is—when backed by a universal law of nature—plausibly considered (nomically) necessary, since the cause is linked to the effect by a nomic necessity (or so I assume for the sake of argument).[8] But it simply does not follow that either term in the relation is necessary or that the effect (the second term) must occur. My action, then, can be nomically caused, that is, "determined," without being nomically necessary.

---

[8] For criticism of the necessity view of laws, see Berofsky, *Freedom from Necessity*, which draws fruitfully on Hume in defending the regularity view. Even a regularity view of laws, and thereby of determinism, can sustain some of the plausibility of incompatibilism, but I believe that view is most plausible in the context of some kind of necessity conception.

To see the point another way, recall the logical analogy. Just as the conditional representation of a valid argument from contingent premises to a contingent conclusion is properly interpreted as a necessary conditional whose antecedent and consequent are both contingent, the proper representation of a causal necessity claim about a given cause and some effect of that cause should be (at its strongest) a causally necessary conditional. It can be necessary that if all humans are mortal and Socrates is human, he is mortal, even if his mortality is contingent. It can also be causally necessary that given the causes of my drinking coffee, I drink it, without its being necessary that I drink it. Once the distinctions just made are adequately appreciated, and English modal idioms are understood, it is apparent that one simply cannot infer the causal necessity principle from the plausible-sounding causal necessitation principle and so cannot justify incompatibilism on the basis of the latter.[9]

The modal fallacy that I have been implicitly noting—the *modal transfer fallacy*, as we might call it—can be described as follows. Given the propositions that (1) *p*, and that (2) necessarily, if *p*, then *q*, one may not infer that (3) it is necessary that *q*. In suggesting that some thinkers have been influenced toward skepticism or incompatibilism by the sorts of ambiguities I have noted, I certainly do not mean to imply that these thinkers have explicitly presented arguments committing the modal transfer fallacy or would argue that it is indeed not a fallacy. (The fallacy has in fact been noted in many places.)[10]

[9] For a contrasting view, see Berofsky, *Freedom from Necessity*, esp. pp. 104–5, where he argues that a "contingent necessity" of the consequent is plausibly attributed to reasoning of the kind I interpret as involving necessity only over a conditional (or universal quantification). He finds "a wealth of linguistic evidence that we do the detachment, that we categorically assert that Jones' fall is necessary [given Jones's being thrown from a window], although this truth, like the categorical truths about the world, depends on other contingent facts" (p. 104). I agree that we categorically speak of such events as such that they "must" occur, but hold that in so speaking we are either being elliptical or making a mistake. Note that a parallel argument is not plausible in the syllogistic case, which seems relevantly analogous. Even if there is *some* sense in which Socrates must be mortal (not nomic, however, since indefinite extension of life seems nomically possible even for biological beings), the relevant 'must' appears equally applicable to accidental truths validly derivable from true premises. People would ordinarily agree that if all the coins in my pocket are U.S. coins, and they are all copper, then all of the coins in my pocket must be copper. Indeed, is there less inclination to use 'must' here even if one knows I have a silver coin in my pocket?

[10] It is noted by Berofsky, *Freedom from Necessity*, and by a number of philosophers he discusses. He is probably less interested in the fallacy than I am, in part because he believes that even apart from its commission, there is, given determinism, a contingent

What I claim is that, particularly because English idiom makes it easy to transfer necessities from conditionals to their consequents, one can be influenced by this kind of reasoning, or by a related shift in meaning, even if one does not formulate the relevant arguments or trade on the ambiguities. The influence of a fallacy—particularly one that is so powerfully reinforced by idiom—can survive its recognition. Certainly some incompatibilists have used the language of necessity as if they might be influenced by such a transfer, or by the naturalness of making it, and students coming to the topic for the first time commonly find the distinction between necessary conditionals and conditionals with necessary consequents difficult to discern. Perhaps because the transfer corresponds to a literal reading of the idiomatic forms of the causal necessitation principle, they find it natural to transfer a modality governing a whole conditional to its consequent.[11]

At this point one might argue that there is a weaker version of the necessity principle that is both true and significant for freedom. Suppose that a set of conditions, C, including my motivational states and circumstances, produces an act of type A, say my stretching my arm, and imagine that it is a law that whenever conditions of kind C occur the agent, S, A's. We might now say that, *relative* to C, S's A-ing is necessary. It is not that S A's in all causally possible worlds—as would be so if the action were a non-relative causal necessity; it is simply in all C-worlds S A's, that is, S A's in all situations where both C and the causal laws of this world hold.[12]

I want to make three points about this appeal to relative necessity.

---

necessity to contend with in arguing for compatibilism. In any case, a number of his compatibilist points are complementary to mine.

[11] Even such careful and sophisticated writers as Carl Ginet and William L. Rowe sometimes speak as if actions were unconditionally causally necessary when the grounds for this are simply their being nomically caused. See the references to their work in n. 23 of Chapter 9. Nor are compatibilists always sufficiently aware of misleading modal parlance: Daniel Dennett, for example, comments on the "illicit slide from 'determined' *or* 'causally necessary' to 'inevitable' and cites Ayers, Wiggins, and Chisholm as cases in point (*Elbow Room*, p. 123; italics added to indicate what appears to be an assumption of equivalence). It may be that compatibilists are often so preoccupied with distinguishing causation from *compulsion* that they do not realize the need to distinguish causal necessitation from causal necessity—which incompatibilists are surely right to view as undermining freedom.

[12] This sort of appeal to relative modality is suggested by Tomis Kapitan in "Doxastic Freedom: A Compatibilist Alternative," *American Philosophical Quarterly* 26 (1989), but I cannot here discuss his position specifically.

First, I agree with what I take to be the underlying intuition: that the causal force of C in producing my A-ing on a given occasion is preserved by a law linking factors of type C to A-ing in general. If, say, my desire to stretch has the causal force to produce a powerful stretching that no ordinary person trying to hold down my arms could easily suppress, then the same motivational circumstance will produce the same powerful stretching in parallel cases. Call this the *causal preservation principle.* It says roughly that in the same circumstances causes of the same kind will produce equally *much,* but says nothing about *how* they produce it, for example with or without necessity. Note, however—and this is my second point—that the preservation of a causal force does not elevate it into a compulsion or presuppose that it ever was one. Granted, if I were compelled to stretch in the first place—say because my desire was utterly irresistible—there is a presumption that the compulsion will also be preserved in a parallel case.[13] But the incompatibilist cannot simply assume that every cause compels, and the appeal to relative necessity does not support the view that any caused action is compelled. Indeed, one wonders whether it is not the sense that nomic causation compels that motivates a search for relative necessity once it is seen that nomic necessity does not transfer from the mere occurrence of a cause to its nomically implied effect. My third point is that we can account for the causal force of causative factors without positing a distinct kind of necessity: that force can be measured in terms of, for example, what would be required to resist it. If it is resistible, then there is no need to talk of its imposing a kind of necessity: we can account for its communication to its effects by the causal preservation principle, and so in terms of standard causal necessity.

I believe that the modal considerations discussed above undermine some of the plausibility of incompatibilism, not because there is no case for it that does not run afoul of them, but because the position simply becomes less plausible when it cannot be viewed in the way it is naturally seen when one allows oneself to think of nomically caused events as somehow inevitable, in the sense appropriate to unconditional necessity. In any case, quite apart from the modal points I have stressed, there remain other considerations raised by

[13] It is only a presumption because we have not characterized the causal factors in a way that implies exact similarity of the agents in question, and, owing to, for example, differences in endurance, a force that compels one person may not compel another, as is illustrated by some of the cases in Chapter 7.

the analogy to skepticism and inimical to the idea that we often act freely. Might freedom be defeated, in something like the way in which knowledge might be defeated, by factors we are at least not normally aware of? Here I intend to be briefer and to discuss only the case of action, since I have addressed skepticism at length elsewhere.[14]

There is no denying the abstract possibility that we might be manipulated by beings whose control, though it renders us unfree, is so subtle that we *feel* free. There is, however, no reason to believe that we are thus controlled. I offer no argument on this empirical and existential matter, in part because it would be quite a task to canvass the relevant evidence, but even more because I take the philosophical issue here to be primarily conceptual and normative. It is also the prior issue: if we do not have a clear conception of freedom, we are not in a good position to assess the case for our having it.

From this perspective, we can see that defeaters of freedom include not only compulsions of which we are unaware but also, if Chapter 7 is sound, the absence of appropriate reasons for our behavior. Incompatibilists have tended to worry about our actions being caused at all; compatibilists have worried mainly about their being caused by the wrong thing—most notably compulsions. The point here is that if behavior is not grounded in reasons in a way appropriate to make it an action, then it is not free, even if it seems to the agent to be so.[15] Fortunately, this possibility is normally remote: as I argue in Chapter 6 regarding self-knowledge in cases of actions for reasons, we normally either know why we do what we do or can quite readily come to know this (given a relevant description of the behavior). But it is possible to do something unfreely and for an unconscious reason, yet believe one has done it freely and for a different reason. One could be neurally manipulated in a way that gives one the impression one is doing something freely and for a moral reason, when in fact one is being compelled to do it for a non-moral one, such as an implanted unconscious fear. If much of our behavior is like this, then we act freely less often than we think.

What may be the most problematic kinds of defeater are certain sorts of unconscious motivation, in a broad sense of 'unconscious'

---

[14] In, for example, chap. 9 of *Belief, Justification, and Knowledge,* and chap. 12 of *The Structure of Justification* (Cambridge: Cambridge University Press, 1993).

[15] It may not be *unfree* either, if that entails compulsion, since behavior that does not qualify as action is presumably not a candidate for free action even if it is not compelled.

not tied to Freudian theory (I explicate this sense briefly in Chapter 8, in connection with self-deception). The question of how pervasive such factors are is empirical. But there is no doubt that just as we can gather more evidence, or better scrutinize the evidence we have, in order to reduce the chance of defeated knowledge, so we can do something, by the way we conduct and condition ourselves, to reduce the influence of such unconscious factors. As this suggests, these factors may reduce the *degree* to which we act freely, without constituting a full-blooded compulsion. That many psychological elements do just this—for example, fear, prejudice, and irrational desires—cannot be doubted. When they do not constitute full-blooded compulsions, they do not in general excuse wrongdoing. Indeed, as I argue in Chapter 7 through the example of a guard of a missile launcher, even compulsion proper (though not the maximal degree of it) need not excuse, though it does extenuate. Furthermore, the mere fact that an influence on my behavior is unconscious does not make it irresistible. Unconscious hatred, for instance, may incline one to lie about a rival's merits. But one may feel a mendacious impulse even without knowing its origin; and while an impulse from an unknown origin may catch one unprepared, a surprise onslaught need by no means be irresistible. Commonsense morality recognizes this: a readiness to resist wrongdoing is a standing requirement of sound moral character.

   In the light of the analogy to skepticism, then, we can see how neither some initially plausible modal arguments nor the most plausible defeasibility considerations can be used to show that freedom is incompatible with causation or even, so far as I can see, that there is reason to doubt that we often are free in what we do. These modal arguments do not show that freedom is precluded by causal necessity; and the defeasibility considerations do not show that it is vitiated by internal or external compulsions. Causation too, appears important for assessing incompatibilism, and I turn to it in the next section.

II. Causation as a Threat to Freedom

   Suppose that the premises of the Socratic syllogism discussed above were necessary.[16] Then it *would* follow that, necessarily,

[16] Since the supposition seems impossible (though intelligible), it may be better to say, 'Suppose we substituted a syllogism of the same form with the necessary premises', and proceed accordingly.

Socrates is mortal. The relevant principle—that if it is necessary that *p and* necessary that if *p* then *q*, then it is also necessary that *q*— is valid. Perhaps an argument of this or a similar form can serve incompatibilism. What we would need is a ground for construing the minor premise—that, given determinism, the causes of our actions occur—as necessary. Let us explore this.

One's first thought may be—and the first thought of anyone in the grip of the plausible-sounding but specious reasoning criticized in Section II will be—that since we are considering a deterministic world, the occurrence of the causes of our actions is as "determined" as anything else. Every event is caused, so the causes of action are also determined and "must" occur. This reasoning is fallacious. Determinism says that every event is nomically caused, but that is simply to assert (on the strongest plausible reading) that for every event there is a (causally necessary) covering law and a suitable antecedent condition. It is *not* to imply that the occurrence of any particular event, such as an antecedent impulse, is unconditionally necessary. The relevant laws connect *kinds* of events (or properties—the point here is neutral with respect to how we construe the terms of the nomic relation). These laws imply that *if* an event of one kind occurs, then an event of another kind does; they do not imply that anything actually occurs. It is not even clear that there are *any* singular events that, as a matter of causal necessity, must occur.

This point about singular events bears comment. Let us first ask whether there are any causal laws that entail the existence of a singular event. It might seem that there are. Consider my pen as it has fallen halfway to the floor; surely it is causally necessary that it continue its fall. But look closely: are we not here transferring the modality from a tacit conditional proposition, say the proposition that if, under standard conditions, my pen is released in midair and reaches halfway to the ground, it continues its fall the rest of the way? When we say such things as that water must flow downhill, we commonly presuppose antecedent conditions and tacitly supply covering laws, such as the generalization that unimpeded water on a surface like that of the earth flows to the lowest point it can reach. This generalization is necessary (and by implication, we may suppose, so are its substitution instances). But there is no categorical necessity that my pen should even exist, or that water should ever be on an unobstructed downhill path.

Unless we make the gratuitous—and I think implausible—assumption that it is causally necessary that the world contain some definite set of antecedent events, I do not see how one can conclude, of any specific event, that it is unconditionally required by causal laws. For determinism, at least of the naturalistic as opposed to theological kind, the assumption is more than gratuitous. On this view, every event depends on an antecedent (an earlier or simultaneous causal event), in a way implying that any necessity belonging to an event depends on that of an antecedent. But, for determinism, there is an infinite set of past events causally underlying any actual event, hence no initial event—such as a creation *ex nihilo*—to produce the whole set of consequent events. There are, for determinism, no initial causes in the world, each with its own necessity.[17] Indeed, a creation *ex nihilo* would presumably be an uncaused event, or at least not caused in the natural order. A theological determinism could countenance it; but then, surely, it would not be causally necessary that God, who establishes the natural laws that *ground* causal necessity, create just the initial set of events he did create. Even if it should be necessary in some sense that he create "the best" possible world (roughly, one than which none better can be conceived), it would not follow that there are not two or more different worlds that are equally good. On any plausible kind of determinism, then, it would be at best mysterious why any event should be unconditionally necessary. Causal laws allow alternative worlds, and neither determinism nor, so far as I can tell, any plausible thesis in the philosophy of science implies that any singular event is by itself causally necessary.

Where, then, could an incompatibilist locate the categorical necessity crucial for the kind of valid modal argument I have sketched? One possibility is to work from the unalterability of the past. Even if no law requires that a particular event occur, it surely is (in some strong sense) impossible to alter the past. Now, while unalterability is not the same as causal necessity, it is apparently a strong modal status; perhaps it is (in this context) roughly equivalent to the causal impossibility of being changed (at least by any later event). Moreover, there is surely some plausibility in supposing that if an event is unalterable, and that event nomically implies a second, then the second

---

[17] We may speak of finite causal chains, for example of the chain from my seeing a red light to my stopping my car; but from each actual event there radiates backward an infinite chain of causes. Perhaps, however, a determinist could allow that this does not require an infinite past, but that would not undermine the points made here.

is unalterable.[18] But if this is so, then incompatibilism is established, at least on the assumption that actions are events and that an unalterable action is not free. For given determinism, our actions can be causally traced backward to unalterable past events. Indeed, if the causes of my writing this have occurred and are thus unalterable, and if they nomically imply my writing it, then my doing so is unalterable—indeed, was unalterable as soon as any set of nomically sufficient conditions for it occurred—and so, it would seem, I cannot do otherwise.[19]

It turns out that ambiguity again lurks beneath the surface. To say that the past is unalterable could be to say that it is not possible (at least not causally possible) that there be an event (such as an action) which changes the past. But it might also be to say that every past event has the modal status (or perhaps the essential modal property) of unalterability. The former thesis might be called the *principle of unaffectability;* the latter thesis asserts the essential unalterability of the past and might thus be called the *principle of unalterability* of past events. The former is plausible, and I want to accept it for the sake of argument. The latter does not follow from the former and is not plausible—at least for compatibilists. The unalterability principle may, however, seem to follow from the unaffectability principle, since the latter is very naturally conceived in idiomatic English as the principle that whatever happens now cannot change the past. But a more accurate statement of it would be the following, in which the impossibility modifies not the past or any past event, but our relation to the

[18] This appears to be the line taken by J. R. Lucas in connection with the problem of freedom and divine foreknowledge: "If we take time seriously, we must believe that what is past . . . is unalterable, and in that sense necessary; and then the modal argument is valid . . . and it is necessary that I shall act in a particular way"; see *The Freedom of the Will* (Oxford: Clarendon Press, 1970), p. 74.

[19] It is interesting to compare this with various versions of the much-discussed consequence argument. See, for example, Peter van Inwagen, *An Essay on Free Will* (Oxford: Oxford University Press, 1983), esp. chap. 3. He puts much weight on the locution, 'no one has, or ever had, any choice about whether', in reference to past events in the causal chains leading, on determinist assumptions, to our actions. This is not equivalent to unalterability, but the *interest* of the locution for the problem of free will may depend on taking it and similar locutions as involving unalterability or at least threatening freedom for similar reasons. I have assessed van Inwagen's argument, along different lines than those pursued here, in a critical notice in *Faith and Philosophy* 3 (1986). For another appraisal of the argument, with special emphasis on epistemic conditions for freedom, see Tomis Kapitan, "Ability and Cognition: A Defense of Compatibilism," *Philosophical Studies* 63 (1991). Cf. Patrick Francken, "Incompatibility, Nondeterministic Causation, and the Real Problem of Free Will," *Journal of Philosophical Research* 18 (1993).

past: it cannot be that anything that happens now (including anything we do) *will* change the past. Although in the natural formulation the modality appears to modify past events directly, in the less misleading formulation it can be seen simply to deny the possibility of certain causal connections and therefore the truth of a kind of generalization. From the fact that no current event, such as an action, can change the past, we may infer a necessary relation—unaffectability by—*between* past and present events, but not a modal status, such as the necessity, *of* past events. A past event's unaffectability by any event in the future of this world does not imply the occurrence of that past event in any other world, much less its happening in every causally possible world, as its unaffectability would imply if the event were nomically necessary and so "could not be otherwise."

Similar points apply to other candidates for a modal status of past events (or present ones) from which, given determinism, it follows that our actions "must" occur. In a sense, for example, it is "personally impossible for me now that the past be different," and if that is so then determinism would seem to imply a similar impossibility of an open future.[20] If I have been right, however, the underlying truth in such cases is the unaffectability principle or some similar principle compatible with the possibility of both a different past and a future that is open in the sense required for free action. Just as the relation of necessitation can hold between contingent events, the relation of unaffectability by future events can hold between past events that could have been otherwise and present or future events that can be otherwise.

This brings us to the question of the plausibility of the essential unalterability principle. If unalterability is really a modal status of past events but *not* equivalent to their causal necessity, it is difficult to see what unalterability is. We may categorically say of past events that they are not objects of our present choice; but that attributes to them no modal property which, given determinism, would seem to threaten freedom.

Granted that we cannot make past events otherwise, this does not imply that they could not have *been* otherwise; and, causally, they surely could have been—unless some antecedent of theirs was necessary. But what would that event be? Determinism does not imply that any specific event unconditionally occurs, and we surely have no

---

[20] This formulation was suggested to me by Michael J. Zimmerman.

(non-theological) reason to think this of any natural events. Now if the antecedents of our actions could have been otherwise, why could not our actions caused by them be otherwise as well? Indeed, they *would* be otherwise, according to determinism, if their antecedents had been otherwise (leaving aside overdetermination). It is true that given determinism, even these events, which could have been otherwise, necessitate the future events they cause. But I have already argued that this relation of necessitation does not entail the necessity—above all, the causally necessary existence—of the elements in it. Indeed, why should we not turn the tables and suggest that the modality representing causal contingency—being possibly otherwise—transmits over the nomic propositions linking past events to their future effects? Then, unless one is compelled to A in the sense recognized by compatibilism, one *can* do otherwise.

The points I am making are not tied to the term 'unalterable'. Similar reasoning will show that the notion of the past as, say, "fixed," "inaccessible," or "beyond our control" can cause trouble in the same way. The points are also extendable to a related argument. When we think of actions as nomically caused and assume the presence of their causes, we may come under the influence of an epistemic argument for incompatibilism. Suppose it is true that *given* my desire for coffee and my having the ability and opportunity to drink some, I will, as a matter of causal law, drink some. In saying this, one can easily think of oneself as *knowing* that I have the desire, ability, and opportunity, and as knowing the relevant law (or at least that it holds). But if I know both that p and, at the same time, that if p then q, I presumably know that q.[21] And now there are various directions one may go. One—in which I fear many tend without saying so or even seeing it—is this: if I know that an agent will A, the agent must A, and hence does not do so freely. A second inclination is to think that we simply cannot know in advance what a free agent will freely do, perhaps because the proposition in question is yet to be "made true." The first line of thinking is not plausible once the verity principle concerning knowledge is distinguished from the necessity principle. The second line is very difficult to assess. I shall say only that I see no need to speak of propositions about the future as being made true: we can surely say what we need to say about them by noting

---

[21] This admits of exceptions, as where one does not make the connection, but that will not affect the point here.

that the events in virtue of which they *are* true or false have yet to occur.[22]

In suggesting that the threat to freedom posed by causation is greatly diminished by certain modal distinctions and related points about knowledge and causation, I have not meant to imply that there are no non-modal respects in which determinism (or even the universal causation of action) poses problems for freedom. It is surely puzzling to think of an action as at once free and caused by factors extending indefinitely (or even infinitely) into the past. If my action was already determined before I was born, how can it be free? Can a tree be sustained by the ground we plant it in if its roots go beyond that ground to indefinite or infinite depths? As some philosophers have stressed, for truly free actions the agent seems to have "ultimate" responsibility.[23]

I agree that infinite causal histories seem to undermine this intuitively significant property of free action, but I would stress in (partial) response that even if there is an unending causal history underlying an action, there may be an ultimate explanation in terms of the agent's reasons and values. Call this a *purposively ultimate* explanation, as contrasted with a *causally ultimate* explanation, such as one might have for the existence of the universe by referring it to an uncaused act of God (or at least one not caused by any event). What the compatibilist can plausibly claim is that, just as a tree can derive its nutrients from the ground in which it is immediately rooted regardless of how deep its roots go beyond that, an ultimately grounded chain of reasons, being purposively ultimate, can coexist with an infinite and ungrounded chain of causes. The power of a desire for happiness, for instance, to explain and justify an action does not depend on the absence of an infinite causal chain connecting that desire with the past. It is largely the intentional *content* of the desire that makes an action which the agent performs in order to satisfy that content intelligible and appropriate, and the content can play this (arguably

---

[22] For discussion of this problem, see J. R. Lucas, *The Future* (Oxford: Basil Blackwell, 1989). Some of the points in this essay may bear on his treatment of freedom and divine foreknowledge, but I must leave that intriguing problem aside here. For a wide-ranging discussion of the problem, with a broad survey of the literature, see Linda Trinkhaus Zagzebski, *The Dilemma of Freedom and Foreknowledge* (Oxford: Oxford University Press, 1990), and John Martin Fischer, "Recent Work on God and Freedom," *American Philosophical Quarterly* 29 (1992).

[23] See, e.g., Robert Kane, "Two Kinds of Incompatibilism," *Philosophy and Phenomenological Research* 50, no. 2 (1989), esp. pp. 247–54.

non-causal) explanatory role quite apart from whether the desire is caused, and independently of the length of the causal chain containing the events producing that desire. The causal history of a desire does not rob it of its intentionality; the causation of action by desires and other intentional elements does not undermine the special role played by their content in making our actions intelligible or appropriate.

A related problem for compatibilism is that we want to think of free agency as more "creative" than it seems to be when we conceive action in the context of a deterministic world. But if we are not hankering for creation *ex nihilo*, we may find, on analysis, as much creativity as we are entitled to attribute to ourselves. Once again, the analogy to knowledge can help. No matter how I came to believe *p*, if I now hold it on appropriate grounds, I can know it; I may, for example, injudiciously accept the word of an unreliable gossip, but later get decisive evidence of the truth of *p*. Similarly, it is arguable that no matter how I came to be as I now am, if I am nonetheless a normal person and act on appropriate grounds, say for reasons expressing those grounds or rooted in them, for instance in my ideals, then I do so freely.[24]

To be sure, under certain conditions, as where a well-grounded true belief is instilled directly into me by brain manipulation, I may deserve no credit for discovering the proposition I thereby come to know; and under other conditions, as where I am neurally manipulated to enhance my altruism, I may deserve no credit for the altruism that is praised when I make a sacrifice for others. But these genetic assessments do not imply that the belief is not knowledge, or the deed unfree. If the altruism is so fanatical that I have no control over it, the situation is different. This is one case in which I am not acting on appropriate grounds.[25]

---

[24] This is controversial, especially for certain kinds of cases. For one thing, someone might, against my will, manipulate me so as to change my nature so drastically that my natural tendencies are quite different. If one thinks of the "old me" it may seem that I am not acting freely when I pursue a newly instilled ideal that is contrary to one I had. But if there really is one agent throughout, then I am now very different and, given my present nature, now acting freely. My action and freedom *were* violated at the time of manipulation, but it is not as if the old me were still present and being compelled: that is a different case, in which, for example, new desires are imposed to override the natural ones.

[25] I do not attempt to give a full account of appropriate grounds here, but I make some of the crucial points in Chapter 7, and in Chapter 9 I suggest some of the ways in which one should have a measure of control of one's character in order for one's

There *are* pasts that leave agents impaired and unfree to act, and other pasts that compel actions; but once necessitation is clearly distinguished from necessity and necessity is no longer attributed, tacitly or otherwise, to past events, the past can seem more a source of raw material than of compulsion. Indeed, we may think of the past as such that it would be different if we should do otherwise than we (freely) will, and would have been different if we had done otherwise than we have done. These are not ordinary causal conditionals (if causal at all), and to affirm them is not to deny that we cannot affect how the past actually is; it is to confirm the contingency of the past.

In concluding this section, I want to explore one disanalogy between the epistemic and behavioral cases we have been discussing. Why, in the case of knowledge, is causation not seen as a threat? The answer, I think, is that beliefs taken to constitute knowledge are felt to be, by that very fact, reliable, and reliability is enhanced by the most salient kinds of connections between beliefs and the causal factors sustaining or producing them. Consider perceptual belief: my belief that there is a white surface before me is produced and sustained by that very thing, and so far as I know this is the only cause of such beliefs in me. If a perceptual belief to the effect that a certain object exists cannot (normally) arise from any other source, then the belief is a reliable sign of that source, and that, in turn, implies that it is true. With memory beliefs, the connection to the past is less tight, but insofar as we think of them as caused by past events, we tend to conceive them as reliable signs of those events, and hence as candidates for knowledge of them. By contrast, free actions are commonly conceived as realizations of suitably open alternatives; they do not, on this view, reflect a fixed past or a congealing present; they do not just reflect how things are but *change* them.

If the approach I take in Chapter 7 is correct, this plausible contrast is easily carried too far. If we distinguish acting freely from being free to act, we can see that on reflection we *do* want our actions to reflect the past or present or both: we want them to express our desires, beliefs, ideals, and, in general, our character. It is difficult to see how we can plausibly interpret this notion other than on causal lines. Indeed, it is only when actions are in some sense causally rooted in us that they can express our virtue, as Aristotle saw, or have moral

---

acts in expressing it to be free. I thank Alfred Mele for noting that my points here raise the general problem of how the genesis of motivational variables is related to the freedom of the actions explainable by appeal to them.

worth, as Kant plausibly held.[26] Granted, there is a sense in which we must be free from the past in order to act freely in the present; but this is freedom from compulsions, not disconnection from the appropriate grounds of rational choice.

The point that free actions must be properly grounded in their agents does not imply that freedom *requires* determinism, or even nomic causation of the strong kind we have been considering—a universal lawlike connection between motivational elements and the actions they ground. Even if causation entails the existence of laws, they need not be universal, as opposed to statistical or tendency laws, such as those explicated in Chapter 1. But if we imagine that only chance "determines" what behavior emerges from the motivating reasons in terms of which we explain and justify our actions, we surely do not thereby think of these actions as free. This would imply that our freest actions have the weakest generative connection with our motivation, and that we act more freely in proportion as we are less influenced by our reasons. That corresponds neither with our parlance concerning freedom nor with our ways of determining moral responsibility.

III. Freedom and Compulsion

The remaining task of this chapter is to extend and elaborate the account given in Chapter 7. The strategy of that essay is to take free action to be best explicable in relation to compulsion. Even if this is not the best route to understanding freedom, given the way that freedom is often ascribed to actions with the force of ruling out one or another kind of compulsion, surely one good way to discern its contours is to consider compulsions as foils. Free actions, so conceived, are uncompelled intentional actions, or suitably related to them, as where one non-intentionally but freely annoys one's neighbors in celebrating Independence Day with fireworks. Normally, we do not call an action free unless we are thinking of it as intentional, under something like the description we use or have in mind in sin-

[26] See Aristotle, *Nicomachean Ethics* 1105a30ff. and Kant, *Foundations of the Metaphysics of Morals,* for example [400]. In Chapter 6 I give an account of the way in which intentional actions are rooted in one's motivational system; free (intentional) actions are no exception.

gling it out for appraisal or comment; and we certainly do not so describe an action unless, under such a description, we are thinking of S as at least knowing or having some idea that S is performing it. What I have no idea I may be doing does not appropriately come within the scope of my will.

There are two points, each implying important subsidiary points, that I want to develop in the remaining space. The first concerns the distinction between conditional and unconditional accounts of 'could not have done otherwise', taken to express a high degree of compulsion—what in Chapter 7 I call *strict unavoidability*. The second point concerns the sense in which the notion of free action, by virtue of its tie with moral responsibility, is a moral concept.

Many compatibilists have given conditional accounts of strict unavoidability, for instance by maintaining that S could have done otherwise provided that, if S had chosen to do otherwise, S would have done otherwise. A number of writers have ably attacked such conditional accounts, noting, for example, that one might not have been *able* to choose otherwise, so that even if such a choice would have produced a different action, that alternative path to action was not accessible to one.[27] But—as is less widely realized than it should be—compatibilists are not committed to conditional accounts, and the unconditional account of 'could not have done otherwise' presented in Chapter 7 is not open to the sorts of objections commonly brought against conditional ones. As I see free action, it is not action that the agent could have avoided, *in the sense that,* had conditions been different in a certain way, the agent would have done otherwise; it is instead action that is *explainable* in a certain way, because actually grounded in an appropriate pattern of (non-compelling) motivational factors. In paradigm cases, it is action performed for (non-compelling) reasons that are in some sense part of one's character. *Why* the agent performs it is what is crucial, not what the agent

---

[27] See, e.g., Chisholm, "Freedom and Action," and "J. L. Austin's Philosophical Papers," *Mind* 73 (1964), as well as Austin's "Ifs and Cans," in his *Philosophical Papers,* ed. J. O. Urmson and G. J. Warnock (Oxford: Clarendon Press, 1961). Peter van Inwagen, *An Essay on Free Will,* considers a number of compatibilist accounts, but neither he nor most incompatibilists focus on non-conditional accounts. There are, however, non-conditional accounts of moral responsibility; for a brief sketch (and many relevant references) see, for example, John Martin Fischer and Mark Ravizza, "The Inevitable," forthcoming in the *Australasian Journal of Philosophy.* Their account seems at least largely compatible with my earlier one in Chapter 7, except that they do not distinguish categorical from conditional uses of 'could have done otherwise'.

could have done instead, or would have done in some other possible circumstances.[28]

This non-conditional account of freedom and compulsion has two important, related implications for our understanding of (moral) responsibility and of strict unavoidability taken to entail a degree of compulsion high enough to eliminate responsibility. First, it ties responsibility to the determinants of free action. This is reasonable because responsibility implies the appropriateness (in one sense) of calling the agent to account. That appropriateness is best explained on the assumption that the action expresses something—whether ultimately reprehensible or not—in the agent's motivational system, where the sense of 'express' is partly causal. Second, my account of freedom and compulsion implies that when one could not have done otherwise in the sense relevant to responsibility, it is because of what *actually* determined action, such as a threat of death to innocent children.

The second implication is best appreciated in connection with a well-known line of argument meant to show that responsibility does not imply that the agent could have done otherwise. Suppose, for example, that I am about to sign a petition but, unbeknownst to me, someone with sophisticated brain altering equipment wants to make sure that I do sign it, and can tell if I am the least inclined to waver. Then it may be false that I am not responsible—since I have signed for my own reasons—but true that (in one important sense) I could not have done otherwise—since, as things were, if I had not on my own proceeded to sign, I would have been made to do so (by induction of motivation suitable to make the action an intentional signing).[29] Indeed, I would add that it is as plausible to say that I freely sign as to say that I am responsible for doing so, and for the same reason: my act is grounded in the appropriate way in my motivational system. The sinister manipulator might even appropriately remark, "If he doesn't sign of his own free will, I'll make him do it." But does this sort of case show that responsibility for an action does not imply that one could have done otherwise?

[28] For a recent sketch of how actions are related to the agent's motivating reasons, see Fred Dretske, "The Metaphysics of Freedom," *Canadian Journal of Philosophy* 22 (1992), and for critical discussion of Dretske's approach, see Hugh J. McCann, "Dretske on the Metaphysics of Action," forthcoming in the *Canadian Journal of Philosophy*.

[29] This case is due to Harry Frankfurt, and I discuss it in Chapter 7. Here I extend what was said there.

Once again, I want to disambiguate. Where moral responsibility is at stake and the question arises (e.g. in appraising an excuse) whether S could not have done otherwise, the sense of that phrase is—if I have been right—categorical: it is to be applied or withheld depending on what sort of thing actually explains the deed, not in terms of what would have produced or explained it if things had been different. But when we consider action purely metaphysically and accordingly think in terms of modalities as explicated in relation to closely similar alternative situations (or alternative "worlds"), then whether S could not have done otherwise is a matter of what S does in relevantly close possible worlds. I believe, then, that examples like the guaranteed signing do not show that compulsion, including strict unavoidability, is an inappropriate basis for understanding freedom and, in part, responsibility. The absence of strict unavoidability, categorically construed, can be necessary for moral responsibility even if that of hypothetical unavoidability is not and even where, if S had not spontaneously done the deed in question, S would have been compelled to. The examples do show something else of interest, however: that one can freely do something to which—in one sense—one has no alternative. But even 'no alternative', like 'could not have done otherwise', has an ordinary and a metaphysical use. Until one pursues the possibility of a non-conditional account of 'could not have done otherwise', one can easily miss the distinction between these two uses.

Granted, it is odd to say, of agents who would have been compelled to A if they were not going to do it of their own accord, that they could have done otherwise; but my claim is only that it is not true that, *in* the sense relevant to moral responsibility, they could *not* have done otherwise. It cannot be simply assumed that the use of 'could have done otherwise' in which the attribution is odd expresses the contradictory of the notion of strict unavoidability and so must apply here. Note, moreover, that even in a case of such potential compulsion, I perhaps could have done *something* I did not do, such that if I did it, the compelling sequence would have been activated. Some would take this to imply that in a perfectly ordinary sense I *could* have done otherwise. If so—and for my purposes this may be left open—then the potential compulsion cases do not show something else they appear to establish: that being free *to A* does not imply being able both to do the deed and to abstain from doing it.

We come now to the normative aspect of the notion of freedom. If free actions are to be understood as uncompelled, and if, as I argue in Chapter 7, what constitutes compulsion is in part a question of what is excusing or at least extenuating, then the notion of free action is not just metaphysical, but also normative. This implies that as our conception of what constitutes an excuse changes, our conception of freedom will also change. There is, in this sense, some open space in the notion of freedom: its connection with responsibility is an enduring feature, but the scope of, and conditions for, responsibility are not precisely fixed by the concept.

An advantage of compatibilism, from this perspective, is that it does not force us to take conduct to be less appropriately assessed as responsible in proportion as it is more nearly causally determined. We may, in order to be more humane or because we want to be more enlightened, expand the category of excuses; but we do not need to assimilate causation to compulsion. Causal necessity would indeed be a kind of compulsion,[30] but no one has even come close to showing that any specific action is (unconditionally) causally necessary. What is only conditionally necessary—necessary given its cause—is no more necessary than the cause itself, and we are back to the same issue: is there any reason to think that some event that is a cause of action is itself necessary? Causation of an event by antecedents does not imply necessity. Unalterability does not imply necessity. Nor is the necessity of any particular event implied by even so grand a thesis as determinism itself. The categorical necessity of an action would indeed be mysterious in the light of determinism properly understood.

Nothing said here is meant to suggest that we have good reason to believe that determinism is true. I doubt that we do; but it seems possible that determinism might hold, and in any case if I am right about the importance of modalities for the problem of free will, the nomic causation of actions is plausibly felt to be a threat to freedom even apart from determinism and probably even apart from our actions' having an infinite or indefinite causal history extending before our births. The core of the free will problem, then, might survive the death of universal determinism.

There may be no way to prove that we sometimes act freely, just as there may be no way to prove we have knowledge of an external

---

[30] It is to his credit that Zimmerman takes account of this point by distinguishing between strict and broad freedom. The former is possible even for (in my terminology) an action that is compelled but not causally necessary; it can be broadly, but not strictly, unavoidable. See, for example, his *Essay on Moral Responsibility*, pp. 24–26.

world. But there is no reason to doubt either view, and if the motivational grounds of many of our actions are, as they seem, both noncompelling and responsible for these actions, in a sense implying that we act for the reasons constituted by those grounds, then surely many of our actions are free. Free actions are well-grounded responses to appropriate reasons for performing them, and in virtue of that grounding they at once express something of what we are and change the world in ways that, so far as we can tell, we freely choose.

PART IV

RATIONAL ACTION

Chapter 11

Rationality and Valuation

A major problem in the philosophy of action is what constitutes a rational action on the part of an individual person. This problem is also important in the social sciences, particularly insofar as their tasks may be conceived as conceptual or critical, and in ethics, which has traditionally viewed the relation between rational action and moral action as one of its major problems. Rational action will be a central concern of this essay; but since the rationality of an action is apparently dependent on that of the agent's motivation and cognition, we must also explore what constitutes the rationality of motivational and cognitive elements, and how it bears on that of actions based on them. Thus, beliefs and wants, which may be plausibly conceived as the basic cognitive and motivational elements, will be one of our major concerns. The rationality of values will also be explored. This is in part because there has been so much controversy over whether our basic values can be rational and in part because, if they can be, that is important for understanding rational action.

In Section I, I will assess a highly influential conception of rational action—instrumentalism—and critically compare it with broader views. In Section II, I will consider developments and refinements in instrumentalism, particularly those by Carl Hempel. In Section III, I will briefly consider a contextualist approach to rational action and will address the controversy between Hempel and William Dray. In

Section IV, I will explore an important contemporary account of rational action, Richard Brandt's. Against this background, I will introduce in Section V a largely new conception of rational action. This conception is inspired by the analogy between the theory of action and the theory of knowledge. In Section V, I will develop this conception and indicate some directions for further research. In the concluding section, I will point out some of the ways in which the rationality of actions is related to that of persons and will suggest how our results bear on theoretical work in the social sciences.

I. The Instrumentalist Conception of Rational Action

A natural way to approach the question of what constitutes rational action is to consider what it is to go about realizing one's aims in a rational way. For the question whether an action is rational very commonly arises when it is not clear that the action well serves some aim(s) the agent has in performing it. It usually does not arise when an action can be seen to be a satisfactory way to realize what appear to be the agent's aims in the circumstances. One might think, then, that the crucial mark of a rational action is its appropriateness to the aim(s) of the agent at the time of action. This approach is reinforced by the view, held or suggested by many philosophers, that an action is rational only if it arises from practical reasoning.[1] For it is then natural to construe the rationality of the action in terms of how good a means it is, judged on the assumption of the truth of the premises of the reasoning, to realize the aim expressed in the major premise. To be sure, a proponent of this view might still want to take account of whether the aim and the belief(s) expressed in the premises are themselves rational; but as we shall see, an instrumentalist may argue that this question is not strictly relevant to the rationality

---

[1] This view is not frequently stated, but there are some philosophers who conceive all intentional actions as arising from practical reasoning, and clearly at least the most important kinds of rational actions are intentional. See, e.g., Donald Davidson, "How Is Weakness of the Will Possible?" in Joel Feinberg, ed., *Moral Concepts* (London: Oxford University Press, 1969), p. 110; and Gilbert Harman, "Practical Reasoning," *Review of Metaphysics* 29 (1976): 451 (cf. p. 442). I have assessed both views in "A Theory of Practical Reasoning," *American Philosophical Quarterly* 19 (1982).

of the action. If what is really crucial to rational action is its success as a means to realizing one or more of the agent's aims, then the character of these aims should be irrelevant, except insofar as realizing one may be at odds with realizing another or with maximum realization of the overall set.

On an instrumentalist approach to rational action, one will be especially interested in cases in which the agent, S, has not only one or more aims, but also quite specific beliefs about what constitute his alternatives and their possible outcomes. It is an empirical question how common such cases are, but they have seemed common enough to most instrumentalists and many others to give great interest to the conception of rational actions as, paradigmatically, those that maximize expectable utility. Roughly, an action, A, by an agent S—Sid, let us say—maximizes his expectable utility if, and only if, it has at least as much expected utility as any alternative he supposes he has.[2]

The expected utility of an action, on this view, is computed as follows: one determines (1) the courses of action S supposes he has, (2) what he believes are their possible outcomes, and (3) the subjective value for S (using arbitrarily chosen numbers from negative to positive) of each outcome; one then multiplies the subjective value of each outcome by the subjective probability of that outcome, and adds these products for each alternative action. A rational action for S in such a situation is one with a score at least as high as that of any of S's alternatives. Consider Sue, a surgeon who supposes she has two options: surgery and non-intervention. (The patient, let us assume, has asked Sue to make the final decision.) Sue might regard surgery as having a probability of .60 of curing the patient, an outcome she values at 100; and a probability of .40 of resulting in his death, an outcome she values at −75. She might regard non-intervention as having a probability of .50 of resulting in cure, one of .20 of resulting in death, and one of .20 of yielding long-term partial remission, which she values at 30. We thus have, for surgery, $(.60 \times 100) + (.40$

---

[2] One could restrict this characterization to *actual* alternatives, but one would then have a highly problematic conception of rationality. For one thing, if S had an alternative which he did not *believe* he had, he would presumably lack the required probability beliefs regarding its outcomes. One would need a number of stipulations to work the view out, and I believe that the result would still be a less plausible conception of rational action. For further discussion of both the maximization of expected utility conception of rational action and Hempel's treatment of it (which will be discussed shortly), see Donald Davidson, "Hempel on Explaining Action," in Davidson's *Essays on Actions and Events* (Oxford: Clarendon Press, 1980).

$\times$ -75), that is, 30; and, for non-intervention, (.50 $\times$ 100) + (.20 $\times$ -75), + (.30 $\times$ 30), that is, 44. Thus, the rational action, on this model, is non-intervention.

There are various ways of interpreting subjective probability and subjective utility. For our purposes nothing is lost if we interpret the former in terms of beliefs and the latter in terms of wants. Let us assume, then, that to say that the subjective probability, for S, of an outcome's occurring, is n, is to say that S believes the likelihood of its occurring to be n. This belief may of course be dispositional. Hence S need not have the corresponding thought, at the time of action or any other time. Similarly, to say that the subjective utility of an outcome is n is to say that n is the degree to which S wants it, or, in the case of negative utility, wants to avoid it.[3] In both cases, it appears that one need presuppose only ordinal scales; but this weak presupposition appears appropriate, since the notion of a rational action does not have to be conceived as quantitative in any sense implying the possibility of interval or ratio measurement of the rationality in question. What is crucial is that we be able to rank actions, not determine precisely how rational they are.

It has been widely recognized that the particular instrumentalist conception of rational action just sketched applies only in special cases. But there seems to have been a tendency, in some quarters, to exaggerate the frequency of such cases in ordinary behavior, including problem-solving behavior generally considered prima facie rational. A main reason for this tendency may be the assumption that if, on considering the question of how probable a possible outcome of A-ing is, Sid *would* assign a probability, then he believes, at least dispositionally, that its occurrence has that probability. But as I have elsewhere argued, this assumption assimilates dispositionally believing to a disposition to believe.[4] To illustrate, one may be cognitively so constituted that if someone asked whether there was a brass band playing in one's backyard, one would immediately dissent. It does not follow that, prior to entertaining this proposition, one believed it false. A machine analogue may help here: the difference is like that between a computer's being so designed that, immediately upon being "asked" the distance between London and Berlin, it calculates

[3] That *wanting* is a suitably broad concept for this purpose is strongly suggested by my arguments for its breadth, as a general motivational notion, in Chapter 2. I have explicated this broad notion of wanting in Chapter 1.
[4] In my "Believing and Affirming," *Mind* 91 (1982).

this from its cartographic tables and displays the figure, and, on the other hand, this figure's *already* being in its memory bank.

It is quite similar with probability beliefs. We are often so disposed that on contemplating a possible event we form a probability belief about its occurrence; but it does not follow that we already had such a belief. This point applies especially to assignments of probability S would make to alternative possible outcomes of his action *after* he has acted and realized one. For the experience of realizing the outcome often evokes beliefs about how likely it was given the means taken to produce it. Moreover, a reasonably cautious person may be very reluctant to make such probability assignments and is often forced to hypothesize instead a *range* of values, such as between .50 and .75. Recall our surgeon. Even if she has statistics on the incidence of death from the kind of surgery in question, each patient is different, and she might well form only the cautious belief that the chance of death from the surgery is better than even. Somewhat paradoxically, the better one understands probability and the complex field of future possibilities, the less often one's behavior satisfies the maximization of expected utility conception of rational action (other things being equal). For one becomes increasingly cautious about forming beliefs regarding the precise probabilities of the relevant outcomes. This is emphatically not to suggest that rational agents do not take account of probabilities or often form beliefs about ranges of probabilities. But my point is only that the maximization of expected utility conception seems to presuppose the formation of beliefs a rational agent would often be unlikely to have.

A natural reply here would be that while it may be important to see that the applicability of this conception is severely limited, I have still shown no deficiency in it for those cases to which it does apply. Indeed, I have not. But there surely are deficiencies. To see some of them, let us consider the resources of a sophisticated elaboration of this conception, by Hempel.

II. A Modified Instrumentalist Conception of Rational Action

Hempel's most general statement of his position on the nature of rational actions is perhaps this:

To qualify a given action as rational is to put forward an *empirical hypothesis* and a *critical appraisal*. The hypothesis is to the effect that the action was done for certain reasons, that it can be explained as having been motivated by them. The reasons will include the ends that the agent presumably sought to attain, and the beliefs he presumably entertained concerning the availability, propriety, and probable effectiveness of alternative means of attaining those ends. The critical appraisal is to the effect that, judged in the light of the agent's beliefs, the action he decided upon constituted a *reasonable* or *appropriate* choice of means for achieving his end.[5]

Clearly Hempel is adding at least one important element to the instrumentalist conception set forth above, namely, the requirement that a rational action be explainable in terms of relevant beliefs and wants (I take wants to represent the ends of which Hempel speaks). He is quite aware, however, that his characterization does not apply to actions under uncertainty, that is, those such that while S has definite beliefs about what her alternatives are and what are their possible outcomes, she does not (or cannot) assign probabilities to the latter. Hempel discusses some possible strategies for characterizing rationality in these cases, including the maximin and maximax rules. But he not only does not endorse these; he even warns us against the "assumption that the idea of rationality, or of the best way to act in a given situation, is reasonably clear."[6]

Our later discussion will bear on how clear a conception of rationality we should expect to be able to attain. But a prior task is to examine Hempel's defense of his instrumentalist conception of rational action where the conception does apply. In this section, I will simply consider his case for ignoring the rationality or irrationality of the beliefs and wants that determine an agent's (subjective) probabilities and utilities. In the next section, I will take up Hempel's requirement that (in my terminology) these beliefs and wants must explain the relevant action.

After Hempel raises the question whether, if S's A-ing is rational, the belief(s) on the basis of which S A's must be supported by evidence, he says that

[5] Carl G. Hempel, *Aspects of Scientific Explanation* (New York: Free Press, 1965), p. 463.
[6] Ibid., p. 469.

if we wish to construct a concept of rational action that might later prove useful in explaining certain types of human behavior, then it seems preferable not to impose on it a requirement of evidential support; for in order to explain an action in terms of the agent's reasons, we need to know what the agent believed, but not necessarily on what grounds.[7]

Similarly, he says that he "will not impose the requirement that there must be 'good reasons' for adopting the given ends and norms: rationality of an action will be understood in a strictly relative sense, as its suitability, judged by the given information, for achieving the specified objective."[8]

These remarks call for several comments. First, although Hempel defends his rejection of an evidence requirement by appeal to the aim of constructing an explanatory concept of rational action, he begins his paper on rational action with the suggestion that he is explicating an antecedently available concept (and in one of the statements I have quoted seems to identify acting rationally with "the best way to act" in the relevant situation). If *that* is a main part of his aim, he needs a direct argument to the effect that the relevant concept implies no evidence requirement. For surely there is no familiar concept of rational action for which it is clear that no evidence requirement applies, particularly a weak and merely negative requirement to the effect that the belief(s) responsible for a rational action are not held in blatant disregard of what S sees is significant counterevidence. Such a requirement is especially plausible if one thinks of rational actions as the best thing, or even a good thing, for the agent to do. Second, and more important, surely a concept of rational action which does embody an evidence requirement can be explanatory, in what seems the relevant sense: that its application to an action implies that the action is explainable in terms of certain sorts of reasons, namely, by appeal to the sorts of wants and beliefs we have described. Beliefs based on evidence, and wants based on reasons, can explain actions at least as well as beliefs and wants with no rational basis.

Granted, without any evidence requirement the concept of rational action will doubtless apply to more actions, and more of them will

---

[7] Ibid., p. 463.
[8] Ibid. On this point and others, it is interesting to compare the views of R. M. Hare; see esp. his "What Makes Choices Rational?" *Review of Metaphysics* 32 (1979), esp. p. 635.

thus qualify as explainable by appeal to the sorts of beliefs and wants that Hempel takes to underlie rational action. Thus, the *explanatory scope* of the concept of rational action would be greater. But the *explanatory power* of the concept, where it does apply, would be no greater. Hempel does not explicitly distinguish these two aspects of explanatory usefulness, and there is no good reason to consider the former more important, particularly given that the action-explaining relevance of both concepts of rational action is derivative in the same way from that of wants and beliefs. In both cases what is explanatorily crucial is that calling an action rational implies that there was something S wanted, to which, in some way, he believed the action would contribute (for example be a good means).

In any event, whether or not considerations of explanatory power favor omitting an evidence requirement from an instrumentalist conception of rational action, there may be good instrumentalist reasons for imposing *some* requirement on the rationality, or at least the nature, of the relevant want(s) and belief(s). For even a thoroughgoing instrumentalist need not suppose, as Hempel in some places seems to, that the rationality of our actions should be subordinate to just any beliefs and wants of the sorts that figure in calculations of expected utility. Let us consider wants and beliefs in turn.

It is presumably our intrinsic wanting—roughly, wanting something for its own sake—that is the crucial source of subjective utilities, even for a thoroughgoing instrumentalist. Suppose, for example, that by virtue of a psychological abnormality, Sid could want to jog for the sake of strengthening his legs yet not want, for its own sake, either to strengthen his legs or to achieve anything to which he takes it to be connected as a means. This might occur where S somehow has an ungrounded chain of wants, say where (a) through motivational inertia, his instrumental wants fail to disappear when the intrinsic want(s) to which they are subordinate do, or (b) where—if this is possible—S has an infinite or circular chain of wants connected by instrumental beliefs (wanting x as a means to y, y as a means to z, etc.). In case (1), S would want to strengthen his legs, but not in virtue of properties he takes to be intrinsic to doing so, nor on the basis of any instrumental properties he takes doing so to have. We would thus have a want that is neither instrumental nor, properly speaking, intrinsic. In case (2), we would have a want not connected by instrumental beliefs to any intrinsic want.

Supposing that either (1) or (2) is possible, should an instrumentalist say that S's jogging would be rational provided S believed it would strengthen his legs and jogged for precisely that reason? An instrumentalist certainly *need* not say this. For one thing, the action is at least psychologically abnormal. Moreover, since it is not, given S's beliefs, a contribution to fulfilling any of his basic ends, that is (roughly), those he would want to realize even if (other things equal) he did not believe their fulfillment to be a means of realizing any other ends of his, there is nothing he has, as an unconditional (even if revisable) end, to provide an adequate answer to the question why the jogging is worth while for him. The point is not that an instrumentalist must posit a set of final ends which all rational agents must seek; it is that even on an instrumentalist view the rationality of an action is plausibly relativized to *some* end wanted for its own sake *in the context.*

An instrumentalist may plausibly go further and maintain that the sorts of ungrounded wants we have considered are neither rational nor capable of rendering rational any action performed in order to realize them. Even supposing instrumentalists do not take this last step, however, they should certainly grant that an action may fail to be rational because of the irrationality of an *instrumental* want on which it is based. I may, for example, have an instrumental want on the basis of which I unwittingly act to the detriment of an intrinsic want, merely for the sake of an instrumental one. Suppose I want to save money, purely as a means to furthering my daughter's education, which I intrinsically want to further. I might discover that I can save money by not buying her certain books which are available at a library, and then, in order to save money, and with no thought of my ultimate reason for wanting to do so, decline to buy the books. By doing so, I might act rationally in a narrow instrumentalist sense, namely that, relative to the wants and beliefs of which I am aware and on the basis of which I assign utilities and probabilities, I maximized expected utility. If, however, the damage to her education from not owning the books obviously outweighs—and should have been seen by me to outweigh—the benefits to her of the saving, the action is not rational from the broad instrumentalist point of view of maximizing my *basic* aims.

An appropriate instrumentalist reply here is that I simply ignored a relevant outcome, the negative effect on my child's education. Granted, but this move raises the problem of how one decides the relevance of outcomes, given that many of our actions have significant consequences for basic wants of ours to which we would not readily see their connection. Here I want to bypass that troublesome problem. My point is that if—following what is suggested by the formulation quoted from Hempel—we consider only the aim by which I am actuated in the circumstances, then we should have to call my declining to buy the books rational, since relative to *that* aim (saving money) it is optimal. Moreover, presumably even instrumentalists may say that in the circumstances my want to save money on the books is not rational, since it should be obvious to me that realizing it will detract from realizing the want on which it is ultimately based. The sense of 'rational' here is perhaps not purely instrumentalist; but my point is simply that even on a strongly instrumentalist view the non-rationality of an actuating want is relevant to the rationality of the action it explains.

It is also worth stressing that the point is not simply a matter of want strength. For if we imagine that somehow S's instrumental want to save money became, at the time, stronger than his want to further the child's education, it does not follow that either the former want or the action it produces is instrumentally rational. The action would still be, one wants to say, a means to the wrong end. Thus, even on an instrumentalist view, the rationality of an action is not simply a matter of its producing the greatest amount of want satisfaction possible on the agent's beliefs at the time. Intrinsic wants are, in a limited context, privileged and can serve as a basis for judging the rationality of extrinsic wants and of actions based on the latter. This is why, for example, an instrumentalist cannot allow assigning, to something wanted merely as a means, a positive utility *in addition* to the utility it has by virtue of its probability of realizing an intrinsic want. If Sue wants to go to the drugstore only to get medicine, and wants medicine only to get well (which she intrinsically wants), going to the drugstore may not be given a utility both for its contribution to getting medicine and its contribution to getting her well.

Now consider the role of beliefs in determining rationality. Suppose that S irrationally believes that jogging will strengthen his legs, against the evidence both of experience and expert testimony, though he does have a rational want to strengthen his legs. Must an instrumentalist say that the action is rational? It would seem not: S ought to see that in so acting he is not advancing his basic ends, or indeed any end of his. S's jogging, in this case, may be excusable, but it is by no means clearly rational.

I am not suggesting that an instrumentalist must adopt the requirement that there really be (objective) evidence *for* the relevant belief(s), or good grounds for wanting the relevant states of affairs. That might be appropriate to a conception (on which I shall comment later) of the objectively rational thing to do, but it is not appropriate here. The point is rather that when S—whether he has positive evidence or not—believes something *against* which he has enough evidence to dissuade a rational person in his position, and then acts on that belief, the rationality of his action can be undermined even from an instrumentalist point of view. The same applies, as I have argued, to acting on an extrinsic want whose realization would be obviously undesirable from the point of view of the intrinsic want(s) to which it is subordinate. Hempel's conception of rational action, then, represents a quite restricted option even for an instrumentalist. So far, however, we have said nothing about his requirement that the factors in terms of which an action is rational must bear an explanatory relation to it. This requirement is controversial and has been attacked, at least as Hempel conceives it, by contextualists, most notably William Dray. Let us explore the issue in some detail.

III. Causalist versus Contextualist Conceptions of Rational Action

On Hempel's conception of rational action, the reasons in virtue of which an action is rational must be sufficient to explain why the agent so acted. The central idea, I think, is that an action is rational only if the belief(s) and want(s) from which it derives its rationality also play an explanatory part, either as initiating or as sustaining factors (presumably in a broadly causal way). Hempel takes this sort of view to be challenged by Dray. According to Dray, the goal of rational explanation, which he conceives as the sort that displays the rationale of the action in question, "is to show that what was done was the thing to have done for the reasons given, rather than merely the thing that is done on such occasions, perhaps in accordance with certain laws."[9] On Dray's view, it appears that the

---

[9] See William Dray, *Laws and Explanation in History* (Oxford: Clarendon Press, 1957), p. 124. Dray's views are developed by him in later work, for example, "'Explaining What' in History," in Patrick Gardiner, ed., *Theories of History* (New York: Free Press, 1959). For another contextualist perspective, see Michael Scriven, "Truisms as Grounds for Historical Explanations," also in Gardiner.

sense in which reasons must explain the action whose rationale they indicate is non-causal. What the relevant sort of explanation requires is neither causal nor nomic connections, but, apparently, a placement of the action in a context of reasons such that, in the light of them, it is the reasonable thing to do.[10]

Hempel resolutely rejects this as a conception of explanation *why* something is the case:

> For any adequate answer to the question why a certain event occurred will surely have to provide us with information which, if accepted as true, would afford good grounds for believing that that event did indeed occur—even if there were no other evidence for its occurrence.[11]

This proposed necessary condition on explanations of why something is so has been challenged by philosophers of science as well as action theorists, and the issues it raises cannot be discussed here.[12] Fortunately, we can narrow the problem to the specific question whether the belief(s) and want(s) in virtue of which an action is rational must play *some* role in bringing about or sustaining it even if their occurrence is not taken to be sufficient to provide, by itself, good reason to expect the agent to do the thing in question. It seems to me that this is the minimal thesis which should be held by theorists taking a covering-law approach to explanation and to rational action. For it seems the weakest plausible thesis that (apparently) requires a covering law linking the agent's reasons to the action that is rational on the basis of them. Even this weak view is controversial, and Dray seems to deny it as well as its stronger cousins.

I cannot assess this view in detail here; but I believe that if we observe an important distinction not brought to bear by either Hempel or Dray (and often overlooked in the literature), we can reasonably judge the view. Consider Tom, who is (irrationally) afraid of heights. Suppose that as a result of his fear he impulsively takes an ugly

---

[10] See, for example, Dray, *Laws and Explanations in History*, pp. 124–26 and 132. Cf. G. E. M. Anscombe's remark that "to give a motive . . . is to say something like 'See the action in this light'. To explain one's own actions by an account indicating a motive is to put them in a certain light"; see *Intention*, 2d ed. (Ithaca: Cornell University Press, 1963), p. 21.

[11] Hempel, *Aspects of Scientific Explanation*, pp. 470–71.

[12] I have discussed them in detail and considered other positions concerning them, in Chapter 5 and in "Inductive-Nomological Explanations and Psychological Laws," *Theory and Decision* 13 (1981).

route to visit a friend, thereby avoiding a safe but mountainous road. Assume further that whereas on the mountain route he would not *see* the land below in a way that frightens him, on the ugly route he will have to negotiate many dangerous curves. If he knows this, yet, fearing just being high up, takes the ugly route against his better judgment, his doing so would be irrational. For the motivating fear is irrational, and in addition he chooses, against his better judgment, the route he knows is significantly dangerous. It might be, however, that he knows that the ugly route is somewhat shorter, though this factor is, for him, too insignificant to affect his actual motivation to take the ugly, shorter route. It is thus no part of the reason why he in fact takes the shorter route. For all that, it is easy to imagine his answering 'Why did you take the ugly road?' with 'It is shorter.'

This reply would be a clear case of *rationalization:* he has rationalized his action, not explained why he performed it. May we conclude, then, that while Hempel is roughly right about explanation, Dray and other contextualists are right about rational action? That would be premature. For there is an immense difference between the action-*type*, taking the shorter route, being a rational thing to do, and the action-token, Tom's taking the shorter route at a given time, t, being rational.[13] The distinction can be seen by recalling something forcefully maintained by Kant: one can do the right thing for the wrong reasons; and when one does, one is not acting morally. I suggest that Tom's case is similar. He does a rational (type of) thing for the wrong reasons, and his doing it (the token) is thus not rational. It is one thing for one's doing a particular thing, A, to be rational; it is quite another for A-ing to be both a rational kind of thing to do and something one in fact does rationally. Doing a rational kind of thing does not entail that one's doing of it is rational. I doubt the converse entailment as well. One could, for good reasons—such as credible testimony from generally reliable people—rationally do something (say, try to swim in a rapids) that is in fact not a rational kind of thing to do, discovering only afterwards that one was cleverly deceived.

What, then, is the connection between rationalization and rationality? What does a rationalization of one's action—if it cites a good

---

[13] As used here, the type-token distinction does not prejudge the ontological question whether individual actions at a given time are 'concrete' particulars or something quite different, to be individuated non-extensionally. One could instead speak of the kind of thing S does, as opposed to his doing something of precisely that kind on a particular occasion. But this has no clear ontological advantage and is less convenient.

reason one had for the action—show to be rational? On my view, it is at best the relevant action-type, not the token, that such rationalizations show to be rational. Taking the ugly, shorter route might be shown to be the rational thing to do by what Tom says, but what he says does not show that *his* taking it is rational: he does it on the basis of irrational fear and against his better judgment. Unfortunately, it is easy to conflate the rationality of types with that of tokens because, for one thing, we have so many locutions that apply to both. We speak of rational action, acting rationally, a rational thing to do, rational choice, approaching a problem rationally, and so on. Any of these phrases can refer either to the type of thing S has done or to his particular doing of something of that type.

Once we steadfastly distinguish these two kinds of things, we can see that much (though not all) of what Dray says about rational action applies to types, whereas Hempel's points against him apply mainly to tokens. Now there may be a kind of explanation which reasons that rationalize a type of action provide: they yield understanding of why one might do something of that type. Max Weber may have been suggesting something similar to an explanation of this sort in some of his famous discussions of ideal types.[14] But even if there are reasons, in a given context, in virtue of which *A*-ing is the (or a) rational (type of) thing for S to do, and even if S has these reasons for *A*-ing—since he knows of them and of their bearing on *A*-ing—if they play no initiating or sustaining role in his *A*-ing, then they do not render that particular action rational. He may rationalize, but not explain, his *A*-ing by appeal to them; but he is no more rational in his particular *A*-ing than a person who, purely for selfish reasons, does what morality requires, is acting morally in doing the particular thing in question. The difference is very much like the Kantian distinction between, on the one hand, acting out of a sense of duty, and thereby following a moral rule, and on the other hand merely acting in accordance with duty or with a moral rule.

My conclusion in this section, then, is that if we are to distinguish rational actions from *rationalizable* ones, a particular action should be considered rational in virtue of a set of beliefs and wants expressing reasons for it, only if these wants and beliefs play a role in generating

---

[14] Max Weber, *Wirtschaft und Gesellschaft*, 4th ed. (Tübingen: Mohr, 1956), first published in 1922. Relevant parts are available in English in Weber, *Selections in Translation*, ed. W. G. Runciman, trans. E. Matthews (Cambridge: Cambridge University Press, 1978).

or sustaining it. This does not, however, give us the makings of a sufficient condition for rational action. For one thing, even if I *A* because of a rational want which conflicts with no other wants of mine, and because of a rational belief that my *A*-ing is necessary to realize this want, my *A*-ing may still fail to be rational owing to a wayward causal chain supplanting the normal connection between these motivational elements and the actions they produce. These elements might, for example, cause another agent with control of my behavior to make me *A* in such a way that my *A*-ing is neither voluntary nor rational.[15] It is no easy matter to explicate such chains, but there is a locution we can use to imply their absence. If *S A*'s (wholly) *for the reason*(s) expressed in the explaining want(s) and belief(s), they do not waywardly cause it. One sufficient (but not necessary) condition for acting rationally, then, might be acting (wholly) for a good reason. How this might be interpreted will be considered in Section V. Our conclusion in this section is simply the necessary condition thesis that if a reason in virtue of which *S A*'s renders his *A*-ing rational, then he *A*'s at least in part *for* that reason.[16]

IV. The Information-Responsiveness Conception of Rationality

So far, we have seen reason to doubt that purely instrumentalist conceptions of rational action, particularly a narrowly instrumentalist maximization of expected utility conception, can be adequate to the concept of rational action implicit in our common-sense reflective criticism and description of action. This is an important conclusion. I take it to be at least in the spirit of a number of philosophers, including Aristotle, Kant, and Mill, and to be suggested by Max Weber, when, for example, he distinguished between a kind of instrumental rationality and a kind involving intrinsic evaluation: whereas "A person acts rationally in the 'means-end' sense when his action is guided by consideration of ends, means and sec-

[15] This problem has been widely discussed. See, for example, Alvin I. Goldman, *A Theory of Human Action* (Englewood Cliffs, N.J.: Prentice-Hall, 1970), and Raimo Tuomela, *Human Action and Its Explanation* (Dordrecht: Reidel, 1977).

[16] The causal sustaining requirement implicit in this condition is argued for in my "Rationalization and Rationality," *Synthese* 65 (1985).

ondary consequences. . . . When, on the other hand, he has to
choose between competing and conflicting ends and consequences,
his decision may be rational in the sense of being based on his conception of absolute values."[17] But how can we determine when a person's
valuing (or wanting) something intrinsically[18] is rational? Determining this will be crucial for understanding rational action if the
rationality of an action is in part a matter of the rationality of some
intrinsic value (or want) to which it can be traced.

This problem has been addressed in great detail by Richard Brandt,
who has developed a powerful action-guiding conception of rational
action. His strategy is to propose what he calls reforming (as opposed
to lexical) definitions. First, he characterizes a broadly instrumentalist
conception of rational action; then, using this conception, he defines
stronger conceptions:

> I shall call a person's action 'rational' in the sense of being rational to a
> first approximation, if and only if it is what he would have done if all
> the mechanisms determining action except for his desires and aversions
> (which are taken as they are)—that is, the *cognitive* inputs influencing
> decision/action—had been optimal as far as possible . . . Second, I shall
> call a desire or aversion 'rational' if and only if it is what it would have
> been had the person undergone *cognitive psycho-therapy*. . . . Finally, I
> shall say that an action is 'rational' in the sense of fully rational if and
> only if the desires and aversions which are involved in the action are
> rational, and if the condition is met for rationality to a first
> approximation.[19]

Methodologically, this procedure is attractive. Brandt starts with a
plausible strengthening of the maximization of expected utility view,
and then argues that if a fully rational action is to represent the best
thing one can do (or at least something to which no alternative is
preferable), then even actions rational by the strengthened criterion
are not fully rational. To be fully rational an action must be based

---

[17] Weber, *Selections in Translation*, p. 29 in the Runciman and Matthews edition. Note
the prima facie causal phrases here: 'guided by' and 'based on'.

[18] Very roughly, S values x (purely) intrinsically if and only if he values it for its own
sake, i.e., for properties intrinsic to it and in such a way that he does not value it on
the basis of valuing anything to which he believes its realization would (or might)
lead.

[19] Richard B. Brandt, *A Theory of the Good and the Right* (Oxford: Clarendon Press,
1979), p. 11. Presumably the sense in which Brandt takes the relevant wants and beliefs
to be "involved in the action" is causal.

not only on minimally adequate cognitive inputs, but on minimally adequate desires or aversions. Minimal adequacy occurs when the cognitive inputs (for example beliefs) and the agent's desires and aversions would survive were "every item of *relevant available* information . . . present to awareness, vividly, at the focus of attention, or with an equal share of attention."[20] Now

> A piece of information is relevant if its presence to awareness would make a difference to the person's tendency to perform a certain act, or to the attractiveness of some prospective outcome to him. Hence it is an essentially causal notion. . . . Second . . . I prefer to define 'all available information' as the propositions accepted by the science of the agent's day, plus factual propositions justified by publicly accessible evidence (including testimony of others about themselves) and the principles of logic.[21]

These ideas are developed at length by Brandt, and I cannot do him justice here. My aim is simply to bring out some central features of his approach by examining three topics: available information, relevant information, and unextinguishability as a sufficient condition for rational desire.

Given Brandt's rather inclusive notion of available information, even his conception of action rational to a first approximation is quite strong. For there are surely many things we do that are well planned, and even quite efficient in accomplishing reasonable goals, which we would not have done if we had all the information relevant in his sense. Often, for example, there is an even more efficient procedure which we do not know of, though more experienced people do. But if the difference between the alternatives is not highly significant, the action still seems, in a common and important sense, rational. Brandt is doubtless aware of this, and my point is not that his proposed definition is somehow mistaken, but simply that it sets a high—perhaps idealized—standard of rational action. Doubtless this is appropriate *if* we think of a rational action as the *best* thing to do in the circumstances.

Brandt's notion of relevance is harder to assess. One would expect the relevance of information to a belief or desire to be at least mainly a matter of a semantic or epistemic relation to its content. Why does

[20] Ibid.
[21] Ibid., pp. 12–13.

he characterize the relation causally? There seem to be at least three reasons: relevance is extremely hard to explicate semantically or epistemically; a causal criterion is naturalistic and thus avoids evaluative notions of the kind he wishes to explicate by using his definition of 'rational'; and if information is not relevant in Brandt's causal sense, an agent can hardly be faulted for not taking account of it, and hence may still be said to have done the *best he could.* If these are not among Brandt's reasons for using a causal criterion of relevance, they are at least plausible reasons.

Let us start with a prima facie counterexample. Suppose that Sid's brain has been manipulated by a diabolical neurosurgeon in such a way that S is no longer moved by coming to believe certain propositions which seem clearly relevant to some intrinsic desire of his. To take a consideration which Brandt himself views as highly relevant to the rationality of an intrinsic desire, suppose S's brain is altered so that his realization that an intrinsic desire of his is artificial has no tendency to extinguish the desire, where intrinsic wants or aversions are artificial if they "could not have been brought about by experience with actual situations which the desires are for and the aversions are against . . . for instance, a non-prestige occupation like garbage collection or marriage to a person of another race, religion, or nationality."[22] I agree with Brandt that if S realizes that, say, his intrinsic desire to avoid marrying someone of another nationality could not have arisen from the relevant kind of experience, this should tend to extinguish the want and is relevant to its rationality. But would it be any less relevant if S could not react appropriately to it? That seems doubtful, at least if 'rational' is commendatory. One would think that a desire should never be commendable simply because the person cannot alter it.

The problem arises because unextinguishability implies rationality, but artificiality, which the unextinguishable desire in question exhibits, implies, for Brandt, irrationality. Such a desire is possible, I think, because the criterion of relevance is too narrow. Even apart from that, however, it appears that a person could have a non-rational (even irrational) desire that would survive cognitive psychotherapy. Brandt must call it rational. He might reply that since the imagined surgery is surely not unalterable in a sense making it nomically impossible for S to react appropriately, it is not impossible for S's desire

[22] Ibid., p. 117.

to extinguish through cognitive psychotherapy. But even if it is not nomically impossible for S to react appropriately under *some* conditions, it could be nomically impossible for cognitive psychotherapy to produce the desired results. Moreover, we may still ask about the (presumably) logically possible case in which S nomically cannot react appropriately. There, too, the information would still appear relevant. S's inability to respond to a relevant criticism surely does not make it irrelevant. S's prejudice may be 'wired in' and thereby evoke our sympathy, but it still seems an irrational attitude.

In any event, I believe that Brandt's way of dealing with this problem does not depend on moves of this sort. He says at one point, "If a desire will not extinguish, then it is not irrational. This result is consistent with the general view that a desire (etc.) is rational if it has been influenced by facts and logic as much as possible. Unextinguishable desires meet this condition."[23] The central idea here seems to be that rationality results when facts and logic have done all they possibly (nomically?) can. Thus, to say that an unextinguishable want can be irrational is to demand more than is possible for S on the basis of his using logic and grasping facts. If S cannot be moved to cease intrinsically wanting x by any amount of exposure to logic and facts, surely we should conclude that *for him* the want is rational. The point can be supported by appeal to the distinction, stressed above, between the rationality of tokens and that of types: we can say that while this particular want is rational, it does not follow that the type it represents is, in the sense that by and large wants of that type are rational.

This position is certainly defensible, but let me offer an alternative. Just as we can distinguish acting rationally from acting merely excusably, we can distinguish having a rational desire from having an excusable one. Now clearly an unextinguishable desire is (for S) excusable, since there is nothing he can do (using logic and facts) to uproot it. But why must we then use the commendatory, action-guiding term 'rational'? For Brandt, the reasoning might run, in part, as follows: since 'rational' is taken to mean 'not irrational',[24] and what is irrational in S is presumably such that he is criticizable for it,

---

[23] Ibid., p. 113.

[24] Ibid., p. 112. Brandt's position here is not merely terminological. He seems to conceive rationality as occurring where one has not made (and would not make, upon appropriate reflection) certain mistakes. It then becomes natural to treat 'rational' as equivalent to 'not irrational', since the latter suggests mistakes or similar deficiencies.

whereas one is presumably not criticizable for what is excusable, un-extinguishable desires are not irrational, and hence are rational.

This raises the question whether 'rational' and 'irrational' should be regarded as contradictories. I think no. For one thing, one is commendatory, the other condemnatory, yet the things—such as actions, values, and wants—to which they apply vary, in the relevant respects, along a continuum. There are more good reasons, for instance, for some of the things we do, and want, than for others; and both our actions and our wants are *influenced* by reasons to different degrees. There should thus be cases to which neither term appropriately applies. This does not entail that Brandt is unjustified in using 'rational' and 'irrational' as contradictories; but if he does, we must at least conclude that in some possible cases, such as that of the diabolical surgery, 'rational' is not commendatory. The victim ought to try to resist the influence of the artificial desire, even though he cannot extinguish it. If we must say, with Brandt, that the desire is (fully) rational, we are at least hard pressed to explain why he ought to try to resist acting on it and, toward that end, to strengthen competing wants.[25]

These points should not be allowed to obscure my substantial agreement with Brandt in many things he says. Indeed, I believe he has made a major advance beyond instrumentalist views. Moreover, his book provides a convincing case against viewing uncritically, as some instrumentalists may have, Aristotle's point that we do not deliberate about ends,[26] and against Hume's narrow view of the senses in which desires can be called unreasonable.[27] A number of Brandt's points will be reflected in the alternative views about rationality which I shall develop in the next section.

V. Rationality as Well-Groundedness

Central to Brandt's conception of rationality are at least two notions: that of responsiveness to relevant available information, and

[25] Brandt is aware of this problem and speaks to it on p. 122 in relation to intrinsic desires for money, caused by its perceived usefulness in realizing intrinsic wants. He seems to think that if a want is either wired in or is causally inevitable on the basis of a rational want (such as an extrinsic want for money), it is rational. "This is simply what I'm like," *S* might say to a critic of the intrinsic want. But would such inescapability imply rationality?

[26] See, for example, Aristotle, *Nicomachean Ethics* 1112b.

[27] See, for example, Hume, *Treatise*, 2.3.3. Weber is not committed to a Humean position, but his position on this issue does not seem fully worked out.

that of optimality: roughly, being as responsive as possible to available relevant information. The first notion is used to specify the sort of thing required for rationality, namely, information-responsiveness; the second specifies the appropriate degree of information-responsiveness. A quite different way to conceive rationality, however, is on analogy with the (epistemic) justification of belief. It appears that 'rational belief' has one use in which it is equivalent to 'justified belief', and the two phrases are commendatory in very similar ways. To be sure, justified belief may be no easier to understand than rationality; but there is at least a rich epistemological literature to draw on, and even apart from that it is surely desirable to unify our theories of rational action and rational motivation with our theory of rational belief. This is a task for which I now want to lay some groundwork.

The Epistemological Analogy

To begin with, I shall assume that we may explicate justified belief using the notion of *well-groundedness*. In outline, the idea is this. Some beliefs on the part of S, such as certain introspective, perceptual, and a priori beliefs, may be conceived as directly justified by virtue of being well-grounded in something—such as an appropriate experience or a certain sort of apprehension or the self-evidence of the proposition believed—not in need of justification, or even amenable to it. Any other justified beliefs of S's may be conceived as indirectly justified (and indirectly grounded) in relation to the former, the directly justified beliefs. On one plausible view, indirectly justified beliefs need not derive all their justification from the directly justified ones, but will derive enough of it from them so that even if the indirectly justified beliefs ceased to have whatever justification they derive from other sources, they would remain justified, in the sense that they would still be epistemically reasonable, that is, S's retaining them would be more reasonable than his withholding belief from the relevant propositions. This allows that some degree of justification arise from coherence; it simply rules out coherence's being an independently necessary condition for justification.

The view is a version of moderate foundationalism, and because it is moderate it does not imply that directly justified beliefs are, say, infallible or indubitable, nor that it is only through deductive inferences that they can transmit justification to superstructure beliefs based on them. The view is controversial; but I have elaborated and defended it elsewhere,[28] as have others, and my purpose here is simply to suggest how it may illuminate rational action and the rationality of valuations, wants, and other propositional attitudes that motivate action.

Clearly, a fully developed foundationalist theory of justified belief must provide accounts of direct justification and of the transmission of justification from foundational beliefs to superstructure beliefs, that is, beliefs that are appropriately based on the former. In both cases, there are many possibilities. For our purposes, just two sorts of account need be mentioned in each case. First, regarding the justification of foundational beliefs, one might hold that they are justified by virtue of being produced by a reliable process, such as the process by which the ring of one's telephone normally causes one to believe that one's telephone is ringing.[29] Another possibility is to conceive direct justification as accruing to certain beliefs by virtue of their content, for example, by virtue of their being a certain kind of belief about one's immediate experience.[30] Concerning the transmission of justification, a foundationalist might require that for a foundational belief, say, that p, to justify a superstructure belief, say, that q, the propositional object of the former must entail that of the latter (for example, p would have to entail q). A weaker view would countenance transmission of justification without such entailment, for example, with a nomic relation or a suitably strong probabilistic relation between p and q. Since moderate foundationalists hold the weaker view regarding transmission, that is the one we shall consider. It will be necessary, however, to consider both of the above conceptions of direct justification.

The notion of a well-grounded action seems to presuppose that of

---

[28] In, for example, my "Psychological Foundationalism," *Monist* 62 (1978), and "Axiological Foundationalism," *Canadian Journal of Philosophy* 12 (1982). See also Mark Pastin, "Modest Foundationalism and Self-Warrant," *American Philosophical Quarterly Monograph Series* 9 (1975); and William P. Alston, "Two Types of Foundationalism," *Journal of Philosophy* 73 (1976).

[29] For representative reliability theories of (empirical) knowledge and of justified belief, see Fred I. Dretske, "Conclusive Reasons," *Australasian Journal of Philosophy* 49 (1971), and *Knowledge and the Flow of Information* (Cambridge: Bradford Books and MIT Press, 1981), esp. chaps. 4 and 5; and Alvin I. Goldman, 'What Is Justified Belief?' in George S. Pappas, ed., *Justification and Knowledge* (Dordrecht: Reidel, 1980).

[30] This characterization seems applicable to Descartes, and a highly qualified form of the view is illustrated by R. M. Chisholm in "A Version of Foundationalism," in his *The Foundations of Knowing* (Minneapolis: University of Minnesota Press, 1982). It is not necessary, however, for a proponent of the view to be a Cartesian.

vs psychotic motivated elts

well-grounded motivational elements. Wants, conceived broadly, are the most common cases of such elements, but there are other cases, including valuation, that is, roughly, a person's valuing of something. The next section will take up the rationality of motivational elements, with valuations—which are of special interest because of their connections with problems in ethics—as the central case.

Rational Intrinsic Valuations

It seems obvious that valuations, like wants, may be appropriately assessed as rational or not rational. I shall also assume (more controversially) that the objects of valuations and wants are states of affairs, but nothing significant for our main purposes will turn on this. Valuations, wants, and beliefs are the only propositional attitudes I shall consider, but much of what is said should apply to at least many other propositional attitudes. For instance, if we can use the notion of well-groundedness to explicate rational valuations and wants, quite parallel points will apply, I think, to rational intentions and to other propositional attitudes.[31]

How might a valuation be well grounded? If we begin with intrinsic valuations—valuations of something for its own sake—and draw on the analogy with directly justified beliefs, we should find that some intrinsic valuations are directly grounded, and well grounded, in the experience (or apprehension) of the relevant kind of state of affairs, say one's viewing a painting. This leaves open what it is for an intrinsic valuation to be well grounded. To begin to solve that problem we need to distinguish two cases.

First, there are cases in which S justifiably believes something appropriate about the valued state of affairs, such as his viewing (certain sorts of) paintings. S might believe that it is worthwhile, enriching, pleasant, or a beautiful experience. We might call such properties *desirability* characteristics, since (in the present scheme) they are conceived as the sorts of properties in virtue of which a state of affairs really is valuable (or desirable). S's belief might also be *de re*; for example, he might justifiably believe, of the viewing of a certain painting and the property of being pleasant, that the former has the latter, in which case S (who may be a small child) need not conceptualize either paintings or pleasantness in the (presumably richer) way re-

---

[31] Some of the relevant points are made in my "Axiological Foundationalism."

quired for *de dicto* belief. Thus, a quite wide range of beliefs may serve here (depending on what restrictions are needed to enable the belief to ground the rationality of the relevant intrinsic valuation). In either case, we may speak of *cognitive grounding*, since the relevant beliefs are the basis of the rationality of the valuation.

There seems to be at least one other kind of grounding through which an intrinsic valuation can be rational. Suppose that I simply enjoy viewing paintings in virtue of experiencing the desirability characteristics of such viewing, for example, the perception of balance, the sense of color contrasts, and so on. Could this not render my intrinsic valuing of viewing paintings rational, even if I form no belief to the effect that my viewing them has these qualities? It would seem so. Indeed, it may be that this second kind of grounding—*experiential grounding*, we might call it—is more basic than the first. Perhaps if I could not intrinsically value viewing paintings simply for the desirable qualities of such viewing, my intrinsic valuation of viewing them could not be rational because I believe my viewing them to have those qualities.

How might an epistemic conception of the rationality of an intrinsic valuation account for its rationality? One possibility is to give well-groundedness for intrinsic valuations a *reliabilist* interpretation analogous to a reliabilist interpretation of what justifies direct, that is (roughly), non-inferential, empirical beliefs. Consider cognitive grounding first. Just as a belief, such as that there is paper before me, can apparently be justified by virtue of being causally generated, in a reliable way, by an experience of the paper which the belief is about and in virtue of whose presence it is true, so a belief that viewing a certain painting is a beautiful experience might be reliably produced by an experience of the design, contrasts, colors, and other relevant properties of the painting in question, and can, in turn, reliably produce an intrinsic valuation of viewing the painting *for* those qualities.

The idea is roughly that just as the belief that there is paper before me is justified because it is produced, by that very paper, through a reliable process and is hence *likely to be true*, the valuation is rational because it is produced, via the justified belief about the desirability characteristics of the experience, by a process reliable in the sense that valuations generated, by something valuable, through that process, are likely to be *correct*, that is, to be directed toward what actually *is* valuable. (Similarly, wants, including desires, that are generated, by something desirable, through such a process, are likely to be, as I suggest we might put it, *sound*, that is, to correspond to (to be wants or desires for) what actually is desirable.)

For extrinsic valuations whose rationality depends on that of at least one instrumental belief, the suggested account must be complicated. (Some of the required criteria will be indicated shortly.) In neither case, however, am I suggesting an *analysis* of justified belief or rational valuation. I am simply sketching a partial theory, available to an epistemic account of rationality, of what constitutes their rationality, at least for direct (empirical) beliefs and cognitively grounded intrinsic valuations.

Experiential grounding also (and perhaps more readily) admits of a reliabilist interpretation. It appears that an intrinsic valuation might be reliably produced by the relevant qualities of one's viewing a painting without the mediation of a belief that it has these qualities. Such a valuation would be a closer analogue of a directly justified perceptual belief than would be cognitively grounded intrinsic valuation. Rather as the belief arises from perceptual experience, the valuation arises, on this conception, in a similarly direct way, from aesthetic experience. When it is reliably produced by properties of the experience in virtue of which the experience is valuable, the intrinsic valuation of the experience is likely to be correct and is rational. Neither its rationality nor its correctness, however, implies an analogue of incorrigibility: on the view suggested, even the rationality of intrinsic valuations is defeasible under special conditions.

In both the cognitive and the experiential cases this epistemic conception of rational intrinsic valuations anchors them 'to the world'. They are grounded in the world either directly, via experience of something, or indirectly, via a belief that is itself justified by virtue of being grounded in the world. Despite appearances, this conception of rational intrinsic valuations does not entail a naturalistic conception of either rationality or value or desirability, though it does entail realist, as opposed, for example, to emotivist, notions of value and desirability, since if nothing really is valuable or desirable, intrinsic valuations (and wants) can hardly be rational through being reliably produced by properties in virtue of which the thing in question is valuable or desirable. Naturalism is not entailed, however, because value and desirability can be real properties even if they supervene on natural properties but are not themselves natural properties.[32] (These points presuppose, of course, that there is a distinction between natural and non-natural—for example, normative—properties. I am inclined to believe that there is, but cannot try to show that here.)

If value and desirability are not natural properties, however, then there is a problem for the reliabilist interpretation. For it is not obvious that non-natural properties can enter into causal relations, hence not clear that they can reliably produce an intrinsic valuation of something for such properties. We do speak of being moved by the beauty of a painting, and perhaps such locutions can be taken to imply recognition of direct causal connections. But it may be that what actually moves us is the relevant combination of design, color, contrast, and so on, and that is apparently a set of natural physical properties. Let us suppose this for the sake of argument. It is crucial to see that these are just the sorts of natural properties on which the beauty of paintings supervenes, and that all the reliabilist needs here is the thesis that these properties appropriately produce our intrinsic valuing of viewing the painting. For one thing, if a painting is beautiful in virtue of them, then its having them is clearly a reliable indication of that beauty. Notice also that even in certain perceptual cases there is an analogue of this point. When one perceptually believes, through sight, that there is a person before one, it is presumably not personhood, but some of the visual properties in virtue of which (in part) the individual one sees is a person, that produce one's belief. Thus, whatever the (admittedly substantial) difficulties in explicating the relevant kind of reliability, we need not conclude that reliabilism is simply inapplicable to relations between non-natural properties and intrinsic valuation.

This is a good place to reiterate that the justification of foundational beliefs *need* not be construed along reliabilist lines. Thus, the valuational (and conative) analogy can also be detached from reliabilism. Perhaps, for example, it is simply a constitutive principle of reason that it is rational to value (and want) intrinsically (say) pleasurable experiences. Could a rational person *not* value such experiences to *some* degree? And if someone does not value (or want) something he

---

[32] For defense of a realist conception of value properties, see Panayot Butchvarov, "That Simple, Indefinable, Nonnatural Property *Good*," *Review of Metaphysics* 36 (1982); and for an account of supervenience relevant to our discussion here, see Jaegwon Kim, "Psychophysical Supervenience as a Mind-Body Theory," *Cognition and Brain Theory* 5 (1982).

believes is pleasurable, do we not expect an explanation, say in terms of its bad effects, or perhaps other special qualities? Normally we do not allow for the possibility that such experiences are not intrinsically valued qua pleasurable.

To be sure, the rationality of intrinsically valuing pleasurable experiences is not quite self-evident. But it is at least quite plausible to take such valuations as rational. The same holds for intrinsic valuations of (and wants for) one's own happiness, as Aristotle apparently believed. Note, for instance, that we normally take the fact that S enjoys something both to explain why he values it intrinsically and to exhibit the valuation as natural for him in a sense implying that it is at least prima facie rational. We may wonder *why* S enjoys whatever it is, or think he *ought* not to enjoy it. But if he does, it seems prima facie rational for him to value it intrinsically. Similarly, it might be held to be an a priori truth that if viewing a beautiful painting really is intrinsically valuable—say because it is a beautiful experience—then intrinsically valuing viewing it on the basis of the properties in virtue of which it is a beautiful experience, is prima facie rational.

There are other possible views a realist about value and desirability might take to preserve the epistemological analogy, but there is no need to outline them here. We should, however, ask whether the analogy can be made out on a noncognitivist interpretation of sentences of the form of 'S's intrinsic valuation of x is rational', where 'rational' is treated like 'morally good'. Let us proceed to this question.

The main problem here is that for the noncognitivist there is no property of (intrinsic) value or desirability and thus no analogue of truth. If the noncognitivist thinks of the relevant sentences as, say, expressing attitudes, it will still be possible to distinguish between good and bad grounds for having (or expressing) these attitudes. Presumably beliefs could be crucial to these grounds. A kind of cognitive grounding would thus be possible. One might, for example, say that if I justifiably believe that viewing a painting gives me pleasure, I am prima facie rational in holding, on that ground, the positive attitude I would express by, for example, 'My intrinsic valuing of viewing it is rational'. We would have, then, a structural but not a substantive epistemological analogy. This would be significant and would help to undermine the irrationalist interpretation sometimes given to noncognitivism. But however that may be, I shall not pursue noncognitivism further. If the epistemological analogy I am developing is plausible, we shall have less reason to give a noncognitivist interpretation to terms like 'rational' in the first place.

The Rationality of Extrinsic Valuations

We must now ask how the rationality of extrinsic, that is, instrumental, valuations is to be understood on the well-groundedness conception. The basic idea is that their rationality (or at least enough of it to render them reasonable) is transmitted from well-grounded intrinsic valuations. Consider a simple case in which S has only one relevant intrinsic valuation, namely one of playing the piano well, and extrinsically values playing scales (as a means to playing well). A paradigm of transmission of rationality from the former to the latter valuation would occur where (1) the latter is wholly based on the former (for example because playing scales is valued *only* as a *means* to playing the piano well) and (2) S *justifiably* believes that playing scales will lead to playing the piano well. Parallel points hold for intrinsic and extrinsic wants, and it should be noted that a rational extrinsic valuation can be grounded in a suitable intrinsic *want* as well as in an intrinsic valuation. (I take it that valuations embody wants in any case, though they do not seem reducible to wants.)

This transmission of rationality from foundational (hence intrinsic) valuations to superstructure valuations is of course analogous to the inferential justification of a belief, and as in that case there are many varieties and many subtleties. All I can add here is that the transmission of rationality from well-grounded intrinsic valuations may pass through many elements. We then have a *valuational chain*. The length of such chains is theoretically unlimited, but in practice they often seem quite short. It is important to see, however, that only the first valuation after the foundational one need be directly based on it, that is, such that S values the relevant object on the basis of what he believes to be its contribution to realizing the intrinsic valuation, for example, to producing the intrinsically valued experience. The valuational basis relation is non-transitive: each element, except the foundational one, must be directly based on its predecessor; but none need be directly based on any other besides its predecessor. One could conceivably value playing the piano well wholly on the basis of valuing one's playing good music, and value playing dull exercises wholly on the basis of valuing playing well, yet never form any belief to the effect that playing the exercises will contribute to one's playing good music. The valuation of playing the exercises would thus not be (directly) based on one's valuation of playing good music.

To be sure, *S* may have two well-grounded intrinsic valuations such that, given his rational beliefs, incompatible extrinsic valuations would be at least prima facie rational (where incompatible valuations are valuations that cannot be jointly satisfied, for example valuations of talking [now] exclusively with Jane and talking [now] exclusively with John). Similarly, one might rationally want to practice one's tennis now as a means to playing well, and rationally want to weed one's garden now as a means to eating well. These possibilities should not be surprising; analogues apply in the domain of belief, for example in certain cases where *S* has evidence for incompatible propositions each of which is prima facie justified for him. There are many ways of deciding which extrinsic valuation (or want), if either, is more rational. Other things equal, the one grounded in the stronger intrinsic valuation is more rational and, in action, should (and will tend to) prevail; for example, if *S* values eating well more than playing tennis well, we would expect, and approve of, his weeding the garden rather than playing tennis if we expect either. But other things need not be equal; one of the intrinsic valuations may be more rational, or more important to *S*'s overall system of values, than the other. The problems raised here are complicated; but they or their counterparts beset any plausible theory of rational valuation (or wanting), and there is no need to try to solve them here.

Rational valuations, then, may be plausibly conceived as well-grounded valuations understood along the lines suggested. The same points hold, mutatis mutandis, for wants. There is much to be said to clarify this conception, but at least the core of the idea is now before us. Rather than go into a detailed discussion of rational valuations and wants, I want now to extend the suggested conception to actions.

Rational Action

This section will concern only intentional actions. Some non-intentional actions, such as those knowingly performed *in* doing something intentionally—the sort Bentham called obliquely intentional—may also be rational; but they may presumably be accounted for on the basis of an adequate conception of rationality for intentional actions. In outlining a conception of rationality for intentional actions,

I shall simply assume that they are explainable in terms of the agent's wants and beliefs, and that the rationality of wants can be understood along the lines just indicated. If so, then perhaps actions can be conceived as rational in relation to intrinsic wants rather as extrinsic valuations and wants are rational in relation to intrinsic valuations and wants (beliefs play a crucial part in all three cases). A rational action, then, might be conceived as a well-grounded one. I refer, of course, to tokens, not types. Our subject is the rationality of particular actions, not that of a type for a person.

Let us explore the suggested conception of rational action. Suppose first that the foundational rational wants are those that are directly grounded, and well grounded, either in certain justified beliefs or in appropriate experiences. Some actions may be directly based on these, that is, performed in order to realize them. If S believes, with respect to an action he is considering and a basic rational want of his, that the former is certain to realize the latter, and on this basis performs the action, the action is prima facie well grounded. In this way, regularly practicing the piano could be well grounded for S relative to his rational intrinsic want to play well. Again, we have an analogue of inferential justification. Indeed, some writers have held that there is always a practical inference mediating between motivational wants (or other motivational elements) and the actions they explain.[33]

It may be, of course, that an action is only indirectly and distantly based on a foundational want. We then have a *purposive chain*, analogous to a valuational chain: S A's in order to realize x, wants to realize x in order to realize y, and so on, until we reach something S wants intrinsically. As in the case of the valuational basis relation, this in-order-to relation, which I shall call the *purposive connecting relation*, is non-transitive. I can jog in order to maintain my health, and maintain my health in order to enhance my chances of a good life, yet not—if I do not 'make the connection' between the first and third elements— jog in order to enhance my chances of a good life. But in both cases the terminal element is well grounded only if rationality is adequately transmitted from the foundational element(s), and this presumably requires that every *connecting belief*, such as the belief that jogging will

---

[33] See the references in n. 1. While I believe this view is too strong, I accept the underlying idea that practical arguments represent the *structure* of the relation between intentional actions and the wants and beliefs on which they are based.

help maintain my health, is justified. A single action may, of course, be grounded in *more* than one rational intrinsic want, say a want to enhance one's chances of a good life and a want to complete marathons. It may thus be rational in virtue of coterminous purposive chains. Coherence criteria may also play a role; take, for example, the overall appropriateness of the action to S's total system of motivation and cognition. The conception being developed simply makes well-groundedness central; it need not be the only source of rationality.

It should also be stressed that, as in the case of rational extrinsic desires, an epistemic conception of rational action may employ varying sorts of transmission principles. An approach modeled on moderate foundationalism is unlikely to allow any action to be indefeasibly rational, that is (roughly), rational in such a way that the agent could not have had a set of wants and beliefs in the light of which it would not have been rational. Certainly there should be room for an action to fail to be rational because, although it is grounded, by a purposive chain, in a rational intrinsic want, w, a condition like one of the following occurs: (1) an alternative action would have been preferable for S because it would have been, and he could have readily seen that it would be, grounded in a stronger competing intrinsic want, w', or (2) S has a belief, which he has temporarily forgotten, than an alternative would more readily satisfy w.

Alternatives (1) and (2) can each be further specified, and there are defeasibility conditions that cannot be discussed here. But something must be said about cases in which S mistakenly but justifiably believes that his *A*-ing is rational in the relevant sense. It seems natural to call such an action *subjectively rational*. Beliefs may be subjectively rational (or subjectively justified) in a parallel sense. But just as such beliefs, if true, do not represent knowledge, subjectively rational actions lack something: they might be said not to be, from the overall point of view of rationality, the right thing for S to do. Here, too, there are distinctions we cannot develop. Two common ways in which the rationality of an action is defeated are these: S might *A* on the basis of a *non*-rational want which he justifiably believes his *A*-ing will realize, or on the basis of a rational want which he *un*justifiably believes his *A*-ing will realize. In these cases he may or may not believe his *A*-ing is rational, but we might still want to speak of a kind of subjectively rational action. An adequate epistemic account of rational action, then, will have to be complicated. I believe, however, that other plausible accounts of rational action, such as Brandt's, are on balance at least equally complicated.

VI. Well-Groundedness versus Other Conceptions of Rationality

The epistemic approach to rationality provides an interesting basis for comparing different conceptions of rationality. From an epistemic perspective, for example, one might say that on the sort of maximization of expected utility conception of rational action discussed in Sections I and II, the only appropriate criteria of assessment in the rationality dimension are *coherence criteria*. It does not matter what is the content of one's wants, nor whether they or one's beliefs are rational; the rationality of an action is entirely relative to the agent's wants and his instrumental beliefs. An action may, for instance, be irrational because it shortchanges the agent on the criterion of intrinsic want satisfaction, but not because of any defect in an intrinsic want which it efficiently satisfies, or even because the relevant probability beliefs are not rational.

The epistemic perspective also puts us in a good position to see how the view that well-groundedness is what is central to the rationality of intrinsic wants differs from the Brandtian account of their rationality. First, Brandt does not require any close analogue of grounding. For him, rational intrinsic wants need not have any particular kind of content or type of origin in experience, for example, being based on appropriate beliefs or appropriate experiences. They are rational if they would pass a certain test. Undoubtedly, Brandt would suppose that in fact few if any intrinsic wants (and valuations) are rational unless they *do* rest on such beliefs or experiences. My point is simply that his view contains no positive conceptual requirement corresponding to well-groundedness. Second, the notion of well-groundedness admits of degree; so, on the well-groundedness conception, a rational intrinsic desire need not be optimally grounded. Third, the well-groundedness conception is neutral with respect to naturalism, whereas Brandt's view, properly understood, is naturalistic.

Speaking from an epistemic perspective, then, we may say that unlike the maximization of expected utility view, Brandt's is not happily conceived as purely coherentist. For his criteria of rational wants and rational belief are by no means purely coherence criteria, and he also strongly restricts the sorts of wants and beliefs in virtue of which *S*'s *A*-ing may be rational: roughly, *S*'s wants must be capable of surviving cognitive psychotherapy, and his beliefs must reflect adequate information. But if Brandt's view is foundationalist, it is, at least as regards wants, a *procedural foundationalism:* rational intrinsic wants, the foundational motivating elements, need not have any particular content or type of content; they must simply be capable of surviving exposure to appropriate information. This in turn leaves open the sort of action that may be rational (even if Brandt's view of justified belief should be a version of foundationalism—a matter on which I offer no interpretation of him). The question of what wants will survive such exposure is empirical. In principle, they might be egoistic or altruistic, hedonistic or puritanical, democratic or oligarchical.

By contrast, while I have attributed to the epistemic conception of rationality no theses about the sort of wants and beliefs that are rational, even a moderate foundationalist conception of rationality will presuppose that some particular wants, such as intrinsic wants for one's own happiness, and some specific beliefs, such as those about certain aspects of one's current immediate experience, are, under appropriate conditions, rational. Different theories will give different accounts of such foundational rationality and will differ as to what is foundationally rational. But a fully worked out epistemic theory of rationality will try to reflect certain plausible intuitions as to what sorts of elements are rational and which among these are properly taken to be foundational.[34] In any case, let us apply to some examples a few of the contrasts between Brandt's view and the epistemic view outlined in this essay.

[34] In *A Theory of Justice* (Cambridge: Harvard University Press, 1971), John Rawls conceives certain goods, for example freedom of the person, imagination, and vigor, as *primary goods,* and he maintains that rational persons want these whatever else they want. See, for example, p. 62 and chap. 3, sec. 25. Rawls certainly represents these goods as valuable as means, but this is consistent with holding—what seems plausible at least for certain natural primary goods, such as self-respect, and health—that they are also intrinsically desirable. It is an interesting question (which unfortunately I cannot pursue here) to what extent Rawls might regard some things as intrinsically desirable (or intrinsically valuable) and might conceive certain wants or valuations regarding them as capable of playing a foundational role, such as I have outlined, in the motivational system of a rational person. I am grateful to Dagfinn Føllesdal for suggesting that Rawls might possibly be interpreted as holding a moderate foundationalist view somewhat of the sort I have been exploring.

Take first the question of what determines the relevance of a consideration to the rationality of intrinsic desires. Returning to our victim of diabolical surgery, regardless of whether his intrinsic desire concerning marriage will extinguish, it need not be well-grounded. He neither has a justified belief, nor any appropriate experience, in virtue of which the desire is rational. This can explain why it is not rational, whereas, if cognitive psychotherapy will not extinguish it, Brandt's view must, implausibly, I think, take it to be rational. The well-groundedness view can also explain why obviously contradictory states of affairs cannot be rationally wanted intrinsically: S cannot have experienced them, nor (presumably) can he justifiably believe them to have desirability characteristics. Suppose, on the other hand, that S researches pianos and buys a good one at a good price, yet overlooks information available to him which would have led to his getting a slightly better price. On the well-groundedness view, one could explain why S did not act optimally, yet still conceive his action as well-grounded to a high degree and thus as rational. On Brandt's scheme, the action must be called irrational (though it should be pointed out that some irrational actions are not far from rational). No doubt there are other cases of intrinsic wants, and of actions, whose rationality or lack of it would be differently characterized on the well-groundedness conception than on Brandt's theory, though extensionally I would expect the two views to be close. This is not to imply that we can establish precise, uncontroversial criteria of well-groundedness for all intrinsic wants (or valuations). But for at least a great many we can give some account of their rationality, or lack of it, by appeal to cognitive or experiential grounding conceived in the ways suggested in this essay.

Moreover, while on a realist conception of value and desirability a want or valuation may be in some objective sense unsound, a realist epistemic conception of rationality may grant that two people may have well-grounded intrinsic wants for mutually incompatible states of affairs, for example one for a predominance of classical music on the radio, one for a predominance of popular music on the radio. Some proponents of the conception might argue that these wants cannot both be *maximally* well grounded, but that view is not essential to the position, any more than the claim that a maximally justified belief must be true is essential to a realist conception of epistemic justification. The position certainly allows for the joint possibility that Jane, for example, has a fully rational intrinsic desire to listen (herself) to classical music, while Tom has a fully rational intrinsic desire to listen (himself) to popular music. They may, for instance, have different response patterns and different capacities. Thus, a kind of relativity is compatible with the well-groundedness view. For Brandt, on the other hand, there is a stronger relativity: if the two incompatible wants imagined (regarding radio broadcasting) do not change under appropriate exposure to information—as it seems they might not—there is no room for the view that one may be better grounded and in a sense more rational.

From much of what has been said it will be apparent that the main variables determining rationality on the well-groundedness conception admit of degree. The belief that a kind of experience has a certain desirability characteristic may be more or less justified. How much one wants a kind of experience may result from differing intensities of one's experience of, or differing degrees of apprehension of, its desirability characteristics. Connecting beliefs, such as that A-ing will realize a want, may be more or less justified. They may also be an inadequate basis for action even if justified: if I justifiably believe A-ing will realize my want, but should see that B-ing instead would realize it much more efficiently, I am overlooking a preferable and incompatible alternative, and my A-ing would be at best prima facie well grounded. Thus, not only does well-groundedness admit of degrees; a want, valuation, or action may be sufficiently well grounded to be rational, yet nowhere near maximally rational.

VII. Conclusion

Much work must be done to develop the well-groundedness conception of rationality as a critical and descriptive tool in the theory of action and, particularly, in the social sciences. That project is impossible here, but I can point out some implications of the conception which suggest that the project is quite worth doing.

First, the well-groundedness conception of rationality is psychologically realistic and connects the rationality of actions, values, and other elements, with psychological properties of persons—such as their beliefs and wants—that are important for understanding human behavior in general, individual and social. The conception is realistic because it does not make rationality something few if any persons can often achieve, nor does it require that all rational actions, rational valuations, or rational wants be backed by *actual* reasoning processes, such as episodes of practical reasoning, or even that all rational propositional attitudes be conscious. Often rational elements do emerge from such processes; and they may derive rationality from the relevant premises and other factors. But often rational actions are 'automatic', and frequently rational valuations are spontaneous. The well-groundedness conception makes this easy to understand. For neither valuational nor purposive chains need be constituted by explicitly inferential links, nor is self-consciousness or deliberation required for transmission of rationality from foundational to superstructure elements. It may, for example, be rational for S to do exercises because he believes exercising is appropriately connected with his leading a certain kind of life, one which S intrinsically and rationally values, even if he has not connected the former to the latter by a series of inferences, or self-consciously evaluated either exercising or the kind of life to which (however indirectly) the exercising is connected by his instrumental beliefs.

Given this view of the transmission of rationality—which accords with, but does not entail, a reliabilist conception of its transmission—the well-groundedness conception of rationality may differ from many traditional ones. But it is important to realize that in other respects the conception may be taken to be a plausible extension of Aristotle's foundationalist notion of rational desire and, implicitly, rational valuation, as I have elsewhere argued.[35] Much the same may be said about Mill, who seems to be quite Aristotelian on this point,[36] and there are surely other historically influential figures whose conception of rationality can be explained, or at least reconstructed, along the lines I have indicated.

If the well-groundedness conception of rationality has the psychological connections I have stressed, one might think that, as Hempel maintains, rationality is an explanatory concept. There is an ambiguity here. If an explanatory concept of rationality is one such that we can explain why certain events or states occur by saying that they are rational, then Hempel's contention is not quite correct. What one may claim, both for Hempel's notion of rational action and for the much

---

[35] I have spelled out the case for this, referring to the *Nicomachean Ethics* 1097a15–1097b20, in my "Axiological Foundationalism."

[36] I have developed this idea in "The Structure of Motivation," *Pacific Philosophical Quarterly* 61 (1980), with reference to *Utilitarianism*, esp. chap. 4.

broader concept of rationality I have sketched, is that they are *obliquely explanatory,* in the sense that their application to an action or propositional attitude entails that it *can* be explained in a certain way. For instance, if an action is rational, then there is a want-belief (intentionalistic) explanation for it; and if a valuation is rational, it is explainable, at least in part, either in terms of a valuation (or want) prior to it in a valuational chain or (when it is intrinsic) in terms of a well-grounded belief or an appropriate experience.

Rationality, then, for all the rational elements we have discussed, entails that they are embedded in an explanatory framework. Does this also apply to the rationality of persons, or to that of social actions on the part of institutions or groups of people? I should think so. For surely the rationality of persons is at least mainly determined by the rationality of their actions, action tendencies, and propositional attitudes; and presumably the rationality of group or institutional action (tokens) is at least mainly determined by that of individual action (tokens).

These points might be thought to imply that human actions, individual and social, admit of causal explanation. They do not imply that. The nature of the relevant explanations is left open by the well-groundedness conception of rationality. I do believe, however, that the relevant explanatory framework is *nomic*[37] and that everyday want-belief explanations of action may be conceived as tacitly appealing to laws. But at least some of these laws are special. For one thing, they employ dispositional rather than event properties to explain events, most notably actions. For another, the kind of dispositions that figure in them, propositional attitudes, have special properties, such as intentionality. In part for these reasons, we need not conceive the relevant explanations as causal, nor collapse the distinction between reasons and causes. Thus, on the overall conception of rationality I propose, the social sciences may be regarded not only as appropriately studying rational human actions rather than mere human behavior, but as studying action, with the goal of discovering a nomic— even if non-causal, non-mechanistic—theoretical framework for its interpretation.

I have argued that a purely instrumentalist conception of rationality

---

[37] This idea is developed in Chapter 5. Cf. Goldman, *A Theory of Human Action;* Tuomela, *Human Action and Its Explanation;* and Irving Thalberg, *Perception, Emotion, and Action* (Oxford: Blackwell, 1977), esp. chap. 3, "Are Reasons We Act On Causally or Logically Connected with Our Deeds?"

is too narrow and that the contextualist account cuts rational actions off from the systems of propositional attitudes from which, by virtue of an explanatory connection, they derive their rationality. Brandt's full-information, optimality conception of rationality is far superior to either approach, and it embodies a number of ideas that any plausible view of rationality should incorporate. But I have argued that his causal criterion of relevant information is inadequate and that we seem well advised not to take 'rational' as an absolute term with such strong necessary conditions. The contrasting proposal I have been exploring conceives rationality as a kind of well-groundedness. The resulting theory enables us to unify our concept of rational action with our concept of rational belief and indeed of rational propositional attitudes in general; and for all of these cases it provides a way to distinguish rationality from rationalizability, and to articulate a range of variables in terms of which we can develop a reasonably clear comparative concept of rationality. The view also enables us to conceive rationality in an explanatory framework that seems essential in the social sciences, whether we conceive it as nomic or in some other way. And it enables us to anchor the rationality of actions, values, wants, and persons themselves, to our experiences in a shared world.[38]

[38] This essay was written for the Berlin Symposium on Analytical and Sociological Theory of Action, held in 1982. I benefited from discussing the essay at the symposium, as well as the Universities of Nebraska and Oklahoma. I particularly want to thank my Berlin commentators, Rainer Döbert and Wilhelm Vossenkuhl, for their helpful critical assessments. I have also benefited from discussing the penultimate version with members of the National Endowment for the Humanities Seminar that I directed in 1983. I also thank William Alston, Richard Brandt, Albert Casullo, John King-Farlow, Eric Kraemer, Don Locke, Alfred Mele, Mark Overvold, Louis Pojman, and Allison Nespor.

Chapter 12

Weakness of Will
and Rational Action

Weakness of will has been widely discussed from at least three points of view. It has been examined historically, with Aristotle recently occupying center stage. It has been analyzed conceptually, with the question of its nature and possibility in the forefront. It has been considered normatively in relation to both rational action and moral character. My concern is not historical and is only secondarily conceptual: while I hope to clarify what constitutes weakness of will, I presuppose, rather than construct, an account of it. My chief aim is to assess the bearing of weakness of will on the rationality of actions that exhibit it—*incontinent actions*. Philosophers have tended to assume that incontinent action is a paradigm of irrationality, and none to my knowledge has seriously criticized this assumption. I challenge it and in doing so try to clarify rationality in general.

I. A Conception of Weakness of Will

There is at best limited agreement on just what weakness of will is, but a common element in most recent accounts is the notion of action against one's better judgment. The idea underlying this notion is that to act against one's better judgment is to do something intentionally, such as take another drink, while in some sense aware of one's judging that doing something else would be better. More explicitly, an agent, *S*, acts against *S*'s better judgment, in *A*-ing, provided (1) *S* *A*'s intentionally (or at least knowingly), (2) there is at least one other action (type) *B* which *S* takes to be an alternative and with respect to which *S* has judged, or makes or holds the judgment, that it would be better to *B* (3) *S* has not abandoned this judgment, and (4) *S* is aware of (2) and (3).[1] The relevant kind of awareness need not involve entertaining the judgment; but if there is no sense in which *S* is aware of holding the judgment, then *S* cannot be said to act *against* it in the way required for incontinence. The following contrast will help to explain this point.

Acting against a judgment is different from acting merely *inconsistently* with it, which is possible through sheer ignorance of what one is doing, as where, not realizing someone's sensitivity on a touchy subject, one unwittingly offends despite judging one must not. An action merely inconsistent with one's better judgment may show folly, recklessness, or forgetfulness, but not weakness of will; that requires some awareness of one's judgment—the directive supposed to govern the will. One cannot act against a directive of which one is unaware, any more than one can oppose a foe of whose existence one has no idea.

Our better judgment need not be our *best*, in either of the senses of 'best judgment' most relevant to incontinence. *S*'s best judgment in the *attributive sense* is one to the effect that an option *is best;* such judgments attribute a kind of optimality to the action in question. *S*'s best judgment in the *epistemic sense* is simply *S*'s *best warranted* practical judgment concerning what to do in the situation, regardless of how the judgment rates any option *S* considers open: it might be just that one should *A*, or that *A*-ing is prima facie a good option. Incontinent action need not go against one's best judgment, in the attributive sense, because *S* can exhibit weakness of will in *A*-ing, against a

<hr/>

[1] This is based on my "Weakness of Will and Practical Judgment," *Noûs* 13 (1979): 174. For a brief statement of many other views of and about weakness of will, see Arthur F. Walker, "The Problem of Weakness of Will: A Critical Survey of Recent Literature," *Nous* 23 (1989). Other recent treatments bearing on issues in this essay include David Wiggins, "Weakness of Will, Commensurability, and the Objects of Deliberation and Desire," in Amelie O. Rorty, ed., *Essays on Aristotle's Ethics* (Berkeley and Los Angeles: University of California Press, 1980); Frank Jackson, "Weakness of Will," *Mind* 93 (1984); David Pears, *Motivated Irrationality* (Oxford: Oxford University Press, 1984); Alfred R. Mele, *Irrationality* (Oxford: Oxford University Press, 1986); and Alan Donagan, *Choice: The Essential Elements in Action* (London: Routledge & Kegan Paul, 1988).

judgment that *B*-ing would be better, even if *S* does not think that *B*-ing would be *best*. *S* may not even have a candidate for the best alternative. Nor must incontinent action contravene a judgment that is best in the epistemic sense (*S* may not even hold such a judgment, as opposed to two or more equally warranted ones). I can act incontinently in serving myself more beef even if my judgment that I should abstain is not only less than my best warranted but *un*warranted. A judgment can play the crucial *directive* role whether warranted or not, and I can exhibit weakness of will in failing to follow the directive even if the judgment is unwarranted. I might well exhibit it even if I *believe* the judgment is unwarranted, assuming that I can genuinely hold a practical judgment under this condition. This epistemic belief may challenge the appropriateness of the judgment's playing its normal directive role, but it does not eliminate that role; hence, acting against the judgment should still count as incontinent. To be sure, the incontinent action may be less criticizable in other ways, for instance morally; and *S* may be more criticizable in some respects, say for simultaneously holding both the judgment and the belief that this judgment is unwarranted. But these are different points.

If incontinent action implies going against one's better judgment, it is not precisely equivalent to action against one's better judgment. Incontinent action must also be uncompelled. This is largely because compelled action is not criticizable in the way incontinent action is.[2] I believe, however, that we may take incontinent actions to be *uncompelled actions against one's better judgment*. I rule out compulsion in part because "the will" does not exhibit weakness (of the relevant kind) in not preventing a compelled act. In acting under compulsion, after all, one "can't help oneself." It is true that incontinence may imply some *pressure* to act, say from passion or appetite, and that the degree of pressure, for instance the severity of a threat, which compels one person might not compel another. One reason for this is different strengths of will. A threat that would compel Jim might simply annoy Jane or perhaps cause her to act (freely) against her better judgment, as where, to avoid embarrassment, she yields confidential information she judges she ought to withhold. Nonetheless, where an agent is genuinely compelled—which, to be sure, may imply that a person

[2] I argue for this in "Weakness of Will and Practical Judgment," esp. on pp. 179–180.

of *normal* will power relative to the situation would also be unable to forbear—the action is not incontinent.

The inclination to countenance compelled incontinent acts may stem from conflating *weakness of the will*—which is roughly a failure to conform to an appropriate directive of practical reason—with *weakness in the will*—which is a different notion: a low level of strength in the overall faculty of will, such that, as compared with people of stronger will, there are more deeds (or more deeds of relevant kinds) which one can be compelled to do even if one judges one should not.[3] Jim, who suffers from weakness in the will, might often be coerced into doing things he judges he should not, though given a phlegmatic temperament and good fortune he might never be incontinent. Jane, who is sometimes incontinent, might have a very strong will—but simply lack sufficient strength of will to resist her own powerful impulses. Compared with Jim, she would tend to be the harder to compel by threat; but neither would exhibit weakness of will proper—incontinence—through being brought, under *compulsion*, to do something he or she judged to be on balance wrong.

My final point in this section concerns the scope of weakness of will. If incontinent action is uncompelled action against one's better judgment, then it should not be surprising if incontinence extends beyond action. After all, if taking more beef against one's better judgment exhibits weakness of will, surely forming the *intention* to do so may indicate a similar failure, even if, because the supply has just run out, one cannot indulge. But forming an intention is at least not typically action. Similarly, if one judges one should go out in a storm to help someone free a stuck car, and one then *fails* to form the intention to go out, is this not incontinence in the same way as the (intentional) failure itself, the reprehensible *act* of omission? I think so, and I would argue that parallel points apply even to one kind of motivation that does not entail intention, namely, wanting on balance: wanting something more than one wants anything one believes incompatible with it. For if I want, in this way, to eat more beef, then I want it more than, say, to hold my weight. I am thus readily *disposed* to eat more when I get a chance; hence, in my forming such a want (or not preventing its formation), I exhibit some degree of volitional failure to direct myself in the correct path. The general

[3] Someone *sufficiently* strong-willed exhibits neither kind of weakness; but one can suffer from weakness in the will without being incontinent: circumstances being favorable, volitional weakness as a *feature* need not be reflected in volitionally weak *action*.

idea is that not only actions, but also the sorts of motivational dispositions that typically yield them, can go against one's better judgment and thereby exhibit a kind of weakness of will.[4]

II. The Irrationality of Incontinence

The conception of weakness of will just articulated makes it easy to see why incontinent actions are prima facie irrational: they contravene one's judgment of what one should do and thus exhibit a kind of inconsistency between one's action and one's assessment—which is often backed by good reasoning—of what one's action should be. The same applies, of course, to other forms of weakness of will, such as incontinent intention. But this section considers only incontinent actions and leaves implicit how its points bear on other kinds of weakness of will. Moreover, while the conception of weakness of will sketched above will be presupposed, much of what is said about the rationality of incontinent action can be defended from the perspective of other views of weakness of will, particularly those taking it to imply going against one's better judgment or in some other way opposing "reason."

Most philosophers writing on weakness of will have implied that incontinent action is at least prima facie irrational. Aristotle, for example, treats incontinence as a vice involving ignorance, speaks of it as both "to be avoided and blameworthy," and says that, whereas the "continent person seems to be the same as one who abides by his rational calculation . . . the incontinent person seems to be the same as one who abandons it."[5] Granted that in speaking of incontinence as a vice he is thinking of weakness of will as a *trait*, he also takes its manifestations in action to merit the kind of disapproval he here expresses, and probably to be irrational. Another view is that "weakness of the will involves a failure to achieve full autonomy" and that while weak-willed actions may carry out one's decisions, these deci-

---

[4] This application of weakness of will to intentions and wants is developed in my "Weakness of Will and Practical Judgment," pp. 181–85.

[5] Aristotle, *Nicomachean Ethics* 1145b10–11; see also 1146b–1148b14; the translation is Terence Irwin's. Wiggins remarks that "almost anyone not under the influence of theory will say . . . the weak-willed man acts not for *no* reason at all . . . but irrationally" in "Weakness of Will, Commensurability," p. 241.

sions are not in accord with what on reflection one would have deter-mined one ought to do.[6] For people want whatever success they have to be in part due to them: *"They* want to determine what happens to them."[7] Incontinent actions, however, bespeak a failure to determine, in the relevant sense, what happens to one.

It has even been thought that incontinent action, conceived as in-tentional, is impossible. For suppose that (1) if *S A*'s intentionally, *S*'s *A*-ing can be rationally explained by *S*'s reasons, (2) if *A*-ing is ratio-nally explainable by the agent's reasons, then it is rational, and (3) it is *ir*rational to act against one's considered best judgment, as is im-plied by incontinence.[8] It follows that incontinent actions are, qua intentional, rational and, qua actions against one's considered best judgment, irrational. If we think there are incontinent actions, we must qualify at least one of these plausible assumptions.

There is a further, though related, reason for taking incontinent actions to be irrational. They seem to manifest a *malfunction:* the will is not carrying out its proper function—to produce conformity between action and practical reason. Since this is a basic rational function, incontinent action reveals a deficiency in the agent's rationality and as such is irrational. For convenience, I speak metaphorically in terms of a subagent, the will. But the functional view does not require such homuncularism: talk of the will here is simply a way to refer to a range of human capacities, and those, in turn, may function well or poorly.

There are other reasons to consider incontinence irrational, but the four specified enable us both to assess this view and to learn some-thing about rational action in general. Appraising these reasons is the main business of the next section. Section IV will provide a wider treatment of the relation between weakness of will and rationality.

III. Incontinent Behavior and Rational Action

We have seen four kinds of arguments to show that inconti-nent action cannot be rational: arguments from practical inconsis-

---

[6] Norman O. Dahl, "Weakness of the Will as a Moral Defect," presented at the Central Division Meetings of the American Philosophical Association, 1987.

[7] Ibid., p. 19.

[8] David Charles, "Weakness of the Will: Ancient and Modern Approaches," pre-sented at the Central Division Meetings of the American Philosophical Association, 1987.

tency, from impaired autonomy, from inexplicability, and from malfunction. Let me start with the argument from inexplicability, since, if it is sound, there *are* no incontinent actions. This argument is disarmingly simple: incontinent action cannot occur because it is intentional and thus rationally explainable, hence rational; yet, as going against one's considered best judgment, incontinent action is *irrational*. The apparent simplicity conceals an ambiguity: the phrase 'an intentional action is rationally explainable' might mean that (i) an intentional action can be explained as performed *for* a reason, or that (ii) an intentional action is explainable *by* a reason in a way implying that it is rational, for example explainable as based on a good reason for it. (i) is plausible, but something like (ii) is needed to support the principle that what is rationally explainable is rational. (ii) will not stand scrutiny, for at least the following reasons.

Surely there is such a thing as an intentional action performed for a bad reason. One might also fail to act rationally because, though one has an adequate reason to do what one does, say to buy a certain stock, one is culpably overlooking a much better reason to do something else which, on even slight reflection, one would much prefer. There are several cases of acting for a bad reason. *S* may, for instance, *A* in order to bring about an end, say to alter a corporation's policy in South Africa, while only *irrationally* believing the action will contribute to this end. Alternatively, the end may be one *S* would not pursue except on the basis of an irrational belief, as where *S* would not want to alter the corporation's policy except on the foolish assumption that doing this would undermine apartheid. The end itself may also be one that *S* should, on the available evidence, see *cannot* be realized; thus, devoting hours to trying to square the circle might be intentional action for a bad reason. Arguably, a morally outrageous end might be still another kind of bad reason for acting. But it is clear that people can intentionally act to realize such ends. To be sure, we might take 'rational' so minimally that any action intelligible enough to be seen as intentional is thereby automatically rational; but in that case, incontinent actions will cease to seem irrational. The term 'irrational' is a contrary of 'rational', not the contradictory; and there are surely many actions—doubtless including admirable spontaneous expressions of affection or delight—which, while not rational, are also not irrational.

The argument from impaired autonomy also fails. Granted that typically action against one's better judgment violates one's autonomy, it is not self-evident that going against one's autonomy is always irrational. Supposing that it is so, however, we must still bear in mind that the judgment against which one acts is—at its strongest in directive content—one's best only in the attributive sense and not necessarily in the epistemic sense. This raises the possibility that one might be unwarranted in holding the judgment. Ironically, it might itself represent a kind of *doxastic incontinence*, in the sense (roughly) that it goes against one's assessment of what, on one's available evidence, one ought to believe: one believes against one's better evidential judgment. Perhaps here—i.e., in acting against one's doxastically incontinent better judgment—one's autonomy would *not* be well served by the continent action, the action in favor of which one judges. Much depends on what constitutes autonomy, of course, and I shall return to this issue. My point here is that considerations of autonomy yield only prima facie reasons to think that an incontinent action must be irrational.

Once we see that there is nothing sacrosanct about a practical judgment simply in virtue of its providing a directive whose violation is incontinent, we can also question whether the discord between such a judgment and action against it must make the action irrational. There is *something* amiss when incontinence occurs, but why must the action be the locus of our main criticism, or deserve the charge of irrationality? The action may, after all, yield the agent great pleasure—or, in less typical cases, a high degree of conformity with some cherished ideal—in a very efficient way and with no foreseeable bad effects. If it does, and if the judgment (however firmly held at the time) is itself one the agent would not accept on careful reflection, why must the action be, on balance, irrational? I cannot see that it must be.

Similarly, even if the normal and proper function of practical judgment is to guide action, why must every action against it be irrational? We can agree that one who acts incontinently is not functioning normally, or even that such agents are not functioning at all well. But it is a further step to the conclusion that the action itself is irrational. Practical judgment is, after all, fallible, even when "considered"; and the function it serves may be impaired *before* one makes it—say, by an intellectual error in reasoning that underlies the judgment—as well as later in behavioral deviance from it. Again, we get only an argument for the prima facie irrationality of incontinent action.

IV. Three Models of Rational Action

In framing a general conception of rational action, I want first to consider a related standard for the rationality of forming intentions: given the desires on the basis of which S thinks it most desirable to A, the "acquisition of new intentions is rational only if their satisfaction is consistent with the satisfaction of this set of desires."[9] This principle can help us understand why certain incontinent actions are irrational; for the very intention to perform them is not consistent with the satisfaction of the desires, say moral desires, grounding one's practical judgment, for example that one should keep an onerous promise.

The principle that rational intention must be consistent with standing desires on the basis of which one forms it is plausible and often holds true. It is a practical expression of what we might call a *fidelity to premises model of rationality.* The parallel view of theoretical reason would be (roughly) that acquisition of a belief is rational only if the belief is consistent with any beliefs one already holds on the basis of which one forms it. But what if the desires grounding the practical judgment are themselves highly irrational, or not representative of one's overall desires, interests, or ideals? After all, even in acting reflectively we may not take adequate account of our overall perspective, our perspective as determined by certain of our basic beliefs and desires, especially those crucial in our world view. Could there be, then, an action against one's better judgment which, through its accord with (the relevant parts of) our overall perspective, *is* rational? If so, we should reject the common assumption that incontinent actions are all irrational. Let us pursue this issue in relation to moral decision.

Consider John, a practiced and conscientious retributivist. He believes that he should punish his daughter for talking hours on the phone when she knew she should study. On reflection, he judges that he should deny her a Saturday outing. But a day later, when it comes time to deny her the outing, he looks into her eyes, realizes that she will be quite upset, decides to make do with a stern rebuke, and lets her go. He feels guilty and chides himself. It is not that he changed his mind; he was simply too uncomfortable with the prospect of cracking down. Suppose, however, that he also has a strong

[9] Ibid.

standing belief that he must be a reasonable parent and is well aware that the deprivation would hurt the child and cause a rebellious reaction. He might be so disposed that if he had thought long enough about the matter, he would have changed his mind; but that is perfectly consistent with the assumption that if his will were stronger, he would have punished her. Thus, his letting her go may still be incontinent. But is it irrational? I cannot see that it is. The following considerations indicate why it need not be.

To begin with, note that John's action is not *passional incontinence*— the most typical kind—and is not in any other way tainted by irrational appetitive influences. Moreover, it is backed by good reasons rooted deep in his character, for example his desire not to hurt his daughter and not to provoke a rebellion so severe as to undermine the good moral effect of the punishment. But even though his incontinent action accords with a civilized and generally admirable compassionate desire, it *does* go against his standing better judgment and its underlying retributive desires. Still, the overall rational basis of that judgment is too narrow and is outweighed by the larger rational considerations producing the incontinent action and apparently rendering it rational.

It might be objected that John must have made another practical judgment favoring mercy; hence, what we really have is a conflict of (presumably prima facie) practical judgments, and the action is continent with respect to one but not the other. Since the epistemically better judgment is the merciful one, John's merciful action is rational, and, as according with that judgment, not incontinent. This is a possible case and important in its own right. But continence does not follow from the action's being based on an *epistemically* better judgment: the punitive judgment might, for example, be ingrained and far stronger, and so represent the overall disposition of practical reason at the time of action.

Moreover, John *need not* have made two judgments: desire and other motivational features can produce action *without* the mediation of practical judgment,[10] and that is my case. Particularly when one acts in the service of passional or appetitive influences, one can act intentionally without doing so on the basis of practical reasoning or even forming a judgment which favors the action in question. If, in

[10] This is controversial, and what follows goes only partway toward an adequate defense. For further supporting considerations, see E. J. Bond, "Reasons, Wants, and Values," *Canadian Journal of Philosophy* 3 (1974), for example pp. 333–36.

anger over his child's headlong assertion of independence in planning a dangerous trip, John reminds her of a deeply embarrassing, misbegotten venture that he had agreed never to mention, he may do so intentionally and for a reason: to shame her into backing down. But he need not have judged that this was a good thing, or in any way reasoned to a conclusion favoring it. Indeed, the most common incontinent actions are not reasoned at all, nor favored by any kind of evaluative judgment. In the case of the waived punishment, if John had reflected enough to form the opposing, merciful judgment, he would probably no longer hold the judgment against which he acts, and so would not have acted incontinently at all. In general, even intentional action need not await reflection or reasoning, and if it did there might be much less incontinence in the first place.

It is also instructive to ask whether John's waiving the punishment is autonomous. Here we are pulled in two directions. It is not *directly autonomous*, since it goes against the present deliverance of his practical judgment; but perhaps it is *indirectly autonomous*, since it is grounded in central elements of John's character which, had he been sufficiently in touch with them, would have led him to a different practical judgment. We might also distinguish between actions that are *judgmentally autonomous*—grounded in what, at the time, one judges, or would on briefly considering the matter judge, one should do—and actions that are *holistically autonomous*: grounded in what, given a correct understanding of one's overall relevant desires and ideals, such as moral and parental desires and standards, one would judge one should do. Incontinent action need not violate one's overall autonomy, holistically conceived.

The tension we feel in deciding whether John's action is autonomous is closely related to the question of its rationality. The fidelity to premises model of rationality has been suggested as one relevant line of inquiry, and it can help us understand the tension. For insofar as we take as decisive for rationality the premises John *consciously uses*, his action is inconsistent with them and as such prima facie irrational; yet insofar as we interpret the model more broadly and take as decisive the premises—in the wide sense of 'grounds for action'—that he *has* by virtue of believing the relevant propositions, his action is consistent with them and thereby prima facie rational. As this suggests, one trouble with the fidelity model as I am describing it is its unclarity about what premises are decisive for rationality: just those used, those *S has* in one or another sense, or some combination.

I thus want to set out another model of rationality (though I here apply it only to action) that can capture what is plausible in the fidelity model, but does not have its main deficiencies. I begin with a narrower model that contrasts with both.

On this narrower model of rational actions—which I shall call the *executive model*—rational actions are those grounded in one's practical judgment (or at least all such actions are rational). Practical reason delivers a guiding judgment; behavior conforms. Autonomy, on this model, is proportional to the extent to which one's overall conduct is under executive control, and it is thus easy to see why incontinent action is neither rational nor autonomous. Indeed, this model makes it easier than any I am aware of to see why incontinent action might be thought irrational. But there is another, broader model which yields a better account of rational action, whether incontinent or not. I describe it briefly here and develop it in Section V.

This third, *balance of reasons model*, is holistic: a rational action is one that is grounded, in the right way, in sufficiently good reasons of the agent, regardless of whether they figure in premises leading to the making of a judgment that favors that action. Here are three points central to the associated conception of (objectively) rational action: these reasons must meet minimal objective standards (for example in terms of the quality of the agent's evidence for the belief(s) involved); they must motivationally explain the action (so that they do not just provide a rationalization for it); and they must be sufficiently harmonious with the agent's overall framework of beliefs and wants, since action based on reasons, such as certain fleeting emotional desires one disapproves of, discordant with the agent's overall makeup, even if not irrational, is not clearly rational. To take a simple illustration, suppose that John wants above all to be moral, and that this desire expresses a carefully considered set of ideals and principles to which he is single-mindedly devoted. A paradigm of a rational action on his part would be one he performs on the basis of this desire and in the reasonable belief that it is his overall obligation. If one takes his governing ideal to be rationally acceptable and his belief that it requires the action to be in some way objectively justified, one may consider the action rational in some objective sense. If one takes the ideal or belief (or both) to be acceptable only from his point of view, one may regard the action as rational only in some subjective sense. The model is neutral between various kinds of objective and subjective conceptions of rationality.

Often the executive and balance of reasons models agree; for we are so constructed that commonly our practical judgments do appropriately reflect our overall system of reasons. But even when we take time to reflect, we can make a practical judgment which is out of line with our most important beliefs and wants relevant to the action. If these beliefs and wants, in an appropriate way, then determine action against our better judgment, we may thereby exhibit incontinence without irrationality.[11]

V. Generalization of the Holistic Model

Much can be learned from exploring how rational incontinent action is possible. In part, the explanation is that the rational authority of practical judgment derives from the agent's overall set of beliefs and desires in the same way as does the rationality of the actions themselves. Given that point, it should be expected that where an action accords with those overall grounds of rationality better than does a practical judgment it contravenes, the action may be rational despite its incontinence. Here, incontinent action, far from a failure to do what is better or best, may be the best option, and may eventually be seen by the agent to be so.

If, following the executive model, one thinks that the business of the will is to obey the intellect and that practical judgment represents the proper disposition of the intellect, action against one's practical judgment will of course seem irrational. This impression is reinforced if one thinks of the judgment as *closer*—as it normally in some sense is—to the overall grounds just cited as crucial for rationality. But the executive model is mistaken; and even if what is closer to the proper grounds of rationality tends to be more rational than what is further, this correspondence does not always hold. Indeed, a practical judgment may itself be passional, foolish, or even incontinent, in the sense of going against one's assessment of what the total evidence bearing on one's options indicates one should do. However, even where the judgment is warranted by the premises on which it based,

[11] The appropriate way must be non-wayward. Attempts to clarify wayward chains and to show how actions are non-waywardly rooted in agents are given in Myles Brand, *Intending and Acting* (Cambridge: MIT Press, 1984) and Chapter 6 of this volume.

they themselves may be defective from the overall point of view central to the agent's rationality, and in that case an incontinent action may turn out to be rational. Like the executive model, the fidelity model yields the right results only where—as in the most usual case—the premises underlying practical judgment are consistent with the overall thrust of the agent's system of reasons as it bears on the context of action.

Nothing I have said is meant to deny that when a rational action is incontinent, its incontinence counts to *some* degree against its rationality. But without being rational to the highest degree, an action may still be rational on balance. I also grant that incontinence counts against the rationality of the *agent:* one is not fully rational at a time at which one acts incontinently, and Aristotle was right to conceive the trait of incontinence as uncharacteristic of rational agents. Moreover, even though an incontinent action can be rational, it is not rational to *cultivate* incontinence as a trait or disposition; for it tends to undermine one's rational self-control. But these points are consistent with my main thesis: that rationality must be holistically conceived and that when it is, some incontinent actions may be seen to be rational.

What has emerged concerning the possible rationality of incontinent actions also applies to that of incontinent intentions and desires, and to incontinent failures to form intentions or desires. For the rationality of these items too should be understood in the same holistic way. Furthermore, as doxastic incontinence shows, the balance of reasons model also applies to the domain of belief better than does its executive counterpart. Just as a practical judgment may poorly represent one's overall reasons bearing on one's options, one's assessment of the weight of evidence may be inadequate to guide one's beliefs. If, in such a case, one believed a proposition that one's overall grounds *do* best support, despite one's appraising some other proposition as better supported by them, the spontaneous belief may be not only rational but also an expression of one's rational nature—perhaps a triumph of habitual responsiveness to good reasons over a self-conscious assessment of what, in the light of arguments, one ought to think.

Similar points apply to desire and valuation, indeed to all the propositional attitudes. For in every such case there may be a disparity between one's assessment of the states of affairs to be desired, valued, or whatever, and the desires or valuations actually best supported by one's grounds. Nature has given us the capacity to appraise our alternatives and to judge what, in the light of our appraisal, we should do, or want, or value. She has so constructed us that normally we abide by such judgments; and typically, we stray from them at our peril. But she has not entirely trusted us to our own judgment, and our natural reasonableness can sometimes prevail over even our careful assessments.

A great deal remains to be said to develop the balance of reasons model, the fidelity to premises model, or even the executive model, fully. I would speculate that it may be in part the influence of the Platonic notion of the tripartite soul, with sovereign reason issuing authoritative directives, that makes the executive model plausible, and, in turn, makes incontinent action appear intrinsically irrational. Similarly, it may be in part the influence of a naive linear foundationalism that gives plausibility to the fidelity to premises model and so makes incontinent actions seem invariably to deviate from reason. But I do not think they need to be irrational, and I suggest that a holistic conception of rationality of the kind set out here helps us both to understand how weakness of will is possible and to assess the actions, intentions, desires, and other propositional attitudes that manifest it.[12]

[12] Part of this essay developed from a paper given at the 1987 Central Division Meetings of the American Philosophical Association, where I benefited from discussions with the other symposiasts, David Charles, Norman Dahl, and Deborah Modrak. Earlier versions of the essay were given in 1988 at Calvin College, Loyola University of Chicago, and Memphis State University. These audiences provided valuable criticism. I also thank Hugh J. McCann and readers for the *Australasian Journal of Philosophy* for helpful comments.

Chapter 13

An Internalist Conception
of Rational Action

The distinction between internalist and externalist theories is a major topic in contemporary epistemology. This essay assumes that there are extensive parallels between epistemology and the theory of action, and its central task is to articulate the same distinction in the domain of action and to determine whether an internalist position in action theory can explicate rational action. It will be argued that the distinction between internalism and externalism is not only applicable to action, but raises questions in action theory similar to the issues it generates in epistemology. Indeed, it raises problems whose resolution may be possible only by a general theory of rationality applicable both to actions and to the propositional attitudes. Section I will briefly set out a version of epistemological internalism to serve as a basis for developing a similar position in action theory. Section II will formulate an internalist conception of intentional action and explore some problems which this conception, like its epistemological counterpart, must solve. Against this background, Section III will sketch an internalist view of rational action. The concluding section will summarize the main results of the essay and bring out some remaining issues.

I. Internalism in Epistemology

In its most general form, epistemological internalism is the view that what justifies a belief—say a visual impression of white paper before one—is something to which the believer has internal access, in the sense that by reflection, including introspective reflection, the believer could become aware of it. The following points will clarify the view.

First, one need not be able to become aware of the justifier under any particular description, though there are limits to the range of appropriate descriptions. A minimal internalism, in perceptual cases at least, would not even require that the awareness be conceptual, in the sense that one is aware of the justificatory ground under any concept.

Second, so long as the awareness is introspective as opposed to, say, observational, it need not even be *direct*. An internalist might hold that we are not directly aware of our beliefs in the phenomenal sense of 'direct,' which precludes mediation by other objects of awareness. Granted, in the inferential sense of 'direct', we may know directly that we have beliefs; but that is consistent with our awareness of them being mediated by, say, direct awareness of some manifestation of them.

Third, the appropriate reflection may be extended, so long as it reveals elements that already justify our belief and it does not substitute new justifiers, for instance, through inferentially extending our knowledge in such a way as to yield premises that were not previously believed and now provide new support for the belief in question. The appropriate kind of reflection, then, is *revelatory* rather than *generative.* To be sure, it may be incidentally generative: one may discover, in the process of reflection, grounds one did not have for the belief in question; and one may acquire new reasons to hold it. But if the belief is justified in the way internalism requires, then one must already *have* accessible grounds for it. It is not enough that an adequate ground be accessible to one by generative reflection. That would be sufficient for *justifiable* belief; it is not sufficient for justified belief.

A major motivation for internalism is the idea that what justifies a belief is somehow available to one to use in *justifying* it.[1] A further motivation is the conviction that even if a Cartesian demon caused us to hold false beliefs, we would remain justified in holding those

[1] Some discussion of how and why grounds of justification must be available to an agent, *S*, is provided in my "Justification, Truth, and Reliability," *Philosophy and Phenomenological Research* 49 (1988).

of them suitably based on internal grounds. What other appropriate standard, after all, is available to us? Internalists hold that there is no acceptable alternative standard of justification, and they conclude that in demon cases there is no basis for calling the relevant internally well-grounded false beliefs unjustified. They thus see internal grounds as the central element in justification.

Much depends on the *scope* of the accessibility requirement central to internalism. The guiding idea is that justified belief requires access to *what justifies* the belief,[2] for example to a visual experience. I shall call this view *first-order internalism*. By contrast, a strong internalist might require introspective access to *how what justifies does so*, where this implies a capacity to know how it does, or at least a capacity, regarding some way it justifies, to form a justified belief that it does so in that way. Call this *second-order internalism*, since in effect it implies that one does or can know (or justifiably believe) something *about* one's belief, say that it is sustained by one's impression of warmth, or that its truth is probabilistically implied by that of a premise one believes. Notice that the distinction of orders here is made on the justification side; it is roughly a matter of awareness simply of a justifier as opposed to a higher-order awareness both of some justifier and of how it plays this role. On the belief content side, first-order internalism would allow justification of a second-order belief, such as my belief that I now believe there is white paper before me, where this self-ascriptive belief is justified by my awareness of, say, a certain attitude toward its propositional object.

It may seem, however, that first-order internalism implies second-order internalism. Certainly if I am aware of what justifies my second-order belief, for instance of an assenting attitude toward the proposition that there is white paper before me, I am in a good position to form other second-order beliefs about *how* this awareness justifies my belief that I believe there is such paper before me. Yet I need not form any second-order beliefs, and perhaps I may not even have the capacity to form any that are justified, or to know how what justifies me does so. For one thing, I can be aware of *my ground* for a belief without being aware of it *as a ground;* and for another, I may be hopelessly confused regarding justification, or pathologically self-deceived regarding certain of the beliefs or mental states in question.

---

[2] Paul K. Moser suggests such a view in *Empirical Justification* (Dordrecht: Reidel, 1985).

Moreover, suppose the person in question is a child with insufficient conceptual resources to have the relevant kind of belief. Then first-order, but not second-order, internalism allows the person to have justified beliefs. Thus, while someone who meets the first-order internalist conditions for justified belief will frequently also meet the second-order conditions for it, this need not be so.

A further point essential here is that while internalism is closely connected with the doctrine of privileged access, it does not imply such access. One could be an internalist without holding even a weak form of the doctrine, and one could consistently hold even a strong doctrine of privileged access without being an internalist. Access is what internalists are committed to, not its privilege. Nonetheless, it is useful to locate internalism in relation to the doctrine of privileged access; there are both historical connections and conceptual parallels. The classical form of that doctrine has two sides; roughly, one thesis is that we are omniscient about a certain range of our mental properties, the other that certain of our beliefs attributing such properties to ourselves are infallible or of some other high epistemic status.[3] It is essential that we distinguish the kind of accessibility that goes with a qualified omniscience thesis—in implying a high degree of spontaneous cognitive receptivity to one's epistemic grounds—from the kind that goes with a qualified infallibility thesis—in implying that those beliefs (if any) which one forms about such grounds have a high degree of reliability. Let me develop this contrast.

Call the first kind of accessibility *occurrent accessibility:* a justifier is occurrently accessible provided it is luminous in a way that implies that one need at most be "looking" in the right direction to become aware of it; one need not search. One tends to be aware of it at the time it does its justificatory work. Thus, my experience of white before me as I read is either such that I cannot help being aware of the white, or at least need only turn my attention in the right direction to become aware of it.[4] As this illustrates, there are two main cases. The awareness is *focal* if, even without my specially attending to it, the object in question, like a car I am looking right at as I drive behind

---

[3] For a related, brief account of privileged access, see my *Belief, Justification, and Knowledge* (Belmont, Calif.: Wadsworth, 1988), chap. 3.

[4] Paul K. Moser's awareness internalism seems to be of this sort; see, for example, his *Knowledge and Evidence* (Cambridge: Cambridge University Press, 1990). For an assessment of Moser's internalism and a valuable discussion of internalist versus externalist views, see William P. Alston, "An Internalist Externalism," *Synthese* 74 (1988).

it, is focused in my consciousness. The awareness is *peripheral* if, like my consciousness of trees on the roadside, it is not focused; yet to achieve at least some degree of focus on its object I need only attend to it, as opposed to changing my field of view. If, for instance, one tree suddenly fell, I would be aware of its falling even if I kept looking at the car in front of me, and I could focus on it by turning my attention to it.

By contrast, *dispositional accessibility* requires only that if, in the right introspective way, you search, you shall find; and finding is both becoming aware of what you find and coming to be in a *position* to know or justifiably believe certain truths about it. In the move from occurrent to dispositional accessibility, what can't be missed gives way to what can be seen; luminescence is supplanted by luminability. One can be, but does not automatically tend to be, aware of dispositionally accessible justifiers at the time they play their justificatory role. To be sure, searching for one thing may yield discovery of quite another, or lead to both the quarry and more of its kind; and what is not sought may be more valuable than what is. But this is not a problem for internalism. As I have noted, the appropriate introspective reflection may be *incidentally* generative: what internalism minimally requires is only that there *be*, accessible to reflection and not merely creatable by it, a sufficient internal ground for every justified belief.

There are degrees of dispositional accessibility, depending on how readily the ground(s) of the justified belief would come to the person upon appropriately considering the matter, as in pursuing the question why one believes that one owes someone a letter. Different versions of internalism may thus require greater or lesser degrees of such accessibility; and any plausible internalism will allow differences in degree corresponding to such variables as the complexity of the belief and the agent's grasp of relevant concepts. It should also be stressed that when, in the normal, non-observational way, one pursues a question like why one believes one owes someone a letter, this self-examination counts as the relevant kind of introspective reflection whether or not one is "looking within" in the sense appropriate to consciousness of phenomenal states. This point is especially important for understanding how internalism applies to *inferentially* justified beliefs, whose grounds are other beliefs rather than phenomenal states.

On the other hand, perceptually justified beliefs are especially good illustrations for internalism because of vivid parallels of an external kind. Thus, in our driving example, external, observational access to the trees may parallel internal access to one's phenomenal grounds for beliefs about those trees. It might be, for instance, that one need only think about the trees to become aware that they are tall and thin; one might or might not be able to slow down enough to discern the shape of their leaves; and one might or might not need to reflect and draw inferences to ascertain whether they stand in a straight line. One's access to memorial images might be variable in this way, whereas one's access to one's steady auditory impressions of a symphony might be as focal as one's visual image of the conductor's moving hands.

One further point of clarification, which also has a parallel in action theory, is in order before we proceed to the next section. What is not itself introspectable may be readily knowable *through* what is introspectable, as one may know one is worried through the imagery and agitation one notes in oneself. Nor need the mediation be inferential: one can know (or justifiably believe) that one wants something *by* one's assentingly considering the proposition that one does, or by one's sense of pleasure in contemplating realization of the want, even if one does not *infer* that one wants it from the second-order proposition that one *is* assentingly considering this, or from the proposition that one is contemplating the realization of the state of affairs with a sense of pleasure. What is known *by* some mark need not be *inferred from* the premise that it *has* that mark.

II. Internalism in the Theory of Action

In formulating an internalist conception of intentional action, it might seem that we must restrict our focus to rational action, since that is the closest behavioral parallel to justified belief. This is not so; for intentional action itself, as opposed to mere behavior, is already based on one or more reasons in a sense that at least normally implies prima facie justification. It is the counterpart of inferential belief, roughly, belief held for one or more reasons, though the case for inferential beliefs' being (in general) prima facie justified may perhaps be weaker.[5] I shall thus start with an internalist view of intentional action in general, and then proceed to develop an internalist conception of rational action.

Consider first the following major parallel between epistemology and the theory of action. Rather as we do not justifiably believe a proposition, *p*, unless we both *have* a ground for it and believe it (causally) *on* that ground, we do not act (intentionally) unless we both *have* a reason for acting and act *for* that reason, in a sense of 'for' implying causal production or sustenance—causal generation for short.[6] Thus, just as, if we do not have introspective access to the ground of a justified belief, we lack internal access to what justifies that belief, so, for parallel reasons, if we do not have a similar access to our reasons for our actions—notably to our wants and beliefs—we lack internal access to those actions. The notion of action, by contrast with that of mere behavior, is apparently an internal concept in much the same way the notion of a belief for a reason (an inferential belief) is. If a belief is *based on* a reason, as opposed to merely caused by one (strictly, by the propositional attitude expressing the reason), the person has at least some kind of access—minimally, a fallible dispositional access—to that reason.

The parallel also holds in the normative cases: justified and rational actions are quite like justified beliefs in requiring the person to have internal access to grounds. The crucial difference is that, whereas in the non-normative case of mere intentional action and mere belief for some reason, there must be access to an appropriate causal ground (one expressing the de facto reason whether good or not); in the latter the access must be to a normatively *adequate* ground, one that justifies, or renders rational, the belief or action based on it.

In both the normative and the other cases, the access is commonly *non-inferential:* we normally do not need to infer from premises, even if we must realize *through* awareness of manifestations, what consti-

---

[5] There is a case, however: for if inferential beliefs are, as they seem, beliefs *for a reason*, and if even a bad reason must meet *relevance* requirements in virtue of which it has *some* prima facie evidential force, then it has some minimal capacity to support a belief based on it. Cf. Jaegwon Kim, "What Is Naturalized Epistemology?" in *Philosophical Perspectives* 2 (1988).

[6] I argue for this—allowing for the possible exception (not relevant here) of actions performed for their own sake—in Chapter 6, and there refer to many others who take action to be similarly causally grounded in one or more reasons. A similar parallel holds between mere inferential belief (as opposed to justified inferential belief) and intentional action; but my purposes here are better served by discussing the parallel between justified inferential belief and rational action.

tutes the ground(s) of an inferential belief or of an action for a reason. Still, internalism does not require that the relevant access be non-inferential; what is crucial is that it be internal and, if it is inferential, that it not substitute new grounds or justifiers, as opposed to revealing those already present. As justifiable belief is not equivalent to justified belief, rationalizable action is not equivalent to rational action. Internalism allows that we may have to dig to find our justifying grounds, so long as we do it on our own, by a reflective or an introspective method, and, in the process, do not change their composition, or produce new grounds in their place. We may, in the process, find supplementary grounds, perhaps even better grounds than our original ones; but if we were justified to begin with, the original grounds must have been adequate, however readily they may be extended, supplemented, or even replaced.

The contrasting externalist view in action theory would be, in outline, that an action is intentional when it *in fact* is produced or sustained in an appropriate way by a suitable set of one's wants and beliefs, say non-waywardly produced or sustained by an overriding want for something and a (rational) belief that the action is necessary for achieving it. This condition may hold even if, in principle, one could not introspectively come to know or justifiably believe that one has those grounds for action. Such *behavioral externalism* appears to me a mistake; it cuts us off from our actions in a way that seems to make us more like spectators of our own doings than their agents. Agents can normally know (or at least form justified beliefs concerning) what they are about, in a sense implying a capacity to know for what reason(s) they are acting; they are not in the position of observers whose only route to such knowledge (or justified belief) is observational.[7]

Two objections must be addressed immediately. I shall deal with them first in the epistemological case and then indicate the parallel resolution in action theory. First, what entitles us to maintain, as many epistemologists do, that a belief is justified *by* a ground only if it is held *on* that ground, and so produced or sustained by the ground? Second, supposing this causal requirement on justification is correct, how does it square with internalism, since we apparently do *not* have the required internal access to the relevant causal production and sustenance relations? Let me address these points in turn.

[7] In Chapter 6, I argue (in different terms) that we do at least *tend* to have non-inferential access to a reason for which we act.

In response to the first objection, I shall make just two points, since I have treated the matter at length in other essays.[8] One is that if we distinguish, as many have not, between *situational justification*—roughly, justification for believing *p* (which is possible even if one does not in fact believe it)—and *doxastic justification*—roughly, justifiedness of an actual belief that *p*—there is much less inclination to resist the causal requirement. For this requirement applies only to doxastic justification. The second point is that if we do not hold the causal requirement, we cannot adequately distinguish between justified beliefs and merely rationalizable ones. The latter are above all beliefs for which the agent can adduce reasons despite holding them for other reasons that are patently inadequate to justify: deliverances of an unreliable crystal ball, for instance. These points are not decisive as stated; but reflection on them will at least show that the causal requirement is prima facie plausible. If the requirement is sound, then precisely parallel points hold for action: there is a distinction, for example, between *situational rationality*—roughly, the rationality, for an agent at a time, *t*, of performing an action of the type, *A*-ing—and behavioral justification—roughly, an agent's rationally *A*-ing at *t*. The latter, like doxastic justification, applies to tokens, specifically, to action-tokens; the former, like situational justification, applies to types, specifically, to action-types.

There are some who would protest that the imagined kind of rationalization does justify. I agree that it justifies the *proposition* that *p*, or the performance of *A*, for us; but this falls short of justifying our actual *belief* that *p*, or our actually *A*-ing. Consider, for instance, our providing a good, but *non-motivating* reason for a deed like keeping an onerous promise, when the promise is actually kept wholly *for* selfish reasons. This justifies the action-type, doing of the deed, by us, but not, as I think Kant saw, *our* doing of it. When the type is rational in this way, the token is rationalizable by appeal to the reasons for doing something of that type; but the token's rationalizability does not imply its rationality. The same holds for belief-types in relation to belief-tokens.

The parallel goes further. Just as we may be *epistemically excusable*

[8] I defend a causal requirement on inferentially justified belief and suggest (implicitly) reasons for a similar requirement on non-inferentially justified beliefs in my "Causal Structure of Indirect Justification," *Journal of Philosophy* 80 (1983). A more general causalist requirement, particularly for actions, is defended in my "Rationalization and Rationality," *Synthese* 65 (1985). Relevant essays by me and by others are also cited there.

for holding a belief (whether it is situationally justified or not) on grounds which do not render it doxastically justified—say where we believe it because we are irresistibly in the grip of superstition— we may be *behaviorally excusable* for something we do wholly for selfish but irresistible reasons. These points are important. But to take them to imply justified believing or rational action, as some epistemically deontological views may, owing to the agent's having violated no epistemic duties, is to assimilate justification to excusability.[9] Justification and rationality are positive in a way excusability is not, and they are causal in a way rationalizability is not. As applied to particular beliefs and actions, they require appropriate causal grounding in adequate reason(s); the availability of reasons to supply a good rationalization is not sufficient for justified belief or rational action.

The second objection also has profound theoretical implications. Its crucial presupposition is that an internalist who holds a causal requirement on justification must claim that the agent has internal access to the causal connection between the justifying ground(s) and the justified belief. The main reason for thinking this is presumably the objector's assumption that if the relevant causal connection is a conceptually necessary condition on the belief's justification, then internalism about such justification implies the agent's having access to that connection. But this assumption is a mistake. First-order internalism, which is the kind that concerns me here, requires internal access to *what* justifies, not to *how* it does.

In support of this last point, we might perhaps say that it is the supervenience base of justification that must be accessible, and this need not include all the conceptually necessary conditions for justified belief. The central idea is that the agent must be capable of becoming aware of the appropriate grounds, and this requirement in turn is motivated largely by the sense that if one justifiedly believes *p*, then one can, on suitable reflection, point to what it is in virtue of which one has that justification. One would need access to the causal connection in order to *show* one is justified, but not just to *give* one's justification. One could give it, in fact, as a small child might when

[9] Some such assimilation may be encouraged by certain versions of the maximization of expected utility view of rational action. The view is not usually stated with any causal requirement linking the action to the basis, in the agent, of utility or subjective probability. An exception is Carl G. Hempel, "Rational Action," in his *Aspects of Scientific Explanation* (New York: Macmillan, 1965). Cf. Graeme Marshall, "Action on the Rationality Principle," *Australasian Journal of Philosophy* 59 (1981), esp. pp. 58–59.

asked to explain a belief, without realizing that one *is* giving a justification. This is not in the least to grant that we do not have a significant, if fallible, introspective access to the relevant causal connections; but that is not implied by internalism in general.[10]

I suggest, then, that a causalist internalism is plausible in the theory of action as well as in epistemology. Internal access to one's intentional action apparently requires such access to the reasons for which one performs it. The access need not be occurrent, of course; and since the crucial grounds of justification—wants and beliefs—are dispositional elements rather than phenomenal or other occurrent states, it is likely that often the access is dispositional. (As this suggests, one can have occurrent access to a dispositional state, as when one is aware of a phenomenal state, or of an event, directly manifesting it.) The point that often our access to our reasons for action is dispositional is illustrated by our frequent need to think for a moment before saying why we have done certain things. Given that our access to our reason(s) for action is frequently dispositional, the claim that we in fact have the internal access to the reason(s) for our action can be seen not to be unrealistically strong. One might well also have the appropriate kind of access to *why* one does the things one intentionally does, through introspective access to the causal connections between one's wants and beliefs and the actions based on them; but while this kind of access would yield a more powerful internalism in the theory of action, it is not required for the first-order internalism I am developing.

If an internalist conception of intentional action is plausible, it is natural to wonder, as some philosophers have, how it may be connected with the internalism commonly discussed in moral psychology: *internalism about motivation.* Neither position is so called because of a direct connection with the other. They do, however, belong to the same spectrum of views: those that affirm our autonomy and self-sufficiency as rational beings, especially in the internality of the basis of normative concepts that apply to us as agents. Generically, motivational internalists hold that motivation is internal to, and thereby belongs to the concept of, the *judgment* (or belief) that one should do something (at least where one takes this to express obligation *on*

---

[10] In "Causalist Internalism," *American Philosophical Quarterly* 26 (1989), I explore the prospects for introspective access to causal conditions and for second-order internalism.

balance); and on most versions, the degree of motivation is such that if, in trying to abide by the judgment, the agent performs the action, it is at least in part produced or sustained *by* that judgment. Thus, motivational internalism takes a degree of motivation, a degree that in practice is often substantial, to be both intrinsic to something internally accessible and grounded in a potentially rational element in the agent.

For motivational internalism, then, one has as good access to a ground of one's action as to one's judgment favoring it; and particularly where the judgment is consciously arrived at and becomes a focus of awareness, this access seems to be very good. Moreover, since causal power is built into the motivating judgment, we apparently have as good introspective access to that power as to the judgment itself and to our effort to abide by it—which is plausibly considered quite good access. When we act, then, normally we can know, by reflection, both what our ground (or at least one ground) for action is and that we acted *for* the reason expressed by our judgment favoring the action. It might thus seem that internalism about motivation promises to support both internalism about our grounds for acting and at least a modest claim of internal access to causal connections between those grounds and our actions.

I believe that Kant was attracted to this twofold internalist conception of action, or at least of moral conduct; but he also saw some of its difficulties, notably that one might only *think* one acts *from* a given judgment, such as a moral one, when one really acts, causally, from another motive and merely in accord with the judgment. Thus, while motivational internalism lends some support to the first-order internalist view of intentional action I have proposed, it does not provide good reason for positing, as a second-order internalism would tend to, internal access to causal connections between those grounds and our actions based on them. We must go beyond motivational internalism if we are to show the possibility of introspective knowledge, not just of the *causal power* of motivational factors, but of their *causal action*. Awareness of a potential cause of one's acting is simply not sufficient for knowledge or justified belief that it actually *is* a cause. Fortunately, internalism in the theory of action does not require our having an introspective route to such knowledge or justified belief. I might add that motivational internalism, even apart from leaving much action out of account and making it at best hard to understand weakness of will, seems mistaken.[11]

III. Internalism in the Theory of Rational Action

It is a short step from the proposed internalist view of intentional action to an internalist conception of rational action. I have already emphasized that behavior is intentional in virtue of having an appropriate, partly causal, relation to its grounds in the agent's motivation and cognition. On the basis of this view, it is natural to employ a concept of rationality in general, and of rational action in particular, that reflects the central role which is played, normatively and causally, by grounds. On this view, rationality is equivalent to *well-groundedness*. This conception is quite general; it applies not only to all the propositional attitudes, but also to actions, whose rationality it takes to be derivative from their relation to propositional attitudes, most notably believing and wanting.

As applied to actions, the basic idea of the well-groundedness view is this: rational actions are those grounded in the right kind of way in the right kind of reason. The right kind of way is being performed *for* the reason(s) in question; the right kind of reason is (undefeated) *rational* motivation, guided by (undefeated) rational belief. Defeaters of the rationality of wants include conflicting wants equal in strength and rationality to those they defeat; defeaters of the rationality of beliefs include both awareness of counterevidence (of potential over-riders) and having reason to doubt the plausibility of one's grounds (hence reason to suspect an underminer), where the having of such a reason may be a matter of what one believes or something less straightforward, such as what, as a rational person, one should be-

---

[11] For one thing, not all intentional action emerges from practical judgment or from the commonest route to such judgment, viz. practical reasoning—a point I have defended in detail in my *Practical Reasoning* (London: Routledge, 1989), chap. 5. That motivational internalism in any but a weak form is mistaken and is not needed to account for weakness of will is argued in my "Weakness of Will and Practical Judgment," *Noûs* 13 (1979). For a detailed statement of a different causalist approach to intentional action and weakness of will, see Hector-Neri Castañeda, *Thinking and Doing* (Dordrecht: Reidel, 1975), and "Practical Reason, Reasons for Doing, and Intentional Action: The Thinking of Doing and the Doing of Thinking," *Philosophical Perspectives* 4 (1990).

lieve, say because the proposition is an obvious inference from what one does believe, or its truth is plainly displayed in one's visual field and the proposition merely needs one's attention to yield belief of it. Being undefeated does *not* require indefeasibility. An action may be rational on the basis of a ground even if it is not impossible that anything defeat the rationality produced by that ground, or by grounds of that kind. It may yet be true that some grounds for action *are* indefeasible, as Aristotle and Kant apparently thought.[12] But the existence of indefeasible grounds is not essential to the internalist conception of rational action I am sketching.

What in particular might it be rational to want intrinsically? Here are some central cases. One's own happiness is a paradigm of something it is rational to want intrinsically, though not necessarily under that description or under any conception embodying the notion of happiness itself. But rational motivation need not be limited to such wants: perhaps, as Kant may have believed, it is also rational to want others' happiness for its own sake. And perhaps the flourishing of art and music can also be so wanted. In this respect, my view is apparently more pluralistic than Aristotle's, though clearly he took the constituents of happiness (sometimes translated 'human flourishing') to be so various that what is put forward with the sound of a eudaemonistic monism may be better regarded as a hierarchical pluralism with intellectual activity at its pinnacle. Moreover, I agree with Aristotle and Kant that some of the things it is rational to want for their own sake may be rationally considered better than others, though I leave open (as at least Aristotle apparently did not in the case of happiness) whether there are some ends that *cannot* (or cannot rationally) be wanted instrumentally, that is, for the sake of something further. There are surely some, however, including one's own happiness, that are not naturally wanted for the sake of anything further.

Let me simply illustrate the well-groundedness conception as applied to actions. Some rational actions are well grounded *directly*, that

---

[12] Aristotle, for example, took happiness to be a final and complete end; and although he explicitly said only that no one seeks it for a further end, he apparently thought that one cannot so seek happiness and conceived it as analogous to the *indemonstrable* (not merely undemonstrated) foundations he required, in *Posterior Analytics* 72b, as ultimate foundations of knowledge. For Kant, at least, some ends given by reflection in the light of the categorical imperative seem best construed as indefeasible: that they are ends binding on all rational beings is a priori, necessary, and showable by reasoning at least as intuitive as any that could be brought against the view.

is, they are performed in order to realize a basic rational end, for instance the pleasures of intellectual activity (compare the way in which certain non-inferential beliefs are well grounded in, say, perceptual experience). Others are well grounded *indirectly*, by virtue of resting on at least one basic rational end through at least one *purposive chain* (rather as certain inferential beliefs are well grounded in justified non-inferential beliefs); that is, through a chain of in-order-to connections, the kind illustrated by purchasing a ribbon in order to print a paper and printing the paper in order to send it to someone.

There are also epistemic requirements on well-groundedness. If the crucial instrumental beliefs, such as the belief that intellectual conversation will promote one's happiness, are unjustified, this tends to undermine the rationality of the action in question. I say 'tends to' because there are complications. For instance, one might justifiably believe, of such an unjustified belief, that it *is* justified, and acting on it might then be rational. As this suggests, some rational actions may be better grounded, and thus more rational, than others.

Rational action has often been thought to be a special case of action based on practical reasoning that concludes in favor of that action.[13] On the basis of similar considerations, rational action has often been thought to be necessarily intentional. In closing this section, I want to examine both these views, beginning with the second.

It does seem plain that an *un*intentional action cannot be rational, that is, it cannot be behaviorally rational: obviously one can unintentionally do something which is rational *for* one to do, as where one accidentally leaves a bet on a number that one has excellent reason to think will win. But there are some things we do neither intentionally nor unintentionally. If, when I intentionally telephone colleagues on important business, I realize I must wake their late-sleeping teenage boy, I do not wake the boy unintentionally; I do it knowingly, yet neither intentionally nor unintentionally. If I do it in the light of an urgent reason to call them, it may be a perfectly reasonable thing to allow myself to do. Might we not also call the action rational? I think so. But if not, imagine a case where rationality is more directly at issue, for instance where I set back my interests considerably by rejecting an article that I must judge as a potential publication. If I do

[13] See Donald Davidson, "How Is Weakness of the Will Possible?" in Joel Feinberg, ed., *Moral Concepts* (New York: Oxford University Press, 1969), and Gilbert Harman, "Practical Reasoning," *Review of Metaphysics* 29 (1976).

it knowing, but also regretting, that it will alienate a friend of the author, yet do it *only* in order to support the cause of quality publication, then, while alienating the friend might be called irrational by an acquaintance who thinks I should somehow compromise, I might, in reply, surely characterize my alienating the author's friend as rational in the light of the relative importance of editorial justice.

Regarding rational action in relation to action based on practical reasoning that concludes in favor of that action, I have elsewhere argued that not all intentional action so arises: even if all intentional action is *action for a reason*, it is not all *reasoned action*.[14] In any case, action based on practical reasoning need not be rational, in part because bad reasons may figure in the premises, or, although the premises do provide some reason to *A*, a vastly superior alternative action is overlooked. Thus, suppose I reason: I want to get this letter to New York as soon as possible; using special delivery is a good way to achieve that; hence I'll use it. If, from years of habit, I am simply temporarily forgetting express mail, which is much faster, this action, though supported by a good prima facie reason, is not rational, and I might admit, to someone surprised at what I did, that it was not rational (or stupid) as I recall my error on the way back from the post office. By contrast, if I used express mail all the time and from sheer habit sent the envelope to the post office so marked in order to get it to New York as soon as possible, then my action would be rational even though it was merely habitual and sprung from no piece of practical reasoning that concludes in favor of it.

These points are not meant to minimize the importance of practical reasoning in understanding rational action. While not all rational actions are based on such reasoning, clearly rational actions, conceived as well grounded, are of a *kind* that always can be so based (at least if they are performed for a further end); and when they are based on practical reasoning, the agent will (at the time) almost certainly have ready access to the relevant grounds, since the grounds will have figured in a conscious process of reasoning specifically directed toward the action in question. The constraints on what constitute rational grounds set the standards for assessing the motivation expressed in the major premise; the constraints on what constitute justified means-end beliefs—which I call *connecting beliefs* because they link one's ac-

---

[14] This point is developed in chap. 5 of my *Practical Reasoning*. This section is indebted, moreover, to chap. 8, sec. 4, of that same work.

tion to one's goal—determine the standards for assessing the cognition expressed in the minor (connecting) premise. The process of practical reasoning, moreover, can be seen in this framework to be a route to *discovery*, not just to retrospective explanation or justification, or to prospective self-encouragement. For in setting oneself an end and seeking a means, one often discovers—by reflection or association or luck or whatever—a good means to that end; and one's so settling on that means may help to motivate one to take it.

We can see, then, that it is natural, though not always necessary, for a rational agent to engage in practical reasoning in determining what to do. The concluding practical judgment is justified provided it is well grounded in the agent's acceptance of the premises. Such grounding implies that the agent justifiedly believes the premises. If, in addition, they are correct and the underlying argument is valid, or of sufficient inductive strength, the reasoning is cogent. If the end and the connecting belief they express are well grounded, and the agent acts for that reason, that is, in order to achieve this end, the action is prima facie rational. It is more rational in proportion to *how* well grounded the underlying motivation and cognition are and how thoroughly it is based upon them. It can be seen to be rational in the light of this underlying motivation and cognition and thereby to be well grounded.

From an internalist point of view, success of the reasoning is a matter of how well it directs the agent by standards for which the agent has adequate reason, where the notion of having adequate reason is construed in the way an epistemological internalist would view it. Thus, if the reasoning is successful, then the response is a rational approach to the practical problem: what to do. If the problem remains intractable and the action does not solve it, the *agent* is not successful. But if the action is optimally well grounded, then failure here is not the agent's fault. The action is fully grounded in practical reason.

By contrast, an externalist view of rational action might take certain objective failures, say to satisfy one's relevant desires, to count against the rationality of the action. It would certainly take some such objective failures to count against an action's rationality in a way an internalist account would not. I grant that some objective failures to achieve one's end, even though they occur despite the agent's having good reasons for the action, from an internal point of view, are prima facie evidence of irrationality; but I prefer the internalist view that lack of external success does not necessarily count against the rationality of an action, just as falsehood does not necessarily count against the rationality of a belief.

IV. Conclusion

If the foregoing points are sound, then internalism in the theory of action is plausible, and an internalist conception of rational action can be defended in ways parallel to those appropriate to defending an internalist view of justified belief. But I do not claim to have established either view. My aim has been mainly to extend internalism to action theory and to show that plausible versions can be formulated in that domain. While I think that externalism is probably less plausible in action theory than in epistemology, I do not claim to have shown it mistaken in either field. Indeed, I have formulated it only in outline and do not doubt that more plausible versions can be articulated. I should add this much, however: just as, for knowledge, externalism is more plausible than it is for justification—and quite plausible indeed[15]—so for *successful* action, as opposed to rational action, an externalist view seems highly plausible. If that notion is not entirely external, we may at least suppose that it has a substantial externalist component, presumably to the effect that the successful action actually yields the desired result, or a result that would under certain conditions be desired. This is a condition whose fulfillment will be external except in cases in which the object of the desire is appropriately internal, say, thinking about the nature of justification.

Skepticism is another source of remaining problems. It may be argued that we never do know what our grounds for action are, or at least never know this simply through what is accessible to introspective reflection. Similar skeptical claims might be made about justified belief regarding what our grounds are. But except on unreasonably strong skeptical assumptions, these skeptical views seem even less plausible than their epistemic counterpart. Even Humean skepticism allows us knowledge of our own mental states (at least the occurrent ones).[16] It should also be stressed that first-order internalism need

[15] For reasons indicated in my "Justification, Truth, and Reliability."

[16] In the *Treatise*, for instance, Hume says that "since all actions and sensations of the mind are known to us by consciousness, they must necessarily appear in every particular what they are, and be what they appear. Every thing that enters the mind,

only posit access to grounds, not to grounds conceived *as* such, nor, especially, to *how* the grounds of justification justify. In any case, it should be plain that if we are to be skeptical about internal access in epistemology, we must either be skeptical about internal access to grounds of actions or show why one need not be a skeptic there too. With respect to skepticism, as in other ways, action theory turns out to be significantly parallel to epistemology.

There remain many problems in specifying just what kind of access introspection gives us to what we want and believe. If wants and beliefs can be unconscious and can still yield intentional action, there is some question whether, in those cases, there is access at all. But if I have been right in thinking that a plausible internalism may be fallibilistic, it is reasonable to hold that agents have the required kind of access; for even in the cases in which one acts on the basis of unconscious motivation or cognition, there is at least a tendency for one to be able to figure out, by adequate reflection, what one's reasons are. This is all that fallibilistic internalism requires for intentional action. One need not be able to identify the relevant grounds the moment one's reflection starts, or always be correct or justified in one's identification, even after reflecting some time. The concept of rational action is internal; but not every rational action need actually stem from grounds the agent can actually become aware of: a de facto barrier between the agent and the grounds may in special cases remain impervious, so long as, in principle, it is not impenetrable to the agent. Moreover, we may even generally have introspective access to the causal connections between our grounds and actions performed on them. But this is not a requirement on a successful internalist theory. Whether it holds or not, the rationality of actions, like the justifiedness of beliefs, remains rooted in what is appropriately accessible to the agent.[17]

---

being in *reality* as the perception, 'tis impossible any thing should to *feeling* appear different. This were to suppose, that even where we are most intimately conscious, we might be mistaken"; see *A Treatise of Human Nature*, ed. L. A. Selby-Bigge (Oxford: Oxford University Press, 1888), p. 190.

[17] This chapter has benefited from discussions with many people, particularly William P. Alston, Richard Foley, Paul K. Moser, David K. O'Connor, and Philip L. Quinn.

Index